Law and Markets

Law and Markets

Alex Robson
Senior Research Fellow, SMART Infrastructure Facility,
University of Wollongong, Australia

palgrave
macmillan

First published 2012 by
PALGRAVE MACMILLAN

Palgrave Macmillan in the UK is an imprint of Macmillan Publishers Limited, registered in England, company number 785998, of Houndmills, Basingstoke, Hampshire RG21 6XS.

Palgrave Macmillan in the US is a division of St Martin's Press LLC, 175 Fifth Avenue, New York, NY 10010.

Palgrave Macmillan is the global academic imprint of the above companies and has companies and representatives throughout the world.

Palgrave® and Macmillan® are registered trademarks in the United States, the United Kingdom, Europe and other countries.

ISBN 978–0–230–24799–4

This book is printed on paper suitable for recycling and made from fully managed and sustained forest sources. Logging, pulping and manufacturing processes are expected to conform to the environmental regulations of the country of origin.

A catalogue record for this book is available from the British Library.

A catalog record for this book is available from the Library of Congress.

10 9 8 7 6 5 4 3 2 1
21 20 19 18 17 16 15 14 13 12

Printed and bound in Great Britain by
CPI Antony Rowe, Chippenham and Eastbourne

For Megan, Ruby, Edie-Rose and Scarlett

Contents

List of Figures

List of Tables

Preface

In his three-volume treatise *Law, Legislation and Liberty*, Nobel Laureate F.A. Hayek notes that:

> The rules of just conduct which the lawyer studies serve a kind of order of the character of which the lawyer is largely ignorant; and this order is studied chiefly by the economist who in turn is similarly ignorant of the rules of conduct on which the order that he studies rests.

Economics is primarily concerned with incentives, the mutual benefits from exchange, the gains from specialisation, and the role of the market as an institution which helps individuals realise those mutual gains. Incentives, costs and benefits therefore matter a great deal. Costs and benefits – as assessed subjectively by market participants – motivate human action and are integral to all economic problems and policy issues. Without an understanding of incentives, costs and benefits, it is impossible to understand economics.

Legal rules allocate economic costs and benefits between parties engaged in both market and non-market transactions. In doing so, legal rules create powerful economic incentives which affect individual behaviour, market outcomes, and ultimately the overall size of net economic benefits.

This book applies the standard principles and tools of microeconomic theory to examine the economic effects of different legal rules on individual incentives, market outcomes, and economic well-being. The book is primarily intended for economists who are seeking a broader and deeper economic understanding of the relationship between markets, legal rules and legal institutions. The book studies the economic aspects of some of the most fundamental institutions in modern market economies, including private property rights, tort law, contract law, criminal law, corporate law, employment law, environmental regulations, antitrust law, and the economics of litigation and settlement. It is not the intention of this book to teach law to economists, or economics to lawyers. Indeed, all legal concepts are introduced along the way, so no prior legal knowledge is required.

In each of these topics the book attempts bring a market focus to the analysis from the very outset, imbedding the examination of legal rules and institutions within a broader demand and supply framework, where market prices can adjust to changes in legal rules, firms can enter and exit industries, and consumers may substitute towards some goods and away from others in response to price changes. Different market structures such as oligopoly and monopoly are also considered, in order to illustrate how different market structures may or may not alter particular conclusions regarding the overall incentive and welfare effects of different legal rules. The overall focus and the substance of the book are therefore deliberately different from most texts in the field. Nevertheless, the coverage of topics is similar to most existing books.

What Makes This Book Different?

This book began its long evolution as a set of lecture notes for the undergraduate and postgraduate law and economics courses I taught in the School of Economics at the Australian National University over the last decade. The book builds substantially upon these early draft lecture notes, adding important insights from older and more recent literature, as well as some of the results of my own research. The end result is much more than a textbook. Over the years in these courses I assigned most of the books that have been published in the field, either as compulsory texts or as reference material. Whilst most books are very good at what they do, they did not do all that I wanted them to do. I found that there was a sizeable gap between their coverage and the core first- and second-year microeconomics curriculum at the ANU, which focuses on market analysis, the paradigm of perfect competition, the gains from trade, incidence and welfare analysis of government policies, shifting demand and supply curves, imperfect competition, and externalities in market settings. These standard market-analytic tools of microeconomic theory are powerful and useful, but tend to be relegated to the background in many existing law and economics books.

The goal of the book is to build a tighter link between the core material of microeconomics and the key topics of law and economics, and to put the market paradigm front and centre. The ultimate purpose is to show how the standard tools of microeconomics can be applied in a wide variety of settings (such as accidental harm in market settings, contract law, and markets for illegal goods) and to appreciate just how useful standard microeconomic analysis can be in analysing issues in law and economics. Legal rules and institutions affect individual incentives on both the demand and supply side of the relevant markets, and therefore affect market outcomes, including prices, quantities and welfare. Moreover, there are important but subtle differences between the ways in which legal rules affect outcomes in settings where there is no market or economic relationship between the parties, compared to outcomes when such a relationship is present. These subtleties are widely known in the literature but mostly ignored in many books, and yet much of the policy discussion around market regulation these days focuses on precisely these settings.

In addition to the focus on markets, this book has several key differences from most of the books in the field:

- Most books contain a cursory application of the standard microeconomic theory of markets and welfare economics and the power of these tools for assessing legal rules. This book puts markets, efficiency, costs and benefits front and centre.
- Many books contain what I find to be an inadequate treatment of the Coase Theorem. In particular, the treatment and consequences of transaction costs is rather poor, and the issue of whether Coase Theorem holds when there are more than two parties is usually completely ignored.
- Most books have an inadequate treatment of the role of market forces in both tort law and contract law. Product liability rules within oligopolistic and monopolistic market settings (let alone under perfect competition) are rarely discussed or considered in detail.
- Most books contain inadequate treatments of the economics of private property rights, which together with free markets and the rule of law, are the cornerstone of modern market economies and economic prosperity. Whilst overlapping usage rights are discussed in most books, the problems that arise when there are overlapping exclusion and disposal rights – and the welfare costs that these can lead to – are not treated with the importance that I think they deserve. In addition, in most texts the economic costs of insecure property rights – one of the most serious problems in many economies throughout the world today – are completely ignored.
- Most books have an inadequate treatment of the economics of crime and public law enforcement. In particular, there is little or no coverage of the economics of illegal markets and the range of examples that the economic model of crime and punishment and public law enforcement can be applied to, including to competition law.
- Most books have an inadequate treatment of modern bargaining theory and its place in the economics of litigation and settlement. There has been a great deal of progress in bargaining theory and cooperative game theory which can be brought to bear on this topic.

This book explores all of these issues and more.

Structure of the book

Like most other areas of economics, the field of law and economics has become enormous. The book is therefore not intended to be an encyclopaedic reference to the entire subject; nor is it a summary of the latest developments in the field. For those wanting an encyclopaedic treatment of topics, I recommend Newman (1998), Bouckaert and De Geest (2000) or Polinsky and Shavell (2007).

The book is structured as follows. Chapter 1 sets out the four main propositions which guide the focus of the book, introduces the basic competitive paradigm and the efficiency properties of competitive markets, and examines some of the legal and economic assumptions that underpin the first fundamental theorem of welfare economics. The chapter also contains a detailed analysis of transaction costs. Chapter 2 contains an economic analysis of the legal system and legal rule-making under various assumptions about how the legal system operates. Chapter 3 presents and analyses the Coase Theorem, and includes an examination of the case where there are more than two parties. Chapters 4 and 5 study the economics of accident law, focusing primarily on market settings. Chapter 6 extends this analysis by examining product liability rules under different market structures. Chapter 7 studies the economics of private property rights, including the economics of insecure property rights, whilst Chapter 8 contains an economic analysis of contract law, also in a market setting. In Chapter 9 we present a model of crime and punishment that can be used to study a wide variety of issues, including optimal fines and imprisonment terms, optimal enforcement, plea bargaining, and behaviour in markets for illegal goods and services. Chapter 10 applies some of the lessons of the previous chapters to study issues in corporate law and competition law. Chapter 11 concludes by examining the economics of litigation and settlement, the market for lawyers, and the efficiency hypothesis of the common law.

Acknowledgements

Writing this book has been more of a marathon than a sprint. Many individuals have contributed indirectly to the development of the book in one way or another.

I would first like to thank Marc Poitras at the University of Dayton and Stergios Skaperdas at the University of California, Irvine for their friendship and many helpful discussions and advice over the years.

As Head of the ANU School of Economics, Ben Smith was instrumental in bringing the Law and Economics course back to life at the ANU. Ben's successors Steve Dowrick and Martin Richardson helped to keep the course going. I would also like to acknowledge the several hundred students who have taken the course at ANU over the years.

Part of this book was written while I was a Visiting Fellow at the Crawford School of Economics and Government at the ANU and also a Senior Research Fellow at the SMART Infrastructure Facility at the University of Wollongong. Thanks go to Jeff Bennett and Gary Bowditch, at these two institutions respectively.

Chris Jones, Henry Ergas and Mark Harrison have provided me with a great deal guidance of encouragement over the years, for which I am deeply grateful.

I would also like to thank Taiba Batool and Ellie Shillito at Palgrave Macmillan for their patience and assistance throughout this project.

Finally I would like to thank my wife Megan for her love, support and encouragement – this book would literally not have been written without her.

1 Introduction

1.1 The legal foundations of markets

The legal system and its rules and norms facilitate the formation of formal and informal markets on which voluntary, value-creating exchanges and resource movements can take place. As Coase (1991) notes, 'without the appropriate institutions no market economy of any significance is possible'. Just as understanding markets, the process of trade and the gains from trade are all central to understanding economics, understanding the role that legal rules and institutions play in facilitating economic exchange is a vital part of understanding of the very same phenomena.

Legal rules influence market outcomes by altering the incentives faced by individuals participating in the market process. Rules, remedies and punishments send 'price' signals to consumers and producers in the form of expected damages and other remedies (in the case of private law), or fines, imprisonment terms and other punishments such as the death penalty (in the case of public and criminal law). In an efficient legal system, legal rules, remedies and punishments maximise the net economic benefits of the market process.

Some legal institutions and rules are more important than others. Private property rights, contract law and accident law all play a vital part in market economies in influencing the efficiency or otherwise of resource allocation. Some legal rules can boost the gains from trade, some can hinder trade and detract from economic well-being, and some – very surprisingly – may be completely irrelevant for determining observed market outcomes.

The field of law and economics – the focus of this book – studies how the legal rules that govern interactions between individuals can affect market outcomes and the allocation of scarce resources, and how these rules alter individuals' incentives, well-being, and the gains from trade and specialisation. Law and economics focus on four separate but related propositions, all of which are explored in this book:[1]

1. **The Invisible Hand Theorem (also known as the First Fundamental Theorem of Welfare Economics):** Under certain assumptions, competitive markets produce efficient outcomes.
2. **The Efficiency Version of the Coase Theorem**: If transaction costs are sufficiently low and legal rights are well defined, legal conflicts (which would otherwise arise over uncompensated costs and benefits that are due to activities which generate external effects) are resolved in an efficient manner via mutually advantageous, voluntary exchange.
3. **The Economic Role of the Legal Rules (Normative Version)**: If transaction costs are not sufficiently low, so that the conclusion of the Coase Theorem does not hold, then legal rules should be designed in such a way to ensure an efficient allocation of resources.
4. **The Economic Role of Legal Rules (Positive Version)**: The system of legal rules developed under the common law (that is, the system of judge or court-made law which is based on precedent, as opposed to statute-based law) in fact evolves over time to ensure an efficient allocation of resources.

1.2 Competitive markets and efficiency

We begin our analysis with the concept of a *perfectly competitive market* for a good, which is defined as a market in which (in addition to assumptions about property rights and contract law which we examine throughout the book) it is also the case that:

- The costs of transacting are low;
- All firms and consumers are price takers;
- Firms can freely enter and exit the industry; and
- Firms sell identical goods, and both firms and consumers have enough information to accurately estimate the quality of the product and the prices that are charged by other firms.

The forces of competition create powerful individual incentives which lead to an allocation of resources which maximises net benefits.

To illustrate the link between competition and efficiency, consider a market in which all consumers are identical, and that consumers have identical quasi-linear utility functions, with the benefits of consumption of Q units of the good denoted by $u(Q)$. Suppose that there are n identical firms (where n is determined endogenously in the long run), each with a cost function of $C(q)$. Thus, total welfare in this economy is

$$W = u(Q) - nC(q) = u(qn) - nC(q)$$

Under these conditions, maximising total benefits minus total costs is equivalent to maximising the sum of consumer surplus (that is, willingness to pay) and producer surplus. We will refer to an allocation which maximises the sum of consumer surplus and the producer surplus as an *efficient* allocation. This is the efficiency concept we will use throughout the book.

In this setting, efficiency requires two conditions. First, for a given number of (identical) firms, it must not be possible to increase welfare by having each firm produce more. This means that:

$$\frac{dW}{dq} = n^* \ u'(q^* n^*) - n^* C'(q') = 0 \tag{1.1}$$

or:

$$u'(q^* n^*) = \ C'(q^*)$$

That is, marginal consumption benefits must equal marginal costs.

Second, for a given quantity, it must not be possible to increase welfare by changing the number of firms. This means that:

$$\frac{dW}{dn} = q^* u'(q^* n^*) - C(q^*) = 0$$

or:

$$u'(q^* n^*) = \frac{C(q^*)}{q^*}$$

This states that marginal consumption benefits must also equal *average* costs. Since the consumer equates marginal benefits with price P, welfare maximisation requires price = marginal cost = average cost.

1.2.1 The invisible hand theorem

A *long-run competitive equilibrium* in this setting is a market quantity $Q^* = q^* n^*$ and a market price P such that:

- Consumers take the price as given and equate the marginal consumption benefits $u'(q^* n^*) = P$ with the price of the good;
- Producers take the price as given and each firms chooses q to maximise its profits, so $C'(q^*) = P$ for each firm;
- The market price P adjusts to *clear* the market, so that demand for the good equals supply. At market-clearing prices, consumers do not want to purchase any more units of a good, and producers do not want to supply any more units; and
- There is free entry and exit so that the equilibrium number of firms n^* in the industry adjusts until profits are zero, so $P = \frac{C(q^*)}{q^*}$ for all firms.

In a long-run competitive equilibrium, since $P = \frac{C(q)}{q}$ and since marginal cost also equals price, we must have marginal cost equal to average cost. This only occurs at the minimum of the average cost curve. The long-run competitive equilibrium is shown in the diagram below. The long-run market supply curve here is assumed to be flat and is equal to the minimum of the average cost curve. The demand curve is the marginal benefit curve, $u'(Q)$.

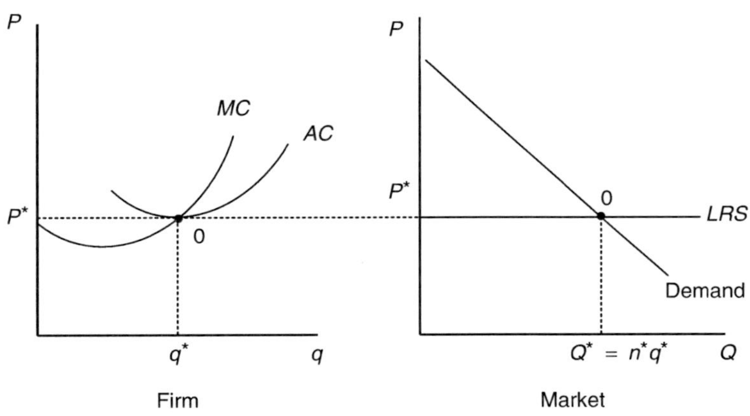

Figure 1.2.1 Long-run competitive equilibrium

Notice that at point Q^*, the marginal benefit of an additional unit of the good is equal to the marginal cost of an additional unit. Since the market demand curve reflects marginal consumption benefits, and since the slope of the long-run market supply curve reflects marginal opportunity costs, and since in a competitive equilibrium the two are equal to each other, this must be the case. But if marginal benefits equal marginal costs, this means that welfare must be maximised. Thus, a competitive equilibrium leads to an outcome that maximises welfare.

In a perfectly competitive market, consumers take prices as given and maximise their net benefits, and producers also take prices as given and maximise profits. The market price adjusts and reconciles consumer demands and producer supply. Higher prices send a signal to consumers to reduce their consumption, and for producers to bring forth more supply. Lower prices send the opposite signals. Market prices adjust until no more gains from trade are possible. This result is a version of the 'invisible hand theorem' or, more formally, the *first fundamental theorem of welfare economics*.

1.2.2 Analysing the welfare effects of policy interventions – the long-run effects of a specific tax

Much of the analysis in this book blends positive and normative analysis. To illustrate the basic approach, suppose that our market is initially in a long-run competitive equilibrium with a market price of P^*, and with each (identical) firm producing q^* units of the good. The equilibrium number of firms is denoted by n^*. As discussed above, this price must equal marginal cost and average cost.

Now suppose that a specific tax of $\$t$ is imposed on production, and that this tax is paid by firms in the industry. Total costs for each firm are now $C(q)+tq$. This tax adds therefore an amount t to each firm's marginal costs and average costs. Marginal costs are now $C'(q)+t$ and average costs are $\frac{C(q)}{q}+t$.

In the short run, with the market price still at P^*, each firm's marginal costs are equal to $C'(q^*)+t > P^*$. Firms produce less, make a loss, and as a result some firms exit the industry. As firms exit the long-run supply curve shifts up, which pushes up the market price as well as the quantity supplied by each individual firm that remains in the industry. In the long run, each remaining firm continues to produce what it did originally, since the quantity that minimises the new average costs

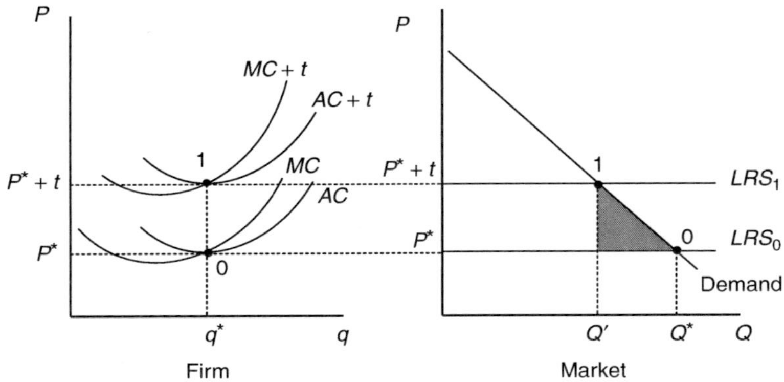

Figure 1.2.2 The long-run effects of a specific tax

$\frac{C(q)}{q}+t$ also minimises the old average costs $\frac{C(q)}{q}$. The new long-run equilibrium market price is:

$$P^* + t = C'(q^*) + t = \frac{C(q^*)}{q^*} + t \qquad (1.2)$$

This is simply the original price, plus the tax. In the long run, the economic incidence of the tax falls entirely on consumers, even though the legal incidence falls entirely on producers.

The initial and final long-run competitive equilibria are illustrated in Figure 1.2.2. The initial market quantity is Q^* and the final quantity is Q'. The tax shifts the average and marginal cost curves up for each firm by the amount of the tax. Each firm continues to produce q^* in the new long-run equilibrium. The new long-run supply curve is LRS_1.

The welfare loss of the tax is shaded in the right-hand panel, and is the difference between the loss of consumer surplus and the revenue raised from the tax, which is tQ'.

1.3 Key assumptions of the invisible hand theorem

There are some key assumptions in the invisible hand theorem which we failed to make explicit earlier. Before we discuss these assumptions, it is important to note that they are *sufficient* rather than *necessary* conditions – in other words, relaxing the assumptions does not *automatically* mean that the invisible hand result will not hold. On the other hand, if the invisible hand result does *not* in fact hold and we observe some inefficiency in a market, it *must* be because one or more of the following assumptions do not hold. Thus, examining these assumptions provides us with some important insights into the role of the legal system in influencing economic outcomes and economic well-being.

As will be discussed further in Chapter 2, the *normative approach* to law and economics attempts to justify legal rules based on some normative consequentialist criterion (usually the efficiency criterion). This approach recognises that efficiency is a powerful and unifying concept. However, inefficiency of existing institutional or legal arrangements does not automatically justify government intervention, the alteration of an existing legal rule, or the imposition of a new legal rule. Outcomes under existing arrangements need to be carefully compared on a like basis with alternatives that are proposed. Failure to do so can lead to the 'nirvana fallacy', which Demsetz (1969) has explained as follows:

> The view that now pervades much public policy economics implicitly presents the relevant choice as between an ideal norm and an existing 'imperfect' institutional arrangement. This nirvana approach differs considerably from a comparative institution approach in which the relevant choice is between alternative real institutional arrangements. In practice, those who adopt the nirvana viewpoint seek to discover discrepancies between the ideal and the real and if discrepancies are found, they deduce that the real is inefficient. Users of the comparative institution approach attempt to assess which alternative real institutional arrangement seems best able to cope with the economic problem; practitioners of this approach may use an ideal norm to provide standards from which divergences are assessed for all practical alternatives of interest and select as efficient that alternative which seems most likely to minimize the divergence.[2]

Efficiency analysis which compares existing arrangements with some theoretically 'perfect' ideal set of institutional arrangements is an inappropriate framework for real world policy design. This book uses efficiency analysis as a unifying analytical concept to illustrate the kinds of costs and benefits that different legal rules can create. However, throughout the analysis, the nirvana fallacy should always be kept in mind. Like markets and the individuals who participate in those markets, regulatory agencies, policy institutions, courts and the legal system are not perfect and are not infallible. Legal rules and institutions are themselves subject the same kinds of failures that may affect markets (that is, imperfect knowledge, informational asymmetries, distorted incentives, and so on). It is important to realise that just as *market failures* exist and may indeed be pervasive, *government and regulatory failures* also exist.

1.3.1.1 Transaction costs

The previous section analysed a setting with frictionless markets. But there are many situations in which there may be costs of arranging exchanges (including transport costs, search costs or production inspection costs) or other non-monetary costs that buyers and sellers may face. As Coase (1991) states: 'There are negotiations to be undertaken, contracts have to be drawn up, inspections have to be made, arrangements have to be made to settle disputes, and so on. These costs have come to be known as transaction costs.'

As Chapter 3 will illustrate, transaction costs are of vital importance in law and economics. For consumers, the full price that is paid to consume a good includes money prices and the non-money costs that are incurred. Similarly, for producers, the monetary price that is received from the sale of a good is reduced by the costs that are incurred in obtaining that money price. When there are no transaction costs in a market, then the market-clearing price is that which is exchanged in money terms between buyers and sellers. Buyers or demanders pay a money price of P_D and this money price is also received by sellers, so $P_D = P_S$. However, when there are transaction costs, this equality of full prices paid breaks down.

1.3.1.1.1 Per unit transaction costs in competitive markets. There are many forms of transaction costs that are imaginable. One of the most straightforward to understand are transaction costs which are the equivalent of a monetary amount per unit of a good consumed or produced. This section analyses these kinds of costs in some detail. Other forms of transaction costs are examined in Chapter 3.

On the buyer side of a market with transaction costs, we now distinguish between the *money price* that the consumer pays and the *full price* that the consumer pays. The former is simply the amount of cash that is handed over to the seller. The latter is the money price that the buyer pays, plus any other costs that the buyer incurs in actually purchasing the product. That is:

$$P_D = P_D^M + t_D$$

where P_D is the full price paid by demanders of the good (i.e. buyers), P_D^M is the money price paid by demanders, and t_D is the additional costs incurred by the buyer (that is, the per unit transaction costs). These additional costs drive a wedge between the full price P_D that buyers pay for the good, and the money price received by sellers, which is P_D^M.

For example, suppose that the consumers' willingness to pay for a good is given by the following marginal utility curve:

$$u'(Q_D) = a - Q_D$$

When non-money prices are introduced, the consumer would now consume up to the point where marginal benefit is equal to the *full* price:

$$P_D^M + t_D = u'(Q_D) = a - Q_D$$

and so the demand curve is

$$Q_D = a - P_D^M - t_D$$

On the seller or supply side, we again distinguish between the money price that the producer physically receives from the buyer, and the *net realised selling price* that the producer actually gets to keep after the transaction is completed. The former is simply what is handed over to the seller. The latter is the price that the seller receives, net of any other costs that the seller incurs (not including direct production costs) in actually selling the product. We have:

$$P_S = P_S^M - t_S$$

where P_S is the seller's *net* realised selling price, P_S^M is the money price physically paid to the seller, and t_S is the additional per unit transaction costs incurred by the seller. Again these additional costs drive a wedge between the price that buyers pay for the good, and the price received by sellers.

For example, suppose that the supply curve is:

$$Q_S = P_S$$

With transaction costs the supply curve in terms of the full price is now:

$$P_S = P_S^M - t_S = Q_S$$

and so the supply curve in terms of the money price is:

$$P_S^M = Q_S + t_S$$

1.3.1.1.2 Long-run equilibrium in a competitive market with per unit transaction costs. A competitive equilibrium in a market with transaction costs is defined in the same way as a market without transaction costs, but with full prices now playing an adjustment role. The full prices paid by buyers and received by sellers now adjust until the quantity demanded at the buyer's full price is equal to the quantity supplied at the seller's net realised selling price, with the additional property that the amount of money that is exchanged (that is, the two money prices) must be equal. In other words,

$$P_S^M = P_D^M \equiv P^*$$

and these prices adjust until $Q_S = Q_D$.

To illustrate, let us continue with our simple example of linear demand and supply curves. To find the competitive or market clearing equilibrium, we equate demand with supply, and set the money prices equal to a single money price that is common between the two sides of the market:

$$Q_S = P_S^M - t_S = a - P_D^M - t_D = Q_D$$

Thus, if $P_S^M = P_D^M \equiv P^*$, we have:

$$P^* - t_S = a - P^* - t_D$$

or:

$$P^* = \frac{a - t_D + t_S}{2} \tag{1.3}$$

This means that $P_D = P^* + t_D = \dfrac{a + t_D + t_S}{2}$ and $P_S = P^* - t_S = \dfrac{a - t_D - t_S}{2}$. The equilibrium is illustrated in Figure 1.3.1.

The analysis of competitive markets with per unit transaction costs is similar to the analysis of specific commodity taxation in competitive markets, with a few subtle but important differences. Most notably, although a tax collects revenue, activities which consumers and producers regard as transaction costs may not. For example, if market transaction involve search, waiting in queues, or travel then there may be little or no revenue collected from any economic actor as a result of such activity. Nevertheless, the analytical similarities between per unit transaction costs and specific taxes lead to several very interesting and important conclusions:

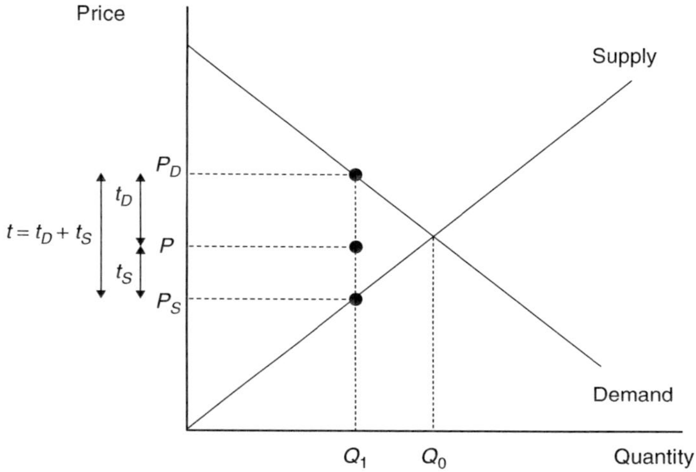

Figure 1.3.1 Long-run competitive equilibrium in a market with per unit transaction costs

- First, in terms of equilibrium market quantities, what matters is not the individual transaction costs faced on each side of the market, but the *sum* of these transaction costs. In other words, if the sum of the transaction costs does not change, then the equilibrium market quantities do not change, and economic welfare does not change.
- Second, (as with taxation) the *economic incidence* of the transaction costs is independent of the *physical* or *legal* incidence of the transaction costs. The former describes the extent to which each party is affected in *economic* terms by transaction costs; the latter is the extent to which each party is *physically* burdened by transaction costs.
- Third, the less elastic side of the market bears the larger fraction of the economic burden of transaction costs, and this fraction is independent of the physical incidence of transaction costs.

To see the first two results, suppose that only buyers physically face transaction costs of t_D, but that these costs are equal to the sum t illustrated in Figure 1.3.2. In this diagram, buyers face transaction costs of $t_D = t$ which are equal to the sum of the transaction costs in Figure 1.3.1. Note that the market quantity does not change: the transaction costs t simply drive a wedge between the full buyer and the money price that they pay. Since the size of the overall wedge is assumed not to change, the market quantity does not change either.

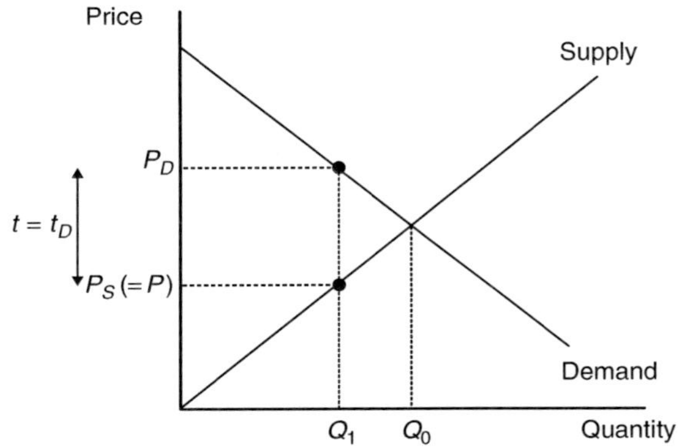

Figure 1.3.2 Only buyers face transaction costs equal to t

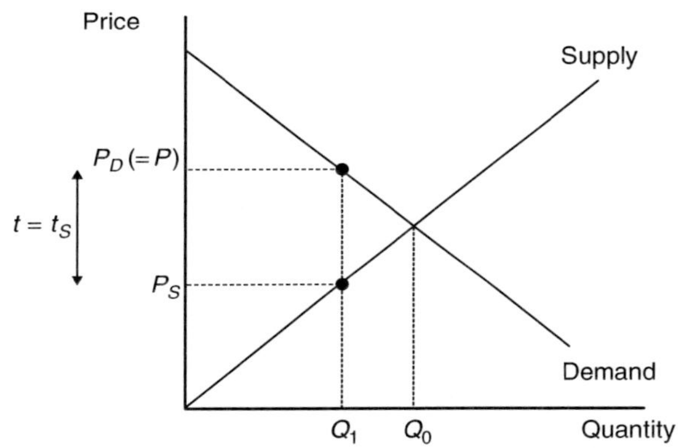

Figure 1.3.3 Only sellers face transaction costs of $t > 0$

Now consider the opposite situation, in which only sellers face transaction costs of t. This situation is illustrated in Figure 1.3.3. In this figure, sellers face transaction costs of $t_S = t$ which are equal to the sum of the transaction costs in Figure 1.3.1. Note that once again, the market quantity does not change: the transaction costs t again simply drive a wedge between the full buyer and the money price that they pay. Since the size of the overall wedge is assumed not to change, the market quantity does not change. The sum of the transaction costs do not change, then the equilibrium market quantities do not change, and economic welfare does not change.

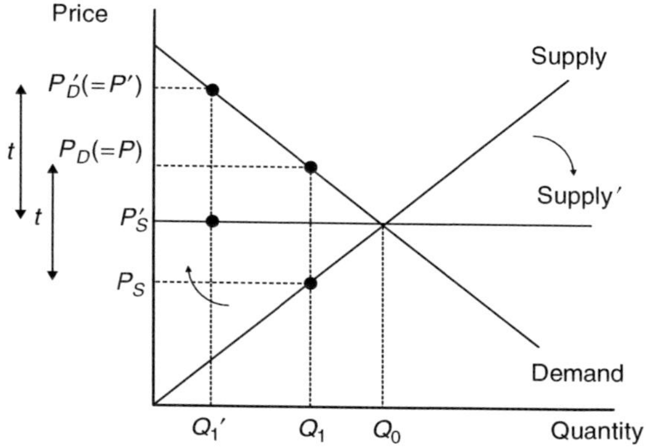

Figure 1.3.4 Transaction cost incidence when the supply curve is perfectly elastic

Note also that in Figure 1.3.2 and Figure 1.3.3 the *physical* incidence of the transaction costs differed completely. And yet the *economic incidence* of the transaction costs did not change: the well-being of both buyers and sellers was the same in each situation. This illustrates the second point above.

To see the third result, consider Figure 1.3.4 above. In this diagram we consider the original situation in which the seller physically bears the burden of the transaction costs *t*, and then compare this to the situation where the seller's marginal cost curve is perfectly elastic. Even though the seller physically pays the transaction costs *t*, the buyer bears the entire economic burden when the seller's supply curve is perfectly elastic.

Tax incidence analysis also provides us with an exact formula for predicting the economic incidence of changes in transaction costs when those changes are sufficiently small. Let t be the sum of the transaction costs. Let P_D and P_S be the full buyer price and net realised seller price respectively. By definition we have $P_D = P_S + t$, and in a competitive equilibrium we have:

$$Q_S(P_S) = Q_D(P_D)$$

or:

$$Q_S[P_S(t)] = Q_D[P_S(t) + t]$$

Differentiating with respect to t, and noting that in an equilibrium markets clear, we have:

$$\frac{dQ_S}{dP_S}\frac{dP_S}{dt} = \frac{dQ_D}{dP_D}\left(\frac{dP_S}{dt}+1\right)$$

and so:

$$\frac{dP_S}{dt} = \frac{\frac{dQ_D}{dP_D}}{\frac{dQ_S}{dP_S} - \frac{dQ_D}{dP_D}} \tag{1.4}$$

At the point where transaction costs are zero, we have $P_S = P_D$ and $Q_S = Q_D$ and so this formula collapses to:

$$\frac{dP_S}{dt} = \frac{\varepsilon_D}{\varepsilon_S - \varepsilon_D} < 0 \tag{1.5}$$

where $\varepsilon_D = \frac{dQ_D}{dP_D}.\frac{P_D}{Q_D}$ and $\varepsilon_S = \frac{dQ_S}{dP_S}.\frac{P_S}{Q_S}$ are the price elasticities of demand and supply respectively. Since $\frac{dP_D}{dt} = \frac{dP_S}{dt} + 1$, we also have:

$$\frac{dP_D}{dt} = \frac{\varepsilon_S}{\varepsilon_S - \varepsilon_D} > 0 \tag{1.6}$$

Further, since the terms $-dP_S/dt$ and dP_D/dt add to 1, each expression can be interpreted as the fraction of the burden borne by each side of the market. If, for example, the supply curve is perfectly elastic as in Figure 1.3.4, then $\varepsilon_S = \infty$ and so $\frac{dP_D}{dt} = \lim_{\varepsilon_S \to \infty} \frac{\varepsilon_S}{\varepsilon_S - \varepsilon_D} = 1$ and $\frac{dP_S}{dt} = \lim_{\varepsilon_S \to \infty} \frac{\varepsilon_D}{\varepsilon_S - \varepsilon_D} = 0$.

1.3.1.1.3 The influence of transaction costs on the money prices paid by consumers. We are now in a position to analyse the effect of transaction costs on the money price that is exchanged between buyers and sellers. Recall that:

$$P_D = P_D^M + t_D$$

where P_D is the full price, P_D^M is the money price, and t_D are the additional per unit transaction costs incurred by the buyer. This means that:

$$P_D^M = P_D - t_D$$

and so, holding t_S constant, we have:

$$\frac{dP_D^M}{dt_D} = \frac{dP_D}{dt} - 1 = \frac{dP_S}{dt} = \frac{\varepsilon_D}{\varepsilon_S - \varepsilon_D} < 0 \tag{1.7}$$

This inequality states that an increase in t_D, holding t_S constant, *reduces* the money price paid by buyers. Similarly, a reduction in t_D, holding t_S constant, *increases* the money price paid by buyers.

This result is illustrated in Figure 1.3.5 below, where t_S is held constant but t_D falls to $t_D' < t_D$. The money price is initially P. The transaction costs are initially t_D and t_S, and are identical to the transaction costs in Figure 1.3.1 above. The full price paid by buyers is $P_D = P_D^M + t_D = P_S^M + t_D = P_S + t_S + t_D$.

Now suppose that transaction costs faced by buyers fall to $t_D' < t_D$. The new full price paid by buyers is $P_D' = P_S + t_S + t_D'$, and the new money price is $P' = P_D' - t_D' > P$. *The full price paid by consumers falls, but the money price paid by consumers rises*. As expression (1.7) indicates, money prices *always* respond to changes in buyer transaction costs in this way.

If we were to ignore transaction costs and full prices and instead focus only on money prices, then a situation like Figure 1.3.5 would present great difficulties. Money prices would rise (which, in the absence of a consideration of transaction costs, would indicate that consumers would be worse off), but quantity demanded would also

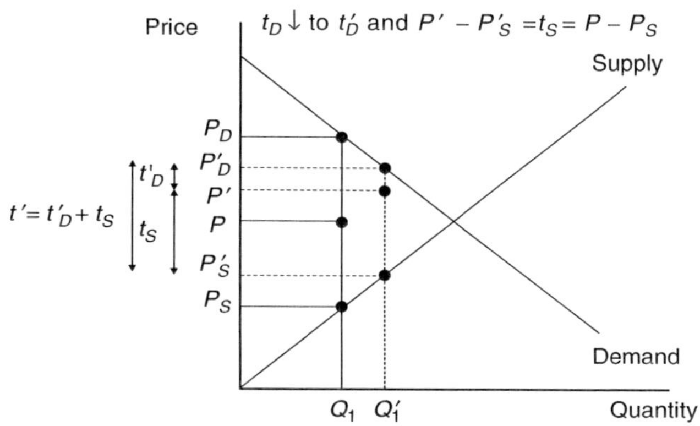

Figure 1.3.5 A reduction in the transaction costs faced by buyers increases the money price paid

rise. Failing to account for transaction costs would therefore give a very misleading picture of changes in both economic behaviour and economic welfare.

What about the effect of changes in the transaction costs faced by sellers? Recall that $P_D^M = P_D - t_D$. Thus, holding t_D constant, we have:

$$\frac{dP_D^M}{dt_S} = \frac{dP_D}{dt} = \frac{\varepsilon_S}{\varepsilon_S - \varepsilon_D} > 0 \tag{1.8}$$

Thus, holding t_D constant, an increase in t_S *increases* the money price paid by buyers. Combining all of these results, we can state the following. If both t_D and t_S increase at the same time, then:

- The full price paid by consumers must rise (unless demand is perfectly elastic); and
- The effect on the money price paid by consumers is ambiguous, and is given by:

$$\begin{aligned} dP_D^M &= \frac{dP_D}{dt}dt - dt_D = \frac{dP_D}{dt}(dt_D + dt_S) - dt_D = \frac{\varepsilon_S}{\varepsilon_S - \varepsilon_D}(dt_D + dt_S) - dt_D \\ &= \left(\frac{\varepsilon_S}{\varepsilon_S - \varepsilon_D} - 1\right)dt_D + \frac{\varepsilon_S}{\varepsilon_S - \varepsilon_D}dt_S \\ &= \frac{\varepsilon_D}{\varepsilon_S - \varepsilon_D}dt_D + \frac{\varepsilon_S}{\varepsilon_S - \varepsilon_D}dt_S \end{aligned} \tag{1.9}$$

This is a weighted average of the change in the transaction costs faced by the buyer and the seller. The first term is negative, but the second term is positive. The overall effect on the money price depends on the relative elasticities of supply and demand, and the size of the change in the transaction costs faced by both buyers and sellers.

1.3.1.2 Property rights and externalities

The invisible hand result assumes that all goods and services and factors of production are privately owned, and that property and other legal rights and obligations (including contractual rights) are well defined and enforced. In other words, the invisible hand result assumes that there is a legal system in place which defines and enforces these rights and obligations. The main purpose of this book is to explain why this set of assumptions matters so much and why legal rules play such an important role in market economies. Chapter 7, for example, explores in detail why the assumption of well-defined private property rights matters for efficiency.

Suppose that in the model of the perfectly competitive market examined above, there are no private property rights over one of the factors of production that are used by firms to produce output. Specifically, suppose that land, which we assume to be a key input, is not privately owned, but is instead able to be accessed without cost by each firm in the industry. In contrast, private property rights typically include a right to exclude others. Land is scarce, and when each firm in this hypothetical industry uses land and there are no private property rights, this imposes an unpriced cost on the other firms. In the language of economics, firms impose a negative externality on each other. Competition will result in a situation where the marginal willingness to pay for land is far below its opportunity cost, and the land will be inefficiently overused. The invisible hand theorem fails in this instance not because of competition and markets, but because of an absence of private property rights over some goods or services.

1.3.1.2.1 Pareto-relevant and -irrelevant externalities. More formally, an *externality* is said to exist whenever the benefit or profit of one person or firm (known as a *bystander*) is directly affected by the actions of another person or firm, and the bystander is neither compensated nor pays compensation. Externalities can be both positive and negative – but this is not the most important distinction. For the purposes of examining the consequences of the existence of externalities for the invisible hand theorem and for the role of the legal system, we will distinguish between two classes of externalities:[3]

- **A Pareto-relevant externality:** This kind of externality exists when the extent of the activity may be modified in such a way as to make the damaged party better off without making the acting party worse off. That is, the activity can be modified in such a way that a Pareto improvement is possible.
- **A Pareto-irrelevant externality**: This kind of externality exists when the extent of the activity cannot be modified in such a way as to make the damaged party better off without making the acting party worse off. One party's benefit or profit may still be affected by the other's actions in the aggregate, but there is no change that could be undertaken so as to make a Pareto improvement.

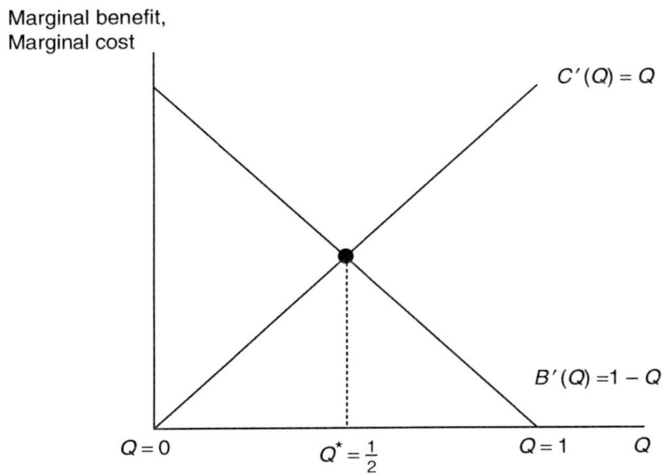

Figure 1.3.6 A negative externality

To understand this distinction, suppose that there are two individuals, 1 and 2. Suppose that person 1 undertakes an activity (the level of which, Q, is chosen by him), which yields him benefits of $B(Q) = Q - \frac{Q^2}{2}$. Suppose, however, that this activity leads to an uncompensated cost of $C(Q) = \frac{Q^2}{2}$ being imposed on individual 2. The efficient outcome here equates marginal benefits, which are equal to $B'(Q) = 1 - Q$ with marginal costs, which are $C'(Q) = Q$. Therefore, $Q^* = \frac{1}{2}$ is the efficient level of Q. The situation is illustrated in Figure 1.3.6.

This example implies two further conclusions:

- At any other point (say, for example, $Q = 0$ or $Q = 1$), there is a way to make at least one of these individuals better off, without making the other worse off. In other words, at any point other than $Q = 1/2$, the externality is Pareto relevant; and
- At the point $Q^* = \frac{1}{2}$, individual 2 is still negatively affected by Q (his cost would be lower if Q were lower), but this negative externality is now Pareto irrelevant: the extent of the activity cannot be modified in such a way as to make the damaged party (individual 2) better off without making the acting party (individual 1) worse off.

By definition, the welfare economist need only be concerned with Pareto-relevant externalities – that is, the first kind examined in this example, rather than the second.

The presence of Pareto-relevant externalities can cause the invisible hand theorem to fail. To see this, apply the previous example to a market setting. That is, suppose that there is a competitive market in which each firm has a zero marginal cost of production, and that type 1 individuals consume the good, with a demand curve of $B'(Q) = 1 - Q$. Suppose that production of Q imposes a cost of $C(Q) = \frac{Q^2}{2}$ on type 2 individuals, who do not consume the good. The competitive equilibrium here is where price equals marginal cost, which is where $Q = 1$. But the efficient outcome is $Q^* = \frac{1}{2}$. Thus, the competitive market outcome is inefficient.

1.3.1.2.2 Pecuniary externalities. Non-economists often make the mistake of thinking that *every* activity that generates an uncompensated reduction of an individual's utility level (that is, every externality) is a candidate for government intervention and regulation. But a moment's thought reveals that this view cannot be sustained.

First, some actions cause harm that is so trivial (relative to the costs of regulation) that it is appropriate, from an efficiency point of view, for the law to ignore them. Second, and more importantly, not all acts which harm others are Pareto relevant. Consider, for example, changes in prices. Increases in prices certainly tend to hurt consumers and tend to benefit producers. The opposite is true for price reductions. But do we really want to treat such price changes as externalities that are worthy candidates for regulation and intervention?

The answer, of course, is no. To see why, consider a perfectly competitive industry, and suppose that all producers experience a rise in marginal costs due to an increase in the price of an input. In the long run, this cost increase will be completely passed on to consumers in the form of an equal rise in prices. The costs of production have risen, so this will certainly reduce society's well-being – that outcome is unavoidable. The question is who should bear these costs so that the overall negative effect of higher costs is minimised. If prices rise, consumers are certainly worse off: they consume fewer units of the good, and for the units that they continue to consume, they pay a higher price. But the law does not force producers to compensate consumers for this price rise. Why not?

The reason is that the price rise is efficient: relative to a situation where prices do not rise, the price rise confers a benefit on producers that exceeds the cost to consumers. Moreover, the size of the price rise that occurs in a competitive market minimises the overall loss to society. To see this, consider Figure 1.3.7 below. Initially, firms face a marginal and average production cost of c_0, which is also equal to the market price. At this price, consumers purchase Q_0 units of the good. Then, suppose that marginal costs rise to $c_1 > c_0$. Suppose first that producers were enjoined (prevented) from passing on the price increase. Then consumers would continue to consume Q_0 units, but producers would experience a loss of A + B + C, which is greater than the loss to consumers if producers did increase prices (i.e. the change in consumer surplus of A + B). Thus, a law preventing producers from passing on price increases would reduce society's overall well-being by the additional amount C.

Now consider an alternative rule which allowed prices to rise but which forced producers to compensate consumers for the reduction in consumer surplus. Relative to the situation where the price rise is not passed on, producers gain A + B + C from increasing prices, since they avoid this loss. Thus, they would be willing to compensate consumers by the amount A + B, instead of not reducing prices and facing the loss of A + B + C. But all that the law has achieved here is to alter the distribution of costs and benefits: producers, rather than consumers, have been forced to bear the cost of the rise in input prices. There has been no overall welfare gain at all, because the price rise was actually an efficient response by producers to changing cost conditions.

Moreover, the price signal provided important information to consumers: it 'told' them to consume less of a good whose costs have gone

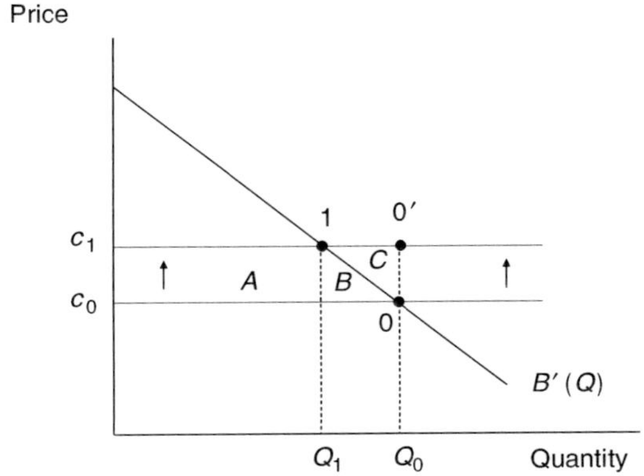

Figure 1.3.7 A pecuniary externality

up, and to consume other goods instead. When some goods become more costly (or more scarce), that is exactly the signal that we want consumers to heed. In other words, price changes provide an incentive for economic actors to shift resources from low-valued to high-valued uses, which is exactly what is required for efficiency. Market prices tend to convey this information far more effectively than courts or regulators – that, after all, is the point of having markets.

Finally, it is very doubtful that such a law would be able achieve its aims. Production conditions and costs are changing all the time. Under the legal principle discussed above, what is meant to happen if producer costs fall? In a competitive market, the market price would fall and consumers would gain. Using the same legal principle, is the law then supposed force consumers to compensate producers for the fall in prices? Again, there would be no benefit to the community from such a rule, and very likely great costs. From an efficiency point of view, there is no role for the legal or regulatory system in dealing with the effects of pecuniary externalities.

1.3.1.3 Informational imperfections and asymmetries

Another important assumption of the invisible hand theorem is that both consumers and producers have enough information to accurately estimate the characteristics of the goods they are consuming. Chapter 6 explores the importance of this assumption. The basic idea is as follows. Suppose that there is a competitive market for a good which can be produced in two varieties: safe and unsafe. Consumers' incremental marginal willingness to pay for a safe good exceeds the incremental cost of producing a safe good, so it is efficient for the safe good to be produced. Suppose that there is a rule of *caveat emptor* (buyer beware) in place. Finally, suppose that consumers do not have enough information to accurately estimate the harm that a good can cause. Specifically, suppose that consumers estimate that all goods are harmless. Then, since consumers believe that all goods are safe, and firms are not liable for harm, and since it is less costly to produce unsafe goods, the competitive equilibrium in this market will result in all firms producing an unsafe good, which will have a very low price. The inability of consumers to estimate expected harm in this example – combined with the legal rule - drives the market towards an inefficient outcome.

1.3.1.4 Market power and barriers to entry

A third important condition in the invisible hand result is that both consumers and producers are assumed to take prices as given, so that neither have any *market power*. This means that neither producers nor consumers can *profitably* move prices away from the prevailing market price. If firms use their market power, however, then the market outcome can fail to be efficient (although sometimes only a single firm in the industry can be enough to guarantee an efficient outcome). The basic idea is that if a firm has market power, it may be willing to increase price (and lose some – but not all – of its customers), thereby lowering revenue but also lowering costs, which could increase the firm's profit. But if price no long equals marginal cost, then some gains from trade have been left unexploited, which means that the outcome cannot be efficient. As Chapter 10 shows, the connections between the number of firms in an industry, the extent of market power, and the ensuing efficiency losses can often be tenuous.

Finally, the invisible hand result assumes that there are no barriers to entry or exit. The importance of this can be seen in our analysis of long-run competitive equilibrium explored earlier. If there are barriers to entry, then the long-run market supply curve is effectively just the short-run supply curve, which is the sum of individual short-run marginal cost curves and is generally upward sloping. If demand increases for some reason, then in the presence of barriers to entry, new firms will not be able to enter the market, and greater demand will be rationed with higher prices. Firms will be able to earn economic profits in the short run. However, these profits may eventually be dissipated away as the prices of scarce inputs rise and profits are bid down to zero. In this case, the owners of those scarce factors of production would earn economic rents. Relative to a situation without entry barriers, overall welfare would be lower.

1.4 Notes

This chapter began with a brief discussion of the legal foundations of markets. Hayek (1994) is a three-volume examination of the role and functions of law and legislation in free societies. The literature on property rights and contract law is vast. Bethell (1998) and Pipes (2000) are excellent book-length examinations of broader issues surrounding property rights. Barzel (1997) is a useful book-length examination of the economics of property rights.

Harberger (1971) is a classic reference on applied welfare economics. Friedman (1990, chapter 15) contains an excellent discussion of different efficiency concepts. Nicholson and Snyder (2009, chapter 8) provides a good overview of competitive markets and long- and short-run equilibrium. Boadway and Bruce (1991), Johansson (1987) and Johansson (1991) contain useful discussions of the basic principles of welfare economics. Jones (2005) is an advanced treatment.

The analysis of per unit transaction costs in this chapter is inspired by Alchian and Allen (1983, pp. 48–50). Spulber (1999) is a book-length examination of endogenous transaction costs and the role of intermediaries and middlemen. Stavins (1995) contains an excellent analysis of transaction costs in the context of markets for tradeable pollution permits.

1.5 Exercises

1. Consider the following model of the market for petrol, which is perfectly competitive and has the demand and supply curves:

$$Q_d = 18 - P \text{ (Demand)}$$
$$Q_s = P \text{ (Supply)}$$

where Q_d is quantity of petrol demanded, Q_s is the quantity of petrol supplied, and P is the market price of petrol.

(a) What does it mean for markets to clear? Find the market-clearing price and quantity of petrol.

(b) Define the concepts of consumer surplus and producer surplus. What is the consumer and producer surplus at the market-clearing price?

(c) Define the concept of point elasticity of demand and supply. At the market-clearing price and quantity, what is the point elasticity of demand? What is the point elasticity of supply?

(d) Suppose that the government puts a tax of \$4 on each unit of petrol consumption. How much revenue tax does this tax raise? What is the deadweight loss of the petrol tax?

(e) Now suppose that instead of taxing consumption, the government puts a tax on production of each unit of petrol. Repeat part (d). Define the concept of the incidence of a tax. Who bears the burden of a petrol tax on consumption or production: consumers or producers? If the demand curve for petrol was less elastic, and the supply curve for petrol was more elastic, what would happen to the incidence of the petrol tax? Explain, using a diagram.

(f) Define the concept of a negative externality. Suppose that petrol consumption causes pollution, and that there is a negative external marginal cost of \$2 associated with the pollution that occurs as a result of petrol consumption. What is the efficient quantity of petrol consumption and production? In the absence of the petrol tax, is the free market outcome efficient? Explain. What is the total cost of pollution at the efficient quantity? Carefully explain why, even though petrol consumption causes pollution and that there is a negative external marginal cost of \$2 associated with petrol consumption, the efficient level of petrol consumption is not zero.

(g) With the petrol tax of \$4 in place, is the market outcome efficient? What is the deadweight loss of the \$4 petrol tax in this situation?

2. Suppose that the market for insulation batts is perfectly competitive and can be described by the following demand and supply curves:

$$Q^D = 50 - P$$

$$Q^S = 10 + P$$

(a) Draw the demand and supply curves based on the above equations.
(b) Find the market-clearing price and quantity of insulation batts.
Now suppose that the government implements a policy of subsidising insulation batt purchases. The subsidy is set at \$10 and is paid to consumers.
(c) Find the new market-clearing quantity. With the subsidy in place, what price do consumers pay? What price do producers receive? What is the change in consumer surplus? What is the change in producer surplus? How much revenue does it cost for the government to run this subsidy scheme? What is the deadweight loss of the insulation subsidy, and why does it arise in the case of a subsidy?
(d) What is the incidence of the subsidy? In general, how do the incidence and deadweight loss of a subsidy depend on the elasticities of demand and supply? (Hint: Draw a diagram to show your answer).

3. Suppose that there are two markets, A and B. These goods are neither substitutes nor complements, so an increase in the price of one good as no effect on demand for the other good, and vice versa.
The supply curves for both goods are perfectly elastic, with marginal costs constant and equal to 1 in both markets.
The demand curves for these two goods are as follows:

$$Q_D^A = 10 - P_A$$

$$Q_D^B = 5 - P_B$$

(a) Find the initial market-clearing prices and quantities in each market. At these market-clearing prices, what is the point elasticity of demand in each market?
(b) Suppose that the government introduces a tax of \$1 in market A, and \$1 in market B. How much revenue does this combination of taxes raise? What is the deadweight loss of this combination of taxes?
(c) Now suppose that you wanted to raise the same (or more) tax revenue that you found in part (b), but that you also wanted to reduce the overall deadweight loss of the tax system. Is there some other combination of taxes that allows you to achieve this goal? Explain your answer, using the elasticity of demand.

4. This question considers the effects of government purchases on market prices, quantities and welfare. Consider the market for cars, which is perfectly competitive and is described by the following demand and supply curves:

$$Q_D = 40 - P$$

$$Q_S = P$$

(a) Find the market-clearing price and quantity. What is the producer and consumer surplus at this market-clearing price?
Now suppose that the government needs to purchase 20 cars, no matter what the price it has to pay. In other words, the government's demand curve for cars is perfectly inelastic at the quantity of 20.

(b) The new market demand curve is the horizontal sum of the private demand curve and the new government demand curve. On a diagram, plot the old demand curve, the new demand curve, and the supply curve. Find the new market-clearing price and quantity.

(c) As a result of the government purchase programme, what happens to the producer surplus? What happens to the consumer surplus of those who purchase cars for private use? Who benefits from the government programme to purchase cars, and who loses? Do the benefits outweigh the losses? Explain.

(d) How much does the government spend on car purchases if it has to purchase 20 cars at the new market-clearing price? The amount of government spending is often used as a measure of the economic benefits of that spending. Explain why the amount that the government spends on cars is a very poor and inaccurate estimate of the economic benefits of the car purchase programme.

(e) 'Crowding out' refers to the reduction in private quantity demanded that occurs when government purchases goods on private markets. What is the extent of crowding out in this case?

Some economists use the term 'multiplier' to describe the effect of government purchases on output. The multiplier is defined as the increase in output divided by the increase in government demand. Calculate the multiplier in this case.

(f) How do the multiplier and the extent of crowding out depend on the elasticities of demand and supply? (Hint: draw a diagram to show your answer.) Under what circumstances is the multiplier 1, and what is the extent of crowding out and the economic benefits of the car purchase programme in this case? Under what circumstances is the multiplier zero, and what is the extent of crowding out and the economic benefits in this case?

2
Courts, Legal Rules, and Markets

2.1 Introduction

What role do legal rules and courts play in a market economy? What role *should* they play? Why do courts make the decisions that they do, and what are the some of the problems that arise with collective legal decision making?

This chapter presents a brief overview of the theory of legal decision making, the behaviour of courts, and the production of legal rules. Section 2.2 explores the issue of whether legal rules can properly be regarded as pure public goods, and some of the economic issues surrounding government provision law enforcement activities if this is assumed to be the case. Section 2.3 examines the normative approach to legal decision making, which assumes that courts and judges make decisions based on various public interest criteria, one of which is efficiency. This section also includes a discussion and analysis of procedural and outcome fairness. In section 2.4 we take a step back from allocative efficiency and other criteria, and study a more modest role for courts – as efficient processors of information. We examine the consequences of this assumption when evidence gathering is costly and can be undertaken strategically by parties. Section 2.5 assumes that rather than enhancing efficiency or processing information, courts as biased 'policy makers' where tribunals, judges or juries have their own preferences over legal rules or outcomes. Section 2.6 examines the advantages and disadvantages associated with group decision making (as opposed to individual decision making) in legal settings.

2.2 Legal rules and law enforcement: Private or public goods?

In modern economies individuals and firms supply a wide range of detection and enforcement activities, and these are purchased by consumers on markets, just like ordinary goods. For example, firms hire private security companies to protect their businesses from theft and malicious damage. Companies and individuals hire lawyers to protect their rights. Individuals put locks on their doors to protect their private property, purchase guns to protect their life and liberty.

Some of these activities benefit only the parties that undertake them. An individual who puts a lock on the door of his house largely benefits himself. But individuals also supply goods which benefit others: the individual who catches a thief benefits not only himself but his entire neighbourhood. Because private individuals supply public goods in the absence of government intervention, the relevant questions for policy analysis are: is the amount that is privately supplied efficient? If so, why? If not, how large is the inefficiency, and can anything be done about it?

2.2.1 Example: Reporting a crime

As an example of the how spillover effects and public good characteristics can affect welfare very naturally in a law and economics setting, consider the following example. Suppose there is a community of $M \geq 2$ individuals. Suppose that a crime has occurred in this community. Each individual can either report the crime, or not. Let $s_i = \{0,1\}$ be the strategy space of individual i, where:

$$s_i = \begin{cases} 0 & \text{if individual } i \text{ does not report the crime} \\ 1 & \text{if individual } i \text{ reports the crime} \end{cases}$$

Suppose that there is a non-refundable cost of $c < 1$ that each individual incurs if they report the crime. If sufficiently many people report the crime, then the criminal is caught and each member of the community benefits, irrespective of whether they report it or not. Hence reporting a crime has the characteristics of a public good – it is non-rival (enjoyment of the benefits of reporting by one person does not reduce enjoyment by another) and non-excludable (once a crime is reported, it is not possible to prevent an individual from benefitting).

Normalise the benefit to each individual of the criminal being caught to 1. Let w be the least number of individuals who must report the crime in order for the criminal to be caught and the benefits to each individual to be secured. Let m be the number of individuals who actually end up reporting the crime. The payoff to individual i is then:

$$u_i = \begin{cases} 1-c & \text{if } m \geq w \text{ and } s_i = 1 \\ 1 & \text{if } m \geq w \text{ and } s_i = 0 \\ -c & \text{if } m < w \text{ and } s_i = 1 \\ 0 & \text{if } m < w \text{ and } s_i = 0 \end{cases}$$

Consider a community of two individuals, for example. Suppose that if at least one person reports the crime, then the criminal is convicted and punished. Let the cost of reporting be $c < 1$. In this situation, it is efficient for only one person to report the crime, and total welfare in the efficient outcome is $W^* = 2 - c$. Do individuals have the incentive to behave efficiently? The payoff matrix for this game is shown in Table 2.2.1.

Recall the concept of a *Nash equilibrium* of a strategic game. Define the notation:

s_{-i} = a collection of strategic choices of all other players, except player i

Take any collection s_{-i} of other players' strategic choices. Player i's *best response* $BR_i(s_{-i})$ to s_{-i} is simply the strategy (or collection of strategies) that gives him the highest payoff in that situation. That is, $BR_i(s_{-i})$ solves:

$$\max_{s_i \in S_i} u_i(s_i, s_{-i})$$

where $u_i(s_i, s_{-i})$ is the utility of player i when he chooses the strategy s_i and the other players in the game are choosing s_{-i}. Hence:

$$BR_i(s_{-i}) = \arg\max_{s_i \in S_i} u_i(s_i, s_{-i})$$

Table 2.2.1 The payoff matrix for the crime reporting game

		Individual 2	
		Report	**Don't Report**
Individual 1	**Report**	$(1-c, 1-c)$	$(1-c, 1)$
	Don't Report	$(1, 1-c)$	$(0,0)$

A (pure strategy) *Nash equilibrium* is simply a collection of strategies $s^* \equiv (s_1^*, s_2^*, \dots, s_n^*)$ such that every player *i*'s strategy choice s_i^* is a best response to s_{-i}^*. In other words, the combination $(s_1^*, s_2^*, \dots, s_n^*)$ is a Nash equilibrium if it satisfies:

$$s_i^* = \arg\max_{s_i \in S_i} u_i(s_i, s_{-i}^*) \quad \text{for all } i$$

There are two pure strategy Nash equilibria in the game in Table 2.2.1, in which either individual 1 or individual 2 reports the crime, and the other individual does not. These equilibria are both efficient.

There is a symmetric *mixed strategy* Nash equilibrium as well. To find this mixed strategy equilibrium, consider individual 1. To be willing to use a mixed strategy, he must be indifferent between reporting the crime and not reporting it. Suppose that individual 1 believes that individual 2 reports the crime with probability ρ. Then the expected payoff from individual 1 reporting is $1 - c$, since he is guaranteed to receive that amount from reporting. On the other hand, if individual 1 decides not to report the crime, he may still benefit if individual 2 reports it. Since this happens with probability ρ, individual 1's expected benefit from not reporting the crime is simply $\rho \times 1 = \rho$. Thus, to be indifferent between reporting and not reporting, we must have $1 - c = \rho^*$. This is the intersection of the individual reaction curves as shown in Figure 2.2.1 below.

The expected number of individuals who report the crime in this mixed strategy equilibrium is:

$$(\rho^*)^2 \times 2 + 2(\rho^*)(1 - \rho^*) \times 1 = 2(1-c)^2 + 2(1-c)c = 2(1-c)$$

which shows that in expected terms, if $c > \frac{1}{2}$ the mixed strategy equilibrium is expected to have an inefficiently low number of people report the crime. On the other hand, if $c < \frac{1}{2}$, then we can expect there to be an inefficiently *high* number of individuals reporting the crime.

The expected welfare level is:

$$\begin{aligned} W &= (\rho^*)^2(2 - 2c) + 2(\rho^*)(1 - \rho^*)(2 - c) \\ &= (1-c)^2(2-2c) + 2(1-c)c(2-c) = 2(1-c) < 2 - c = W^* \end{aligned}$$

For any level of c, this is lower than welfare in the efficient outcome. Therefore, even if the expected number of reporters is 1, welfare is still expected to be lower in this equilibrium than in the efficient outcome, for any positive value of c.

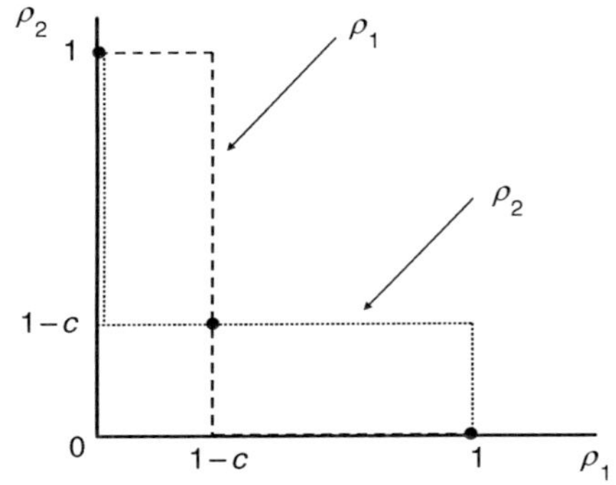

Figure 2.2.1 Reaction curves and equilibria in the crime reporting game

Note that the expected number of individuals who report the crime, expected welfare, and the probability that both individuals will report the crime depends negatively on the cost of reporting the crime. In the extreme case where the cost of reporting the crime is zero, all individuals report. In the other extreme case where the cost of reporting is 1, nobody reports the crime – even though it is still efficient for at least one person to do so.

In addition to issues related to the public good characteristics of certain law enforcement activity, there are a number of other difficulties. As Cowen (1992) points out, foremost among these is the issue of conflict between competing private law enforcement agencies. Suppose that individual A contracts with enforcement company A to protect his rights, and that A's promised punishment for murder is the death penalty. Suppose that individual B is contracted to enforcement company B, which promises to protect its customers from the death penalty. Now suppose that B murders A's son – this now raises the possibility of conflict between the obligations that company A and B promised to carry out on behalf of their clients.

On the other hand, there is a great deal of empirical evidence which shows that throughout history private dispute-resolution markets have developed, in which arbitration services are supplied by private firms and parties agree to be bound by their decisions.[1]

In summary, even if legal rules and enforcement activities are pure public goods, this does not resolve all of the issues that are of interest. It does *not* mean, for example, that it will be always efficient for individuals to supply *no* private enforcement activity themselves, and that the government should undertake all forms of enforcement activity.

It also does not mean that government supply will make a difference to overall levels of enforcement or economic efficiency, or that the marginal benefits of any level of government supply will always outweigh the costs. And it certainly does not mean that governments will automatically supply the efficient amount of the pure public good.

2.3 The normative approach to legal decision making

2.3.1 Courts as efficiency maximisers

Chapter 1 examined the invisible hand theorem and discussed some of the implications that may follow if the assumptions of that result do not hold. One of the main conclusions to emerge there was that if there is an inefficient allocation of economic resources, then it must be because one or more of the assumptions of the theorem do not hold. For example, economic resource allocation might be observed to be inefficient because private property rights over assets are not well defined, which may lead to greater risk, underinvestment and resource underexploitation.

One important approach to justifying and explaining the role of courts and legal decision making is that in such situations, legal rules and decisions can enhance the efficiency of resource allocation. Thus, continuing our property rights example, if private property rights are not well defined, courts and legal rules may assist by better defining these private property rights.[2] This general approach to legal decision making, in which courts and/or legal rules should aim to improve economic outcomes, is broadly known as the *normative* or *public interest* approach. Under this view, the existence of an inefficiency (which may be due to a market failure or the existence of inefficient legal rules) justifies intervention and a change in current legal rules by governments, regulators or courts. The only remaining question is: which interventions or rules should be chosen?

The normative approach proceeds by applying a test of market failure and the tools of cost–benefit analysis. The approach is usually comprised of the following five elements:

1. Define some suitable *efficiency criterion.*
2. Analyse the market, and *determine whether inefficiencies exist.*
3. Determine the *magnitude and extent* of the inefficiency.
4. Determine which interventions are *appropriate* and which are *feasible.* This entails *identifying possible legal rules* that directly or indirectly address the alleged market failure. Such appropriate, feasible rules may not actually exist.

5. Weigh up the incremental benefits and costs of the change (relative to an appropriately specified baseline) and show that the expected benefits of the proposed rule outweigh the expected costs. The *direct costs* associated with rule are the expenditures associated with the proposed rule (for example, the costs to firms and consumers in the market under consideration, etc.). The *indirect costs* include rule-induced inefficiencies (that is, possible misallocations in other markets and other general equilibrium effects).

2.3.1.1 Normative as positive theory (NPT) and the role of legal precedent

Some economists take the normative approach a step further and argue that the legal system (and, in particular, the common law system of rules) *in fact* evolves over time to produce efficient rules. The basic idea of this *efficiency hypothesis* is that legal rulings set precedents for possible future disputes between parties. If a court sets a precedent that leads to inefficient outcomes, then in certain circumstances there will be gains to parties if they contest that decision and attempt to get the inefficient decision overturned. Thus, the *normative* concept of efficiency leads to *positive* predictions regarding the behaviour of courts and the evolution of legal rules over time. This efficiency approach to the evolution of the common law is a version of the 'normative as positive' (NPT) theory of regulation,[3] and has been proposed most forcefully by Posner (2007) and analysed in detail by Rubin (1977). The efficiency hypothesis will be examined in further detail in Chapter 11.

2.3.2 Legal rules and institutions: Coordination devices or restraints on behaviour?

In most examinations of legal systems, legal rules are viewed as restraining the behaviour of consumers and firms as they behave within market settings. For example, private property rights and nuisance law deter individuals from imposing uncompensated negative external costs on others. Contract law restrains opportunistic behaviour when unforeseen contingencies or unanticipated events occur. Using efficiency as the benchmark, the goal of the normative approach is to show that such restraints will lead to benefits which outweigh costs, relative to alternative rules and institutional arrangements.

An alternative but closely related view – which still sits firmly within the overall normative approach – is that legal rules serve as *coordination devices* between individuals, rather than as devices that restrain individual behaviour.[4] Consider, for example, speed limits for automobiles.

One obvious role for speed limits is to restrain individuals from driving too fast. But another possible role is to coordinate behaviour. Lave (1985), for example, shows that there is a statistically significant relationship between the fatality rate and the *variance* of speed, rather than average speed, and suggests that this supports the view of speed limits as coordination devices, rather than restraining devices.

To understand the difference between the two possible ways in which legal rules may operate, consider the strategic game in Table 2.3.1. There are two individuals, 1 and 2. They both benefit if they drive at a fast speed, and their benefits are slightly lower if they both drive at slow speeds. But the worst outcomes occur when they drive at *different* speeds – if individual 1 is driving fast, then individual 2's slow driving imposes a negative externality on individual 1, since the flow of traffic is slower and it takes 1 more time to get to where he wants to go. Similarly, if individual 2 is driving at a slow speed, then individual 1's fast driving imposes a negative externality on individual 2.

The efficient outcome here is for both individuals to drive at a fast speed. But this is only one of two pure strategy Nash equilibria here. Setting a speed limit which drivers obey may serve as a *coordination device* for participants and does not alter their payoffs; it simply helps them choose among multiple equilibria, providing a focal point for individuals so that they voluntarily choose the best equilibrium action.

On the other hand, suppose that the role of speed limits is to restrain drivers from behaviour that would endanger others. Suppose that an accident is more likely if both drivers drive at a fast speed. In the game in Table 2.3.2, individual 1 benefits if he drives fast and individual 2 drives slow, but individual 2 is made worse off as a result of this. The efficient outcome is for both to drive at a slow speed, but the equilibrium is for both to drive at a fast speed. The role of speed limits in Table 2.3.2 is very different from the previous example: it is to somehow change the expected payoffs of individuals and restrain them, inducing them not to choose the equilibrium actions or to change the payoffs of the game so as to alter incentives and induce the players to choose the efficient outcome as an equilibrium.

Table 2.3.1 Payoffs from driving at different speeds: The coordination game

		Individual 2	
		Fast	**Slow**
Individual 1	**Fast**	(100,100)	(20,10)
	Slow	(10, 20)	(50,50)

Table 2.3.2 Payoffs from driving at different speeds: The restraining game

		Individual 2	
		Fast	Slow
Individual 1	Fast	(30,30)	(60,10)
	Slow	(10,60)	(50,50)

2.3.3 Law and social norms

The coordinating role of speed limits discussed in the previous section is an extreme example of how formal legal rules can interact with more informal standards of individual behaviour. It is important to note that throughout this book, when we refer to 'legal rules' we are not referring exclusively to formal legal rules. Some of the most important legal rules are not formal at all – they take the form of social norms or standards of behaviour which evolve over time. Becker (1974) and Becker and Murphy (2000, chapter 2) show how *strong complementarities* between individual and group behaviour can lead to 'social multipliers' which, in a legal setting, can reinforce (or work against) the individual effects of formal legal rules. We can interpret these situations as occurring when social norms have strong influences on individual behaviour, which may override or reinforce the effects of formal legal rules.

To see how these social norms can operate in a legal setting, suppose that there is a continuum of individuals, and that individual i is considering the level of 'illegal activity' in which he will engage. Let this level be denoted by x_i. The benefit of illegal activity to individual i is $B(x_i, X)$, with $B_{x_i} = \frac{\partial B}{\partial x_i} > 0$ and $B_{x_i x_i} = \frac{\partial^2 B}{\partial x_i^2} < 0$, and where $X = \int x_i di$ is the aggregate level of illegal activity. The continuum assumption simply formalises the notion that each individual has a negligible effect on X, although acting together individuals have a significant effect. We will assume that X affects individual i's benefit negatively (although, as we will see, this assumption is not required for the analysis that follows), so that $B_X = \frac{\partial B}{\partial X} < 0$. If the individual chooses to commit illegal activity of x_i, we assume that he faces an expected fine of $\rho f x_i$, where ρ is the probability of being caught and punished, and f is the marginal fine (that is the fine per unit of illegal activity). Thus the individual's expected gain from choosing x_i is:

$$B(x_i, X) - \rho f x_i$$

The individual equates marginal benefits with expected marginal costs, so the individually optimal level of illegal activity, denoted by x_i^*, solves:

$$B_{x_i}(x_i^*, X) = \rho f \tag{2.1}$$

and we can write:

$$x_i^* = x_i^*(X, \rho f)$$

The presence of *strong complementarities* in this context simply involves an assumption that holding other variables constant, the individual's choice of illegal activity depends positively on the aggregate level of illegal activity X – that is, on what all other individuals do. In this sense, X can be regarded as a social norm or a standard of behaviour, which influences individual behaviour.[5] For example, there may be a social norm not to respect private property rights, so that an individual's choice of whether to commit theft depends strongly on his own benefits from theft, as well as the aggregate level of theft – even though a higher aggregate level of theft makes each individuals worse off. Analytically, strong complementarities depend on the sign of $B_{x_i X} = \dfrac{\partial^2 B}{\partial x_i \partial X}$, not on the sign of B_X. To see this, hold the expected fine constant, and totally differentiate equation (2.1), which yields:

$$B_{x_i x_i} dx_i^* + B_{x_i X} dX = 0$$

so that:

$$\frac{dx_i^*}{dX} = -\frac{B_{x_i X}}{B_{x_i x_i}}$$

Since $B_{x_i x_i}$ is assumed to be negative, the sign of $\dfrac{dx_i^*}{dX}$ turns on the sign of $B_{x_i X}$, which is the effect of X on the individual's *marginal* (not total) benefit of illegal activity. If this is positive, then strong complementarities are said to be present.

To see how these strong complementarities or social norms can interact with the formal legal system, suppose that the expected fine is increased, either by increasing ρ, f or both. In the presence of social norms, there are now two effects that need to be considered. The first is the partial effect of the increased fine on individual behaviour, $\dfrac{\partial x_i^*}{\partial(\rho f)}$. Holding X fixed, this is negative. The second effect is the reinforcing effect of social norms on individual behaviour.

The change in the expected fine affects all individuals and so affects the aggregate, and this feeds back into individual choices. The effect on the total level of illegal activity is therefore given by:

$$\frac{dX}{d(\rho f)} = \frac{d}{d(\rho f)}\int x_i^*(X,\rho f)\,di$$

$$= \int \frac{d}{d(\rho f)} x_i^*(X,\rho f)di = \int \left[\frac{\partial x_i^*}{\partial X}\frac{dX}{d(\rho f)} + \frac{\partial x_i^*}{\partial(\rho f)}\right]di$$

so that:

$$\frac{dX}{d(\rho f)} = \frac{\int \frac{\partial x_i^*}{\partial(\rho f)}di}{1-\int \frac{\partial x_i^*}{\partial X}di} \tag{2.2}$$

The numerator in equation (2.2) is the sum of the partial effects of an increased fine on individual behaviour, holding X fixed. The denominator is the 'social multiplier' effect, which boosts the change in aggregate illegal activity above and beyond the effect that would occur in the absence of any social norms. If $0 < \int \frac{\partial x_i^*}{\partial X}di < 1$, then the increase in the expected fine may have a significant effect on aggregate illegal activity, even though the partial effect on individuals $\frac{\partial x_i^*}{\partial(\rho f)}$, may be quite small. On the other hand, if there are no strong complementarities present (so that $\frac{\partial x_i^*}{\partial X} < 0$) then the denominator in equation (2.2) would exceed unity, and the deterrence effect of the increase in the expected fine on individual behaviour would be less than the sum of the partial effects on individual behaviour.

2.3.4 Courts as implementers of 'fair' or 'just' economic outcomes

Efficiency is clearly not the only criterion which may be relevant for courts. 'Fairness' or equity may also be important. There are two concepts of fairness that we consider here. The first is *procedural fairness*. Under this definition of fairness, a fair outcome is one that occurs as the result of a fair process. Suppose, for example,[6] that two individuals with identical wealth levels agree to bet on the outcome of the toss of an unbiased coin. The loser pays the winner \$100. After the result is known, the outcome may be perceived by an outside observer (who is only interested in outcomes) to be unfair, since it involves a more uneven distribution of wealth. But the process by which this occurred could hardly be said to be unfair.

On the other hand, now suppose that the losing individual steals \$100 back from the winner. To our outside observer, the outcome in terms of distribution of wealth may appear to be fairer in terms of wealth distribution – but it was clearly obtained by an unfair process. Moreover, as we will see in Chapter 10, even if theft was acceptable from a fairness point of view, it would have significant (negative) efficiency consequences. Indeed, in this second example there is unlikely be a trade-off between equity and efficiency: if the entire set of negative economic consequences of not punishing or deterring theft are traced through, then the outside observer (who only cares about equality of outcomes) may also end up concluding that theft is undesirable.

Moving the focus away from outcomes and resorting to notions of procedural fairness is not required to reach the conclusion that theft is undesirable. The same considerations apply to many of the issues discussed in this book. For example, consider accident law. Those concerned with procedural fairness would argue that not allowing a victim to claim damages from an injurer as a result of accidental harm caused by the injurer's lack of care (that is, a rule of no liability) is inherently 'unfair'. However, as we will see in Chapter 4, it is also the case that a rule of no liability leads to inefficient outcomes. Again, there is no need to appeal to notions of procedural fairness to reach the conclusion that a rule of no liability is undesirable.

As a result of these and other considerations, there is considerable debate in the literature over the appropriate definition of the concept of economic fairness or equity. While many economists do not regard such questions as lying within the domain of economics, the actual development of many legal rules, judgements and decisions that affect economic outcomes (and their implementation) are almost always the subject of criticisms (or endorsements) based on notions of 'fairness' and 'equity'.

2.4 Courts as interpreters of evidence: The economics of updating of information

Legal rules and the decisions taken by courts can influence market outcomes by creating 'price' signals and altering individual incentives. One minimalist way of viewing courts (or judges or juries) is simply as arbiters who process information and in doing so provide information to others in the economy.

To understand this "information processing" role and some of its consequences, consider the following simple example. Denote by G the event that an individual has committed a criminal act, and I the event that the individual has not. The judge (or jury) does not know for sure whether the individual is guilty or not, but the parties to the dispute each know whether the individual is guilty. The judge (or jury) has no preferences over the outcome itself, although they may incur costs if the decision turns out to be wrong.

Suppose that in the absence of evidence, the court's unconditional probability or *prior belief* of guilt is $\rho(G)$. The presentation of *evidence* before a court conveys information about guilt or innocence. Suppose that there is a piece of evidence E which is suggestive of guilt, but is not conclusive. The event of no evidence arising is denoted by *NE*. The probability of observing evidence and that the defendant is guilty is $\rho\ \rho(G \cap E$. The probability that the evidence arises if the individual has committed the act is:

$$\rho(E \mid G) = \frac{\rho(E \cap G)}{\rho(G)} \tag{2.3}$$

On the other hand, the probability that the evidence arises if the individual has *not* committed the act is

$$\rho(E \mid I) = \frac{\rho(E \cap I)}{\rho(I)} \tag{2.4}$$

The probability that evidence will actually emerge is therefore:

$$\begin{aligned} \rho(E) &= \rho(E \cap G) + \rho(E \cap I) \\ &= \rho(E \mid G)\rho(G) + \rho(E \mid I)r(I) \end{aligned} \tag{2.5}$$

The court updates its prior beliefs by computing the probability of guilt, conditional on evidence of guilt having been presented, through the use of Bayes' rule. This probability is denoted by $\rho(G \mid E)$, and is equal to:

$$\rho(G \mid E) = \frac{\rho(G \cap E)}{\rho(E)} = \frac{\rho(E \mid G)\rho(G)}{\rho(E \mid G)\rho(G) + \rho(E \mid I)\rho(I)}.$$

2.4.1 Strategic evidence gathering

Consider the previous Bayesian updating framework, and suppose that there are two parties – a plaintiff and a defendant – to a legal dispute. Suppose that they gather evidence and produce to the court the evidence pair $E = (e_P, e_D)$. The cost of obtaining e 'units' of evidence is simply assumed be \$$e$. Suppose that:

$$\frac{\rho(E \mid G)}{\rho(E \mid I)} = \frac{\rho(e_P, e_D \mid G)}{\rho(e_P, e_D \mid I)} = \frac{e_P}{e_D} \tag{2.6}$$

The ratio $\dfrac{\rho(e_P, e_D \mid G)}{\rho(e_P, e_D \mid I)}$ is called the *likelihood ratio*, and is defined as the ratio of the probability of observing the evidence pair $E = (e_P, e_D)$ when the individual is actually guilty to the probability of observing the evidence pair $E = (e_P, e_D)$ when the individual is innocent. Note that the likelihood ratio can take on any positive value.

The assumption in equation (2.6) simply states that this ratio is proportional to the ratio of expenditure on the production of evidence by each party. If this is the case, then $\rho(E \mid G) = \rho(E \mid I)\frac{e_P}{e_D}$, and:

$$\text{Prob (Plaintiff Wins)} = \rho(G \mid E)$$

$$= \frac{\rho(E \mid I)\frac{e_P}{e_D}\rho(G)}{\rho(E \mid I)\frac{e_P}{e_D}\rho(G) + \rho(E \mid I)\rho(I)}$$

$$= \frac{\rho(G)e_P}{\rho(G)e_P + \rho(I)e_D} \tag{2.7}$$

If the court has *uniform* prior beliefs, so that $\rho(G) = \rho(I)$, then this collapses to:

$$\text{Prob (Plaintiff Wins)} = \rho(G \mid E) = \frac{e_P}{e_P + e_D} \tag{2.8}$$

Equation (2.8) states that if the court is an efficient processor of information and has uniform prior beliefs, and if the likelihood ratio is proportional to the ratio of expenditure on the production of evidence by each party, then the party that spends more resources on evidence production at trial is more likely to win the case, irrespective of whether the defendant is actually guilty or not. On the other hand, if the court has non-uniform priors and instead has some predetermined bias of guilt [so that $\rho(G) \neq \rho(I)$], then the probability that the plaintiff wins is given by equation (2.7) above.

Even though courts in this example are efficient processors of information, the probability of either outcome occurring depends on the evidence-gathering ability of the two sides in the legal contest and is influenced by the way the evidence-gathering game is set up. Suppose that the marginal cost of producing evidence is 1 for each party. If the judgement has a value of $J to the plaintiff, and the defendant stands to lose $J if the plaintiff is successful, and if they are both risk neutral, then the expected net benefits to the plaintiff are:

$$B_P = \frac{e_P}{e_P + e_D}J - e_P$$

and

$$B_D = -\frac{e_P}{e_P + e_D}J - e_D$$

for the defendant. Question 2 at the end of this chapter asks you to find the equilibrium of this game.

2.5 Courts as biased policy makers

Whether we like it or not, judges and tribunals have their own preferences and they often act as policy makers implementing their own preferences over outcomes. This section therefore considers the extreme case, where a judicial decision maker has their own preferences over outcomes and makes decisions based *only* on these preferences.

There are again two parties to a legal dispute: the plaintiff (P) and the defendant (D), who do not know what the judge's true preferences are. Each party has to submit an outcome to the judge. A party wins the case if it is closest to the judge's true preferences, which are only revealed after the case is concluded. The judge's decision rule is very simple: he simply implements the outcome announced by the parties which is closest to his own true preference.

The rules of this game mean that the parties to the dispute will be influenced by their beliefs about the judge's true preferences, and will modify their positions accordingly. However, because the utility of the parties depends on the outcome, they will also take their own payoffs into account.

To illustrate what can occur, consider a simple example. Suppose that a *judicial decision* is simply a parameter J on the interval $[\underline{J}, \overline{J}]$. This could be a policy outcome which has wider ramifications, or it could simply reflect the judge's own preferences about what is 'just' or 'fair' (or, indeed, efficient) in the particular case before him. The only role of the judge is to announce a decision J.

The game proceeds by each party simultaneously announcing a position on the interval $[\underline{J}, \overline{J}]$, and then the judge chooses the position that is closest to his preferred position. The parties then receive payoffs when this announcement is made.

Assume that the parties are diametrically opposed to each other: the plaintiff's utility is increasing in J, and the defendant's utility is decreasing in J. Suppose that, as far as the parties are concerned, every judge is *ex ante* identical, with favourite policy J°. Neither party knows the true value of J°. Suppose that both parties have no information about the biases of the particular judge before them, so that, as far as they are concerned, and any value of J° is possible with equal probability. Hence parties' beliefs about J° are uniformly distributed on $[\underline{J}, \overline{J}]$. Since the plaintiff's utility is increasing in J, and the defendant's utility is decreasing in J, the plaintiff's most-preferred outcome is $J_P^\circ = \overline{J}$, and the defendant's most-preferred outcome is $J_D^\circ = \underline{J}$. Finally, suppose that the parties are risk neutral.

Let J_P and J_D be the announcements that each party make. The judge awards the case to the party which is closest to his true preferences. The probability that the plaintiff P wins the dispute is:

$$\begin{aligned}&\Pr\,(J_P - J^\circ < J^\circ - J_D)\\ &= \Pr\left(\frac{J_D + J_P}{2} < J^\circ\right) = 1 - \Pr\left(J^\circ \le \frac{J_D + J_P}{2}\right)\\ &= 1 - F\left(\frac{J_D + J_P}{2}\right)\end{aligned}$$

where $F(\cdot)$ is the cumulative distribution function of each parties' belief. If beliefs are uniformly distributed on $[\underline{J}, \bar{J}]$, then $F(x) = \dfrac{x - \underline{J}}{\bar{J} - \underline{J}}$. Thus, the plaintiff believes he will win with probability:

$$1 - F\left(\frac{J_D + J_P}{2}\right) = 1 - \frac{\frac{J_D + J_P}{2} - \underline{J}}{\bar{J} - \underline{J}} \tag{2.9}$$

and the defendant believes he will win with probability:

$$\frac{\frac{J_D + J_P}{2} - \underline{J}}{\bar{J} - \underline{J}} \tag{2.10}$$

Let the parties be risk neutral, and suppose that their benefit functions are $B_P(J) = J$ and $B_D(J) = -J$. The winning party gets to implement their announced policy. Then the expected benefits are:

$$\begin{aligned}\mathrm{E}[B_P] &= \Pr(\text{P wins})B_P(J_P) + \Pr(\text{D wins})B_P(J_D)\\ &= \left[1 - F\left(\frac{J_D + J_P}{2}\right)\right]J_P + F\left(\frac{J_D + J_P}{2}\right)J_D\end{aligned}$$

and:

$$\begin{aligned}\mathrm{E}[B_D] &= \Pr(\text{P wins})B_D(J_P) + \Pr(\text{D wins})B_D(J_D)\\ &= -\left[1 - F\left(\frac{J_D + J_P}{2}\right)\right]J_P - F\left(\frac{J_D + J_P}{2}\right)J_D\end{aligned}$$

More concretely, suppose that $[\underline{J}, \bar{J}] = [0,1]$. Then $F\left(\dfrac{J_D + J_P}{2}\right) = \dfrac{J_D + J_P}{2}$, and we get:

$$\mathrm{E}[B_P] = \left[1 - \left(\frac{J_D + J_P}{2}\right)\right]J_P + \left(\frac{J_D + J_P}{2}\right)J_D$$

and:

$$\mathrm{E}[B_D] = -\left[1 - \left(\frac{J_D + J_P}{2}\right)\right]J_P - \left(\frac{J_D + J_P}{2}\right)J_D$$

In the announcement game outlined above, in a Nash equilibrium, the first-order conditions are:

$$\frac{\partial \mathrm{E}[B_P]}{\partial J_P} = 1 - \frac{1}{2}J_D - J_P + \frac{1}{2}J_D = 0$$

and

$$\frac{\partial \mathrm{E}[B_D]}{\partial J_D} = \frac{1}{2}J_P - \frac{1}{2}J_P - J_D = 0$$

and so we get the unique Nash equilibrium:

$$J_P^* = 1, \quad J_D^* = 0$$

The plaintiff and the defendant each announce their most favoured outcome, and there is therefore an equal probability that the judge will announce either outcome as his decision. If the judge's actual preference is $J^\circ > \frac{1}{2}$, then he will award the case to the plaintiff, whereas if $J^\circ < \frac{1}{2}$ he will award the case to the defendant. The expected payoffs of the parties are $\mathrm{E}[B_P^*] = \left[1 - \frac{1}{2}\right]1 = \frac{1}{2}$ and $\mathrm{E}\,[B_D^*] = -\left[1 - \frac{1}{2}\right]1 = -\frac{1}{2}$.

2.6 Aggregation of individual judicial or juror decisions

Up to this point we have analysed courts or legal decision making 'as if' the individuals engaged in that process have clear, rational objectives – regarding efficiency, fairness, or some other criteria. But legal decisions – and in fact many, if not most forms of economic policy – are often undertaken as *collective* decision-making processes. Legal rules and precedents are often formed as a result of a mechanism that attempts to develop a *consensus* between judges, jurors, or tribunal members. More formally, courts or judicial bodies (such as juries) often take decisions based on an *aggregation rule*. An aggregation rule simply takes the individual decisions or preferences of individuals over a set of outcomes and produces an aggregate or group ranking of those outcomes. An alternative way to think about an aggregation rule is that it takes information from individual decision makers regarding the desirability of alternatives, processes it, and produces a summary of this information, which is then used to provide a picture of the 'overall' desirability of each of the alternatives.

This section explores some of the issues involved in aggregation. There are several major complications which arise in the analysis of such aggregation rules or procedures:

1. There may be very few (if any) aggregation rules whose outcomes obey a 'reasonable' or desirable set of properties or axioms;
2. The outcome of some aggregation rules may be very sensitive to the choice of rule, even though underlying preferences do not change and even though the rule is changed in relatively minor ways;
3. Some rules may be highly susceptible to strategic preference manipulation by certain individuals.

A complete analysis of all of these issues is beyond the scope of this book. We instead conclude this chapter by studying one of the most important arguments as to why group decisions may be superior to individual decisions.

2.6.1 Are group decisions better than individual decisions? The Condorcet Jury Theorem

One of the earliest justifications for the superiority of group decisions over individual decisions is due to Condorcet (1785/1976). The idea of the *Condorcet Jury Theorem* is that whilst individuals may make judgemental mistakes or have individual biases, if there are a sufficient number of individuals, these mistakes and biases tend to 'cancel each other out', producing more accurate decisions than would be achieved by an individual decision maker. One possible conclusion of this result is that group decisions and aggregation may preferable to individual legal decision making.

More formally, suppose that there is a group of n jurors or legal decision makers (where n is odd) choosing between two alternatives (for example, the guilt or innocence of a defendant), each of which have equal likelihood of being correct, a priori. Suppose that each juror has the same probability ρ of making the correct decision, with $\frac{1}{2} < \rho < 1$, and that jurors make decisions independently and sincerely. Then the probability that the group makes the correct decision using simple majority rule of aggregation is:[7]

$$\rho_n = \sum_{h=(n+1)/2}^{n} \frac{n!}{h!(n-h)!} \rho^h (1-\rho)^{n-h} \tag{2.11}$$

This probability ρ_n approaches unity as $n \to \infty$. That is, as the group becomes larger, the group decision becomes more accurate than the individual decision of any of its individual members. This result is proved in the Appendix to this Chapter.

To see the intuition behind this result, suppose that there are three jurors: A, B and C. Suppose that the correct decision is that the defendant

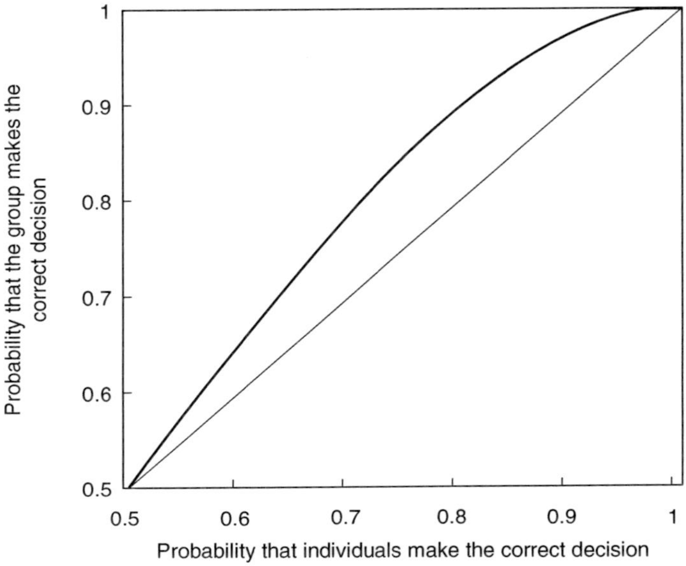

Figure 2.6.1 If $\rho > \frac{1}{2}$, the probability that a group of three jurors will make the correct decision exceeds ρ

is guilty. Let $\rho > \frac{1}{2}$ be the probability that each juror believes that the defendant is guilty. Finally, suppose that each juror votes sincerely and that decisions are made by simple majority rule. The probability that the defendant is found guilty is the probability that at least two of the jurors will vote to convict. This can happen if either A and B vote guilty, A and C vote guilty, B and C vote guilty, or A, B and C vote guilty. The probability that exactly two jurors will vote guilty is:

$$3(1-\rho)\rho^2 = \frac{3!}{2!1!}(1-\rho)\rho^2$$

whilst the probability that exactly three decision makers will vote guilty is simply:

$$\rho^3 = \frac{3!}{3!0!}\rho^3$$

Hence, the probability that the defendant will be found guilty by the group is:

$$\frac{3!}{2!1!}(1-\rho)\rho^2 + \rho^3 + \frac{3!}{3!0!}\rho^3 = \sum_{h=(n+1)/2}^{n} \frac{n!}{h!(n-h)!}\rho^h (1-\rho)^{n-h}$$

which corresponds to equation (2.11) above. As Figure 2.6.1 shows, even for a group of three jurors, the quantity ρ_3, which is the probability

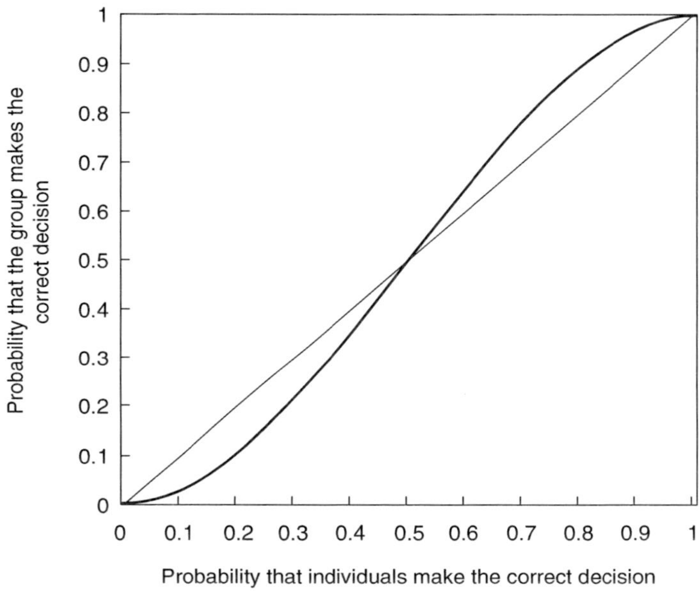

Figure 2.6.2 If $0 < \rho < \frac{1}{2}$, the probability that a group of three jurors will make the correct decision is less than ρ

that the group of three jurors will make the correct decision (the thick solid curved line), exceeds ρ, the probability that any single juror will make the correct decision (the thin straight line). In other words, even for small numbers of jurors, the group has a better chance of making the correct decision than any single individual.

Note that there are several key assumptions that are involved in this result:

- There are only two alternatives from which to choose. If there are three or more alternatives, the result breaks down.
- The result assumes that $\rho > \frac{1}{2}$ for each juror. But if $\rho < \frac{1}{2}$, so that each juror's belief is biased towards making the wrong decision, then $\lim_{n \to \infty} \rho_n = 0$ and adding more jurors makes the incorrect decision even more likely. This happens even if ρ is only slightly lower than $\frac{1}{2}$. Moreover, as Figure 2.6.2 shows, even if there is a small group of jurors, when $\rho < \frac{1}{2}$ the probability that the group will make the correct decision is *less* than the probability that any individual juror

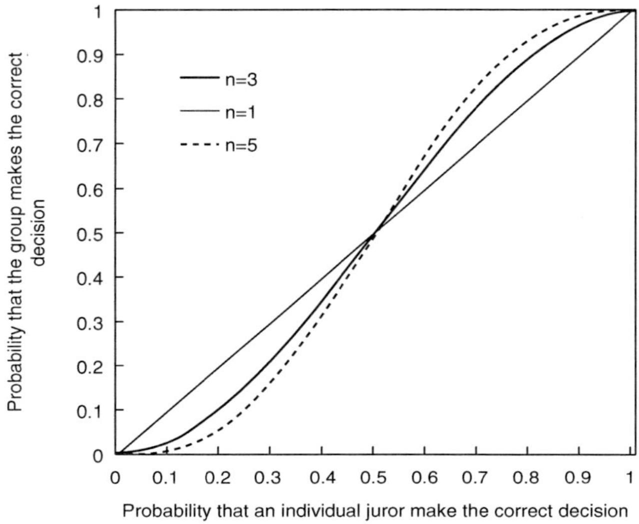

Figure 2.6.3 Larger groups are more accurate than smaller groups if $\rho > \frac{1}{2}$, but are less accurate if $0 < \rho < \frac{1}{2}$

will make the correct decision. Figure 2.6.3 shows that the extent of the inaccuracy gets worse, rather than better, as more individuals are added to the group. In this case, collective decision making is inferior to individual decision making.

- The result assumes that decisions are taken by majority rule, rather than by unanimity. What about other voting procedures?
- The result assumes that voting decisions are independent. But what if they are correlated?
- The result assumes that voting decisions are *sincere*. But some or all voters may not have an incentive to vote sincerely if not doing so makes them better off.

2.7 Notes

Gibbons (1992), Osborne (2009) and Harrington (2009) are useful references on game theory. The analysis of the mixed strategy equilibria in the crime-reporting game draws on the classic paper of Palfrey and Rosenthal (1984), who examine the general issue of contributions to a discrete public good when contributions can and cannot be refunded. The model of strategic evidence gathering presented in this chapter is due to Skaperdas and Vaidya (2011). The examination of biased judicial decision making is a modified version of Farber (1980). Thorough analyses of preferences aggregation procedures and paradoxes can be found in Mueller (2003) and Saari (1995, 2001a, 2001b). Austen-Smith and Banks (2000, 2005) have an advanced treatment.

2.8 Appendix

This appendix proves the Condorcet Jury Theorem stated in the text. Each juror's decision can be characterised as a Bernoulli random variable X_i, where

$$X_i = \begin{cases} 1 & \text{if individual } i \text{ makes the correct decision} \\ 0 & \text{if individual } i \text{ makes the incorrect decision} \end{cases}$$

The distribution of X_i is as follows:

$$X_i = \begin{cases} 1 & \text{with probability } \rho \\ 0 & \text{with probability 1-}\rho \end{cases}$$

Let $S_n = \sum_{i=1}^{n} X_i$ be the number of jurors who make the correct decision, remembering that juror decisions are statistically independent. The event that at least half of the jurors will make the correct decision is the event that $S_n \geq \frac{n+1}{2}$. We want to show that if $\rho > \frac{1}{2}$, then:

$$\lim_{n\to\infty} \rho_n = \lim_{n\to\infty} \Pr\left(S_n \geq \frac{n+1}{2}\right) = 1$$

To this end, note that:

$$1 - \Pr\left(n - S_n \geq \frac{n-1}{2}\right) = 1 - \Pr\left(S_n \leq n - \frac{n-1}{2}\right) = 1 - \Pr\left(S_n \leq \frac{n+1}{2}\right) = \Pr\left(S_n \geq \frac{n+1}{2}\right)$$

So, to show the result, it suffices to show that $\lim_{n\to\infty} \Pr\left(n - S_n \geq \frac{n-1}{2}\right) = 0$. We use the one-sided Chebyshev inequality [see, for example, Ross (2010) page 403], which states that for any random variable Y with mean zero and variance σ^2, for any positive number a, we have

$$\Pr(Y \geq a) \leq \frac{\sigma^2}{\sigma^2 + a^2}$$

Now the mean of $n - S_n - n + n\rho = 0$, and its variance is $n\rho(1-\rho)$. Hence we have

$$\begin{aligned} \Pr\left(n - S_n \geq \frac{n-1}{2}\right) &= \Pr\left(n - S_n - n + n\rho \geq \frac{n-1}{2} - n + n\rho\right) \\ &\leq \frac{\operatorname{var}(n - S_n)}{\operatorname{var}(n - S_n) + \left(\frac{n-1}{2} - n + n\rho\right)^2} \end{aligned}$$

$$= \frac{n\rho(1-\rho)}{n\rho(1-\rho)+\left(\frac{n-1}{2}-n+n\rho\right)^2} < \frac{n\left(\frac{1}{2}\right)^2}{n\left(\frac{1}{2}\right)^2+\left(\frac{n-1}{2}-n+n\rho\right)^2}$$

$$= \frac{n^{-1}\left(\frac{1}{2}\right)^2}{n^{-1}\left(\frac{1}{2}\right)^2+\left(\frac{n-1}{2n}-1+\rho\right)^2}$$

where the strict inequality follows from the assumption that $\rho > \frac{1}{2}$. The last expression goes to zero as $n \to \infty$.

2.9 Exercises

1. Suppose that statistically, only 0.5 per cent of individuals are criminals. Suppose that this is the court's prior belief. Thus $\rho(G) = 0.005$. Suppose that evidence correctly identifies a guilty defendant 99 per cent of the time. That is, $\rho(E \mid G) = 0.99$. Suppose also that if there is no evidence, this correctly identifies an innocent defendant 99 per cent of the time. Therefore, $\rho(NE \mid I) = 0.99$ This means that $\rho(E \mid I) = 0.01$.
   (a) Use Bayes' rule to find $P(G \mid E)$, the probability that the defendant is guilty, given that evidence has been presented.
   (b) Given that the piece of evidence has been produced, what is the probability that the defendant is innocent?
   (c) Now suppose that evidence is not presented. What is the probability that the defendant is actually guilty, given that there is no evidence of this?
   (d) What is the probability that he is innocent? In other words, find $P(G \mid NE)$ and $P\ (G \mid NE)$.

2. There is a unique Nash equilibrium in the evidence-gathering game presented in this chapter. Find this equilibrium. Show that in equilibrium, the posterior probability is the same as the prior, and so there is no change actual updating of prior probabilities.

3
The Coase Theorem

3.1 Introduction

When do legal rules matter for efficiency? This chapter presents and discusses the Coase Theorem (1960), which is one of the most important and remarkable findings in economics. The theorem states that under certain conditions legal rules will have no bearing on the economic efficiency of resource allocation. As long as there is *some* legal rule in place, then an efficient outcome will ensue.

The Coase Theorem lays the foundation for the entire field of law and economics, because it shows the conditions under which legal rules will matter for economic efficiency, and hence the conditions under which the basic principles of cost–benefit analysis can be brought to bear in the analysis and assessment of the economic consequences of legal rules. The analysis in this chapter will allow us to examine in detail the economic issues involved in the Coase Theorem, and the theorem's implications.

Coase recognised that standard approaches to externalities – which begin from the premise that harm is 'caused' by one party – neglect the fact that when one individual takes costly actions to reduce harm, the other party gains at his expense. The fact that 'harm' can be reduced by taking costly actions which benefit another illustrates the reciprocal nature of externalities. This is not surprising, since *social* costs really are just that: social.

The chapter is structured as follows. Sections 3.2, 3.3 and 3.4 use the Edgeworth Box to present the Coase Theorem. Section 3.5 explores the role of transaction costs in the Coase Theorem and examines two kinds of transaction costs: lump-sum costs and per unit costs. Section 3.6 examines whether the Coase Theorem holds when there are more than two parties, and introduces tools from cooperative game theory to address this question.

3.2 Externalities, the Coase Theorem and the Edgeworth Box

We use the Edgeworth Box to present the Coase Theorem and analyse its consequences. Suppose there are two parties: a factory (F) and a group of residents (R). There are two commodities in this economy: the factory's output, Q, and another good that can be transferred costlessly between the parties, which we shall call money.

Suppose that the factory produces output of $Q \geq 0$. The utility to the factory is:

$$u_F = u_F(Q, M_F) \tag{3.1}$$

where M_F is the amount of money that the factory 'consumes'.[1] We assume that the marginal utility of Q is positive but declining with the level of activity.[2] We also assume that the factory prefers more money to less, but that the marginal utility of money is declining.[3] The factory also starts out with some amount of money, $\overline{M}_F$. A typical indifference curve for the factory is plotted in Figure 3.2.1.

The residents also start out with some amount of money, $\overline{M}_R$. We assume that the production of Q by the factory generates uncompensated disutility for the residents. In other words, the production of Q by the factory generates a negative externality. The residents' utility function is therefore:

$$v_R = v_R(Q, M_R) \tag{3.2}$$

where the marginal utility of Q is now *negative*. The marginal disutility (or, effectively, the marginal cost) is also assumed to increase with the

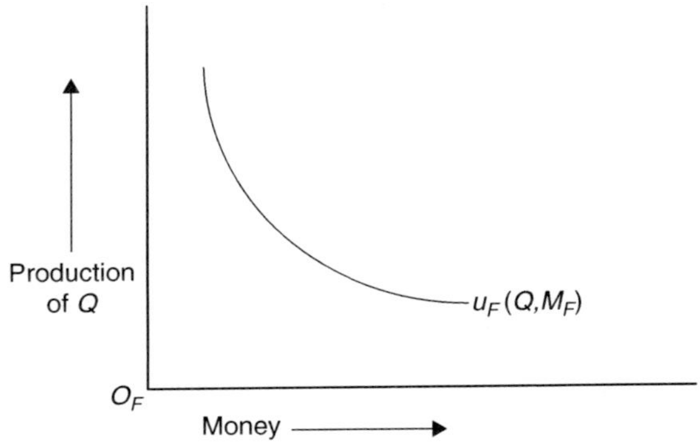

Figure 3.2.1 An indifference curve for the factory

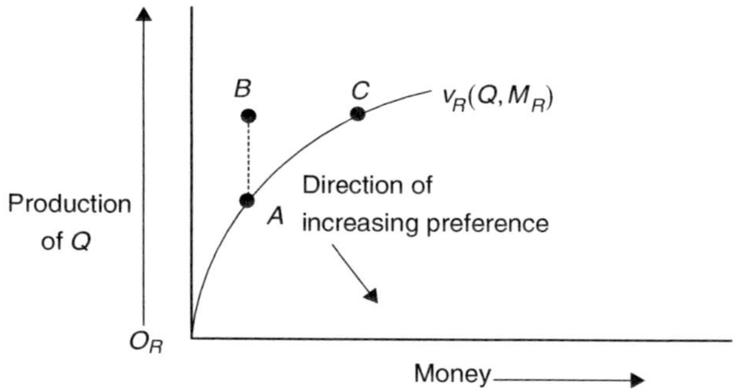

Figure 3.2.2 An indifference curve for the residents

level of activity.[4] Again, we assume that the residents prefer more money to less, but that the marginal utility of money is declining.[5] A typical indifference curve for the residents is plotted in Figure 3.2.2.

To see why the residents' indifference curve is shaped like this, consider a move from point *A* to point *B* in Figure 3.2.2. At point *B*, the residents are consuming the same amount of money as at point A, but output Q is higher. Since the residents dislike Q, this move makes them worse off. The only way that indifference can be restored is if they consume more money (say, point *C*). Thus, the indifference curve must be upward sloping.

To understand why the indifference curve has a concave shape, note that the marginal disutility of Q increases with Q. This means that every additional unit of Q which is produced by the factory requires ever greater amounts of compensation in terms of money in order for the residents to remain indifferent. This means that the typical indifference curve must be increasing and concave as shown in Figure 3.2.2. Finally, suppose that there is some maximum amount of Q that the factory can actually produce (because, for example, of capacity constraints). Let this maximum amount be given by $\overline{Q}$.

Instead of the residents having preferences over Q and money, with Q entering the utility function as a 'bad', define another variable, $\overline{Q} - Q$, to be the *absence* of Q. The variable $\overline{Q} - Q$ then enters the residents' utility or benefit function as a *good* in the standard fashion.

In other words, let us define variables in such a way that:

$$u_R(\overline{Q} - Q, M_R) = v_R(Q, M_R) \tag{3.3}$$

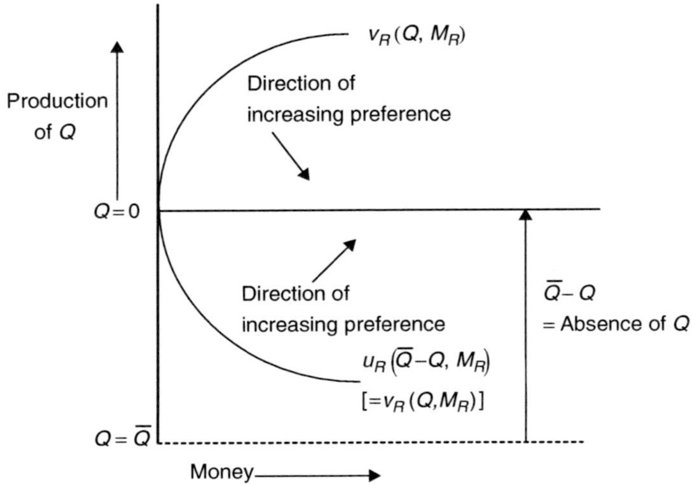

Figure 3.2.3 Preferences for the absence of Q

with:

$$\frac{\partial u_R}{\partial(\overline{Q}-Q)} = -\frac{\partial v_R}{\partial Q} > 0$$

and

$$\frac{\partial u_R}{\partial M_R} = \frac{\partial v_R}{\partial M_R} > 0$$

We can then plot indifference curves for money and the *absence* of Q in the usual way. This is done in Figure 3.2.3.

3.3 Efficiency

Let us characterise the efficient allocations diagrammatically. We can plot both the factory's and the residents' indifference curves on the same Edgeworth Box diagram, with money on the horizontal axis and production and absence of Q on the vertical axis. The total amount of money in this economy is:

$$\overline{M} = \overline{M}_F + \overline{M}_R \tag{3.4}$$

This means that the length of the horizontal axis of the Edgeworth Box is $\overline{M}$. On the other hand, the maximum amount of Q that can be produced in this economy is $\overline{Q}$, so the length of the vertical axis is $\overline{Q}$. We can 'flip'

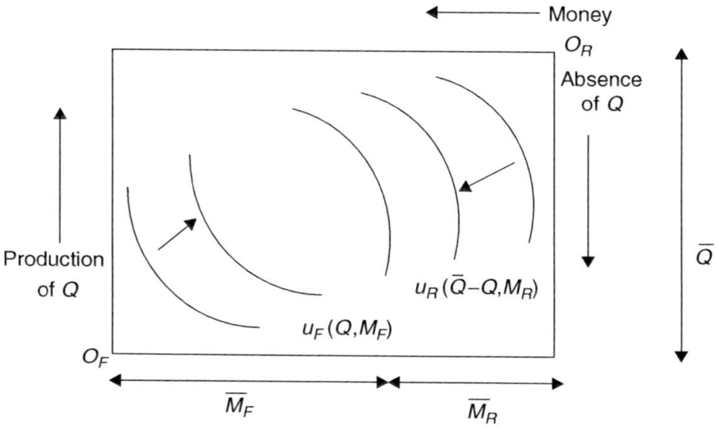

Figure 3.3.1 The Edgeworth Box representation with F's production creates a negative external cost for R

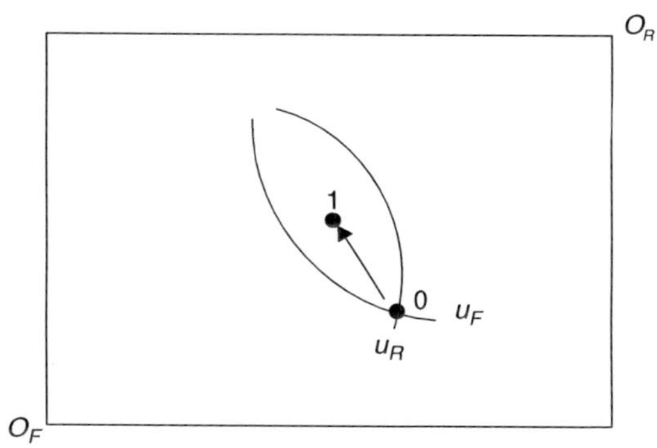

Figure 3.3.2 A move from point "0" to point "1" is a Pareto improvement

the residents' indifference curves and draw them on this Edgeworth Box diagram. This is done in Figure 3.3.1.

We are now in a position to characterise the Pareto-optimal levels of production. An allocation is Pareto optimal if it is not possible to find some other allocation that makes one individual better off without making another individual worse off. Consider a move from point 0 to point 1 in Figure 3.3.2. This move makes both the factory and the residents better off, since each would be on higher indifference curves than at point 0. This move from 0 to 1 constitutes a Pareto improvement, and so point 0 could not have been efficient.

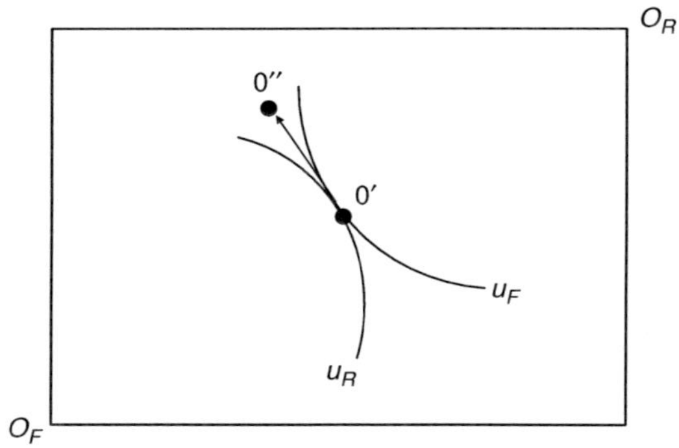

Figure 3.3.3 Point 0′ is Pareto optimal, but point 0″ is not

Note that Pareto-improving moves like this are always possible in this example, unless the indifference curves are tangent to each other, as they are at point 0′ in Figure 3.3.3. Any move away from point 0′ (say, to point 0″) potentially makes both parties worse off, and can certainly not make them better off. Hence, point 0′, where the slopes of the two indifference curves are equal, is efficient.[6]

The slope of the factory's indifference curve at any particular point is the *marginal rate of substitution of money for Q* at that point – the amount of additional production of Q that the factory must be allowed as compensation for a one dollar reduction in the amount of money that they consume:

Slope of Factory's Indifference Curve

$$= MRS^F_{M.Q} = -\frac{dQ}{dM_F}\bigg|_{u_F \text{ constant}} = \frac{\dfrac{\partial u_F}{\partial M_F}}{\dfrac{\partial u_F}{\partial Q}} \tag{3.5}$$

Similarly, the slope of the residents' indifference curve at any particular point is the marginal rate of substitution of money for $\overline{Q} - Q$ at that point. It is the amount of 'absence of Q' (i.e. the reduction in Q) that the resident must be given to compensate them for a one dollar reduction in the amount of money that they consume:

Slope of Resident's Indifference Curve

$$= MRS^R_{M,\overline{Q}-Q} = -\frac{d(\overline{Q}-Q)}{dM_R}\bigg|_{u_R \text{ constant}} = \frac{\dfrac{\partial u_R}{\partial M_R}}{\dfrac{\partial u_R}{\partial(\overline{Q}-Q)}} \tag{3.6}$$

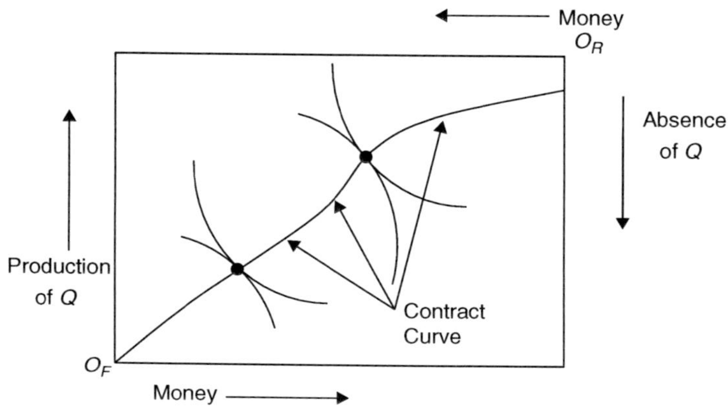

Figure 3.3.4 The contract curve

Figure 3.3.4 suggests that the set of points where these slopes are equal are efficient. In other words, if

$$\frac{\dfrac{\partial u_F}{\partial M_F}}{\dfrac{\partial u_F}{\partial Q}} = \frac{\dfrac{\partial u_R}{\partial M_R}}{\dfrac{\partial u_R}{\partial(\overline{Q}-Q)}} \tag{3.7}$$

then the allocation is Pareto optimal. Note that in general, this condition is sufficient, but not necessary, for efficiency. In other words, there may be other points where this condition does not hold, but which are also efficient.

Notice also that, in general, there are many levels of production of Q at which the marginal rates of substitution are equal. This contract curve is plotted in Figure 3.3.4. It is the set of possible allocations that the parties could reach if they exhausted all potential gains from trade.

3.4 Legal rules in the Edgeworth Box

Different legal rules or property rights define different initial allocations in the Edgeworth Box. For example, suppose that the factory has the right to produce as much Q as it likes (that is, a rule of *no liability*), without being obligated to compensate the residents. Then the starting point for trading between the factory and the residents lies somewhere on the top edge of the Edgeworth Box, as is shown in Figure 3.4.1.

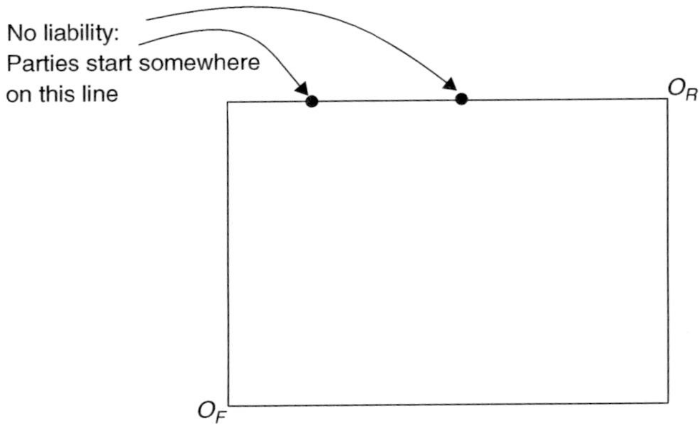

Figure 3.4.1 Possible initial allocations under a no liability rule in the Edgeworth Box

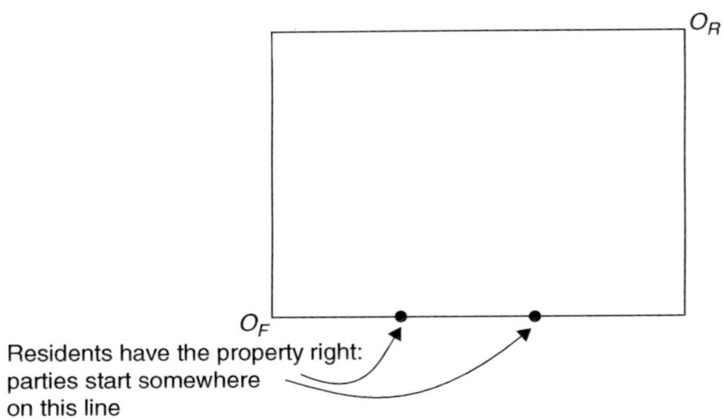

Figure 3.4.2 Possible initial allocations if the residents have the property right

On the other hand, suppose that the residents have the right to prevent the factory from producing, and can demand a payment from the factory in exchange for granting them right to produce. Then, the starting point for trading between the factory and the residents would lie somewhere on the bottom edge of the Edgeworth Box, as is shown in Figure 3.4.2.

How do these different legal rules matter for the well-being of the factory and the residents, for efficiency, and for the production of *Q*? Is one legal rule better than another? If so, why? If not, why not?

We begin to answer these questions in this set-up by stating and proving the Coase Theorem. There are two versions to the Coase Theorem that we will explore:

1. *The Efficiency Version of the Coase Theorem:* If transaction costs are sufficiently low, then the initial legal regime or assignment of property rights will not hinder the parties from reaching an agreement in which all possible gains from trade have been exhausted. In other words, *from an efficiency point of view, if transaction costs are low, no legal rule is preferable to any other. Legal rules don't matter for efficiency.*
2. *The Invariance Version of the Coase Theorem*: If transaction costs are sufficiently low, then the bargaining will always lead to the *same* level of production of Q, irrespective of the initial legal regime or assignment of property rights. In other words, the legal rule has no relevance for determining the level of production of Q that will eventually be chosen by the factory.

These are quite remarkable propositions. Let us investigate them using the Edgeworth Box. Consider Figure 3.4.3 below. Throughout we hold the parties' initial amounts of money constant by assuming that, irrespective of the legal regime, the factory has an initial allocation of money, $\overline{M}_F$, and the residents have an initial allocation of money, $\overline{M}_R$.

3.4.1 Rules favour the factory: No liability

Suppose that the legal regime is one of no liability. Then, in the absence of bargaining between the factory and the residents, the best that the factory can do is to produce at point I in Figure 3.4.3. Clearly this is

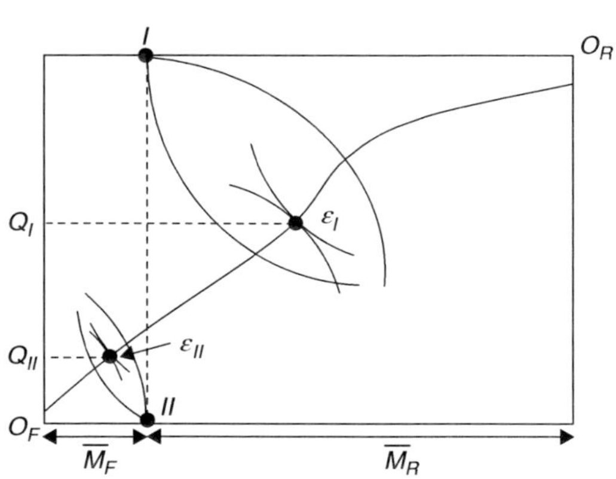

Figure 3.4.3 Bargaining around legal rules and the efficiency version of the Coase Theorem

not a Pareto-optimal outcome – there are other allocations which make both parties strictly better off.

Suppose the residents try to persuade the factory to reduce its production by offering them money in exchange for a reduction in *Q*. Depending on the bargaining power of the parties and in the absence of transaction costs (both of which we examine in detail below), the parties could keep exchanging reductions in *Q* for increases in money until a point like ε_I is reached, where there are no remaining gains from trade. Note that in this example both parties are better off as a result of such trades, and that the final level of production, Q_I, is less than the level that would have been produced in the absence of bargaining. The factory ends up with more money than it initially started with, and the residents do not have to put up with as much *Q*.

3.4.2 Rules favour the residents: The residents enjoy the property right

Now suppose we are in legal regime II, where the residents can demand payment from the factory in exchange for granting the factory the right to produce. Then, in the absence of bargaining between the factory and the residents, the best that the factory can do is to produce at point II in Figure 3.4.3. Again, this is not an efficient outcome – there are other allocations which make both parties strictly better off.

Suppose the factory tries to persuade the residents to increase its production by offering them money in exchange for an increase in *Q*. Depending on the bargaining power of the parties and in the absence of transaction costs (both of which we examine in detail below), the parties could keep exchanging increases in *Q* for decreases in money until a point like ε_{II} is reached, where there are no remaining gains from trade. Note again that this specific example illustrates that both parties are better off as a result of such trades, and that the final level of production, Q_{II} is greater than the level that would have been produced in the absence of bargaining. The factory ends up with less money than it initially started with, and the residents have to put up with more y.

3.4.3 Does the legal regime matter?

The question we now ask is this: does the initial assignment of property rights or legal rights matter, and, if so, how? To answer this question, we compare the two outcomes derived above. From Figure 3.4.3 we can conclude that, in the absence of transaction costs, the efficiency version of the Coase Theorem always holds: as long as initial legal rights are well defined and there are no impediments to trade, parties will reach efficient agreements.

However, it is also clear from Figure 3.4.3 that, in general, *the invariance version of the Coase Theorem does not hold,* since production of Q is higher in legal regime *I* than it is in legal regime II. In other words, in the absence of transaction costs the legal regime does *not* matter for efficiency, but in general, if there is more than one efficient level of production, the legal regime *does* matter in determining *which* efficient point is actually reached – even if there are no transaction costs.

3.4.4 Distribution of utilities and the utility possibilities curve

It is also possible to view the same outcome differently, using the utility possibilities curve (UPC), which shows the combinations of utilities that each of the parties can obtain. The UPC corresponding to Figure 3.4.3 is shown in Figure 3.4.4. The utilities or benefits corresponding to the initial assignments of legal rights are shown as points I and II, whereas the utilities corresponding to the final allocations are shown as points ε_{I} and ε_{II} respectively. Clearly the initial assignment of property rights does not matter for efficiency (as both points ε_{I} and ε_{II} are on the UPC). On the other hand, the residents clearly prefer regime II to regime I, and the factory prefers regime I to regime II. In other words, the legal regime matters for distribution.

The slope of the utility possibilities curve can be computed as follows.[7] Consider a small change in the utility of the residents, du_R along the contract curve. For any such change, it must be true for the residents that:

$$du_R = \frac{\partial u_R}{\partial M_R} dM_R + \frac{\partial u_R}{\partial(\overline{Q} - Q)} d(\overline{Q} - Q) \tag{3.8}$$

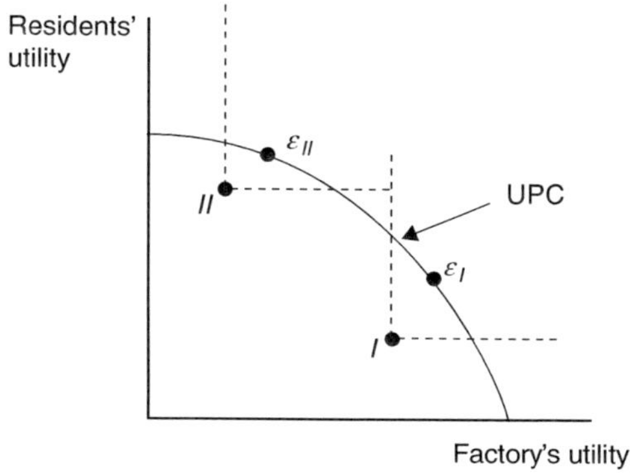

Figure 3.4.4 The utility possibilities curve corresponding to Figure 3.4.3

Dividing both sides by $\frac{\partial u_R}{\partial(\overline{Q}-Q)}$, we obtain:

$$\frac{du_R}{\frac{\partial u_R}{\partial(\overline{Q}-Q)}} = \frac{\frac{\partial u_R}{\partial M_R}}{\frac{\partial u_R}{\partial(\overline{Q}-Q)}} dM_R + d(\overline{Q}-Q) = MRS^R_{M,\overline{Q}-Q} dM_R + d(\overline{Q}-Q).$$

A similar analysis for the factory shows that:

$$\frac{du_F}{\frac{\partial u_F}{\partial Q}} = \frac{\frac{\partial u_F}{\partial M_F}}{\frac{\partial u_F}{\partial Q}} dM_F + dQ = MRS^F_{M,Q} dM_F + dQ.$$

Now $dM_R = -dM_F$ and $d(\overline{Q}-Q) = -dQ$. Therefore, for the residents we obtain:

$$\frac{du_R}{\frac{\partial u_R}{\partial(\overline{Q}-Q)}} = -MRS^R_{M,\overline{Q}-Q} dM_F - dQ = -MRS^F_{M,Q} dM_F - dQ = -\frac{du_F}{\frac{\partial u_F}{\partial Q}}.$$

where the second equality follows from the equality of marginal rates of substitution at points on the contract curve. Since $\frac{\partial u_R}{\partial(\overline{Q}-Q)} = -\frac{\frac{\partial u_R}{\partial M_R}}{MRS^R_{M,\overline{Q}-Q}}$ and $\frac{\partial u_F}{\partial Q} = -\frac{\frac{\partial u_F}{\partial M_F}}{MRS^F_{M,Q}}$, this means that:

$$\frac{du_R}{\partial u_F} = -\frac{\frac{\partial u_R}{\partial(\overline{Q}-Q)}}{\frac{\partial u_F}{\partial Q}} = -\frac{\frac{\partial u_R}{\partial M_R}}{\frac{\partial u_F}{\partial M_F}}. \tag{3.9}$$

The slope of the utility possibilities frontier is equal to the (negative of the) ratio of the marginal utilities of money for the parties. In particular, if the marginal utilities of money are constant, then this ratio is constant and the UPC will be a straight line, rather than the bowed shape in Figure 3.4.4.

3.4.5 When does the invariance version of the Coase Theorem hold? The special case of quasi-linear preferences

In the previous section we investigated the efficiency version of the Coase Theorem and saw that in the absence of transaction costs, parties would bargain over the level of Q until there were no further gains from trade left to exploit. However, that analysis showed that even in the absence of transaction costs, the invariance version of the Theorem does not usually hold.

Let us now investigate the invariance version in a little more detail. It turns out that the invariance version of the Coase Theorem holds if the preferences of the parties take the quasi-linear form. Consider again the utility function of the factory. Suppose that its utility function is:

$$u_F(Q, M_F) = u(Q) + M_F \tag{3.10}$$

where $u'(Q) > 0$ and $u''(Q) < 0$. These are called quasi-linear preferences because they are partially linear in one of the goods – in this case money. The marginal rate of substitution of money for Q is:

$$MRS^F_{M,Q} = -\frac{\dfrac{\partial u_F}{\partial M_F}}{\dfrac{\partial u_F}{\partial Q}} = \frac{1}{u'(Q)} \tag{3.11}$$

which is independent of the consumption of M_F. This means that if we horizontally shift the consumer's indifference curve, for any fixed level of Q, their marginal rate of substitution does not change. Effectively, this means that, for a given set of relative prices or rate of exchange between production of Q and money, changes in money do not change the factory's demand for Q, as shown in Figure 3.4.5. This is often referred to the case of there being *no income effects* or *no wealth effects* present in the demand for Q.

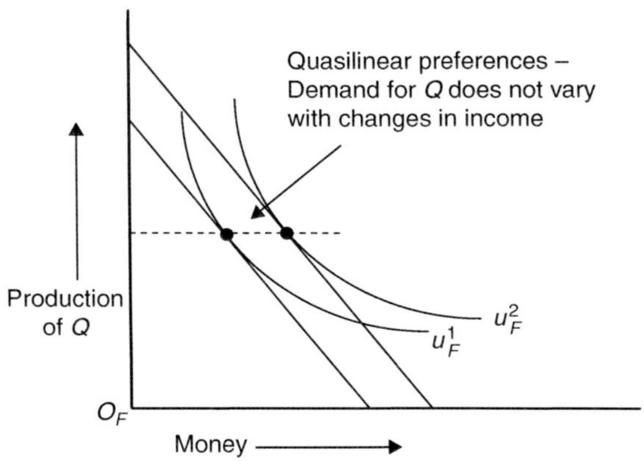

Figure 3.4.5 Indifference curves without income effects

To see how the assumption of quasi-linear preferences matters, consider the following special case: suppose that the residents also have *identical* quasi-linear preferences over money and the *absence* of Q:

$$u_R(\overline{Q}-Q, M_R) = M_R + u(\overline{Q}-Q)$$

and where we assume $u(0) = 0$. Then, the set of points where their marginal rates of substitution must be equal must obey:

$$u'(Q) = u'(\overline{Q}-Q)$$

Since the function $u(\cdot)$ is everywhere increasing, this implies that, along the contract curve we must have:

$$Q = \overline{Q} - Q$$

or:

$$Q = \frac{\overline{Q}}{2} = \text{constant}$$

This situation is illustrated in Figure 3.4.6.

In Figure 3.4.6 it is clear that if both parties have identical quasi-linear preferences, then the invariance version of the Coase Theorem must hold, since, irrespective of the initial allocation, all efficient points lie on the line $Q = \frac{\overline{Q}}{2}$, so the final allocation after all gains from trade are exhausted always has $Q = \frac{\overline{Q}}{2}$. The only difference between legal regimes will be the final allocation of money between the parties.

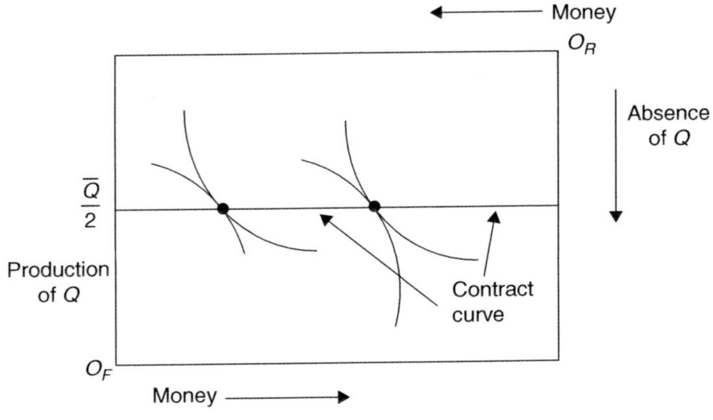

Figure 3.4.6 The contract curve with identical quasi-linear preferences

This analysis has just illustrated a very important result: *if individuals have identical quasi-linear preferences and there are no transaction costs, then both the efficiency version and the invariance version of the Coase Theorem hold.*[8]

Another way to see this result is to plot the marginal rates of substitution of Q (and the absence of Q) for money for both the factory and the residents, which is the inverse of the slope of the indifference curves in Figure 3.4.3. For the factory, this marginal rate of substitution is the amount of money that the factory must be given to accept a one unit reduction in Q. Therefore, it is also the amount of money that the factory would be willing to pay or give up to get a one unit increase in Q. In other words, it measures the factory's *marginal willingness to pay for* Q in terms of money.

Factory's Marginal Willingness to Pay for Q

$$= MRS^F_{Q,M} = \left.\frac{dM}{dQ}\right|_{u_F\ \text{constant}} = -\frac{\dfrac{\partial u_F}{\partial Q}}{\dfrac{\partial u_F}{\partial M_F}}.$$

With diminishing marginal utility for Q, this marginal rate of substitution is decreasing in Q.

Similarly, for the residents this marginal rate of substitution is the amount of money that the residents must be given to accept a one unit reduction in $\overline{Q}-Q$. Therefore, it is also the amount of money that the residents would be willing to pay or give up to get a one unit increase in $\overline{Q}-Q$. In other words, it measures the factory's *marginal willingness to pay for* $\overline{Q}-Q$ in terms of money.

Residents' Marginal Willingness to Pay for Reductions in Q

$$= MRS^R_{\overline{Q}-Q,M} = \left.\frac{dM}{d(\overline{Q}-Q)}\right|_{u_R\ \text{constant}} = -\frac{\dfrac{\partial u_R}{\partial(\overline{Q}-Q)}}{\dfrac{\partial u_R}{\partial M_R}}$$

With diminishing marginal utility for $\overline{Q}-Q$, this marginal rate of substitution is decreasing in $\overline{Q}-Q$.

A special case of quasi-linear preferences has the utility functions taking the quadratic form $u(Q) = aQ - bQ^2$, and $u(\overline{Q}-Q) = a(\overline{Q}-Q) - b(\overline{Q}-Q)^2$. In this case, the marginal rate of substitution of Q (and the absence of Q)

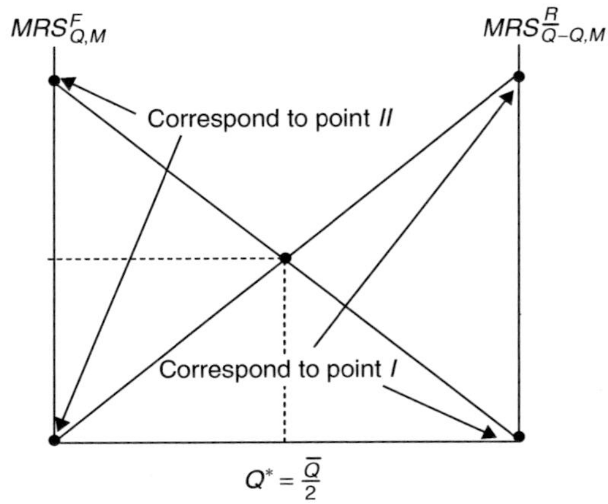

Figure 3.4.7 Marginal willingness to pay under quasi-linear quadratic preferences

for money are linear in Q (and the absence of Q), since $u'(Q) = a - 2bQ$ and $u'(\overline{Q} - Q) = a - 2b(\overline{Q} - Q)$.

This situation is plotted in Figure 3.4.7. The length of the box is the total possible production of Q, which is $\overline{Q}$. There is only one point where the marginal rates of substitution are equal, which is at the point where $Q = \overline{Q}/2$.

Consider an initial legal rule which states that the factory can produce as much Q as it desires, which corresponds to point I in Figure 3.4.3. At this point, the factory has a very low (zero) marginal willingness to pay for additional units of Q, since if the marginal utility was positive it would have produced more. But point I also means that the residents enjoy a zero amount of the *absence* of Q, which means that with diminishing marginal willingness to pay, their marginal willingness to pay for the first unit must be very high. Thus, we get the two points identified in Figure 3.4.7 as corresponding to point I in Figure 3.4.3.

Note that at these two points, marginal willingness to pay differs considerably between the parties, which implies that substantial possible gains from trade exist at point I, as the UPC in Figure 3.4.8 shows. The same applies to point II. The ways in which these gains from trade are split between the parties is examined further in Chapter 11.

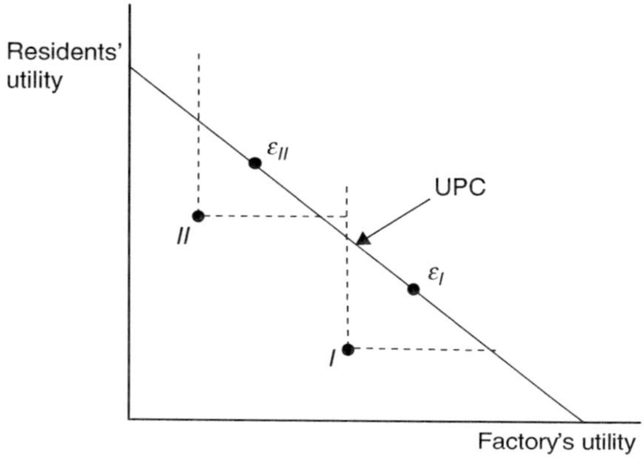

Figure 3.4.8 The UPC when the parties have identical quasi-linear preferences

3.5 The Coase Theorem and the role of transaction costs

What is the role of transaction costs in the Coase Theorem? Transaction costs can take several forms. To illustrate the main ideas, we will classify transaction costs according to the following two types:

- *Lump-sum* transaction costs, which do not depend on the volume of trade; and
- *Per unit* transaction costs, which consist of a cost for each unit of a good that is either supplied or demanded. These can be further classified into *ad valorem* transaction costs, which are a percentage of the market price, or *specific* transaction costs, which are a fixed dollar amount for each unit of the good that is supplied or demanded.

3.5.1 Lump-sum transaction costs

Lump-sum transaction costs shrink the length of the Edgeworth Box by the amount of money that each party incurs in paying for the transaction. Thus the pure efficiency version of the Coase Theorem will not hold, in the sense that the utility possibilities that were previously available in the absence of transaction costs are no longer available in the presence of transaction costs. Nevertheless, the outcome that the parties reach is constrained efficient; that is, it is efficient conditional on the existence of transaction costs.

The important point here is that *the initial legal rule or property right may affect the size and distribution of the lump-sum transaction costs, and therefore may affect the gains from trade*. This means that the presence of such costs could affect the efficiency properties of various legal rules, and that legal rules can, in principle, be ranked according to their efficiency properties.

For example, suppose that the factory initially enjoys the legal right to produce as much as it desires, but the residents must incur transaction costs of C in order to reach a bargain with the factory. However, suppose that no such transaction costs must be incurred when the residents have the right to choose the level of production. Then clearly, in the presence of such lump-sum transaction costs, the legal rule matters for efficiency. Furthermore, since transaction costs are not incurred when the residents have the initial property right, an efficient legal rule will assign them the property right and allow the parties to bargain (costlessly, in this example when the residents have the property right) until the efficient level of production is reached. Thus, a further important implication of this analysis is that *when transaction costs are sufficiently high enough for legal rules to matter, the efficient legal rule minimises the effects of transaction costs*.

Note, however, that in the absence of income effects, these kinds of costs will have no effect on the level of production that the parties agree upon, since that level does not depend on the level of money that each has. The only exception to this is if the lump-sum transaction costs are so large as to 'eat up' all possible gains from trade. In other cases, however, the only question for the design of legal rules is to find the rule that minimises the transaction costs.

On the other hand, in the presence of income effects, the existence of lump-sum transaction costs *will* affect the level of production that the two parties agree upon. We therefore obtain an invariance version of the Coase Theorem in the presence of lump-sum transaction costs: *Suppose that there are no income effects. In the presence of lump-sum transaction costs which do not vary with the legal rule and are not large enough to exhaust all possible gains from trade, then bargaining between the parties will always lead to the* same *level of production of Q, irrespective of the initial legal regime or assignment of property rights. In other words, the legal rule has no relevance for determining the level of production of Q that will eventually be chosen by the factory.*

3.5.2 Per unit transaction costs

Per unit transaction costs are added to each unit of production that the parties negotiate over. As Chapter 1 illustrated, these kinds of transaction costs drive a wedge between the marginal rates of substitution or marginal valuations of the parties. In this section we show that *the existence of per unit transaction costs means that neither the efficiency version nor the invariance version of the Coase Theorem hold.*

3.5.2.1 *A rule of no liability*

To illustrate this result, suppose that each party faces (possibly different) specific per unit transaction costs. We continue to assume identical, quadratic quasi-linear preferences, but the result still goes through with other assumptions about preferences. Suppose that the factory has the right to choose the level of Q. In the absence of any bargaining with the factory, they would choose $Q = \overline{Q}$. Now suppose that the factory and the residents bargain over the level of production of Q. Let the factory face a transaction cost of t_F per unit of production of Q that is negotiated below the initial allocation $Q = \overline{Q}$. Similarly, let the residents face a transaction cost of t_R per unit of production of Q that is negotiated below the initial allocation. This situation is illustrated in Figure 3.5.1.

The marginal benefit received by the factory per unit of reduction in the level of Q now consists of the money price P, *less* the transaction costs t_F it incurs in bargaining with the residents. Thus the price received by the factory is:

$$P_F = P - t_F$$

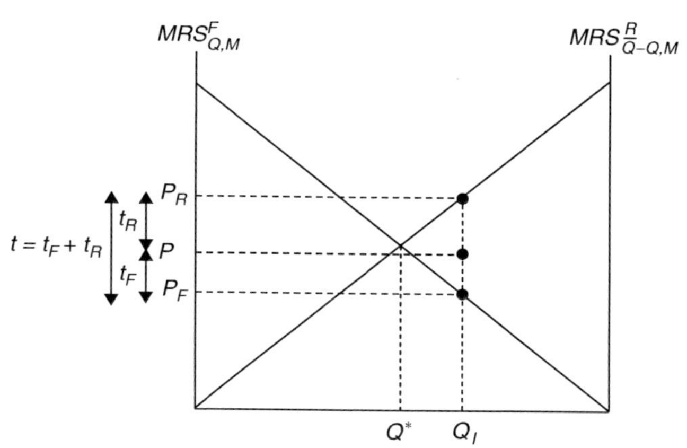

Figure 3.5.1 Per unit transaction costs when the factory has the right to pollute

On the other hand, the price paid by the residents per unit of reduction in the level of Q now consists of the money price P which is paid to the factory, *plus* the transaction costs t_R it incurs in bargaining with the factory. Thus the price paid by the residents is:

$$P_R = P + t_R$$

Note that the gains from trade are still completely exhausted, but in the presence of transaction costs, the gains from trade are now exhausted at the point $Q = Q_I > Q^*$.

The common money price P is determined by the commonality of marginal rates of substitution inclusive of transaction costs:

$$P_F + t_F = MRS^F_{Q,M} + t_F = P = MRS^R_{\bar{Q}-Q,M} - t_R = P_R - t_R$$

The total transaction costs incurred are

$$tQ_I = (t_R + t_F)Q_I = (P_R - P_F)Q_I$$

The aggregate gains from trade to each party are lower than they were in the absence of transaction costs, although the gains to each party individually may be higher or lower than they were in the absence of transaction costs, depending on the bargaining power of each party. The presence of transaction costs may alter the distribution of bargaining power between the parties; indeed, one party could deliberately and strategically impose transaction on itself and the other party in order to improve its bargaining position.

3.5.2.2 *If the residents have the property right*

Now suppose that each party continues to face (possibly different) specific per unit transaction costs, but suppose that the residents have the right to choose the level of Q. In the absence of any bargaining with the factory, the residents would choose $Q = 0$. Now suppose that the factory and the residents bargain over the level of production of Q. Again, let the factory face a transaction cost of t'_F per unit of production of Q that is negotiated in excess of the initial allocation $Q = 0$, where in general $t'_F \neq t_F$. Similarly, let the residents face a transaction cost of $t'_R \neq t_R$ per unit of production of Q that is negotiated in excess of the initial allocation.

In this case, the roles of the parties are reversed. The payment by the factory per unit of increase in the level of Q now consists of the money price P', plus the transaction costs t'_F it incurs in bargaining with the residents. Thus the full price paid by the factory is:

$$P'_F = P' + t'_F$$

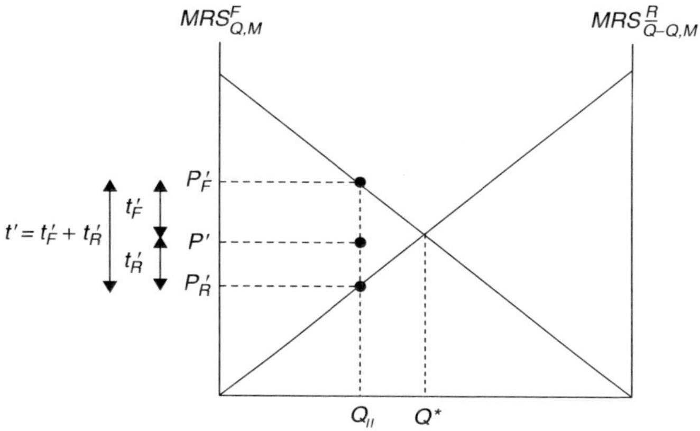

Figure 3.5.2 Per unit transaction costs when the residents enjoy the property right

On the other hand, the benefit received by the residents per unit of increase in the level of Q again consists of the new money price P' which it receives from the factory, *less* the transaction costs t_R it incurs in bargaining with the factory. Thus the price received by the residents is:

$$P'_R = P' - t'_R$$

The common money price P′ is again determined by the commonality of marginal rates of substitution inclusive of transaction costs:

$$P'_F - t'_F = MRS^F_{Q,M} - t'_F = P' = MRS^R_{\bar{Q}-Q,M} + t'_R = P'_R + t'_R$$

Note that the gains from trade are again completely exhausted, but in the presence of transaction costs, the gains from trade are now exhausted at the point $Q = Q_{II} < Q^*$. The total transaction costs incurred are

$$t'Q_{II} = (t'_R + t'_F)Q_{II} = (P'_R - P'_F)Q_{II}$$

The aggregate gains from trade to each party are again lower than they were in the absence of transaction costs, although the gains to each party individually may be higher or lower than they were in the absence of transaction costs.

3.5.2.3 Implications of transaction costs

Several important results follow from this analysis:

- **The Failure of the Invariance Version of the Coase Theorem:** In the presence of per unit transaction costs, the invariance version of the Coase Theorem no longer holds. That is, the final level of production of *Q* depends on the initial legal regime.
- **The Failure of the Efficiency Version of the Coase Theorem:** In the presence of per unit transaction costs, the efficiency version of the Coase Theorem no longer holds. That is, the total transactions costs and the size of the welfare gains which flow from the final choice of the level of production of *Q* depend on the initial legal regime.
- **The Efficient Legal Rule Minimises Aggregate Transaction Costs:** Moreover – and more significantly – both the individual and aggregate gains from trade when the residents have the property right will, in general, differ from the outcome under a no liability rule. Since income effects are absent in both cases, and since the aggregate gains from trade in the absence of transaction costs are the same in each legal regime, *the efficient legal rule minimises the aggregate transaction costs.*
- **If Transactions Costs are High, Legal Rules Should Direct Individuals *Away* from Negotiated Outcomes:** When transactions costs are high, it is better that they not be incurred at all. One way to ensure that transaction costs do not occur is to encourage individuals not to make those transactions at all. In other words, if the market mechanism is costly to use, individuals should be given an incentive *not* to use the market mechanism. For example, consider a rule of *strict liability*, where the factory can produce as much *Q* as it desires, with the proviso that it must compensate the residents. Then the factory will produce up to the point where its marginal gain equals the marginal loss to the residents, which is at the efficient point Q^*. But this transfer is an involuntary, non-market transaction: even though the residents are compensated (assuming that they win in court) they did not consent to the factory's production. Nevertheless, no transaction costs are incurred since the factory does not bargain with the residents. Hence the maximum welfare gains are realised, even though no market exchange has taken place. Here a rule of strict liability not only attempts to mimic or replicate the outcome that the parties would have arrived at but for the existence of high transaction costs. *It also means that those transaction costs are not actually incurred.*
- **The Economic and Legal Incidence of Transaction Costs:** Notice also that the final outcome in each case only depends on the *total* per

unit transaction costs (which are equal to $t = t_R + t_F$ under the no liability rule or $t' = t'_R + t'_F$ when the residents have the property right). For the purposes of determining the final level of production and the total gains from trade, it matters not who bears those costs – what matters is the total transaction costs. In other words, *the economic incidence of transaction costs* (which determines the final outcome) *is independent of the legal incidence* (the identity of the party that bears those costs).

3.6 The Coase Theorem with more than two parties

Let us now return to a world without transaction costs. A natural question is whether the Coase Theorem holds when there are three or more parties. Suppose, for example that there are two factories and a group of residents. The residents must now bargain with both factories if they would like to see a reduction in pollution. Does either version of the Coase Theorem hold in this case?

Even if parties have quasi-linear preferences, the situation now becomes more complicated, relative to our previous example. The reason is that in splitting up the potential surplus that could be realised when the efficient levels of production are chosen, the parties must not only agree on an outcome in which each party receives at least as much as it would if the parties acted alone. The agreement must also be *stable* (in some yet to be defined sense) against possible threats in which two of the parties might reach a superior agreement that gives each of them more than they would receive if the agreement included an additional party. In other words, instead of having just a *single* threat point, each party now has *multiple* threat points, which each can use to their advantage to obtain a better deal. The question we now turn to is whether stable Coasean-type agreements are possible in such a situation, and whether they are invariant to the initial legal rule or allocation of property rights.

3.6.1 Cooperative game theory in law and economics

To analyse agreements between more than two parties, we take a slight detour and introduce the concept of a *cooperative* or *coalitional game with transferable utility*. Consider a set N of *players*, where we also denote the number of players by $N > 2$. A *cooperative game with transferable utility or transferable payoffs* consists of the following:

- A set $N > 2$ of *players* or *parties*;
- A function $v(S)$ that represents the aggregate *value* or *worth* or *benefit* $v(S)$ of each *coalition* or group of players $S \subseteq N$.

The function $v(S)$ is called the *characteristic function*. An *allocation* or *imputation* is simply a collection of payments $\mathbf{x} = \{x_i : i \in N\}$ to each of the participants in the cooperative game with $x_i \geq v(\{i\})$. An allocation is *feasible* if $\sum_{i \in N} x_i = v(N)$. In what follows we will assume that it is efficient for the grand coalition N to form. We say that the imputation $\mathbf{x}$ *dominates* $\mathbf{y}$ *through* S if there exists a coalition S such that:

$$x_i > y_i \quad \text{for all } i \in S$$

We write $x \succ_S y$ if this is the case. In this situation, we also say that the allocation $\mathbf{y}$ is *blocked* by the coalition S.

3.6.1.1 *The core of a cooperative game*

One of the main issues in cooperative game theory is to find an allocation which splits $v(N)$ but which is stable against deviations by individual parties and groups of parties. The main idea of *the core* is to view the values $v(S)$ of each coalition as the *opportunity cost* of that group entering into the grand coalition. For an allocation to be in the core, the benefits that *every* coalition jointly receive must exceed the opportunity cost – the benefit they would receive if they deviated from the grand coalition.

Thus, we say that an allocation $\mathbf{x}$ is *in the core* if it cannot be blocked by any coalition S. In other words, the set of feasible allocations in the core is the set:

$$\text{core}(N, v) = \left\{ \mathbf{x} : \sum_{i \in N} x_i = v(N) \text{ and } \sum_{i \in S} x_i \geq v(S) \text{ for all } S \subset N \right\}$$

Note that the core may be empty. As an example of how cooperative game theory works, consider the *following three-player majority game*. Suppose that there are three players, A, B and C. When they all act together, they can obtain a payoff of \$1. Any two of them acting together can obtain a payoff of θ, where $0 < \theta < 1$. The characteristic function of this cooperative game is:

$$v(S) = \begin{cases} 0 & \text{if } |S| = 1 \\ \theta & \text{if } |S| = 2 \\ 1 & \text{if } |S| = 3 \end{cases}$$

Suppose that the payments x_A, x_B, x_C are in the core. Then these payments must be non-negative, and we must have $x_A + x_B + x_C = 1$ and $x_A + x_B, x_A + x_C, x_B + x_C \geq \theta$. But if this second set of inequalities holds, they must also hold if we sum them together, so we must have:

$$2(x_A + x_B + x_C) \geq 3\theta$$

However, since $x_A + x_B + x_C = 1$, this implies that we need $\theta \leq 2/3$ for the core to be non-empty.

We will use this simple majority game together with the following *0–1 normalisation* of a cooperative game, to understand the conditions under which the Coase Theorem does or does not hold when there are three or more players. The 0–1 normalisation works as follows. Suppose that we have cooperative game with a characteristic function $v(S)$, and which has $v(\{i\}) \neq 0$ for some i, and $v(N) \neq 1$. We seek to transform the payoffs of the game such that it is strategically equivalent to the original game (that is, it has the same structure as the original game), but which has $v(\{i\}) = 0$ for all i, and $v(N) = 1$.

This can be done by adding (not necessarily positive) numbers z_i to the individual payoff of each individual to give them $v(\{i\}) = 0$. In other words, set $z_i = -v(\{i\})$. This number must be added to every coalition of which i is a member. In particular, the new value of the grand coalition must be:

$$K = v(N) + \sum_i z_i$$

Now, divide the new value of every coalition by K. The resulting characteristic function is strategically equivalent to the original game, since each individual's payoff has been scaled up by z_i and divided by a constant K. Moreover, we have $v(\{i\}) = 0$ for all i, and $v(N) = 1$. This normalisation will prove extremely useful in the analysis that follows.

3.6.1.2 Applying the concept of the core: The Coase Theorem with three or more parties

3.6.1.2.1 An example with a non-empty core. To illustrate the main issues involved in situations in which there are three or more parties, consider the following example. There are two factories, F_1 and F_2, and a group of residents, R. Both factories emit pollution and this reduces the well-being of the residents. In the absence of production by the firms, the residents are assumed to enjoy utility of 40. If both firms produce, the residents' utility falls to 24. Therefore, production by both factories imposes a negative external cost of 16 (= 40 – 24) on the residents. If only one firm produces, the utility of the residents increases from 24 to 32. So production by only one firm imposes a negative external cost of 8. The marginal external cost to the residents is therefore constant.

If the factories produce alone, they can earn profits of 3 and 8 respectively. If they merge and produce together, then they can jointly earn profits of 11. Therefore, there are no scale effects in production. Clearly, the efficient outcome here is for both factories not to produce.

Suppose first that the factories can produce as much as they wish. Call this legal regime I. Let the characteristic function of this game be v_I. Denote the value of the grand coalition by $v_I(12R)$. Then $v_I(12R) = 40$, the total utility available to the parties when the factories and the residents agree that the factories should shut down production. Notation for other possible coalitions is defined in a similar fashion. The characteristic function in this situation is:

$$v_I(1) = 3, \quad v_I(2) = 8, \quad v_I(R) = 24, \quad v_I(12) = 11, \quad v_I(2R) = 32,$$
$$v_I(1R) = 32, \quad v_I(12R) = 40$$

Does there exist an efficient agreement between the parties which is stable against all threats? Suppose that the agreement involves payments x_1, x_2 and x_R to each of the players. To be individually rational, the payments must satisfy:

$$x_1 \geq 3, \quad x_2 \geq 8, \quad x_R \geq 24$$

The agreement between F_1, F_2 and R must also be feasible, and if it is efficient it will not waste any resources. This requires:

$$x_1 + x_2 + x_R = 40.$$

In addition, the payments must also be stable against other possible sets of agreements. One possibility is that instead of both agreeing to shut down, the factories F_1 and F_2 merge and continue to produce. To prevent this from occurring, they must be paid at least 11 jointly. In other words:

$$x_1 + x_2 \geq 11$$

Since $x_1 + x_2 + x_R = 40$, this means that we must also have $x_R \leq 29$. Similarly, to prevent other agreements between groups of only two parties from being attractive, we must have:

$$x_1 + x_R \geq 32$$

and:

$$x_2 + x_R \geq 32$$

Again, these two inequalities, together with the feasibility constraint, imply that $x_2 \leq 8$ and $x_1 \leq 8$. The former condition, together with the restriction that $x_2 \geq 8$, implies that $x_2 = 8$. The gains from trade are all shared between factory 1 and the residents. Therefore, any set of agreements which satisfies the following set of inequalities will be stable against deviations by any deviation by a single party, or any deviation by a subcoalition of 2 parties:

$$x_1 = 3+\alpha, \quad x_2 = 8, \quad x_R = 37-\alpha \tag{3.12}$$

where $0 \le \alpha \le 5$. The set of payments in (3.12) is the core of the game when the factories have the legal right to emit pollution.

Now suppose that the factories must first obtain the residents' permission to produce. Call this legal regime II, and let the characteristic function of this game be v_{II}. Denote the value of the grand coalition by $v_{II}(12R)$. Then again we have $v_{II}(12R) = 40$. The characteristic function in this situation is:

$$v_{II}(1) = 0, \quad v_{II}(2) = 0, \quad v_{II}(R) = 40, \quad v_{II}(12) = 0$$
$$v_{II}(2R) = 40, \quad v_{II}(1R) = 40, \quad v_{II}(12R) = 40$$

There is no payment that the factories could make to persuade the residents to let them produce. The core is still non-empty, but has a very simple structure: it is simply the point $x_1 = 0, x_2 = 0, x_R = 40$. Note, however, that the outcome is the same as that under legal regime I, and is still efficient. Hence both versions of the Coase Theorem hold in this example.

Another way of seeing what is going on in this example is to examine the 0–1 normalisation of the game under each legal rule. Consider legal regime I. The 0–1 normalisation has $z_1 + z_2 + z_R = -3 + -8 + -24 = -35$ and $K = 5$, and so:

$$v_I(1) = 0, \quad v_I(2) = 0, \quad v_I(R) = 0, \quad v_I(12) = 0, \quad v_I(2R) = 0,$$
$$v_I(1R) = 1, v_I(12R) = 1$$

Clearly firm 1 and the residents can share the gains from trade between themselves, without giving anything to firm 2. On the other hand, consider legal regime II. Its 0–1 normalisation is $v(S) = 0$ for any coalition. This is as it should be, since there are no gains from trade if the residents already have the property right and this is the efficient outcome.

3.6.1.2.2 Modifying the example. Now consider a slightly modified version of our previous example. Suppose now that if the factories merge, they enjoy joint profits of 12 instead of 11. This could be because there are economies of scale in the production of the good produced by the factories, which makes their joint profits higher than the sum of their profits separately.

Also, suppose that the externalities are not symmetric. Specifically, suppose factory 1 imposes a negative external cost of 9 on the residents, whilst factory 2 imposes a negative external cost of 4. All other values remain the same as in our previous example. The efficient outcome is again for both factories to shut down.

Let us now consider the characteristic functions of the games that are generated by our two legal regimes for this new example. Under legal regime I, we have:

$$v_I(1) = 3, \quad v_I(2) = 8, \quad v_I(R) = 24, \quad v_I(12) = 12,$$
$$v_I(2R) = 36, \quad v_I(1R) = 31, \quad v_I(12R) = 40$$

Does there exist an efficient agreement between the parties which is stable against all threats? We proceed as we did before. Suppose that the agreement involves payments x_1, x_2 and x_R to each of the players. Individual rationality and efficiency require:

$$x_1 \geq 3, \quad x_2 \geq 8, \quad x_R \geq 24 \quad \text{and} \quad x_1 + x_2 + x_R = 40$$

This situation is illustrated in Figure 3.6.1. The diagram is an equilateral triangle with a height of 40. The distance from any point in the triangle to the side *opposite* the vertex labelled with a party represents the payment that the party on that vertex receives. So, for example, the vertex labelled $x_R = 40$ represents set of payments where the residents receive 40 and F_1 and F_2 receive nothing.

In addition to individual rationality and efficiency, the payments must also be stable against other possible sets of agreements. One

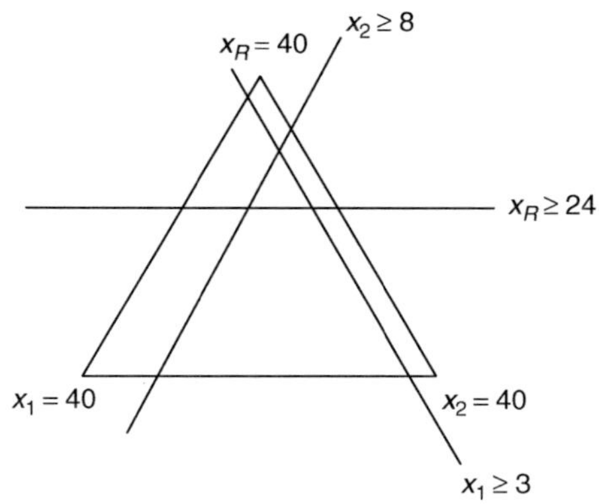

Figure 3.6.1 Diagrammatic representation of the three-party cooperative game

possibility is that instead of both agreeing to shut down, the factories F_1 and F_2 merge and continue to produce. To prevent this from occurring, they must be paid at least 12 jointly. In other words:

$$x_1 + x_R \geq 12$$

Since $x_1 + x_2 + x_R = 40$, this means that we must also have $x_R \leq 28$. Similarly, to prevent other agreements between groups of only two parties from being attractive, we must have:

$$x_1 + x_R \geq 31$$

and:

$$x_2 + x_R \geq 36$$

Again, these two inequalities, together with the feasibility constraint, imply that $x_2 \leq 9$ and $x_1 \leq 4$.

The shaded area in Figure 3.6.2 shows the range of allocations which satisfy all of these inequalities. Clearly, this set is non-empty. For example, the allocation:

$$x_1 = 4 - \alpha, \quad x_2 = 8 + \alpha, \quad x_R = 28$$

where $0 < \alpha < 1$, satisfies all of the inequalities discussed above.

Thus, if the residents pay factory 1 an amount equal to 4 – α, and pay factory 2 an amount equal to 8 + α, they will obtain utility of 40,

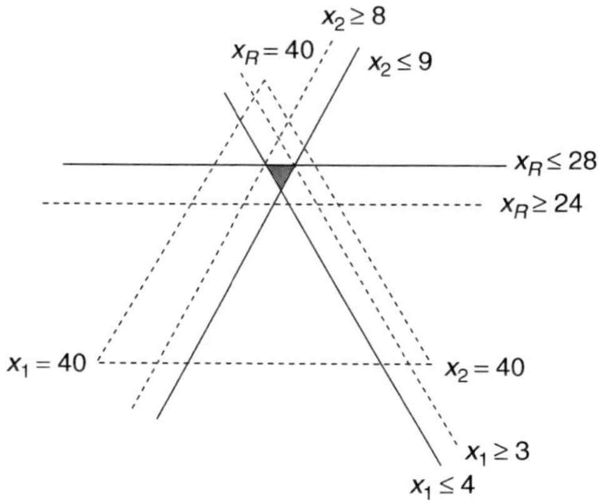

Figure 3.6.2 Diagrammatic representation of the three-party cooperative game with non-empty core

less total payments of 12, giving them final utility of 28. Both factory 1 and factory 2 would accept these payments, since they are both strictly better off than they were producing on their own. In addition, 1 and 2 do not have an incentive to merge and keep producing, since they would not gain from doing so. Similarly, neither the factories nor the residents would have an incentive to break this agreement and negotiate a separate agreement in which only one of the factories agrees to shut down. The 0–1 normalisation of this situation has $z_1 + z_2 + z_R = -3 + -8 + -24 = -35$ and $K = 5$, and so:

$$v_I(1) = 0, \quad v_I(2) = 0, \quad v_I(R) = 0, \quad v_I(12) = 0.2, \quad v_I(2R) = 0.8,$$
$$v_I(1R) = 0.8, \quad v_I(12R) = 1$$

Since $v_I(12) + v_I(2R) + v_I(1R) = 0.2 + 0.8 + 0.8 = 1.8$, any allocation that is in the core will have to have $2(x_1 + x_2 + x_R) \geq 1.8$, which is permissible given that we also have $x_1 + x_2 + x_R = 1$ for allocations in the core.

Now suppose that the residents have the property right to prevent the factories from producing. The residents would choose production levels of zero for both (which is efficient), and there are no payments that the factories could make which would induce the residents to accept a positive level of production. The core again consists of a single point, (0,0,40). Thus, we have illustrated what is actually a more general result: *if the core is non-empty, then the invariance and efficiency versions of the Coase Theorem both hold.*

3.6.1.2.3 Is the result a general one? Searching for examples with an empty core. Does the Coase Theorem still hold if the core is empty? And what does it take in our example for the Coase Theorem to break down? We now show how the result stated above breaks down in the presence of an empty core, and isolate the source of the empty core.

Only a slight modification of the previous example is needed to show this. Consider the same example as in the previous section, but now suppose that if F_1 and F_2 merge, they can realise joint profits of 15 rather than 12. This seems like a trivial modification. After all, our previous example featured economies of scale, this example simply makes those synergies slightly larger. However, as we will see, modifying the example in this way increases the opportunity cost of F_1 and F_2 entering into agreement with the residents. This increase in opportunity cost means that F_1 and F_2 must receive greater compensation for entering such an agreement, which in turn means that the residents' net benefit is lower than in the previous case. As we will show, these changes render any agreement – even though it is efficient – unstable.

Under legal regime I, the characteristic function is now:[9]

$$v_I(1) = 3, \quad v_I(2) = 8, \quad v_I(R) = 24, \quad v_I(12) = 15, \quad v_I(2R) = 36,$$
$$v_I(1R) = 31, \quad v_I(12R) = 40$$

Once again this situation can be illustrated diagrammatically (see Figure 3.6.3 below).

Does there exist a stable agreement between all three parties? Again, to be individually rational, the payments must satisfy:

$$x_1 \geq 3, \quad x_2 \geq 8, \quad x_R \geq 24 \tag{3.13}$$

The agreement between F_1, F_2 and R must also be efficient and feasible, which again requires:

$$x_1 + x_2 + x_R = 40 \tag{3.14}$$

In addition, the payments must also be stable against other possible sets of agreements. One possibility is that instead of agreeing to shut down, F_1 and F_2 merge and continue to produce. To prevent this from occurring, they must be paid at least 15 jointly. In other words:

$$x_1 + x_2 \geq 15 \tag{3.15}$$

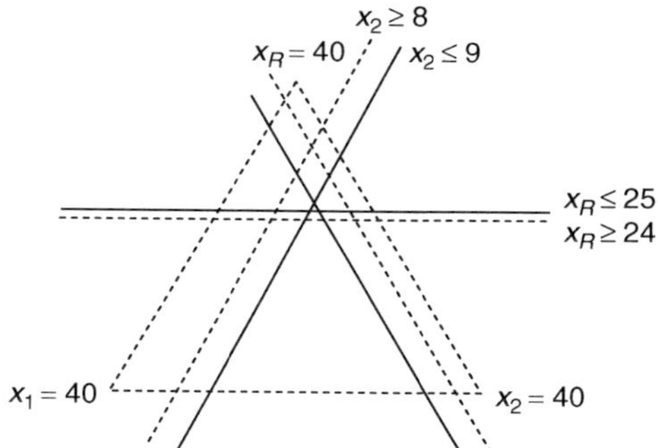

Figure 3.6.3 Diagrammatic representation of the three-party cooperative game with an empty core

Since $x_1 + x_2 + x_R = 40$, this means that we must also have $x_R \leq 25$. Similarly, to prevent other agreements from being attractive, we must have:

$$x_1 + x_R \geq 31 \tag{3.16}$$

and:

$$x_2 + x_R \geq 36 \tag{3.17}$$

Again, these two inequalities, together with the feasibility constraint, imply that $x_2 \leq 9$ and $x_1 \leq 4$. But these last two inequalities are clearly inconsistent with the requirement that $x_1 + x_2 \geq 15$.

Note that in this particular example there are actually *three* externalities at work here. The first two externalities are negative, and are caused by A and B's production reducing C's profit. The second externality is a positive externality – A and B producing together increases the joint profits of both of them. The size of this second externality turns out to be crucial in this example.

To see this even more clearly, adding (3.15), (3.16) and (3.17) gives:

$$2(x_1 + x_2 + x_R) \geq 15 + 31 + 36 = 82$$

which implies:

$$40 = x_1 + x_2 + x_R \geq 41$$

But this is not possible. In other words, if (3.15), (3.16) and (3.17) hold, then (3.14) cannot hold. Conversely, if (3.14) holds, then at least one (and possibly all) of (3.15), (3.16) and (3.17) cannot hold.

In other words, there is no set of payments which is stable here. To illustrate, suppose R pays F_2 not to produce. Then R would offer F_2 a maximum of 36 – 24 = 12. F_2 would accept a minimum of 8, so suppose R pays F_2 \$8. But F_2 and F_1 could come to an agreement in which they both produce, and in which F_2 receives 8.5 and F_1 receives 6.5 > 3. Thus F_2 and F_1 are better off. F_2 has no incentive to sign an agreement with R under the original terms.

But now notice that F_1 and R could form an agreement that makes them both better off than in the situation just examined. In turn, this agreement could be bettered by F_2 and R – and we are back to where we started. In other words, we are in a cycle of endless negotiating and renegotiating. Thus, beginning from a situation of no liability, there are no stable two firm coalitions – and the grand coalition is unstable as well. This outcome is very different from the outcome that would obtain if the residents had the property right. Under this legal rule, the residents would again choose production levels of zero for both factories (which is the efficient outcome), and there are no payments that the factories could make which would induce the residents to accept a positive level of production. Thus, *if the core is empty, neither the invariance version nor the efficiency version of the Coase Theorem hold.*

To gain an even deeper understanding of what is going on here, note that the 0–1 normalisation of this situation has $z_1 + z_2 + z_R = -3 + -8 + -24 = -35$ and $K = 5$, and so the normalised version of this game has the following characteristic function:

$$v_I(1) = 0, \quad v_I(2) = 0, \quad v_I(R) = 0, \quad v_I(12) = 0.8,$$
$$v_I(2R) = 0.8, \quad v_I(1R) = 0.8, \quad v_I(12R) = 1$$

In other words, *the Aivazian–Callen (1981) example is strategically equivalent to a simple majority game in which* $\theta = 0.8 > \frac{2}{3}$. This is illustrated in Figure 3.6.4, where the set of points that satisfy the requirements of the core are inside the triangle which is drawn with a broken line, but lie outside the triangle drawn with a solid line. In other words, there is no allocation which satisfies:

$$x_1 + x_2 \geq 0.8, \quad x_1 + x_R \geq 0.8, \quad x_2 + x_R \geq 0.8 \quad \text{and} \quad x_1 + x_2 + x_R = 1.$$

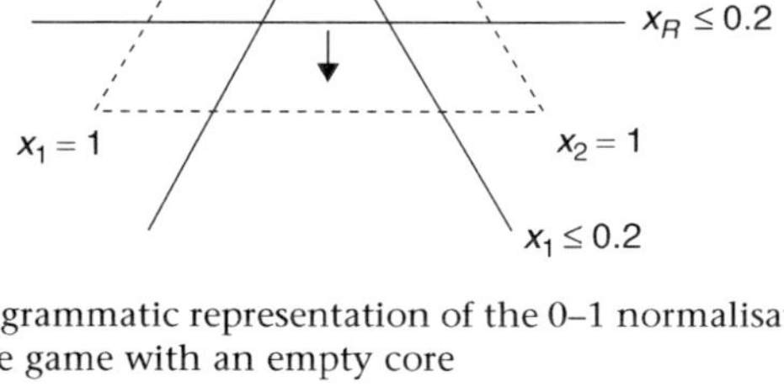

Figure 3.6.4 Diagrammatic representation of the 0–1 normalisation of the three-party cooperative game with an empty core

3.6.1.3 'Rescuing' the Coase Theorem, part I: The existence of multiple externalities requires multiple legal rules

Can the Coase Theorem be rescued in the three-party example? One possibility, following Mueller (2003), is to note the fact that there are really multiple externalities in this example: since the factories can merge and obtain a higher payoff that exceeds the sum of the payoffs they could obtain separately, there is also a positive externality between the factories. However, it is also important to note that it was only when this additional externality became sufficiently large that problems emerged. In any case, recognising this, let us introduce an additional legal rule to address this additional externality. After all, the Coase Theorem states that the legal rule does not matter for efficiency as long as *some* legal rule is in place.

Suppose, then, that we introduce an 'auxiliary' legal rule that addresses the positive externality and governs the actions that F_1 and F_2 are permitted to take on their own. For example, suppose that there is a rule of no liability for pollution, but that this is combined with a legal rule that states that F_1 and F_2 must effectively act as a merged entity and cannot produce separately. This rules out the coalitions $\{F_1\}$, $\{F_2\}$, $\{F_1R\}$ and $\{F_2R\}$. Then, if a no liability rule applies to the factories, agreements between the merged entity $\{F_1F_2\}$ and the residents will be stable and so the efficient outcome will occur.

On the other hand, suppose that the auxiliary legal rule states that F_1 and F_2 *cannot* act as a merged entity and must therefore produce separately, but that they are permitted to enter into contracts with the residents, both individually and separately. This would rule out the coalition $\{F_1F_2\}$. Then, again, if the grand coalition was to form there is an allocation which is stable. For example, the allocation $x_1 = 3+\alpha, x_2 = 9-\alpha, x_R = 28$ where $0 < \alpha < 1$ is stable against deviations from sub-coalition when the coalition $\{F_1F_2\}$ is not permitted to form.

3.6.1.4 'Rescuing' the Coase Theorem, part II: Enforceable contracts penalty clauses

Another possibility for 'rescuing' the Coase Theorem in the three-party example is to follow Bernholz (1997) and Aivazian and Callen (2003) and introduce the concepts of *enforceable contracts* and *penalty clauses.* To understand the role of enforceable contracts and penalties, suppose that contracts, once written, cannot be breached without compensation to the affected parties. Then, in our example, once a contract between any two-player coalition has been agreed to, a party that wishes to break an agreement and negotiate with another party would face a financial cost.

Suppose, for example, that there is a rule of no liability, and that factory 1 signs an agreement with the residents to stop production. Then the residents must receive at least 24 from such an agreement, and factory 1 must receive at least 3, with the joint value equal to 31. Suppose the parties split the gains from trade, so that the residents receive 26 and factory 1 receives 5. Now suppose that the factory 1 wishes to breach this agreement and instead merge with factory 2 and jointly produce. Factory 1 must compensate the residents 26 if he breaches their agreement. But this is not possible, since the joint profits that can be gained from a merger between the factories are only equal to 15 in total, and factory 2 must get at least 8 of those in order for the merger to be worth his while. The gains from breaching the contract are simply not high enough to warrant factory 1 breaching the contract.

Similarly, suppose that the residents wished to breach their agreement with factory 1, and instead form an agreement with factory 2. The available gains are 36. Factory 1 would need to be compensated 5, and factory 2 needs to receive at least 8. So that leaves a maximum of 23 for the residents to enjoy after all compensation has been made. But the residents were already receiving 26 in their contract with factory 1. Therefore, with enforceable contracts in place, there is no incentive for the residents to breach their agreement either. But since neither factory 1 nor the residents want to breach the agreement, it must be stable. Both parties' only option is to then sign an agreement with factory 2, from which there are mutual benefits. Therefore, cycling does not occur and the invariance and efficiency versions of the Coase Theorem again hold.

3.6.2 The core and transaction costs

The example in the previous section showed that even in the absence of transaction costs, the legal rule will, in general, matter for both production and efficiency, unless we add auxiliary legal rules. As we show in this section, introducing general transaction costs into the analysis does not alter this conclusion. The analysis in this section shows that if general rather than specific transactions costs are introduced, a situation in which the core is empty does not transform the outcome into one where we have a non-empty core, just because general transaction costs are present. Moreover, in situations in which the core *is* non-empty, introducing general transaction costs can transform the situation into one in which the core suddenly becomes empty. These results are due to Aivazian and Callen (2003).

Following Aivazian and Callen (2003), let us illustrate these results using the following simple specification of transaction costs:

$$C(S) = \begin{cases} S^k & \text{if } S > 1 \\ 0 & \text{otherwise} \end{cases}$$

where $k > 1$. These transaction costs are illustrated in Figure 3.6.5 for various coalition sizes and various values of k.

Following Aivazian and Callen (2003), consider the following characteristic function:

$$v(i) = 0 \quad \text{for } i = 1, 2, R$$

$$v(12) = a, \quad v(1R) = b, \quad v(2R) = c$$

$$v(12R) = d > \max\{a, b, c\}$$

Suppose that the core is non-empty. A sufficient condition for this to be the case is as follows. Let $x_1 \geq 0$, $x_2 \geq 0$, $x_R \geq 0$ be in the core. Then we require:

$$x_1 + x_2 \geq a$$

$$x_1 + x_R \geq b$$

$$x_2 + x_R \geq c$$

Which, summing across all three inequalities, implies:

$$2d = 2(x_1 + x_2 + x_R) \geq a + b + c$$

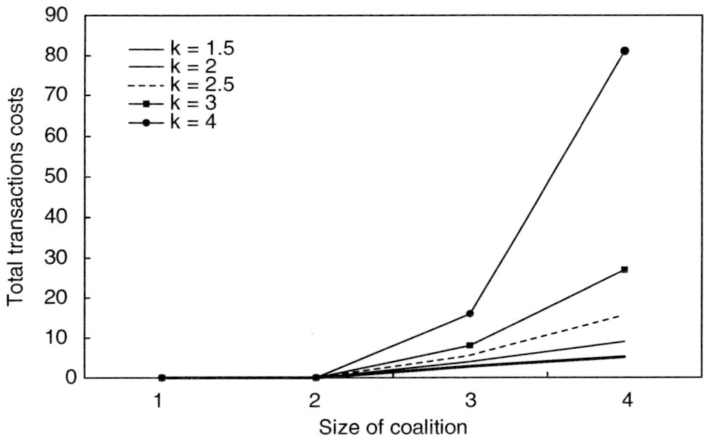

Figure 3.6.5 Transaction costs which increase with the size of the coalition

Thus, suppose that $d \geq \frac{a+b+c}{2}$. To see if the legal rule matters for efficiency here, suppose again that there is a rule of no liability in place and that F_1 and F_2 produce separately. This means that the initial utility levels are $v(F_1) = 0, v(F_2) = 0, v(R) = 0$. To be individually rational, the payments must satisfy:

$$x_1 \geq 0, \quad x_2 \geq 0, \quad x_R \geq 0$$

The agreement between F_1, F_2 and R must also be efficient and feasible. When transaction costs are present this requires:

$$x_1 + x_2 + x_R = d - 3^k.$$

In addition, the payments must also be stable against other possible sets of agreements. One possibility is that instead of agreeing to shut down, F_1 and F_2 merge and continue to produce. To prevent this from occurring, they must be paid at least a jointly, less the transaction costs incurred when they negotiate. In other words:

$$x_1 + x_2 \geq a - 2^k$$

Similarly, to prevent other agreements from being attractive, we must have:

$$x_1 + x_R \geq b - 2^k$$

and:

$$x_2 + x_R \geq c - 2^k$$

Again, adding these inequalities together yields the following condition for the core to be non-empty:

$$2(x_1 + x_2 + x_R) \geq a + b + c - 3.2^k$$

Therefore, for the core to be non-empty, we require:

$$2(d - 3^k) \geq a + b + c - 3.2^k$$

or:

$$d \geq 2.3^k - 3.2^k$$

The right-hand side is positive as long as $k > 1$, which we have assumed to be the case. Thus, if d is positive and less than $2.3^k - 3.2^k$, *even if the core is not empty in the absence of transaction costs, it will become empty once transaction costs are introduced*. In such situations, neither the invariance version nor the efficiency version of the Coase Theorem will hold.

3.7 Notes

The literature on the Coase Theorem is massive – according to Stigler (1988), Coase's (1960) paper is one of the most cited papers in the whole of the social sciences literature. Parisi (2008) provides a useful summary of the history of the debate over the result. The analysis developed in this chapter draws on various sources, including Bergstrom (1976), Ulen (1991), Hurwicz (1995), Chipman and Tian (2011), and Varian (2010, chapter 34). The analysis of the Coase Theorem in a three-person setting (with and without transaction costs) is explored by Aivazian and Callen (1981, 2003).

The diagrammatic analysis of the Coase Theorem with per unit transaction costs is implicit in most of the law and economics literature. The diagrammatic analysis of three-person cooperative games can be found in many good advanced microeconomic theory textbooks, including Mas-Colell, Whinston and Green (1995). Ordeshook (1986) provides an excellent explanation of the 0–1 normalisation of a cooperative game.

3.8 Exercises

1. Consider an economy with two people, 1 and 2. Both individuals initially have 200 dollars. Individuals can make monetary payments to each other, but the total amount of money available in the economy remains constant.

   Person 1 likes loud music (denoted by x), and person 2 does not. There is a daily upper limit of 24 hours on the playing of loud music, and the lower limit is zero hours. Let x_1 denote person 1's legal entitlement to play a specified number of hours of loud music without 2's consent.

   There are three legal regimes, labelled I, II and III:

   - In regime I, $x_1 = 0$, and person 2 enjoys a property right to silence. This means that 1 must obtain, possibly in exchange for a money payment, person 2's permission or consent to play a specified positive number of hours of loud music.
   - In regime II, $x_1 = 24$, i.e. person 1 is legally entitled to play loud music all day and person 2 must pay agent 1 to get a specified number of hours without noise.
   - In regime III, individuals are issued tradeable 'music permits' by the government. The owner of one music permit is legally permitted (but not legally obliged) to play one hour of loud music per day. An individual cannot play loud music without a permit. Suppose that individual 1 is issued with 8 music permits, and individual 2 is issued with 16 music permits.

   Suppose that $u_1 = m_1 + 24x - \frac{x^2}{2}$ and $u_2 = m_2 + 24y - \frac{y^2}{2}$, where $y \equiv 24 - x$ is the absence of loud music.

(a) What is the marginal rate of substitution of loud music for money for person 1? What is the marginal rate of substitution of the absence of loud music for money for person 2? What is the demand curve for loud music for person 1? What is the demand curve for the absence of loud music for person 2? What is the income effect for loud music for person 1? What is the income effect for the absence of loud music for person 2? Find the Pareto optimal allocations of loud music and money in this economy.

(b) The utility possibilities curve plots individual 2's utility as a function of individual 1's utility at all Pareto optimal points. What is the utility possibilities curve in this example?

(c) Suppose that the legal regime is I, and suppose that transaction costs are sufficiently low that individuals can bargain with one another and exploit all possible gains from trade. Describe in words and identify on a diagram the kinds of trades that these individuals might undertake. If all gains from trade can be exploited, how many hours of loud music will be played?

(d) Repeat question (c) for legal regimes II and III. Discuss your results in light of both versions of the Coase Theorem.

(e) Suppose that when the individuals bargain with one another, the bargaining rules state that they must split all gains from trade equally. This is known as the 'split the surplus' bargaining rule. For each legal regime, calculate the utility levels for each individual if all gains from trade are exploited. On the diagram, identify the utility gains that accrue to each individual. Which legal regime does individual 1 prefer? Which legal regime does individual 2 prefer? Does each individual's preference ranking over legal regime depend on the bargaining rule that is in place?

(f) For each of the legal regimes I and II there is an equivalent initial allocation of tradeable music permits. What are these initial allocations?

2. Suppose that there are two factories, F_1 and F_2, and a group of residents, R. Both factories emit pollution and this reduces the wellbeing of the residents.

The parties can reach agreements between themselves to eliminate each factory's pollution. Consider the following characteristic function, which describes the payoffs that the members of each coalition could jointly achieve if that coalition formed:

$$V(\{i\}) = 0 \quad \text{for } i = F_1, F_2, R$$

$$V(F_1, F_2) = a, \quad V(F_1R) = b, \quad V(F_1R) = c$$

$$V(F_1F_2R) = d$$

(a) Under what conditions is it efficient for the grand coalition to form?

(b) Define the concept of the *core* of a cooperative game. Write down a sufficient condition for the core of this game to be non-empty.

(c) Suppose that the core is non-empty. Do the efficiency and invariance versions of the Coase Theorem hold? Explain.

(d) Suppose that the core is empty. Do the efficiency and invariance versions of the Coase Theorem hold? Explain.

(e) Can the existence of transaction costs make an empty core non-empty? Explain. Can you derive an example in which there are transaction costs but in which both versions of the Coase Theorem still hold?

3. *The Shapley–Shubik pollution game* (Shapley and Shubik, 1969) studies the following situation. Suppose that there are $n > 1$ firms around a lake. It costs an individual factory A to treat its waste before discharging it into a lake. On the other hand, if s firms do not treat their waste, it costs each firm sB to purify its water supply. Let $B < A < nB$.

   (a) What are the aggregate costs if all firms treat their water? What are the aggregate costs if no firms treat their water? What are the aggregate costs if s firms do not treat their water? What is the efficient outcome in this situation?
   (b) Suppose that no firms treat their waste. What is the best that an individual firm i can do for itself in this situation? Let the costs that firm i incurs for this individually optimal action be $v(i)$.
   (c) What is the best outcome that the coalition of all firms acting together can achieve? Let the costs that the coalition N incurs for this optimal action be $v(N)$.
   (d) Consider a coalition S which has $N > s > 1$ members. Suppose that all firms who are members of S treat their waste. What is the lowest payoff that the members of coalition S can jointly obtain? Now suppose that all firms who are members of S do not treat their waste. What is the lowest payoff that the members of coalition S can jointly obtain? Compare these two values and find $v(S)$, which is the lowest cost that the members of coalition S can jointly obtain, even if the firms who are not members of S try to do their worst to the members of S.
   (e) Does this game have a core? Discuss.

4
Accident Law and Markets, Part I: The Unilateral Care Model

4.1 Introduction

Chapter 3 examined situations where transactions costs were sufficiently low to render legal rules irrelevant from an efficiency point of view. If these conditions always prevailed and transactions costs were sufficiently low – and if economists cared only about economic efficiency – then the study of law and economics would not be very interesting (and this would be a very short book!). In such a world, parties would always be able to bargain around the law, and as a result of the reasoning embodied in the Coase Theorem, legal rules would simply not matter for efficiency – although they would of course matter for distribution and for the parties involved.

It would be a grave mistake, however, to conclude from our analysis of the Coase Theorem that 'legal rules do not matter', or that 'property rights do not matter'. The reason for this is straightforward: legal rules, property rights and the institutions that support markets matter precisely because transaction costs are usually *not* zero. This chapter and those which follow illustrate the importance of legal rules for efficiency by examining cases where transaction costs are so high as to rule out all forms of bargaining.

In this chapter we examine the opposite extreme case: we analyse situations where transactions costs are high and bargaining between parties is prohibitively costly, so that *no* negotiation is possible. In other words, we rule out situations covered by the Coase Theorem.

The kinds of situations examined in this chapter are typically governed by accident law or tort law. These legal rules aim at drawing a line between those harmful events that should lead to compensation, and others for which the harm should 'lie where it falls'. Throughout the chapter we will distinguish between two parties: the *injurer* and the *victim*. This terminology needs to be used with a great deal of care. As the analysis in Chapter 3 showed, *social costs really are social*. To take the Chapter 3 example, if the residents enjoy a property right and enforce that right without bargaining with the factory, then in a very real sense the residents could be said to be harming the factory, by preventing the factory from producing. This conceptual approach contrasts with the Pigouvian tradition, which views the factory as an injurer whose harmful actions must somehow be constrained and controlled. The Coasean approach strips away this presumption and emphasises the reciprocal nature of harm. This is one of the key insights of Coase's analysis.

This chapter presents a canonical model of accident law, which serves as a baseline model for many of the other topic discussed in this book. There are two important considerations to keep in mind throughout this chapter:

- We will study *accidental* harm, which is essentially *unpredictable*; and
- The chance that harm actually occurs and the damage that is inflicted depends on how much *care* or *precaution* is actually taken.

In other words, the probability of harm occurring depends on the level of care taken by the injurer, and care is costly. This situation is best summarised by the concept of *probabilistic externalities*. An externality is probabilistic if the link between the original action and its effects on bystanders is uncertain, as opposed to an action whose effects are more or less completely foreseeable and deliberate.

The key economic issue explored in this chapter is as follows: when party A undertakes an activity that imposes an (uncertain) and otherwise uncompensated cost on another party B, should A compensate B, or should the damage 'lie where it falls'? Further, if A should compensate B, how much compensation should be paid?

In contrast to most textbook treatments of the issues, the analysis in this chapter also focuses on the economics of accident law in market settings. The point of departure in section 4.2 is the basic unilateral care model, where only one party can take steps to reduce the probability of accidental harm occurring. This model is first examined within a non-market setting. Section 4.3 extends the analysis by applying standard accident laws to a competitive market setting. Section 4.4 studies the special but very relevant case of the unilateral care model in a market setting where injurers are firms in a competitive market, but where victims of harm are themselves also firms in a different perfectly competitive market. Monopoly and oligopoly are examined in section 4.5. Section 4.6 concludes with an examination of the costs and benefits of liability rules in situations where regulators have imperfect information about the position of marginal benefit and cost curves. The insights from this analysis are used to shed light on the relative desirability of pollution taxes versus permit trading schemes.

4.2 The unilateral care model

Suppose that only one party – the injurer – is undertaking some potentially harmful activity and that the level of care in order to prevent harm to others can be described by a positive number $x_i \geq 0$. Assume that the party who may be harmed (the victim) cannot take their own precautions to avoid damage. This is known as the *unilateral care model,* because only one party can affect the probability of an accident occurring and the harm that can occur.

The *probability of harm* that is associated with the injurer's level of care x_i is:

$$\rho(x_i) \quad \text{where } \rho(x_i) \in [0,1] \text{ for all } x_i \geq 0$$

It is natural to assume that the higher the level of care taken, the lower will be the chance that the injurer will harm the victim. Therefore, we will assume that:

$$\rho'(x_i) \equiv \frac{d\rho(x_i)}{dx_i} < 0$$

It is also natural to assume, as with most economic technologies, that there are diminishing marginal returns to care: as more care is taken the marginal reduction in care is positive but gets smaller and smaller. Therefore, we will assume that:

$$\rho''(x_i) \equiv \frac{d^2\rho(x_i)}{dx_i^2} > 0$$

The probability of harm function is therefore downward sloping and convex. Should an accident occur, we will assume that the victim suffers damages or harm with monetary value $h>0$. We will assume that both parties are risk neutral. Thus, the expected damage to a victim, given a level of care equal to x_i is taken by the injurer, is:

$$\begin{aligned}\text{Expected damage} &= \text{probability of accident} \\ &\quad \times \text{harm caused by accident} \\ &= \rho(x_i)\,h \qquad (4.1)\end{aligned}$$

In our economic analysis of accident law, we will call $\rho(x_i)h$ the *expected damage* or *expected harm function*. It could also be the case that the level of damages itself depends on the level of care taken by the injurer, so we could write

$$h = h(x_i)$$

Then, the expected damage function would be:

$$\begin{aligned}\text{Expected damage} &= \text{probability of accident} \\ &\quad \times \text{damage caused by accident} \\ &= \rho(x_i) \times h(x_i) \qquad (4.2)\end{aligned}$$

If we let:

$$\text{Expected harm} = H(x_i) \qquad (4.3)$$

with $H'(x_i) \equiv \dfrac{dH(x_i)}{dx_i} < 0$ and $H''(x_i) \equiv \dfrac{d^2H(x_i)}{dx_i^2} > 0$, then this encompasses both cases in (4.1) and (4.2).

4.2.1 The efficiency of legal rules in the unilateral care model

4.2.1.1 The efficient level of care

Let us address the question of efficient legal rules in the unilateral care model. Efficiency here is interpreted in an *ex ante* sense – we seek to find the allocation of resources which minimises the expected aggregate costs of care. Let us denote such a level (assuming it exists) by x_i^*. Note that in principle there might be more than one such efficient level of care, although our assumptions allow us to rule out such cases. Let $w_i > 0$ be the dollar cost of providing one unit of care (that is, w_i is the marginal cost of care). To find x_i^* we need to solve:

$$\begin{aligned}&\min_{x_i \geq 0} \text{Expected social cost} \\ &\quad = \min_{x_i \geq 0} \{\text{Injurer's cost of care} + \text{Victim's expected damages}\} \\ &\quad = \min_{x_i \geq 0} \{w_i x_i + \rho(x_i)h\}\end{aligned}$$

Note that, in general, the efficient level of care, x_i^* will not be zero (that is, it will always be efficient for the injurer to take some care). However, it is also true that in general it is never efficient to reduce the possibility of harm to zero. The necessary and sufficient first-order condition for this problem is:

$$w_i + \rho'(x_i^*)h = 0$$

or:

$$w_i = -\rho'(x_i^*)h$$

This equation is of the form:

Social marginal cost of care = Expected Social Marginal Reduction in Damages.

The left-hand side is the social marginal cost of care. The right-hand side is the marginal reduction in expected damage (or, alternatively, the expected social benefit of an extra unit of care). Thus, this is just a condition of the usual economic form 'provide care until the social marginal cost of the last unit of care equals the expected social marginal benefit of that last unit'. It follows that, as with any other externality problem in economics, the agents will respond to marginal incentives, rather than total incentives. The solution to this problem is shown in Figure 4.2.1.

Notice that at x_i^*, the injurer still imposes a negative external cost on the victim, since the level of x_i chosen by the injurer still determines both the total and marginal expected damages of the victim. But, in the language of Buchanan and Stubblebine (1962), the externality is no longer Pareto relevant: there are no trades between the injurer and the victim that could take place that would make the victim better off, without making the injurer worse off.

It is straightforward to verify (both analytically and diagrammatically, using a diagram exactly like Figure 4.2.1 below) that the efficient level of care increases (decreases) if the marginal benefit of care rises (falls) and that the efficient level of care decreases (increases) if the marginal cost of care rises (falls).

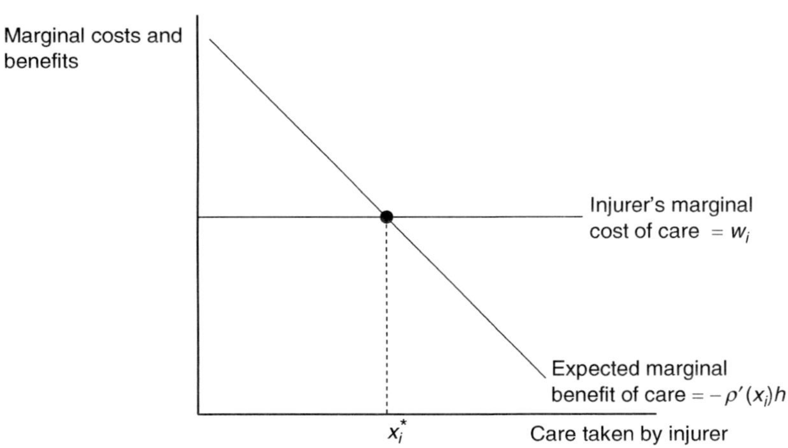

Figure 4.2.1 The efficient level of care

4.2.2 Legal rules in the unilateral care model

Now let us consider three different legal arrangements in the unilateral care model.

4.2.2.1 No liability

Under a no liability rule, the injurer is never responsible for any damage caused to the victim, and is never obligated to pay any damages. Then, letting $w_i > 0$ denote the dollar cost of a unit of care the injurer solves:

$$\min_{x_i \geq 0} w_i x_i$$

The solution is $x_i^{NL} = 0$. That is, the injurer takes no care at all, which is inefficient. This is shown in Figure 4.2.2. The no liability rule creates very poor incentives for taking care, and results in an inefficiently low level of care.

4.2.2.2 Strict liability

Under strict liability, an injurer is obligated to pay all of the victim's damages, irrespective of the amount of care that is taken. Thus, the injurer chooses the level of care that minimises his expected cost of care, which under a strict liability rule is the sum of the cost of care, plus any expected damages to the victim. That is, the injurer solves:

$$\min_{x_i \geq 0} \{w_i x_i + \rho(x_i)h\}$$

The solution to this problem, x^*_{SL}, must obey the first-order condition:

$$w_i + \rho'(x^*_{SL})h = 0$$

This solution is shown in Figure 4.2.3, where total costs rather than marginal costs are shown.

In the unilateral care model, a strict liability rule causes the injurer to internalise the probabilistic externality and take the efficient level of care. Note from the first-order condition for the efficient level of care, and the diagrams above, that this is *exactly the same first order condition as we derived for the rule of strict liability*.

4.2.2.3 A negligence rule or due standard of care

Under a negligence rule, the court sets a level of care $z_i \geq 0$, which is also called a *due standard of care*. If the injurer takes a level of care x_i which *exceeds* the due standard, then he is not liable for any damage to

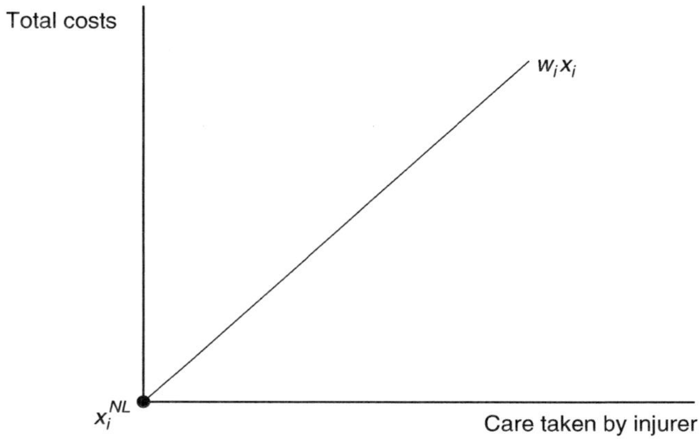

Figure 4.2.2 The injurer's care level under a no liability rule

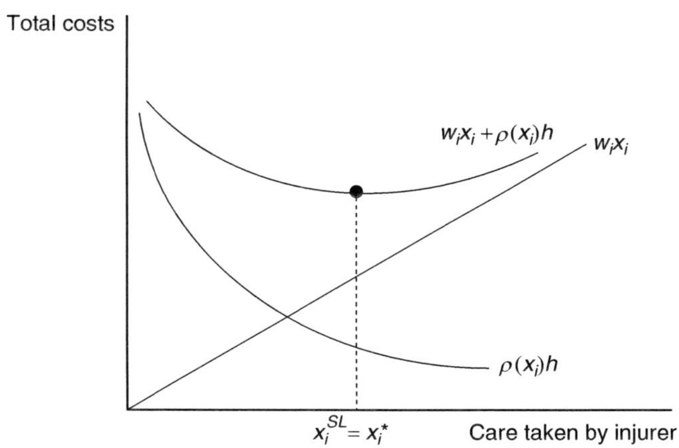

Figure 4.2.3 Injurer care under a strict liability rule

the victim, and his only cost is that which he incurred in taking care. On the other hand, if the injurer *fails* to meet the due standard (i.e. if $x_i < z_i$), then he is liable for all of the victim's damages, in addition to the cost of the care he undertook.

Therefore, the injurer's expected cost function under a negligence rule is:

$$\text{Injurer's expected cost} = \begin{cases} w_i x_i & \text{if } x_i \geq z_i \\ w_i x_i + \rho(x_i)h & \text{if } x_i < z_i \end{cases}$$

The injurer, once again, chooses the level of care that minimises his expected cost. In the diagram below, the choice of the due standard z_i induces the injurer to take exactly an amount of care that is equal to z_i, since this is where the injurer's expected cost under this particular negligence rule is the lowest. This outcome need not always occur under this legal rule.

Suppose that the court knew the benefit and cost functions of the two parties, and that it knew the efficient level of care x_i^* which we found earlier. Suppose that the court set the due standard of care z_i equal to the efficient level of care x_i^*. Then, substituting this into the injurer's cost function that we derived earlier, we have the injurer's new expected cost function under this particular negligence rule:

$$\text{Injurer's expected cost} = \begin{cases} w_i x_i & \text{if } x_i \geq x_i^* \\ w_i x_i + \rho(x_i)h & \text{if } x_i < x_i^* \end{cases}$$

The injurer's cost function when the due standard is set at $z_i = x_i^*$ is shown in Figure 4.2.4.

As the diagram illustrates, with the due standard set at x_i^*, the injurer's expected cost function is minimised by choosing x_i^*, the efficient level of care. This gives us a second important result: in the unilateral care model, a negligence rule which sets the due standard at $z_i = x_i^*$ is

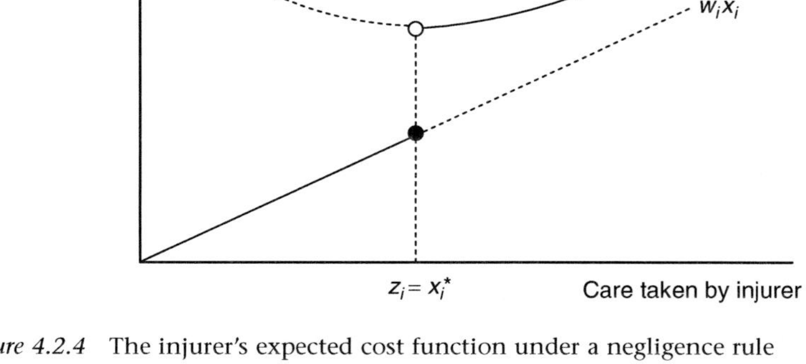

Figure 4.2.4 The injurer's expected cost function under a negligence rule

efficient. There are other efficient negligence rules as well (for example, suppose that the due standard is set at $z_i > x_i^*$ for sufficiently high z^i. This also results in efficient behaviour in the unilateral care model).

4.2.2.4 *Contrast with the Pigouvian approach*

The Pigouvian approach to negative externalities is to levy a tax which is equal to the marginal damage, where this is evaluated at the efficient level of activity. Applying this approach to the unilateral model of accidental harm is straightforward. What tax rate induces efficient behaviour? The tax must be designed in such a way as to induce the injurer to take the efficient level of care. Therefore, it must be conditioned on the injurer's actual level of care. So let the injurer's tax bill be $t_i = t(x_i)$. The injurer's costs are now:

$$w_i x_i + t(x_i) \tag{4.4}$$

whereas total social costs are $w_i x_i + H(x_i)$. To induce the injurer to behave efficiently, we simply set $t(x_i) = H(x_i)$, so that the injurer chooses x_i with the property that $w_i = -H'(x_i)$, which is the efficiency condition. The expected revenue from such a tax is simply $H(x_i^*)$. This is a non-linear tax, which requires knowledge of the entire shape of the expected harm function, but in expected terms is identical to a rule of strict liability.

4.2.3 Applications of the unilateral care model

This section considers some basic applications of the unilateral care model.

4.2.3.1 *Punitive damages and the effects of legal errors*

Punitive damages are those that are awarded to victims in excess of their actual losses; they are designed to 'punish' the injurer. How can we reconcile these kinds of damages with notions of efficiency? One justification is that injurers occasionally escape liability because judges or courts make mistakes, or because of imperfect enforcement. In the context of accident law, legal errors can be divided into two types:

- Type I error: a person who is not liable is mistakenly found liable.
- Type II error: a person who is liable is mistakenly found not liable.

We will focus on the second type of error first. Suppose that there is a rule of strict liability, and consider an injurer who only expects to face liability with probability $1 - e_2$ if an accident occurs, where e_2 is the probability of a Type II error occurring. The injurer's expected costs are now:

$$w_i x_i + (1 - e_2)\rho(x_i)h$$

A higher e_2 lowers the injurer's expected costs, which under a rule of strict liability lowers the level of care that is taken. Now suppose that, if the injurer is found liable for damage, the injurer faces punitive damages D as well as compensatory damages of h. The injurer's expected costs are now:

$$w_i x_i + (1 - e_2)\rho(x_i)(h + D)$$

The level of D that induces efficient behaviour by the injurer is the one which equates his expected costs with social costs. This means that we need to choose D to satisfy:

$$w_i x_i + \rho(x_i)h = w_i x_i + (1 - e_2)\rho(x_i)(h + D^*)$$

which implies that:

$$h = (1 - e_2)(h + D^*)$$

so:

$$D^* = \left(\frac{e_2}{1 - e_2}\right)h$$

The efficient level of punitive damages is increasing in the actual level of harm h, so all else being equal, those harmed by more serious tortious acts should receive higher punitive damages payouts. D^* is also increasing in e_2, the probability of a type II error.

The effects of Type I errors can also be incorporated into this analysis. Suppose again that there is a rule of strict liability, and that the probability of a Type I error is e_1. In this model, a Type I error occurs when the injurer is found liable and is forced to pay damages, but in reality no actual harm has occurred. Such examples frequently arise with so-called 'frivolous' lawsuits, where plaintiffs successfully sue for damages in instances where the harm is trivial or non-existent.

Harm does not occur with probability $1 - \rho(x_i)$. Ordinarily the injurer would not pay damages in this instance, but if there are Type I errors, he will pay h if no harm occurs, and so this occurs with probability $e_1[1 - \rho(x_i)]$. Therefore, the injurer's expected costs (assuming for the moment that there are no Type II errors) are:

$$w_i x_i + \rho(x_i)h + e_1[1 - \rho(x_i)]h = w_i x_i + \rho(x_i)(1 - e_1)h + e_1 h \qquad (4.5)$$

which for any x_i exceeds $w_i x_i + \rho(x_i)h$. The presence of Type I errors increases the injurer's expected damages, but *reduces* the level of care that the injurer takes. This may seem somewhat paradoxical, but is easy to understand once we think carefully about marginal versus average incentives. Type I errors increase the injurer's expected costs (thus affecting average or total incentives), but worsen the injurer's marginal incentives to take care. In the extreme case where $e_1 = 1$, for example, the injurer faces damages with probability 1, irrespective of the level of care taken. In this situation there is simply no point in the injurer taking care, since he cannot reduce his liability by doing so.

Combining the two kinds of errors yields the injurer's expected costs:

$$w_i x_i + [(1 - e_1 - e_2)\rho(x_i) + e_1]h \tag{4.6}$$

Both kinds of errors reduce the incentives to take care, but the combined effect (due to the presence of Type I errors) could end up increasing the expected damages paid by the injurer.

4.2.3.2 The judgement proof problem

In some instances involving compensating victims for accidental harm, injurers are wealth constrained – the injurer's total assets are less than the damage that they might actually cause. This is also known as the 'judgement proof problem'. Suppose that the injurer has assets of $a > 0$, but that $a < h$, where h is the damage caused to victims. Let's consider the unilateral care model of accidents studied in class, and consider the following legal rules:

- No liability
- Strict liability
- Negligence rule

Which of these legal rules can induce injurers to take an efficient amount of care when they are wealth constrained?

4.2.3.2.1 No liability. Under a no liability rule, the injurer's expected costs are:

$$w_i x_i$$

for any level of assets. Thus, the injurer always chooses $x_i = 0$, and so this rule cannot be efficient.

4.2.3.2.2 Strict liability. Under a rule of strict liability, the injurer's expected costs are:

$$w_i x_i + p(x_i)a$$

Because the injurer does not face the full social costs of his actions (he only has to pay $a < h$ when the damage is h), he chooses $x_i < x_i^*$. So a rule of strict liability is also inefficient here.

4.2.3.2.3 Negligence rule. Assuming the due standard is set at $z_i = x_i^*$, the injurer's expected costs are:

$$\text{Injurer's expected costs} = \begin{cases} w_i x_i & \text{if } x_i \geq x_i^* \\ w_i x_i + p(x_i)a & \text{if } x_i < x_i^* \end{cases}$$

Suppose that x_i° minimizes $w_i x_i + p(x_i)a$. Since $a < h$, we know that $x_i^\circ < x_i^*$. But it could be possible that:

$$w_i x_i^\circ + p(x_i^\circ)a < w_i x_i^\circ$$

which could hold if a is sufficiently low. For example, in the extreme case that the injurer has no assets, he will take no care. More generally, suppose, for example, that $a = a_2$ in Figure 4.2.5. Then $x_i = x_i^{\circ\circ}$ (rather than $x_i = x_i^*$) would be chosen by the injurer, since:

$$w_i x_i^{\circ\circ} + p(x_i^{\circ\circ})a_2 < w_i x_i^* \tag{4.7}$$

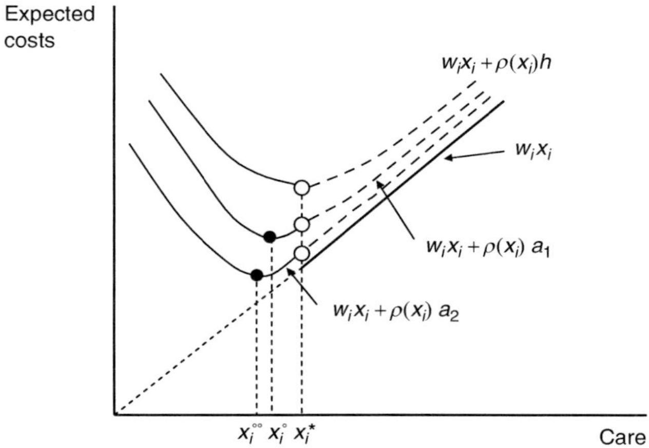

Figure 4.2.5 A judgement proof injurer

4.3 Extending the unilateral care model to a market setting: Liability rules in competitive markets

In most discussions of the unilateral care model, market exchanges are kept in the background. However, the goal of this book is to put markets front and centre. Therefore, this section extends the unilateral model to a market framework.

Consider a perfectly competitive market for a good, and suppose that the production of the good causes external harm to those who do not consume the good (the case where the good causes harm to consumers or purchasers of the good is dealt with in the next chapter). Consumer utility is equal to $u(Q)$. Suppose that there are n identical firms (where n is determined endogenously in the long run), each with a total cost function of $C(q)$. The efficiency conditions and the long-run equilibrium outcome were discussed in Chapter 1.

In contrast to the situation examined in Chapter 1, now suppose that production of the good causes total expected harm of $nqH(x_i)$, where q is the quantity produced by each firm, x_i is the level of care taken by each firm, and $H(x_i)$ is the expected harm per unit of the good produced. Finally, let each firm's per unit cost of care be equal to w_i. Welfare is given by the difference between benefits and costs:

$$W = u(nq) - nC(q) - nq[wx_i + H(x_i)]$$

Welfare maximisation now requires three conditions. First, for a given number of (identical) firms, it must not be possible to increase welfare by having each firm produce more. This means that:

$$\frac{\partial W}{\partial n} == n^*u'(n^*q^*) - n^*[w_i x_i^* + H(x_i^*)] - n^* C'(n^*) = 0$$

or:

$$u'(n^*q^*) = w_i x_i^* + H(x_i^*) + C'(q^*) \tag{4.8}$$

This equation states that the marginal consumption benefits from consuming the last unit of the good must equal the full marginal costs of consumption, where those costs now include the marginal expected harm that occurs as a result of producing the good, as well as the cost of care. In contrast, if the good was harmless, the efficiency condition with respect to q would be $u'(nq) = C'(q^*)$. Thus, when the good causes harm, the efficiency condition with respect to q implies that overall consumption and production should be less than it would if the good was not harmful.

Second, for a given quantity, it must not be possible to increase welfare by changing the number of firms. This means that:

$$\frac{\partial W}{\partial n} = q^* u'(n^* q^*) - q^*[w_i x_i^* + H(x_i^*)] - C(q^*) = 0$$

or:

$$u'(n^* q^*) = w_i x_i^* + H(x_i^*) + \frac{C(q^*)}{q^*} = 0 \qquad (4.9)$$

This condition states that the marginal consumption benefits must also equal *average* expected costs, where these costs again include the expected harm that occurs as a result of the good being produced. Since the consumer equates marginal benefits with price P, welfare maximisation again requires price = marginal cost = average cost.

Finally, efficiency requires that it must not be possible to increase welfare by altering the level of care:

$$\frac{\partial W}{\partial x_i} = -n^* q^*[w_i + H'(x_i^*)] = 0$$

or:

$$w_i = -H'(x_i^*) \qquad (4.10)$$

This states that for the last unit of care that is provided, the reduction in expected harm (which is the marginal benefit of care) should be equal to the marginal cost providing that last unit of care.

4.3.1 Liability rules

This section examines the welfare consequences of various liability rules in a competitive market setting when production causes external harm. We consider three rules: no liability, strict liability and a negligence rule.

4.3.1.1 No liability

Consider a no liability rule, where firms do not have to compensate victims. For any q, each firm's profit is equal to:

$$\pi = Pq - qw_i x_i - C(q)$$

Firms now have no incentive to take care, so they choose $x_i = 0$. They supply q up to the point where price equals marginal cost, so this means that the quantity supplied satisfies $P = C'(q)$. The market equilibrium is identical to the one discussed in Chapter 2, when there was no harm. Marginal private consumption benefits equal marginal private costs, but these costs are less than social costs. Hence the competitive equilibrium under a no liability rule is not efficient.

4.3.1.2 *Strict liability*

Under a rule of strict liability, firms must compensate those harmed for all losses. Since firms must fully compensate victims, each firm's profit is equal to $Pq - q[w_i x_i + H(x_i)] - C(q)$. Each price-taking profit-maximising firm produces at the point where price is equal to marginal cost, so:

$$P = w_i x_i + H(x_i) + C'(q) .$$

Furthermore, for any q, under a strict liability rule, firms are faced with the full social costs of their actions. Therefore they will minimise the costs of care by equating the marginal benefits of care (the reduction in damages that they must pay consumers) with the marginal costs, so that:

$$w_i = -H'(x_i)$$

Note that this is the same as the efficiency condition for care – firms take the efficient level of care under strict liability.

4.3.1.2.1 *Short- and long-run competitive equilibrium under strict liability.* Suppose we are in some long-run equilibrium where there is no liability rule in place. In the short run, suppose the number of firms is fixed at (say) n_0. Now introduce a strict liability rule. Forcing the firm to compensate victims acts like a specific tax on production, where firms get to choose the expected size of the tax by choosing their level of care. In the short run, this rule increases marginal and average cost, and we get an upward shift in the short-run supply curve by $w_i x_i^* + H(x_i^*)$. In the short run the market price rises, but not by the full amount of the costs care plus the expected harm. The extent of the price rise in the short run depends on the elasticity of demand. The *legal* incidence of the rule of strict liability is that firms pay the costs of care and expected harm, but in the short run the *economic* incidence is shared between producers and consumers of the good. In the short run the quantity produced by each firm falls, since they choose production to equate their new marginal cost with the higher price. Relative to a situation with no harm, this situation involves negative profits. Total quantity is lower.

In the long run, firms will exit the industry, driving up the market price until profits are driven back to zero. Thus, in addition to producing at a point where price equals marginal cost, firms earn zero profits, so we also have $P^*_{SL} = w_i x_i^* + H(x_i^*) + \frac{C(q)}{q}$. Thus, price equals full average cost. But once again, since marginal cost also equals price, which in turn is equal to average cost, we must have marginal cost equal to average cost. This again occurs at the minimum of the average cost curve, which now includes social costs: the cost of care and the expected harm.

The long-run competitive equilibrium is shown in Figure 4.3.1 below. The long-run market supply curve is flat and is equal to the minimum of the new average cost curve. Note that for each firm this minimum occurs at the same point as it did when the product was not dangerous: the quantity q^*, which minimises $w_i x_i + H(x_i) + \frac{C(q)}{q}$ is the same quantity that minimises $\frac{C(q)}{q}$. This happens because under a strict liability rule, the marginal and average cost curves shift upward in a parallel fashion. Each firm is forced to pay the cost of care and the expected harm per unit of the good, and this acts like a specific tax as in Chapter 1. Even though firms bear all of the *legal* incidence of the strict liability rule, consumers will bear all of the *economic* incidence of this rule in the long run.

4.3.1.3 *Negligence rule*

Now consider a negligence rule, where the due standard of care is set at the efficient level. For any q, each firm's profit is now equal to

$$\pi = \begin{cases} Pq - q[w_i x_i + H(x_i)] - C(q) & \text{if } x_i < x_i^* \\ Pq - qw_i x_i - C(q) & \text{if } x_i \geq x_i^* \end{cases}$$

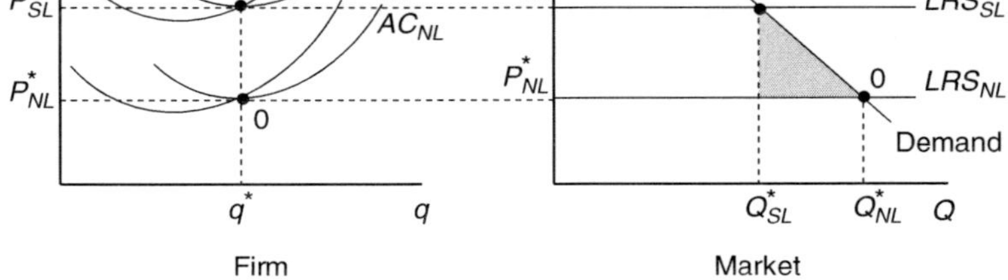

Figure 4.3.1 Long-run competitive equilibrium under a strict liability rule

Firms supply q up to the point where price equals marginal cost, so this means that the quantity supplied satisfies:

$$P = \begin{cases} w_i x_i + H(x_i) + C'(q) & \text{if } x_i < x_i^* \\ w_i x_i + C'(q) & \text{if } x_i \geq x_i^* \end{cases}$$

Since the due standard is set at the efficient level of care, firms can lower their marginal costs and avoid paying damages to the victim by choosing the efficient level of care here. Therefore, each firm chooses $x_i = x_i^*$, and chooses to produce at the point where marginal cost equals price:

$$P = w_i x_i^* + C'(q)$$

4.3.1.3.1 Short- and long-run equilibrium under a negligence rule. In the short run, the number of firms is again fixed at (say) n_0. Consider the same thought experiment as in the previous section. Suppose we are initially in some long-run equilibrium where there is a no liability rule. Now introduce a negligence rule. Each firm's marginal and average costs increase by $w_i x_i^*$ rather than $w_i x_i^* + H(x_i^*)$. This increases marginal and average cost – but not by as much as under the strict liability rule. In the short run we get an upward shift in the short-run supply curve by $w_i x_i^*$. The market price rises, but not by the full amount of the costs of care.

Once again, the extent of the price rise in the short run depends on the elasticity of demand, and once again, the *legal* incidence of the rule of strict liability is that firms pay the costs of care, but in the short run the *economic* incidence is again shared between producers and consumers of the good. In the short run the quantity produced by each firm falls, since they choose production to equate their new marginal cost with the higher price. But this reduction is not as large as it is under strict liability. Relative to the original equilibrium, this situation again involves negative profits.

In a long-run competitive equilibrium, firms will exit the industry and the market price will rise until profits are driven back to zero. Thus, in addition to producing at a point where price equals marginal cost, firms earn zero profits, so we also have $P = w_i x_i^* + \dfrac{C(q)}{q}$. Once again, since marginal cost also equals price, which in turn is equal to average cost, we must have marginal cost equal to average cost. This again occurs at the minimum of the average cost curve, which now only includes the cost of care, but does *not* include the expected harm created by each unit of the good. Thus, the market price does *not* adjust to equal *full* (social) average cost. The long-run competitive equilibrium is shown in Figure 4.3.2 below. The long-run market supply curve is again flat and is equal to the minimum of the average cost curve, where costs now include the cost of care but not the expected harm. Note that this minimum occurs at the same point as it did when the product was not dangerous: the quantity q that minimises $w_i x_i^* + \frac{C(q)}{q}$ is the same quantity that minimises $\frac{C(q)}{q}$. This happens because under a strict liability rule, the marginal and average cost curves shift upwards in a parallel fashion. Each firm pays the efficient cost of care, and this again acts like a specific tax, but the 'tax' is only equal to $w_i x_i^* < w_i x_i^* + H(x_i^*)$. Intuitively, the social cost of a firm entering this industry and producing an additional unit is $w_i x_i^* + H(x_i^*)$. But under a negligence rule, firms only have to pay $w_i x_i^*$ to avoid liability. The result in the long run is excessive market entry: even though each individual firm chooses the efficient level of care and the efficient quantity, an inefficiently high amount of the good is produced in the long-run equilibrium, because there are too many firms in the industry and the market price is too low. In a perfectly competitive market, a negligence rule does not produce efficient results.

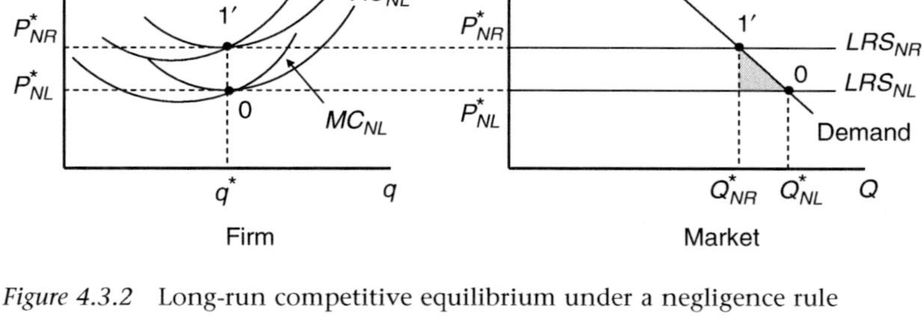

Figure 4.3.2 Long-run competitive equilibrium under a negligence rule

4.3.1.4 *The second-best due standard of care under a negligence rule*

The negligence rule explored in the previous section can be improved upon, however. There is a second-best due standard of care that is not equal to x_i^*, but which can increase welfare. Suppose that the due standard of care is increased to $\bar{x}_i > x_i^*$. Define $\hat{x}_i$ to be the point where $w_i\hat{x}_i = w_i x_i^* + H(x_i^*)$. This point is shown in Figure 4.3.3.

As long as the due standard is set at $\bar{x}_i < \hat{x}$, each firm will decide to meet the due standard $\bar{x}_i$ to avoid liability. Thus, each firm's marginal cost rises. This creates losses, and firms exit the industry. Let $n(\bar{x}_i)$ be the number of firms in a long-run competitive equilibrium when the due standard of care is $\bar{x}_i$. In the long-run competitive equilibrium, each firm continues to produce the same quantity q (for the same reasons as discussed above), and we have:

$$P\left[n(\bar{x}_i)q\right] = \frac{C(q)}{q} + w_i\bar{x}_i$$

Differentiating both sides with respect to $\bar{x}_i$ yields:

$$P'\left[n(\bar{x}_i)q\right]qn'(\bar{x}_i) = w_i$$

Both sides are positive, and $P'<0$, so we have $n'(\bar{x}_i) < 0$, and the number of firms in any long-run competitive equilibrium declines as $\bar{x}_i$ rises. Now total welfare is:

$$W(\bar{x}_i) = u[n(\bar{x}_i)q] - n(\bar{x}_i)C(q) - n(\bar{x}_i)q[w_i\bar{x}_i + H(\bar{x}_i)]$$

and the change in welfare as the due standard changes is:

$$\begin{aligned}
W'(\bar{x}_i) &= u'[n(\bar{x}_i)q]qn'(\bar{x}_i) - n'(\bar{x}_i)C(q) - n'(\bar{x}_i) \\
&\quad \times q[w_i\bar{x}_i + H(\bar{x}_i)] - n(\bar{x}_i)q[w_i + H'(\bar{x}_i)] \\
&= qn'(\bar{x}_i)\left\{u'[n(\bar{x}_i)q] - \frac{C(q)}{q} - [w_i\bar{x}_i + H(\bar{x}_i)]\right\} - n(\bar{x}_i)q[w_i + H'(\bar{x}_i)] \\
&= -qn'(\bar{x}_i)\{H(\bar{x}_i)\} - n(\bar{x}_i)q[w_i + H'(\bar{x}_i)]
\end{aligned}$$

$$= -n(\bar{x}_i)qw_i - q\{n'(\bar{x}_i)H(\bar{x}_i) + n(\bar{x}_i)'H(\bar{x}_i)\} \tag{4.11}$$

Let us examine expression (4.11) term by term. Consider the first term, $-n(\bar{x}_i)qw_i$. As the due standard of care is increased, there is a welfare cost to consumers because the market price of the good rises.

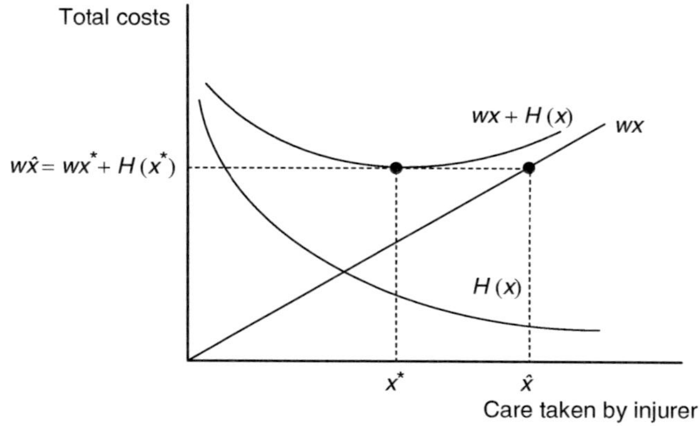

Figure 4.3.3 The second-best negligence rule

As the due standard of care is changed and firms take more care, the marginal change in the market price is simply equal the marginal cost of care, which is:

$$dP = w_i$$

Since the total market quantity is $Q = n\left(\bar{x}_i\right)q$, the change in consumer welfare is:

$$-QdP = -n(\bar{x}_i)qw_i$$

which is the first term in the expression (4.11).

Now consider the second term. It is the derivative of $qn(\bar{x}_i)H(\bar{x}_i)$ with respect to $\bar{x}_i$. But $qn(\bar{x}_i)H(\bar{x}_i)$ is simply the total external harm that production in this industry causes.

In other words, the change in welfare as the due standard of care rises is equal to the reduction in harm caused by production, less the change in consumer surplus from higher prices. The optimal second-best due standard will be above x_i^* as long as $W'(\bar{x}_i) > 0$ for some $\bar{x}_i$.

Notice also that if the due standard is set so that $\bar{x}_i > \hat{x}_i$, each firm will choose *not* to meet the high due standard of care, and will instead choose to be negligent and to minimise costs will choose the efficient level of care, $x_i = x_i^*$. If this happens, firms will be found to be negligent and will have to pay damages of $H(x_i^*)$. But they will also behave efficiently with respect to care. Moreover, this increases marginal and average costs to the level they would be if firms faced a rule of strict liability. In other words, as the due standard is increased, a negligence rule begins to 'look like' a strict liability rule. Therefore, welfare is maximised. Thus, it is possible for negligence rules to achieve full efficiency, as long as the due standard of care is set sufficiently high.

4.3.1.5 Other policies when there is a rule of no liability

When there is a no liability rule in place, there may be supplementary policy instruments which induce firms to increase their care above $x_i = 0$. This section examines one example of such a policy.

4.3.1.5.1 A lump-sum subsidy. Consider a policy which pays firms to take care. Suppose that the government grants a lump sum cash payment to the firm if it takes the efficient level of care, but not otherwise. Thus, the subsidy is equal to:

$$S = \begin{cases} \bar{S} & \text{if } x_i = x_i^* \\ 0 & \text{otherwise} \end{cases}$$

where $\bar{S} > w_i x_i^* q$ for any q. The firm's profit function is now:

$$\pi = \begin{cases} Pq - C(q) - w_i x_i^* q + \bar{S} & \text{if } x_i = x_i^* \\ Pq - C(q) - w_i x_i^* q & \text{otherwise} \end{cases}$$

Since $\bar{S} > w_i x_i^* q$, each firm maximises profits by choosing $x_i = x_i^*$. Each firm's marginal costs are:

$$C'(q) + w_i x_i^* > C'(q)$$

But its *average* costs are:

$$\frac{C(q)}{q} + w_i x_i^* - \frac{\bar{S}}{q} < \frac{C(q)}{q}$$

In other words, the subsidy increases marginal costs but reduces average costs.

The effect of this subsidy on market outcomes is shown in Figure 4.3.4, where the market is initially in a long-run competitive equilibrium with a no liability rule, denoted by point 0. Then the subsidy is introduced. This induces individual firms to choose the efficient level of care. The subsidy therefore increases marginal costs, and the short-run market supply curve also shifts upwards by the cost of care, $w_i x_i^*$.

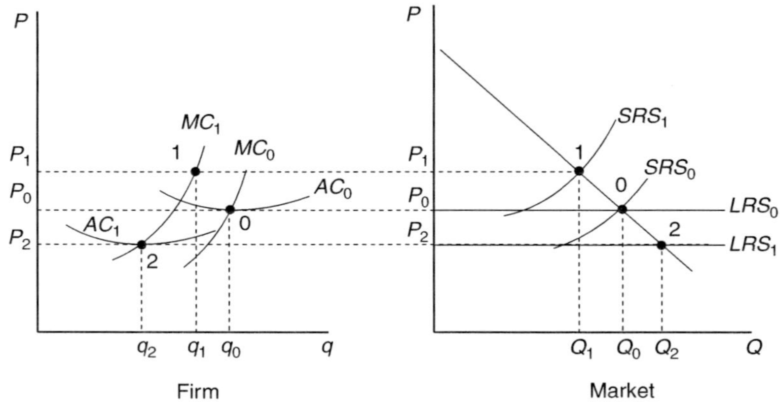

Figure 4.3.4 A lump-sum subsidy to provide the efficient level of care

The intersection of the new market supply curve and the demand curve gives us the new price in the short run. The new short-run equilibrium is at point 1. The economic incidence of the higher costs depends on the elasticity of demand and is shared between producers and consumers.

Since the subsidy paid to firms is designed to exceed the full cost of care, the average costs of each firm fall. Thus, at point 1, after the subsidy is introduced, firms earn positive profits. With free entry into the industry, the number of firms in the market increases. This pushes down the market price, shifting the market short-run supply curve downwards. This continues until the new long-run equilibrium (point 2) is reached, where firms again earn zero profits.

Even though each firm chooses the efficient level of care in the short- and long-run equilibrium, there are too many firms in the industry, the market price is too low, and the total quantity produced is too high. The subsidy is inefficient – and total output is even higher than it is at point 0, under a no liability rule.

Intuitively, the social cost of a firm entering this industry and producing an additional unit is $w_i x_i^* + H(x_i^*)$. But instead of facing firms with this social cost when they produce their first unit, the subsidy encourages entry. The result is excessive market entry: even though each individual firm chooses the efficient level of care and the efficient quantity, an inefficiently high amount of the good is produced in the long-run equilibrium, because there are too many firms in the industry and the market price is too low.

4.4 Legal rules in competitive markets: The case of two industries

The previous sections considered legal rules in market settings when firms in an industry created external harm, but this harm was assumed not to impact on another market or industry. We now relax this assumption. That is, suppose that there are two industries, *i* and *v*. Industry *i* (the 'injuring' industry) imposes a cost on industry *v* (the 'victim' industry). Both markets are perfectly competitive. To simplify the analysis, we make a series of assumptions:

- Consumers of *i* and *v* regard the goods as neither substitutes nor complements. The benefits of consumption of each good are identical, so that the industries have the same demand curves, $Q_i = Q_v \Rightarrow u'(Q_i) = u'(Q_v)$.
- Firms in each industry have identical constant marginal costs of $c_i = c_v = c$.
- As a result of the constant marginal cost assumption, we can treat firms in each industry as a single representative price taking firm. The representative firm in industry *i* produces Q_i units of output, and the firm in industry *v* produces Q_v units of output.
- The marginal costs of care in each industry *i* are constant and equal to w_i per unit of the good produced.
- The expected harm per unit of the good is constant (but obviously depends on the level of care taken per unit), and is equal to $H(x_i)$.

Under these conditions, total welfare is:

$$W = u(Q_i) + u(Q_v) - cQ_i - cQ_v - w_i x_i Q_i - Q_i Q_v H(x_i)$$

Notice that the harm here has the characteristics of a public bad – one unit of output produced in industry *i* affects *all* firms in industry *v*. The situation we have in mind is as follows. Suppose that firms in industry *i* use a production technique which emits pollution into a river system. Industry *v* uses water in the river system to produce beer. The greater the total output of industry *i*, the greater is the total amount of water pollution. Contaminated water harms the beer industry, and beer-producing firms cannot take actions (other than reducing their production levels) to reduce this harm. The per unit costs to the beer industry of water pollution are $H(x_i)$. The *total* harm of pollution rises with the quantity produced in *both* industries.

The efficiency conditions are:

$$u'(Q_i^*) = c + w_i x_i^* + Q_v^* H(x_i^*) \qquad (4.12)$$

$$u'(Q_v^*) = c + Q_i^* H(x_i^*) \qquad (4.13)$$

$$w_i = -Q_v^* H'(x_i^*) \qquad (4.14)$$

Equation (4.12) states that good *i* should be produced up to the point where the marginal consumption benefits equal the marginal costs of care, plus the marginal costs of harm (which depend on the output in industry *v*). Expression (4.13) is similar, and states that good *v* should be produced up to the point where the marginal consumption benefits equal the marginal costs of harm (which depend on output in industry *i*). Equation (4.14) says that care should be taken up until the point where the marginal cost is equal to the sum of the marginal benefits, $-Q_v^* H'(x_i^*)$. Equation (4.14) is therefore a Samuelson-type condition for public goods [see Samuelson (1954, 1955)].

4.4.1 Legal rules

Consider our various legal rules in this setting. First, consider a no liability rule. Firms in industry *i* have no incentive to take any care under this legal rule. Marginal costs are therefore equal to *c*, and equilibrium output satisfies:

$$u'(Q_i^{NL}) = c \qquad (4.15)$$

so that output exceeds the efficient level.

In industry *v*, marginal costs are equal to $c + Q_i^{NL} H(0)$, which exceed the efficient level. The competitive equilibrium quantity satisfies:

$$u'(Q_i^{NL}) = c + Q_i^{NL} H(0) \qquad (4.16)$$

and output is less than the efficient level. The no liability rule is not efficient.

Now suppose there is a rule of strict liability. The profit of the representative firm in industry *i* is:

$$\pi_i^{SL} = P_i Q_i - [c + w_i x_i + Q_v H(x_i)] Q_i$$

Since firms are faced with the full social costs of their actions, they choose the efficient level of care for the level of Q_v that is chosen, and also (conditional on Q_v) choose the efficient level of output. However, since under a strict liability rule firms in industry *v* are fully compensated for all harm, the profit of the representative firm in industry *v* is:

$$P_v Q_v - cQ_v$$

Setting price equal to marginal cost in industry *v* yields $P_v = u'\left(Q_v^{SL}\right) = c$. This results in a level of production of *v* that is too high. The reason is that entry and production in industry *v* is partially responsible for creating harm, but under strict liability firms in industry v face none of these costs. In turn, this results in underproduction of good *i*. For the same reasons, a rule of no liability has a similar outcome: competitive equilibrium in both markets involves over production of good *i* but underproduction of good *v*.

Finally, consider a negligence rule. Suppose the due standard is set at the efficient level, x_i^*. To avoid liability, each firm (for the same reasons discussed in section 4.3.1.3) will choose to take the efficient level of care. But then this will lower the marginal cost in industry *i* to $c + w_i x_i^*$, which is less than the level needed to ensure efficient production and consumption in that market. Hence, the competitive equilibrium will involve overproduction in market *i*, and will again result in underproduction in market *v*.

In section 4.3.1.3 we saw that second-best negligence rules existed, which involved setting due standards of care higher than x_i^*. Is that the case here? Suppose that the due standard of care is set at some level above the due standard, say at $\overline{x}_i > x_i^*$. Then as long as the due standard of care is not set too high, firms in market *i* will choose to take the level of care $\overline{x}_i$ to avoid liability. This will increase marginal costs, which reduces production in market *i*. In turn, this reduces the marginal harm in industry *v*. Both effects result in a welfare improvement over the negligence rule when the due standard of care is set at x_i^*.

4.4.2 Liability rules, Pigouvian taxes and combinations of the two approaches

From an efficiency point of view there are two problems associated with the legal rules analysed in the previous section. First, legal rules such as strict liability and negligence rule involve compensation payments flowing from injurers to victims. This compensation alters marginal costs and incentives in each market, and in competitive markets this affects entry and exit decisions (and therefore overall production) in each industry, leading to inefficient entry and exit. Secondly, the legal rules do not (and cannot) take into account the level of activity in each market, and so ignore information that is vital for efficiency of the long run competitive equilibrium in each industry.

In contrast, an efficient Pigouvian tax simply sets a care-dependent specific tax on firms in industry *i* equal to the marginal harm at the optimum. In other words, consider a tax which is set at at $t_i(x_i) = Q_v^* H(x_i)$. Firms in industry *i* can minimise their tax bill by choosing the efficient level of care. Thus, marginal costs in industry *i* under this tax would be $c + w_i x_i^* + Q_v^* H(x_i^*)$. This would induce efficient production in industry *i*, so $Q_i - Q_i^*$.

Firms in industry *v* would still be harmed, with harm equal to $Q_i^* H(x_i^*)$ per unit of the good. But there is no need to compensate firms for this harm. Indeed, as condition (4.13) shows, facing firms in industry *v* with this harm is exactly what is needed for efficient outcomes in that industry. A no liability rule (that is, a rule which does not compensate victims), combined with a tax of $t_i(x_i) = Q_v^* H(x_i)$ therefore produces efficient outcomes.

Notice that the optimal Pigouvian tax really involves both a tax *and* a legal rule. This suggests that other combinations of taxes and legal rules may be efficient. This turns out to be the case. Consider, for example, a strict liability rule combined with a tax on industry *v*. This would also produce efficient outcomes here. To see this, recall that under a rule of strict liability, firms in industry *i* choose the efficient level of care per unit of the good, which increases marginal cost in the industry and results in efficient production overall, conditional on Q_v. But under this rule, firms in industry *v* would be fully compensated for all harm, which reduces their marginal costs and results in an inefficiently high level of production in industry *v*, and a correspondingly low level of production in industry *i*.

Therefore, to control excessive production of Q_v in industry *v* under this legal rule, a tax equal to $Q_i^* H(x_i)$ would need to be set. This would raise marginal costs in industry *v* to $c + Q_i^* H(x_i)$, inducing efficient production decisions in that industry (since firms in industry *i* would choose the efficient level of care under a strict liability rule), as well as efficient production decisions in industry *i*.

Efficient control of accidental harm is often seen as an 'all or nothing' choice between Pigouvian taxes and legal rules. This is the wrong way to think about Pigouvian taxes. In fact, as this section has shown, a traditional Pigouvian tax really consists of two instruments: a tax on the injurer combined with a legal rule of no liability. But other combinations of taxes and legal rules may produce the same outcomes, and there may be no reason to prefer one over the other. The incentive and efficiency effects of the tax will depend on the characteristics of the legal rule it is being combined with.

Finally, we conclude this section with a word of caution regarding Pigouvian taxes. Note also that our criticism of legal rules – namely, that they ignore levels of production in each industry – can also be levelled at Pigouvian taxes. The taxes explored in this section – and Pigouvian taxes in general – have significant informational requirements. In the above examples, the government must know either Q_i^* or Q_v^*, as well as the shape of the $H(x_i)$ function, and must be able to observe the level of care taken by firms in industry i. In a world of imperfect information there is no reason to expect that the 'correct' Pigouvian tax will be chosen, and therefore no reason to expect that the Pigouvian approach will yield superior outcomes to (say) a negligence rule.

4.5 Extending the unilateral care model to other market situations: Liability rules in imperfectly competitive markets

This section reconsiders some of problems analysed in previous sections, but we now assume that markets are not perfectly competitive.

4.5.1 Monopoly

4.5.1.1 Strict liability

Consider a firm which is a monopolist in the market. Suppose that it produces Q units. The demand curve is still:

$$P(Q) = u'(Q)$$

Under a rule of strict liability, the firm's profits are:

$$\pi = P(Q)Q - C(Q) - [w_i x_i + H(x_i)]Q$$

The monopolist can minimise its costs by choosing the efficient level of care, so $x_i = x_i^*$.[1] Therefore, its profits are:

$$\pi = P(Q)Q - C(Q) - [w_i x_i^* + H(x_i^*)]Q$$

The first-order condition is:

$$P'(Q)Q + P(Q) = C'(Q) + x_i^* + H(x_i^*)$$

or:

$$P = \frac{\varepsilon}{1+\varepsilon}[C'(Q) + x_i^* + H(x_i^*)]$$

where ε is the elasticity of demand and $\varepsilon < -1$ for a profit-maximising monopolist.

One question of interest here is the degree of 'forward cost shifting', which refers to the degree to which consumer prices change in response to a change in the costs of care or changes in the liability rule. *Overshifting* is said to occur if the market price rises by more than the change in costs. Under perfect competition the forward shifting of the costs of care and external harm onto consumers in the short run depends on the elasticity of demand and supply curves. As shown earlier in this chapter, in the long run (assuming that the long-run supply curve is flat), the full amount of the increase in producer costs is usually passed on to consumers. Furthermore, under perfect competition unless the supply curve is downward sloping, the costs of care and harm under a strict liability rule can never be 'overshifted' in the sense that consumer prices rise by more than these costs.

The situation under monopoly is not as straightforward, because the monopolist can choose his price level. Consider the monopolist's first-order condition for profit maximisation in the presence of a strict liability rule. Let $Z = w_i x_i^* + H(x_i^*)$ be the per unit costs of care and harm at the optimal level of care. Then:

$$P(Z) = \frac{\varepsilon}{1+\varepsilon}[C'(Q) + Z] \qquad (4.17)$$

Suppose that Z increases by a small amount. Then

$$P'(Z)(1+\varepsilon) + P\frac{d\varepsilon}{dP}P'(Z) = \frac{d\varepsilon}{dP}P'(Z)[C'(Q)+Z] + \varepsilon\left[C''(Q)\frac{dQ}{dP}P'(Z)+1\right]$$

and so

$$P'(Z)\left\{(1+\varepsilon) + P\frac{d\varepsilon}{dP} - \frac{d\varepsilon}{dP}[C'(Q)+Z] + \varepsilon C''(Q)\frac{dQ}{dP}\right\} = \varepsilon$$

or:

$$P'(Z)\left\{1+\varepsilon + P\frac{d\varepsilon}{dP}\left(1-\frac{1+\varepsilon}{\varepsilon}\right) - \varepsilon C''(Q)\frac{dQ}{dP}\right\} = \varepsilon$$

Therefore, the change in the monopolist's price is:

$$P'(Z) = \frac{\varepsilon}{1+\varepsilon - \frac{P}{\varepsilon}\frac{d\varepsilon}{dP} - \varepsilon C''(Q)\frac{dQ}{dP}} = \frac{\varepsilon}{1+\varepsilon - E - Q'C''\varepsilon} \qquad (4.18)$$

where $E = \frac{d\varepsilon}{dP}\frac{P}{\varepsilon}$ is the *elasticity of the elasticity of demand with respect to price* – that is, E tells us how the elasticity of demand changes as we move along the demand curve. The formula tells us that there will be overshifting of the costs of care and expected harm under certain conditions. For example, if the elasticity of demand is constant and if marginal costs are constant (so that $C'' = 0$), then $E = 0$ and we have:

$$P'(Z) = \frac{\varepsilon}{1+\varepsilon} > 1$$

so that price rises by more than the increase in the sum of the costs of care and the costs of harm that are imposed on the firm under a rule of strict liability.

Intuitively, if the elasticity of demand does not increase much as we move up the demand curve, consumption is not becoming too sensitive to price changes as the price increases. Thus, the monopolist can afford to pass on more of the change in costs under a strict liability rule. Thus, even if marginal production costs are constant, it can easily happen that $P'(Z) > 1$. Note also that forward cost shifting is *less* likely if marginal costs are increasing, since then the denominator becomes more negative. Since the numerator is also negative, this means that the absolute value of the right hand side becomes smaller, and so forward cost-shifting is less likely.

4.5.1.2 *Negligence rule*

Under a negligence rule where the due standard is set at x^*, the monopolist's profits are:

$$\pi = \begin{cases} P(Q)Q - C(Q) - [w_i x_i + H(x_i)]Q & \text{if } x_i < x_i^* \\ P(Q)Q - C(Q) - w_i x_i Q & \text{if } x_i \geq x_i^* \end{cases}$$

The monopolist can again minimise its costs by choosing the efficient level of care, so $x_i = x_i^*$. Therefore, the firm's profits are:

$$\pi = P(Q)Q - C(Q) - w_i x_i^* Q$$

The first-order condition is:

$$P'(Q)Q + P(Q) = C'(Q) + w_i x_i^*$$

or:

$$P = \frac{\varepsilon}{1+\varepsilon}[C'(Q) + w_i x_i^*]$$

Under a negligence rule, the firm will produce more and will charge a lower price than under a rule of strict liability. Again, however, if the marginal cost of care w_i rises, there may be cost overshifting by a monopolist.

4.5.1.3 *A no liability rule*

Under a no liability rule, the firm's profits are:

$$\pi = P(Q)Q - C(Q) - w_i x_i Q$$

The monopolist can again minimise its costs by choosing to provide no care. Therefore, the firm's profits are:

$$\pi = P(Q)Q - C(Q)$$

The first-order condition is:

$$P'(Q)Q + P(Q) = C'(Q)$$

or:

$$P = \frac{\varepsilon}{1+\varepsilon} C'(Q)$$

Under a no liability rule, the firm will produce more and will charge a lower price than under a rule of strict liability or a negligence rule.

4.5.2 Cournot oligopoly

Now consider the Cournot model of oligopoly. Suppose that there are n identical firms, all of whom have the same marginal production costs of $c > 0$. The demand curve is still $P(Q) = u'(Q)$.

4.5.2.1 *Strict liability*

Consider firm i. Suppose that it produces q_i units of the good. Under a rule of strict liability, the firm's profits are:

$$\pi_i = P(Q)q_i - cq_i - [w_i x_i + H(x_i)]q_i$$

For any q_i and any choice of care and quantity by the other firms, firm i can minimise its costs by choosing the efficient level of care, so $x_i = x_i^*$. Therefore, its profits are:

$$\pi_i = P(Q)q_i - cq_i - [w_i x_i^* + H(x_i^*)]q_i$$

The first-order condition is:

$$P'(Q)q_i + P(Q) = c + w_i x_i^* + H(x_i^*)$$

Adding up across all n firms yields:

$$P'(Q)Q + nP(Q) = n[c + w_i x_i^* + H(x_i^*)]$$

or:

$$P = \frac{\varepsilon}{\frac{1}{n} + \varepsilon}[c + w_i x_i^* + H(x_i^*)]$$

where, again, ε is the elasticity of demand.

Let $Z = w_i x_i^* + H(x_i^*)$ be the per unit costs of care and harm at the optimal level of care. Then:

$$P(Z) = \frac{\varepsilon}{\frac{1}{n} + \varepsilon}[c + Z]$$

Suppose that Z increases by a small amount. The change in the oligopoly price is:

$$P'(Z) = \frac{\varepsilon}{\varepsilon + \frac{1 - E}{n}}$$

where once again, E is the elasticity of the elasticity of demand with respect to price. Again, there will be forward cost shifting under a rule of strict liability if the elasticity of demand is not too sensitive to price – but here the extent of cost shifting is also constrained by the number of firms in the market. The above equation shows that as n increases, $P'(Z)$ gets smaller, and as $n \to \infty$ we approach the competitive outcome in which $P'(Z) = 1$.

4.5.2.2 *Negligence rule*

Under a negligence rule where the due standard is set at x_i^*, each firm's profits are:

$$\pi_i = \begin{cases} P(Q)q_i - cq_i - [w_i x_i + H(x_i)]q_i & \text{if } x_i < x_i^* \\ P(Q)q_i - cq_i - w_i x_i q_i & \text{if } x_i \geq x_i^* \end{cases}$$

The firm can again minimise its costs by choosing the efficient level of care, so $x_i = x_i^*$. Therefore, the firm's profits are:

$$\pi = P(Q)q_i - cq_i - w_i x_i^* q_i$$

The first-order condition is:

$$P'(Q)q_i + P(Q) = c + w_i x_i^*$$

Adding up across all n firms yields:

$$P'(Q)Q + nP(Q) = n[c + w_i x_i^*]$$

Or:

$$P = \frac{\varepsilon}{\frac{1}{n} + \varepsilon}[c + w_i x_i^*]$$

Under a negligence rule, each firm will produce more and the market price will be lower than under a rule of strict liability. Again, if the marginal cost of care w_i rises, there can be cost overshifting.

4.5.2.3 A no liability rule

Under a no liability rule, the firm's profits are:

$$\pi_i = P(Q)q_i - cq_i - w_i x_i q_i$$

The monopolist can again minimise its costs by choosing to provide no care. Therefore, the firm's profits are:

$$\pi_i = P(Q)q_i - cq_i$$

And we get the usual Cournot outcome. Under a no liability rule, the industry will produce more and will charge a lower price than under a rule of strict liability or a negligence rule.

4.5.2.4 Discussion and comparison with perfect competition

The usual result in economic theory is that a monopolist or oligopoly that chooses a single price always produces an inefficiently low quantity. This is also true here if we fix the legal rule, and compare outcomes under various market structures: a monopolist facing the same legal rule will always still produce a lower amount than a Cournot industry, which in turn will produce a lower amount than a perfectly competitive industry.

There are two important points to note here, however. First, because firms restrict output under monopoly or imperfect competition, *this may be welfare improving relative to the outcome under perfect competition when output may lead to accidental harm*. The reason is straightforward: in the previous section we saw that under perfect competition under a negligence rule, even though individual firms chose the efficient level of care, market output is inefficiently high. But under our assumptions a monopolist or oligopolist under a negligence rule also chooses the efficient level of care – but both restrict output. Therefore, with a negligence rule, welfare may be higher under monopoly than under perfect competition – even though in both cases firms choose the efficient level of care.

This is illustrated for the case of monopoly in Figure 4.5.1 below, which assumes constant marginal costs of $c > 0$ (so that marginal costs are also equal to average costs). Consider a negligence rule with the due standard of care set at x_i*. Under perfect competition, firms minimise costs by choosing the efficient level of care, and so the market price is equal to $c + wx_i^*$. The competitive quantity is Q, but the efficient quantity is $Q_{NR} < Q$, where price equals $c + w_i x_i^* + H(x_i^*)$, which is marginal production costs plus the costs of care per unit, plus the harm per unit.

If the efficient level of care is chosen, the change in welfare as Q changes is:

$$W'(Q) = u'(Q) - c - [w_i x_i^* + H(x_i^*)]$$

For a small change in Q, this is the shaded area in Figure 4.5.1. The change in the area is zero at the efficient quantity.

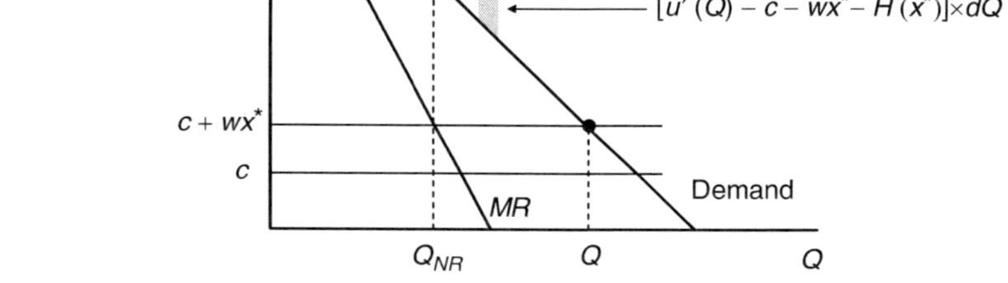

Figure 4.5.1 A monopolist facing a negligence rule

Now consider a monopolist facing the same negligence rule. The monopolist chooses a level of output that is less than the level under perfect competition, but chooses the same level of care. This means that welfare may be higher under monopoly. Figure 4.5.1 shows the special case where the monopolist's pursuit of profit induces him to choose exactly the efficient quantity. This happens if the monopolist's profit-maximising price under the negligence rule happens by accident to be equal to $c + w_i x_i^* + H(x_i^*)$, which is marginal production costs plus the costs of care per unit, plus the harm per unit of output:

$$\frac{\varepsilon}{1+\varepsilon}[c + w_i x_i^*] = c + w_i x_i^* + H(x_i^*)$$

This holds if demand for the good is sufficiently elastic at the monopolist's profit-maximising point:

$$\varepsilon = -1 - \frac{c + w_i x_i^*}{H(x_i^*)}$$

This can also happen with a no liability rule. The monopolist chooses a level of output that is less than the level under perfect competition. Again, this means that welfare must be higher under monopoly. Figure 4.5.2 shows the special case where the monopolist's pursuit of profit again induces him to 'accidentally' choose exactly the efficient quantity. This happens if the monopolist's price happens to be equal to $c + w_i x_i^* + H(x_i^*)$, which happens if:

$$\frac{\varepsilon}{1+\varepsilon}c = c + w_i x_i^* + H(x_i^*)$$

This holds if demand for the good is sufficiently elastic at the monopolist's profit-maximising point:

$$\varepsilon = -1 - \frac{c}{w_i x_i^* + H(x_i^*)}$$

However, although in this case the efficient quantity is chosen, the efficient level of care is not. The efficiency loss in this case is equal to the (efficient) quantity multiplied by the social cost per unit of the good that is in excess of the optimal social cost:

$$DWL = \{H(0) - [w_i x_i^* + H(x_i^*)]\}Q$$

The second point to note is that the standard result of a monopolist *always* producing less than the outcome under perfect competition no longer holds if the monopolist faces a different legal rule to that

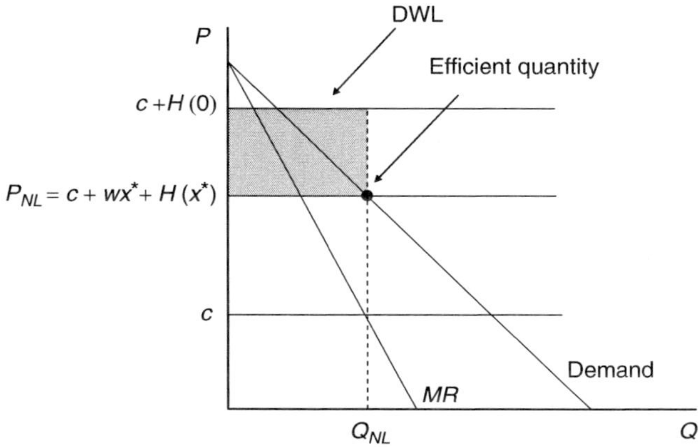

Figure 4.5.2 A monopolist under a no liability rule, producing the efficient quantity

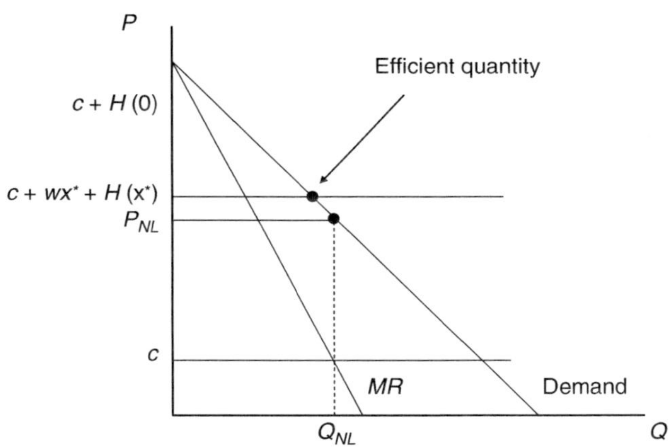

Figure 4.5.3 A monopolist under a no liability rule producing an inefficiently high quantity

which might prevail under perfect competition. For example, consider a monopolist facing a rule of no liability, and compare this against the efficient outcome. Suppose that the costs of care and harm are very high, relative to production costs. Efficiency requires that the firm internalise these costs and produce a relatively low quantity. However, under a no liability rule, the firm avoids paying these costs, and lower costs boost production – even for a monopolist. As Figure 4.5.3 shows, it can easily happen that under a no liability rule (or a negligence rule) a monopolist could produce *more* than the efficient quantity.

4.6 Liability rules versus taxes and quantity regulation

The standard Pigouvian approach to reducing the adverse welfare effects of uncompensated negative external effects is to set a tax equal to the social marginal harm, where the marginal harm is evaluated at the optimal level of production. In some circumstances, this approach may be preferable to a set of liability rules. There are other situations, however, in which liability rules are preferable to taxes. In this section we explore one such situation: where the regulator is uncertain about marginal benefits and marginal costs.

To illustrate the main principles involved, we consider an example based on the classic paper of White and Wittman (1983). Consider an economy with a single firm that produces output of Q. Suppose that regulator knows that the marginal social cost curve is:

$$C(Q) = C_0 + C_1 Q$$

where $C_0 > 1$ and $C_1 > 0$. However, the regulator does not know the exact shape of the firm's marginal benefit curve. Suppose that the actual marginal benefit curve is:

$$B(Q) = B_0 + B_1 Q + v$$

where $B_0 > 0$and $B_1 < 0$. The firm's private marginal costs are zero. The regulator knows the values of B_0 and B_1 but cannot observe v. Suppose that regulator believes that v will take on the following values:

$$v = \begin{cases} -2 & \text{with probability } 1/2 \\ 2 & \text{with probability } 1/2 \end{cases}$$

Let $\overline{Q}$ be the point where expected marginal social benefits equal marginal social costs. Since the expected value of v is zero, this means that at $\overline{Q}$, we must have:

$$C_0 + C_1 \overline{Q} = B_0 + B_1 \overline{Q}$$

So:

$$\overline{Q} = \frac{B_0 - C_0}{C_1 - B_1}$$

Consider the following policy options that are available to the regulator:

- **Quantity Regulation:** Force the firm to always produce at $Q = \overline{Q}$.
- **Tax Regulation:** Impose a Pigouvian per unit tax of t on the production of Q, where t is equal to expected marginal social costs evaluated at the point $Q = \overline{Q}$.
- **Strict Liability:** Make the firm strictly liable for the 'reasonable' social costs that it creates, where 'reasonable' social costs are interpreted as expected social costs.

Let us examine each of these regulatory mechanisms. Before doing so, however, we establish an important result. Consider Figure 4.6.1 below, which plots marginal social benefits and costs that flow from the production of Q. The efficient level of production is where these marginal benefits and costs are equal, at the point Q^*. Other points of production – whether greater or less than Q^* – result in welfare losses. As a general rule, the size of these welfare losses can be computed by calculating the area of the shaded triangle, which is the accumulated difference between marginal benefits and costs for all units that are either produced in excess of Q^*, or which are less than Q^*. To calculate the deadweight loss from not producing Q^*, we therefore simply compute the base of the triangle, which is the difference between Q^* and the level of actual

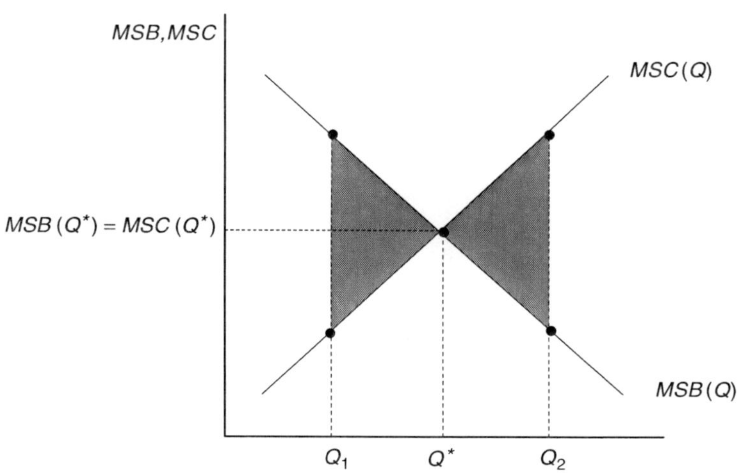

Figure 4.6.1 Efficient production and the computation of deadweight welfare loss

production, and the height of the triangle, which is the difference between marginal benefits and costs at the actual level of production. So, for example, if production was at Q_1 instead of Q^* in Figure 4.6.1, the deadweight loss associated with this level of production would be:

$$DWL_{Q_1} = \frac{1}{2}|Q^* - Q_1||MSC(Q_1) - MSB(Q_1)| \tag{4.19}$$

Similarly, if production was at Q_2 instead of Q^*, the deadweight loss would be:

$$DWL_{Q_2} = \frac{1}{2}|Q^* - Q_2||MSC(Q_2) - MSB(Q_2)|$$

This method of computing deadweight losses will be utilised extensively in the analysis that follows.

4.6.1 Quantity regulation

Under quantity regulation, the firm is forced to produce at $Q = \overline{Q}$. But efficiency requires that for any value of v, the firm produce at Q^*, where this is defined by the condition that *actual* marginal costs equal *actual* marginal benefits:

$$C_0 + C_1Q^* = B_0 + B_1Q^* + v$$

or:

$$Q^* = \frac{B_0 - C_0 + v}{C_1 - B_1}$$

Since $Q^* \neq \overline{Q}$, there will be a deadweight loss from this policy; this is illustrated in Figure 4.6.2.

Applying the method in equation (4.19), we can see that for any value of v this loss is equal to:

$$DWL_{QR} = \frac{1}{2}|Q^* - \overline{Q}||v| = \frac{1}{2}\left|\frac{B_0 - C_0 + v}{C_1 - B_1} - \frac{B_0 - C_0}{C_1 - B_1}\right||v| = \frac{1}{2}\frac{v^2}{C_1 - B_1}$$

The expected value of this is:

$$\mathrm{E}(DWL_{QR}) = \frac{1}{2}\frac{\sigma_v^2}{C_1 - B_1}$$

(which follows from the assumption that v has a zero mean). Now $\sigma_v^2 = \frac{1}{2} \times 4 + \frac{1}{2} \times 4 = 4$ and so:

$$\mathrm{E}(DWL_{QR}) = \frac{2}{C_1 - B_1} \tag{4.20}$$

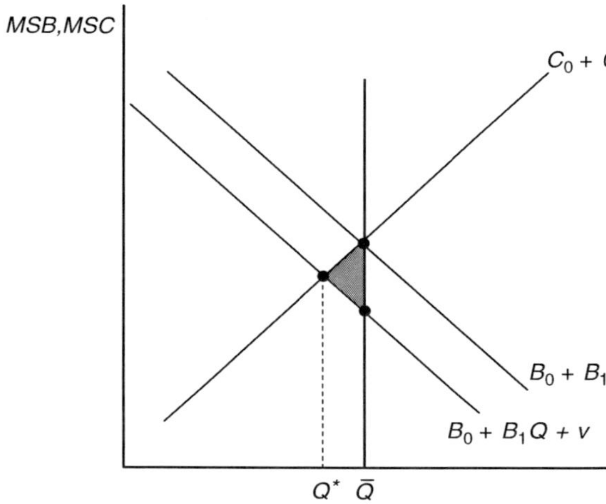

Figure 4.6.2 The deadweight loss of quantity regulation under incomplete information: Social marginal benefits turn out to be less than expected

4.6.2 A Pigouvian tax

Under a Pigouvian tax, the firm faces a tax equal to the expected marginal benefit and marginal cost at $Q = \overline{Q}$. This means that the tax is equal to

$$t = B_0 + B_1\overline{Q} = B_0 + B_1\frac{B_0 - C_0}{C_1 - B_1}$$

For any value of v, the firm will produce at Q' the point where *actual* marginal benefits equal the tax. This means that:

$$B_0 + B_1Q' + v = B_0 + B_1\frac{B_0 - C_0}{C_1 - B_1}$$

So:

$$Q' = \frac{B_0 - C_0}{C_1 - B_1} - \frac{v}{B_1}$$

But efficiency again requires that for any value of v, the firm produce at Q^*, where $Q^* = \dfrac{B_0 - C_0 + v}{C_1 - B_1}$. Thus the difference between actual production and efficient production is:

$$Q^* - Q' = \frac{B_0 - C_0 + v}{C_1 - B_1} - \left(\frac{B_0 - C_0}{C_1 - B_1} - \frac{v}{B_1}\right) = \frac{v}{C_1 - B_1} + \frac{v}{B_1} = \frac{C_1 v}{B_1(C_1 - B_1)}$$

On the other hand, the height of the deadweight loss triangle in this case is:

$$B_0 + B_1Q' + v - (C_0 - C_1Q') = B_0 - C_0 + (B_1 - C_1)\left(\frac{B_0 - C_0}{C_1 - B_1} - \frac{v}{B_1}\right) = \frac{C_1 v}{B_1}$$

and so for any value of v the deadweight loss is:

$$DWL_{Tax} = \frac{1}{2}\,|\,Q^* - Q'\,|\left|\frac{C_1 v}{B_1}\right| = \frac{1}{2}\left|\frac{C_1 v}{B_1(C_1 - B_1)}\right|\left|\frac{C_1 v}{B_1}\right| = \frac{1}{2}\left(\frac{C_1}{B_1}\right)^2 \frac{v^2}{C_1 - B_1}$$

The expected value of this is:

$$\mathbf{E}(DWL_{Tax}) = \frac{1}{2}\left(\frac{C_1}{B_1}\right)^2 \frac{\sigma_v^2}{C_1 - B_1} = \left(\frac{C_1}{B_1}\right)^2 \frac{2}{C_1 - B_1} \tag{4.21}$$

4.6.3 Pigouvian taxation versus quantity regulation: Which is better?

In the previous analysis we derived formulas for the expected deadweight loss under quantity regulation and Pigouvian taxation. The natural question is: under uncertainty, which instrument is better? The answer can be found by simply inspecting equations (4.20) and (4.21). The tax will be better if:

$$\begin{aligned}\mathbf{E}(DWL_{Tax}) &= \frac{1}{2}\left(\frac{C_1}{B_1}\right)^2 \frac{\sigma_v^2}{C_1 - B_1} = \left(\frac{C_1}{B_1}\right)^2 \frac{2}{C_1 - B_1} < \frac{2}{C_1 - B_1} = \frac{1}{2}\frac{\sigma_v^2}{C_1 - B_1}\\ &= \mathbf{E}(DWL_{QR})\end{aligned}$$

which is true if and only if:

$$\left(\frac{C_1}{B_1}\right)^2 < 1$$

or:

$$|C_1| < |B_1| \tag{4.22}$$

This has a simple interpretation: Pigouvian taxes have a lower expected deadweight loss if the *slope* of the marginal social cost curve is less than the slope of the marginal social benefit curve (that is, if the marginal cost curve is relatively flat, compared with the marginal benefit curve).

This result applies more generally. The economic intuition is straightforward and is illustrated in Figure 4.6.4 and Figure 4.6.5 below.

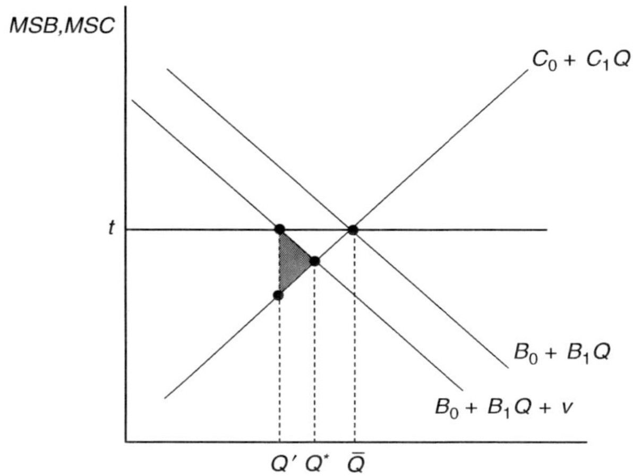

Figure 4.6.3 The deadweight loss of a Pigouvian tax under incomplete information: Social marginal benefits turn out to be less than expected

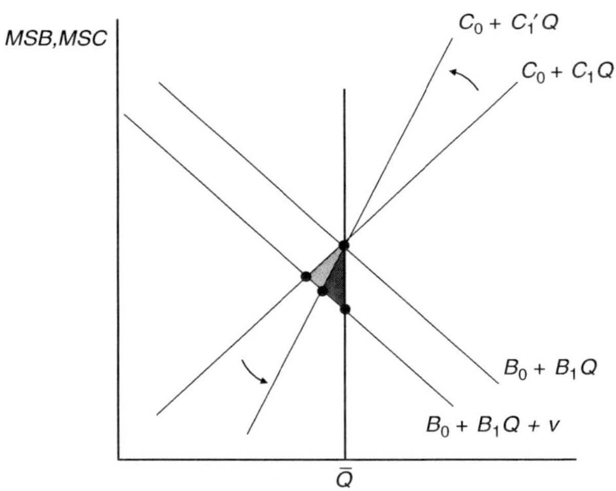

Figure 4.6.4 The expected deadweight loss of quantity regulation falls if the marginal cost curve becomes steeper

Figure 4.6.4 is identical to Figure 4.6.2, except we have now made the marginal social cost curve steeper. As the slope increases, the efficient level of production approaches $\bar{Q}$, and the welfare loss falls. In the

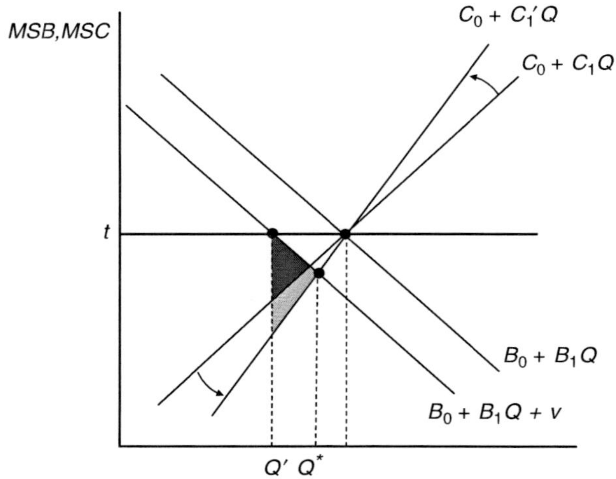

Figure 4.6.5 The expected deadweight loss of Pigouvian taxation rises if the marginal cost curve becomes steeper

limit, if the marginal cost curve is vertical, then quantity regulation perfectly mimics the actual marginal social costs of production, and there is no welfare loss.

On the other hand, consider Pigouvian taxation in Figure 4.6.5, which is identical to Figure 4.6.3 above except we have again made the marginal social cost curve steeper. As the slope increases, the efficient level of production moves towards $\overline{Q}$ and away from Q', the level of production under the tax. The welfare loss rises. In the limit, if the marginal cost curve is vertical, then the welfare loss from Pigouvian taxation increases without bound.

4.6.4 A strict liability rule

Under strict liability, the firm faces a tax equal to the expected marginal costs of its actions. This means that for any x the firm's marginal costs are:

$$C_0 + C_1Q$$

For any value of v, the firm will produce at $\hat{Q}$, which is the point where actual marginal benefits equal its marginal costs under the liability rule. Thus for any v, $\hat{Q}$ is defined by

$$B_0 + B_1\hat{Q} + v = C_0 + C_1\hat{Q}.$$

So for any realisation of v, we have:

$$\hat{Q} = \frac{B_0 - C_0 + v}{C_1 - B_1} = Q^*$$

That is, strict liability is efficient here, and there is no deadweight loss. The reason is that there is no uncertainty over marginal costs, so the strict liability rule (which forces the firm to pay expected costs) also forces the firm to pay **actual** costs. This induces the firm to completely internalise the external costs of its actions, and it behaves efficiently.

This result – that a strict liability rule has a lower expected deadweight loss than both quantity and tax regulation – is more general than this example would suggest. Indeed, White and Wittman (1983) show that even if the regulator is uncertain about the position of both the marginal social cost and marginal social benefit curves, a strict liability rule always dominates the other two instruments, irrespective of the slope of these curves and irrespective of the extent of the regulator's ignorance about the position of the marginal benefit and cost curves (that is, irrespective of σ_v^2). The intuition behind this result is straightforward: the strict liability rule acts like a non-linear tax and is more flexible than the other two regulatory mechanisms. When marginal benefits turn out to be high, the strict liability still contains sufficient incentives for the firm to increase

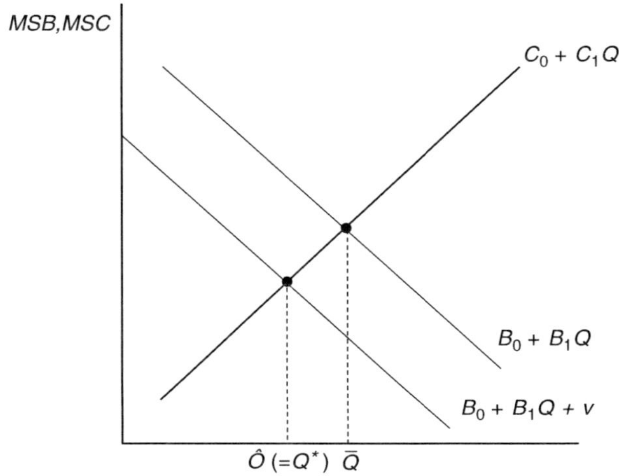

Figure 4.6.6 The deadweight loss of a strict liability rule under incomplete information: Social marginal benefits turn out to be Less than expected

production, which is desirable from an efficiency point of view. Under quantity regulation, increasing production is not allowed, even if it is efficient. On the other hand, under a tax the firm would increase production when marginal benefits are high, but would do so by too much.

If marginal costs turn out to be high, then under strict liability the firm will not reduce its production. But neither will it do so under quantity regulation. And under a tax, the firm reduces production by too much. So again, if the regulator is uncertain about marginal costs, implementing a strict liability rule turns out to be better, on average, than the other two instruments.

4.6.5 Application: The economics of emissions taxes and emissions trading ('cap and trade') schemes

One of the most important points to emerge from the foregoing analysis is that when there is policy uncertainty or ignorance regarding the position of marginal costs and benefit schedules, no policy will be perfect – all instruments will create welfare losses, unless they just happen by chance to be right. So the policy question is therefore: which policy creates the lowest welfare loss on average? Or: which policy creates the lowest expected deadweight loss?

The analysis in section 4.6.3 can be easily applied to the question of the relative desirability of emissions taxes and emissions trading schemes. The key is to realise that instead of thinking about production of a pollutant, we can also think in terms of pollution abatement (that is, the *absence* of pollution). The marginal social *costs* of pollution in Figure 4.6.1 are equal to the marginal social *benefits* of abatement – if producing something results in social costs, then reducing production of it results in marginal social benefits. Similarly, the marginal social *benefits* of pollution in Figure 4.6.1 are equal to the marginal social *costs* of abatement – after all, once again, if producing something results in social benefits, then reducing production of it must result in marginal social costs.

Once we realise this, then applying our previous results to the issue of emissions taxes versus trading schemes becomes trivially straightforward: the results just get switched around. An emissions trading scheme is equivalent to controlling the aggregate quantity of abatement – and therefore the aggregate level of pollution that is produced – at an economy-wide level, rather than at the individual firm level. And an emissions tax is equivalent to a tax on all firms. Hence, applying the results in section 4.6.3, we obtain the following:

- If the marginal social cost curve for production of a pollutant is relatively steep compared to the marginal social benefit curve, then an emissions trading scheme (aggregate quantity regulation) has a lower expected deadweight loss than Pigouvian taxation.

- Hence, if the marginal *benefit* curve for *abatement* is relatively steep compared to the marginal social cost curve for abatement, then an emissions trading scheme (aggregate quantity regulation) has a lower expected deadweight loss than Pigouvian taxation.
- If the marginal social cost curve for production of a pollutant is relatively flat compared with the marginal social benefit curve, then Pigouvian taxation has a lower expected deadweight loss than an emissions trading scheme (aggregate quantity regulation).
- Hence, if the marginal *benefit* curve for abatement is relatively flat compared to the marginal social cost curve for abatement, then Pigouvian taxation has a lower expected deadweight loss than an emissions trading scheme.

Hence, if the marginal cost of abatement curve is very steep and the marginal benefit of abatement curve is relatively flat, then an emissions tax is preferred on the grounds that it has a lower expected deadweight loss.[2]

4.7 Notes

There is a large literature on the economics of accident law. Shavell (1987) and Landes and Posner (1987) are thorough book-length treatments. The analysis of the second-best negligence rule in this chapter is inspired by Polinksy (1980), who studies a slightly different situation in which the harm that is caused by injurers occurs as a lump sum, rather than as a per unit social cost. Shavell (1982) studies the interaction between liability rules and insurance markets. White and Wittman (1983) and Weitzman (1974) are the classic papers on the comparisons of tax and quantity instruments under uncertainty.

4.8 Exercises

1. In this chapter we assumed that all injurers and victims are identical. In reality, this will not be the case. To see how heterogeneity among potential injurers might alter the efficiency properties of simple negligence rules, consider a simple modification of the unilateral care model. Everything else is the same, but now assume that the injurers differ in their marginal costs of care, w.

   For simplicity, suppose that there are only three types of injurers, labelled 1, 2 and 3, and suppose that there is an equal proportion of each type in the population. Assume that type 1 injurers have a marginal cost of w_1, type 2 injurers have a marginal cost of w_2, and that type 3 injurers have a marginal cost of w_3, with:

$$0 < w_1 < w_2 < w_3$$

(a) Let w_2 be the cost of care for a 'reasonable person', and let x_2^* be the efficient level of care taken by a reasonable person. How does the efficient level of care taken by types 1 and 3 compare with x_2^*?

(b) Suppose that the courts cannot observe w directly, and so decide on a 'reasonable person' negligence rule, which operates as follows:

If actual care taken $\geq x_2^*$, then the injurer *is* not liable

If actual care taken $< x_2^*$ then the injurer *is* liable

Will this reasonable person negligence rule induce either types 1, 2 or 3 to take an efficient level of care? (Remember, in general it will be efficient for different types to take different levels of care).

(c) Will a rule of strict liability induce either types 1, 2 or 3 to take an efficient level of care?

(d) In this context, discuss the relative benefits of strict liability versus negligence.

2. In some instances involving accidental harm, the injurer may be uncertain as to the due standard of care that actually applies. This question illustrates some of the issues that can arise when due standards in negligence rules are uncertain. Consider the following table, which describes the probability of an accident and total costs under various situations in the unilateral care model. Assume that an accident leads to a loss of $100.

Level of Care	Marginal Cost of Care	Total Cost of Care	Accident Probability	Expected Loss	Total Social Costs
1	1		0.14		
2	1		0.11		
3	4		0.09		
4	6		0.08		
5	7		0.07		

Consider the unilateral care model, and suppose that there are three possible due standards that the injurer believes he might face: $z_a = 2$, $z_b = 3$ and $z_c = 4$. Let:

$$\pi_a = \Pr(\text{Actual due standard equals } z_a)$$
$$\pi_b = \Pr(\text{Actual due standard equals } z_b)$$
$$\pi_c = \Pr(\text{Actual due standard equals } z_c)$$

be the injurer's perceived probability beliefs of facing each possible due standard, with $\pi_a + \pi_b + \pi_c = 1$. Let x be the level of care chosen by the injurer. Assume that the injurer is risk neutral.

(a) If $x < z_a$, what is the probability that the injurer believes he will be found to be negligent?

(b) If $x = z_a$, what is the probability that the injurer believes he will be found to be negligent?
(c) If $x = z_b$, what is the probability that the injurer believes he will be found to be negligent?
(d) If $x = z_c$, what is the probability that the injurer believes he will be found to be negligent?
(e) If $x = z_c$, what is the probability that the injurer believes he will be found to be negligent?
(f) Given your answers in parts (a)–(e), what is the injurer's expected cost function? Fill in the empty cells in the table.
(g) Would the injurer ever choose the socially optimal level of care? Would the injurer ever choose an inefficiently low level of care? Would the injurer ever choose an inefficiently high level of care?

3. Consider a regulator who is considering regulating an industry in which the production of a good, x, creates a negative externality. A firm produces x, but the regulator does not know the exact shape of the firm's marginal benefit curve or the marginal social cost curve. Suppose that the firm's actual marginal benefit curve is:

$$MPB(x) = B_0 - x + u$$

where u is a random variable which takes on the values 1 and –1 with equal probability. The actual marginal social cost curve is:

$$MSC(x) = C_0 + x + v$$

where v is a random variable which takes on the values 1 and –1 with equal probability. Assume that u and v are statistically independent. The regulator knows the values B_0 and C_0, but cannot observe the realisations of u or v.

Let $\bar{x}$ be the point where *expected* marginal private benefits equal expected marginal social costs, and consider the following three policy options that are available to the regulator:

- **Quantity Regulation:** Force the firm to always produce at $x = \bar{x}$.
- **Tax Regulation:** Set a tax on each unit of the good that firm 1 produces, with the tax set equal to the expected social marginal cost (and expected private marginal benefit) at the point $x = \bar{x}$.
- **Strict Liability:** Make firm 1 strictly liable for any 'reasonable' damages that it causes. That is, force the firm to pay the *expected* social costs of its actions.

For each form of regulation, illustrate the expected deadweight loss diagrammatically, and compute it analytically. In each case, explain how the expected deadweight losses depend on B_0 and C_0, if at all. Rank the policy options according to the expected deadweight loss that they create, and explain why your ranking makes economic sense. For the regulator to choose the efficient policy, does it need to know B_0 and C_0?

5

Accident Law and Markets, Part II: The Bilateral Care Model

5.1 Introduction

Up to this point we have analysed tort laws under the assumption that the victim cannot take any care. Let us now drop this assumption. That is, suppose now that the victim can also take action (in the form of care or precaution) that reduces expected harm. This situation is referred to as *the bilateral care model*. The approach outlined in this chapter not only allows us to study a much wider set of situations; the possibility that a second party can affect the probability and extent of harm introduces new complications and also means that legal rules will potentially become more complex.

The chapter is structured as follows. Section 5.2 outlines the basic bilateral care model. Section 5.3 analyses the legal rules that were introduced in Chapter 4 in the bilateral care model setting using basic game-theoretic tools, and discusses several applications and extensions. Section 5.4 examines the bilateral care model in a setting of perfectly competitive markets. Section 5.5 introduces some new legal rules that can be analysed within the bilateral care model, and provides an example of where such rules prove to be the class of rules that induce parties to behave efficiently.

5.2 The basic bilateral approach

Let $x_v \geq 0$ be the level of care taken by the victim, and let $x_i \geq 0$ be the level of care taken by the injurer. Then we assume the following probability of damage function:

$$\rho(x_i, x_v) \quad \text{where } 0 \leq \rho(x_i, x_v) \leq 1 \text{ for all } x_i, x_v \geq 0$$

Because the victim can now take care, the analysis becomes a little bit more complicated than the analysis of the unilateral care model. The marginal benefit of each party's action now depends on the action chosen by the other party. Thus, when choosing his action, each party must form a view about what the other party will do, because each player can act *strategically* under different institutional arrangements in response to what they believe the other player's best response is.

Let us assume that the injurer can take a level of care $x_i \geq 0$, at a constant marginal cost of $w_i > 0$, and the victim can take a level of care $x_v \geq 0$ at a marginal cost of $w_v > 0$. The probability of an accident occurring, given that care levels are x_i and x_v, is $\rho(x_i, x_v) \in [0,1]$. Generalising this model to allow for the possibility that the level of harm could also depend on the level of care taken by each party, we have $H(x_i, x_v) = \rho(x_i, x_v)\ h(x_i, x_v)$, where we assume:

- $\frac{\partial H}{\partial x_i} < 0$. If the injurer takes more care, the expected harm falls.
- $\frac{\partial^2 H}{\partial x_i^2} > 0$. There are diminishing marginal returns to providing more care by the injurer: more care reduces both the probability and harm from an accident, but the *rate* of reduction falls as more care is provided.
- $\frac{\partial H}{\partial x_v} < 0$. If the victim takes more care, expected harm falls.
- $\frac{\partial^2 H}{\partial x_v^2} > 0$. There are diminishing marginal returns to providing more care by the victim: more care reduces the probability and harm from an accident, but the *rate* of reduction falls as more care is provided.
- $\frac{\partial^2 H}{\partial x_i \partial x_v} > 0$. For any level of care that is provided by the victim, as more care is provided by the injurer, the *marginal* effectiveness of the victim's care falls. And, conversely, for any level of care that is provided by the victim, as more care is provided by the injurer, the *marginal* effectiveness of the victim's care falls. Another way of saying this is – the levels of care taken by each of the players are *substitutes*: when the victim increases his amount of care, this reduces the marginal effectiveness of the injurer's care. To restore the marginal effectiveness to its original level, the injurer reduces his amount care. Conversely, if the injurer *increases* his level of care, the victim will *reduce* his level of care.

This final behavioural assumption need not always be true in reality – it will depend on the nature of the activity in question and the nature of the accident that is being analysed.

5.2.1.1 *Efficient levels of care*

Let us first characterise the efficient levels of care by both parties in this model. Recall that the efficient levels of care minimises the aggregate expected costs of care. The aggregate expected costs here are:

$$w_i x_i + w_v x_v + H(x_i, x_v)$$

There will now be *two* first-order conditions instead of one. At the efficient care levels $(x_i^* > 0, x_v^* > 0)$, these conditions are:

$$w_i = -\frac{\partial H(x_i^*, x_v^*)}{\partial x_i}$$

$$w_v = -\frac{\partial H(x_i^*, x_v^*)}{\partial x_v}$$

Again, these conditions are of the familiar form:

1. Social marginal cost of care by injurer = Expected social marginal reduction in damages due to care by injurer
2. Social marginal cost of care by victim = Expected social marginal reduction in damages due to care by victim

5.3 Legal rules in the bilateral care model

5.3.1 No liability

Consider a rule of no liability: the injurer is never obligated to pay damages to the victim. How much care will each party take? Let us consider the injurer's choice of care. As before, the goal of the injurer is to minimise his expected cost of care. With no liability, the injurer's problem is to solve:

$$\min_{x_i \geq 0} w_i x_i$$

Just as we had in the unilateral care model, the solution to this problem is:

$$x_i^{NL} = 0$$

That is, under a rule of no liability, the injurer takes no care at all. Given this choice, what is the victim's best choice of care? The goal of the victim is to minimise his expected cost of care. Under a rule of no liability (and given the result that we derived above) the victim's problem is:

$$\min_{x_v \geq 0} w_v x_v + H(x_i^{NL}, x_v)$$
$$= \min_{x_v \geq 0} w_v x_v + H(0, x_v)$$

The solution, which we denote by x_v^{NL} must obey the first-order condition:

$$w_v + \frac{\partial H(0, x_v^{NL})}{\partial x_v} = 0$$

or:

$$w_v = -\frac{\partial H(0, x_v^{NL})}{\partial x_v}$$

These choices constitute a Nash equilibrium: given the choice of the other party, neither party wishes to change their behaviour. The question is: how do these levels of care compare to the efficient levels? Recall that at the efficient level of care, we have $x_i^* > 0$. Since we assumed that x_i and x_v were substitutes, and since $x_i^{NL} = 0 < x_i^*$, this means that with a rule of no liability the victim must be taking more care than the efficient level. That is, $x_v^{NL} > x_v^*$. In the bilateral care model, a rule of no liability is inefficient: no care is taken by the injurer, and too much care is taken by the victim.

The result is best seen in Figure 5.3.1. Instead of expected social cost now being a curve, it is shaped like a cup. Imagine that you are looking down on the cup. Each curve in this diagram represents a different level of aggregate expected costs. These costs decrease as we move towards (x_i^*, x_v^*) (the bottom of the cup), and are minimised at the point (x_i^*, x_v^*), the efficient level of care.

With a rule of no liability, the injurer takes a level of care that is equal to zero. For the victim, the point x_v^* no longer minimises his expected costs. The victim effectively now faces the total social costs, and must choose the level of care that minimises total social costs, subject to the constraint that $x_i = 0$. This means the victim chooses the point on the vertical axis for which total social costs are minimised. This occurs at the point $x_v^{NL} > x_v^*$ in Figure 5.3.1.

5.3.2 Strict liability

The analysis for a rule of strict liability – where the injurer is obligated to pay for all damages, irrespective of whether he took care or

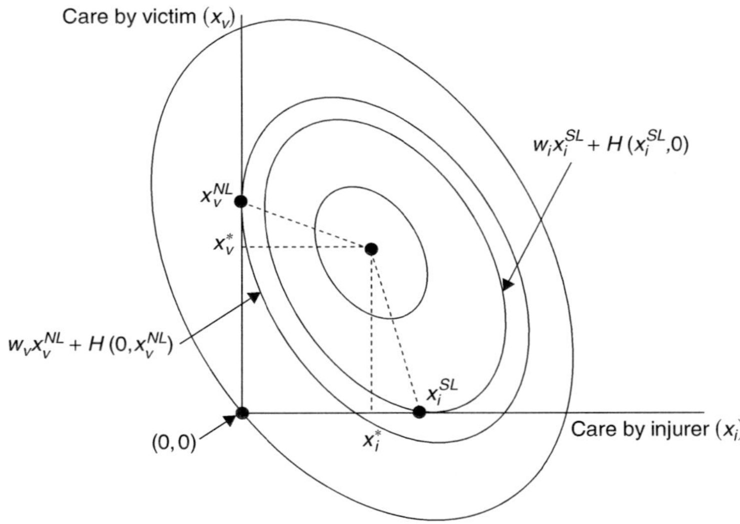

Figure 5.3.1 The bilateral care model

not – is very similar. We consider the victim first. The victim's problem is now:

$$\min_{x_v \geq 0} w_v x_v$$

which gives us:

$$x_v^{SL} = 0$$

The victim takes no care under a rule of strict liability. Given this choice, what is the injurer's best choice of care? Remember, the goal of the injurer is to minimise his expected cost of care. Under a rule of strict liability (and given the result that we just derived for the victim with this rule) the injurer is faced with the full social costs, and so minimises those costs subject to the condition that $x_v = 0$. In other words, the victim's problem is:

$$\min_{x_i \geq 0} w_i x_i + H(x_i, x_v^{SL}) = \min_{x_i \geq 0} w_i x_i + H(x_i, 0)$$

The solution, which we denote by x_i^{SL}, must obey the first-order condition:

$$w_i + \frac{\partial H(x_i^{SL}, 0)}{\partial x_i} = 0$$

or:

$$w_i = -\frac{\partial H(x_i^{SL}, 0)}{\partial x_i}.$$

The question is: how do these levels of care compare to the efficient levels? The argument is the same here as it was for the analysis of no liability. Recall that at the efficient level of care, we have $x_v^* > 0$. Since we assumed that x_i and x_v were substitutes, and since $x_v^{SL} = 0 < x_v^*$, this means that with a rule of strict liability the injurer must take more care than the efficient level. That is, $x_i^{SL} > x_i^*$. In the bilateral care model, a rule of strict liability is inefficient: no care is taken by the victim, and too much care is taken by the injurer.

Again, the result is best seen in Figure 5.3.1. With a rule of strict liability, the victim takes a level of care that is equal to zero. For the injurer, the point x_i^* no longer minimises his expected costs: he increases his level of care in response, above the efficient level.

5.3.2.1 *A negligence rule*

Let us now consider a negligence rule. Recall that in the unilateral care situation, we modelled a negligence rule as a choice by the court of z, the level of care of the injurer. We will not consider all possible negligence rules here. We will only consider a negligence rule which sets the due standard at $z = x_i^*$, the efficient level of care. Suppose that this is the rule. We will show that the efficient levels of care (x_i^*, x_v^*) are a Nash equilibrium. In other words, under a negligence rule, given that the victim chooses x_v^*, the injurer's best response is to choose x_i^*. And, given that the injurer chooses x_i^*, the victim's best response is to choose x_v^*.

To see this, suppose that the victim is choosing a level of care equal to x_v^*. Under a negligence rule where $z = x_i^*$, the injurer's expected costs are:

$$\begin{cases} w_i x_i & \text{if } x_i \geq x_i^* \\ w_i x_i + H(x_i, x_v^*) & \text{if } x_i > x_i^* \end{cases}$$

Since $w_i x_i^* < w_i x_i^* + H(x_i, x_v^*)$, the injurer chooses $x_i = x_i^*$ to minimise his costs.

Similarly, if the injurer is taking care of x_i^*, the victim now faces costs of $w_v x_v + H(x_i^*, x_v)$. These costs are equal to total social costs less $w_i x_i^*$.

Thus, the victim total social costs, subject to the constraint that $x_i = x_i^*$. Diagrammatically, the victim must choose the point on the line $x_i = x_i^*$ with the lowest total social costs. But this is just the point $x_v = x_v^*$. That is, the victim solves:

$$\min_{x_v \geq 0} w_v x_v + H(x_i^*, x_v)$$

The first-order condition is:

$$w_v = -\frac{\partial H(x_i^*, x_v^{NR})}{\partial x_v}$$

But this is exactly the same first-order condition that we had at the efficient level of care. Thus, the victim also behaves efficiently. Therefore in the bilateral care model, a negligence rule in which the due standard for the injurer is set at $z = x_i^*$, is efficient.

5.3.2.2 *'No fault' liability scheme*

We can use our analytical framework of bilateral accidents to analyse different policies which influence the levels of care. Consider, for example, a *no fault liability scheme*. In the simplest example of a no fault liability scheme, the government taxes injurers, and then places the proceeds in a common pool. When an accident occurs, victims are not required to sue injurers, but instead they are compensated for their injuries by drawing from the pool. Injurers therefore do not pay any damages directly, but simply pay taxes in a lump-sum fashion, whether they cause an accident or not.

The cost function of injurers is as follows. Suppose that the government knows what the level of damages h would be in the event that an accident occurs. Injurers are taxed this amount, whether or not an accident occurs. Therefore, the cost function of the injurer is:

$$\text{Injurer's costs} = \begin{cases} w_i x_i + h & \text{if an accident occurs} \\ w_i x_i + h & \text{if an accident does not occurs} \end{cases}$$

$$= \rho(x_i, x_v)(w_i x_i + h) + [1 - \rho(x_i, x_v)(w_i x_i + h)]$$

$$= w_i x_i + h$$

Now the cost function of victims is:

$$\text{Victim's costs} = \begin{cases} (w_v x_v + h) - h & \text{if an accident occurs} \\ w_v x_v & \text{if an accident does not occurs} \end{cases}$$
$$= w_v x_v$$

5.3.2.2.1 Optimal choices of care. The optimal choice of care for the victim is:

$$x_v^{NFL} = 0$$

and the optimal choice of care by the injurer is:

$$x_i^{NFL} = 0$$

The probability of an accident occurring is therefore:

$$\rho(0,0) > \rho(x_i, x_v) \quad \text{for all } x_i, x_v$$

and the aggregate expected social costs under this scheme are:

$$\rho(0,0)h$$

From an efficiency point view, this no fault liability scheme is the worst possible scheme. While victims are always compensated for their damages, the incentive structure that this scheme creates means that the probability of accidents increases, and expected social costs also rise. This outcome can be shown in the diagram below.

Suppose instead that the government does not observe the true amount of harm, but instead underestimates them and taxes injurers an amount $T < h$. The injurer's cost function is still the same, but the victim's cost function is now:

$$\text{Victim's costs} = \begin{cases} (w_v x_v + h) - h & \text{if an accident occurs} \\ w_v x_v & \text{if an accident does not occur} \end{cases}$$
$$= \rho(x_i, x_v)[(w_v x_v + h) - T] + [1 - \rho(x_i, x_v)]w_v x_v$$
$$= w_v x_v + \rho(x_i, x_v)(h - T)$$

where $h - T > 0$ by construction. The injurer still takes no care, but the victim's cost function, given injurer behaviour, is:

$$\text{Victim's costs} = w_v x_v + \rho(0, x_v)(h - T)$$

The victim chooses his level of care to satisfy the marginal condition:

$$w_v = \frac{\partial \rho(0, x_v)}{\partial x_v}(h - T)$$

In general, the level of care that satisfies this condition will not be zero, and so the probability of an accident and expected social costs will be lower when $T < h$. In the extreme case where $T = 0$, we are back to the legal rule of no liability. Thus, in general, a rule of no liability is preferred to this no fault liability scheme. The reason is that incentives for both injurers and victims are completely undermined in a no fault liability scheme, whereas with a no-liability rule (and also with a strict liability rule), at least one of the parties takes some positive amount of care.

5.3.3 Sequential care in the bilateral care model

Up to this point we have assumed that the injurer and the victim move simultaneously. But this may not be a realistic assumption in all situations. In many cases, one party may choose their level of care first, and this may be observed by the other, who then chooses his level of care. This situation can give rise to different incentives than in the simultaneous move case.

Suppose again that there is a victim and an injurer. They can take care of x_i and x_v. The marginal costs of care are w_i and w_v. The expected harm is $H(x_i, x_v)$.

5.3.3.1 If the injurer moves first

We first consider a situation in which the injurer moves first at the victim moves second. We assume that the victim can observe the injurer's choice of care.

The model is solved sequentially, by assuming that the first-mover has chosen some level of care, working out what the second mover will do for each possibility, and then rolling back to the first period to examine what the first mover will do, given that he can anticipate how the second mover will react.

5.3.3.1.1 Strict liability. First, consider a rule of strict liability for the injurer. Suppose that the injurer has chosen x_i. The victim observes this and solves:

$$\min_{x_v} w_v x_v$$

which gives $x_v = 0$. Anticipating this, the injurer chooses:

$$x_i(0) \equiv \arg\min_{x_i} w_i x_i + H(x_i, 0)$$

We have $x_i(0) > x_i^* = x_i(x_v^*)$. A rule of strict liability has the same outcome as if the game was played simultaneously. This is because the victim has a dominant strategy, and so irrespective of whether he can observe what the injurer does or not, under this legal rule he is always fully compensated and will always choose $x_v = 0$.

5.3.3.1.2 No liability. Now consider a rule of no liability. It is easy to see that because the injurer has a dominant strategy (namely, to choose $x_i = 0$), the fact that there is sequential care has no bearing on the outcome under this legal rule. The victim therefore chooses $x_v = x_v(0) > x_v^* = x_v(x_i^*)$.

5.3.3.1.3 Negligence rule. Now consider a negligence rule for injurers, where the due standard is set at $z_i = x_i^*$. We find the subgame perfect equilibrium by first assuming that the injurer has chosen some level of care x_i, and then examine the incentives that this creates for the victim.

In the case of a negligence rule, we split the injurer's possible actions up into two possible classes of outcomes, which depend on whether or not the injurer has met the due standard.

First, suppose that the injurer has chosen $x_i \geq x_i^*$. The injurer would never choose $x_i > x_i^*$, since taking care that exceeds the due standard does not reduce his expected costs. So we must have $x_i = x_i^*$. Then the costs of the accident now full upon the victim, and so the victim's expected costs are:

$$w_v x_v + H(x_i^*, x_v)$$

This is minimised at the point $x_i = x_i^*$.

On the other hand, suppose that the injurer has chosen $x_i < x_i^*$. Then the injurer has behaved negligently, and so will bear the full costs of any accident. Hence the victim's expected costs are:

$$w_v x_v$$

Hence, the victim would choose $x_v = 0$ in response to this.

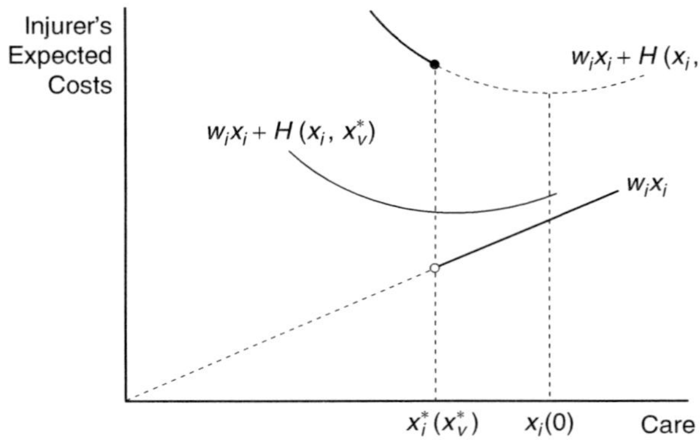

Figure 5.3.2 The injurer's expected costs

Now roll back to the first period. The injurer can anticipate the behaviour of the victim, and so therefore expects his costs to be:

$$\text{Injurer's Expected Costs} = \begin{cases} x_i w_i & \text{if} \quad x_i \geq x_i^* \\ x_i w_i + H(x_i, 0) & \text{if} \quad x_i < x_i^* \end{cases}$$

As Figure 5.3.2 shows, these costs are minimised at the point $x_i = x_i^*$. Therefore, it cannot happen that $x_i < x_i^*$ and $x_v = 0$. We have therefore found a unique subgame perfect equilibrium outcome: in the sequential situation, the negligence rule induces both victims and injurers to behave efficiently. The subgame perfect equilibrium payoffs in this situation are $w_i x_i^*$ for the injurer and $w_v x_v^* + H(x_i^*, x_v^*)$ for the victim.

5.3.3.2 *If the victim moves first*

Now suppose that the victim moves first. The outcomes under strict liability and no liability are the same as before, so we again consider a negligence rule for injurers.

Under a negligence rule for injurers with a due standard of $z_i = x_i^*$, the injurer's expected costs are:

$$\text{Injurer's Expected Costs} = \begin{cases} x_i w_i & \text{if} \quad x_i \geq x_i^* \\ x_i w_i + H(x_i, x_v) & \text{if} \quad x_i < x_i^* \end{cases}$$

We again solve the game by backward induction. Suppose that the victim has chosen x_v. We split the victim's choices into two possible classes. Suppose the victim has chosen a suboptimally low level of care,

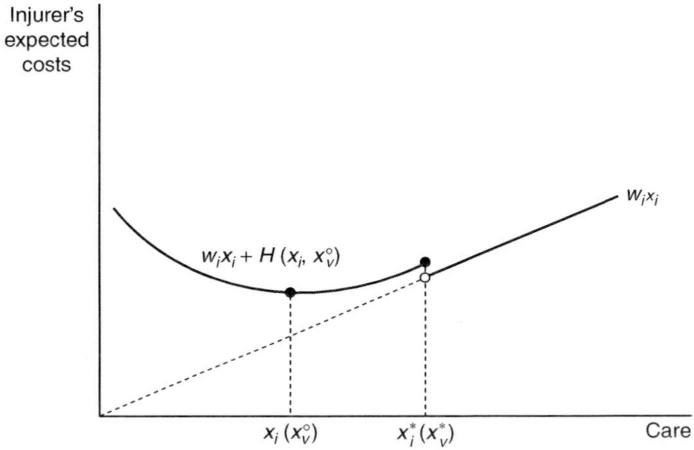

Figure 5.3.3 The injurer's expected costs – injurer prefers an inefficiently low level of care

so that $x_v \leq x_v^*$. Then this means that the injurer will face the efficient level of expected damages if $x_v = x_v^*$, or if $x_v < x_v^*$, this will increase the injurer's costs and he will face an even greater incentive to avoid them. Hence, in this case, the injurer will behave efficiently.

The victim, knowing this, would then face the full costs of his actions, and so would choose $x_v = x_v^*$. Hence, there is a subgame perfect equilibrium in which both parties behave efficiently.

On the other hand, suppose that the victim chooses an inefficiently high level of care, so that $x_v > x_v^*$. Then this reduces the costs that the injurer faces, and there are two possibilities. First, the victim's care may reduce costs by so much that the injurer would rather choose an inefficiently low level of care than meet the due standard. This situation is illustrated in Figure 5.3.3.

But if this is the case, the injurer would be found negligent, and the victim would face no costs. Therefore, he would choose $x_v = 0$ in the first period, which is inconsistent with our original assumption that $x_v > x_v^*$.

On the other hand, the victim's additional care may reduce costs by only a little, making it optimal for the injurer to still meet the due standard of care. But if this is the case, the injurer would not be found negligent, and the victim would face the full costs of the accident. Therefore, the victim would not choose $x_v > x_v^*$ in the first period, which is again inconsistent with our original assumption.

We therefore conclude that if the victim moves first, there is a unique subgame perfect equilibrium in which both parties behave efficiently, with the injurer choosing the efficient level of care, and the victim always bearing the accident costs.

In both cases, then – irrespective of who moves first – we find that a negligence rule for injurers induces a unique subgame perfect equilibrium in which each party behaves efficiently. With a negligence rule, there is no first-mover advantage for either the injurer or the victim.

5.4 The bilateral care model in a market setting

We now extend the previous analysis to encompass a market setting. Consider two perfectly competitive industries, denoted by *i* and *v*. Firms in industry *i* cause harm to firms in industry *v*, but firms in both industries can take actions to reduce expected harm to firms in industry *v*. To simplify the analysis, we make a series of assumptions:

- Consumers of *i* and *v* regard the goods as neither substitutes nor complements. The benefits of consumption of each good are identical, so that the industries have the same demand curves, $Q_i = Q_v \Rightarrow u'(Q_i) = u'(Q_v)$.
- Firms in each industry have identical constant marginal costs of $c_i = c_v = c$.
- As a result of the constant marginal cost assumption, we can treat firms in each industry as a single representative price taking firm. The representative firm in industry *i* produces Q_i units of output, and the firm in industry *v* produces Q_v units of output.
- The marginal costs of care in each industry are identical, so that $w_i = w_v = w$.
- The expected per unit harm function has the following symmetry property: $\frac{\partial H}{\partial x_i} = \frac{\partial H}{\partial x_v} \Rightarrow x_i = x_v$. (For example, this condition is satisfied by the constant elasticity of expected harm function if $\alpha = \beta = 0.5$.)

Under these conditions, total welfare is:

$$\begin{aligned} W(Q_i, Q_v, x_i, x_v) &= u(Q_i) + u(Q_v) - c_i Q_i - c_v Q_v - w_i x_i Q_i - w_v x_v Q_v - Q_i Q_v H(x_i, x_v) \\ &= u(Q_i) + u(Q_v) - cQ_i - cQ_v - w x_i Q_i - w x_v Q_v - Q_i Q_v H(x_i, x_v) \end{aligned}$$

The situation we have in mind is similar to that discussed in Chapter 4, with the added assumption that beer-producing firms can reduce harm by decontaminating the water before using it in beer production. This decontamination process is costly. The per unit expected costs to the beer industry of water pollution are still $H(x_i, x_v)$. The total harm of pollution rises with the quantity produced in each industry. For a given level of total output of industry v (say Q_v units), then the total harm that the industry faces could increase if either (or all) of the following occur:

- Firms in industry i industry each choose a lower level of care (e.g. less decontamination);
- Firms in industry i choose a low level of care;
- Firms in industry i produce more output; or
- Firms in industry v produce more beer.

The efficiency conditions are now:

$$\frac{\partial W}{\partial Q_i} = u'(Q_i^*) - c - wx_i^* - Q_v^* H(x_i^*, x_v^*) = 0 \tag{5.1}$$

$$\frac{\partial W}{\partial Q_v} = u'(Q_v^*) - c - wx_v^* - Q_i^* H(x_i^*, x_v^*) = 0 \tag{5.2}$$

$$\frac{\partial W}{\partial x_i} = -w - Q_v^* \frac{\partial H}{\partial x_i} = 0 \tag{5.3}$$

$$\frac{\partial W}{\partial x_v} = -w - Q_i^* \frac{\partial H}{\partial x_v} = 0 \tag{5.4}$$

The first two conditions in (5.1) and (5.2) relate to the output levels. Given optimal levels of per unit care, the marginal consumption benefit of the last unit of output in industry i should be equal to the full marginal cost, where the marginal cost depends on the production cost, the per unit costs of care, and the marginal cost of harm to firms in industry v. Similarly, the marginal consumption benefit of the last unit of output in industry v should be equal to the sum of the marginal production cost, the per unit costs of care, and the marginal cost of harm to firms in industry v. Note that under our assumptions, we have:

$$u'(Q_v^*) - c - wx_i^* - Q_v^* H(x_i^*, x_v^*) = 0 = u'(Q_v^*) - c - wx_v^* - Q_i^* H(x_i^*, x_v^*)$$

which implies that $Q_i^* = Q_v^*$.

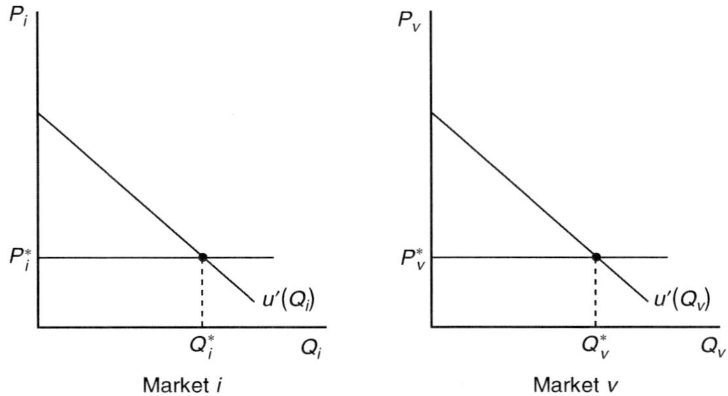

Figure 5.4.1 Efficiency in the bilateral care model in a competitive market setting

The last two conditions in (5.3) and (5.4) relate to care, and simply state that care should be undertaken by firms in each industry up to the point where marginal cost equals marginal benefit, noting that for each industry marginal benefit depends on output levels in the other industry. Note that under our assumptions, we have:

$$-w - Q_v^* \frac{\partial H}{\partial x_i} = 0 = -w - Q_i^* \frac{\partial H}{\partial x_v}$$

which, together with the assumptions on H and the fact that $Q_i^* = Q_v^*$, imply that $x_i^* = x_v^* = x^*$.

Since the demand curves in each industry are $P_i = u'(Q_i)$ and $P_v = u'(Q_v)$, and are equal to each other, the efficiency conditions imply that at the efficient allocation, the efficient prices in each industry must also be identical:

$$P_i = c + wx^* + Q^* H(x^*, x^*) = P_v$$

The efficient outcome is shown in Figure 5.4.1.

5.4.1 No liability

Under a rule of no liability, firms in industry *i* do not have to compensate firms in industry *v*. This rule is inefficient for the same reasons as discussed in the unilateral care model. Firms in industry *i* do not take any care. Their marginal costs are $c + wx_i$, and so to minimise marginal costs firms choose $x_i = x_i^{NL} = 0$. The competitive equilibrium price in industry i is therefore $P_i^{NL} = c$. The competitive quantity in industry i is $Q_i^{NL} = u'^{-1}(c) > Q_i^*$.

On the other hand, marginal costs in industry v are equal to:

$$c + wx_v + Q_i^{NL} H(0, x_v)$$

To minimise these costs, firms in industry v choose a level of care which obeys:

$$w + Q_i^{NL} \frac{\partial H(0, x_v^{NL})}{\partial x_v} = 0$$

Since $Q_i^{NL} > Q_i^*$, the marginal benefit of care by firms in industry v is higher. This would be the case even if firms in industry i were to choose the efficient level of care. In addition, firms in industry choose an inefficiently low level of care, which further increases the marginal benefit of care for firms in industry v. Therefore, $x_v^{NL} > x_v^*$, and $H(0, x_v^{NL}) > H(x_i^*, x_v^*)$, which, together with the fact that $x_v^{NL} > x_v^*$, means that the competitive equilibrium price in industry v must be higher than the efficient price:

$$P_v^{NL} = c + wx_v^{NL} + Q_i^{NL} H(0, x_v^{NL}) > c + wx_v^* + Q_i^* H(x_i^*, x_v^*) = P_v^*$$

which also means that $Q_v^{NL} < Q_v^*$. The competitive equilibrium under no liability is illustrated in Figure 5.4.2.

What is the welfare loss from a no-liability rule here? Producers in industry i still earn zero profits, with all price reductions being passed on to

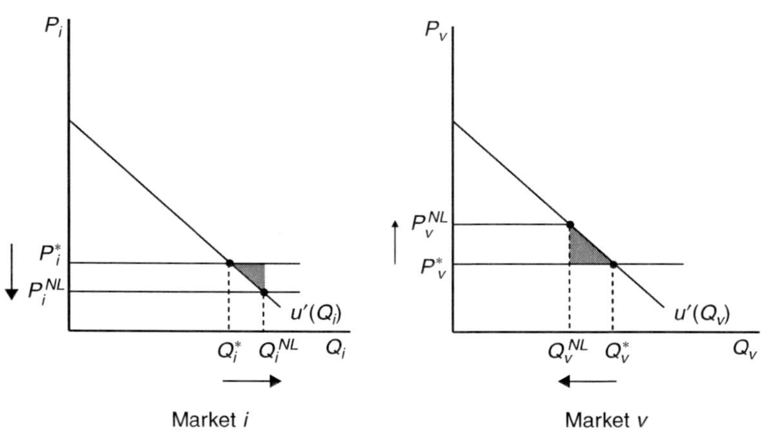

Figure 5.4.2 Competitive equilibrium under a no liability rule

consumers. For each additional unit of good i that is consumed, marginal social cost exceeds the price, and since consumers equate marginal benefits with price, it must be the case that the marginal social cost of each additional unit consumed in market i exceeds the social marginal benefit of each unit. Hence we get a welfare loss from overconsumption in market i.

Similarly, producers in industry v still earn zero profits in equilibrium, with all price increases being passed on to consumers. For each unit of good v that is not consumed, marginal social cost is less than the price, and since consumers equate marginal benefits with price, it must be the case that the marginal social cost of each additional unit consumed in market v is less than the social marginal benefit of each unit. Hence there is also a welfare loss from *under*-consumption in market v. The total welfare loss is the sum of the triangle welfare losses in each market as shown in Figure 5.4.2 above.

5.4.2 Strict liability

A rule of strict liability is also inefficient for the same reasons as discussed in the no liability case. Firms in industry v do not take any care. Their marginal costs are $c + wx_v$, and so firms choose $x_v = x_v^{SL} = 0$. The competitive equilibrium price in industry v is therefore $P_v^{SL} = c$. The competitive quantity is $Q_v^{SL} = u'^{-1}(c) > Q_v^*$.

The marginal costs in industry i are now:

$$c + wx_i + Q_v^{SL} H(x_i, 0)$$

To minimise these costs, firms choose a level of care which obeys:

$$w + Q_v^{SL} \frac{\partial H(x_i^{SL}, 0)}{\partial x_i} = 0$$

Again, since $Q_v^{SL} > Q_v^*$, the marginal benefit of care by firms in industry v is higher, even if firms in industry i chose the efficient level of care. All of the other results discussed above go through, with the role of each industry simply reversed. Moreover, under our special symmetry assumptions the welfare loss under strict liability is identical to the welfare loss under no liability.

5.4.3 A negligence rule

Suppose that each firm in industry i is held liable for harm to firms in industry v if they fail to meet some due standard of care. Suppose that this due standard is set at the efficient level of care, $z_i = x_i^*$. Consider industry v first. Suppose that each firm in industry v believes that all firms in industry *i* will choose the efficient level of care, and that the industry as a whole will also produce the efficient quantity. Then the profit of the representative firm in industry *v* is:

$$\pi_v = P_v Q_v - cQ_v - wx_v Q_v - Q_i^* Q_v H(x_i^*, x_v)$$

Each firm in industry *v* would then choose the efficient level of care. The first-order condition with respect to Q_v satisfies:

$$P_v = c + wx_v^* + Q_i^* H(x_i^*, x_v)$$

and so industry *v* will produce the efficient quantity.

Consider, on the other hand, firms in industry *i*. Suppose that they believe that each firm in industry *v* will supply the efficient levels of care and output. Then each firm's profit is:

$$\pi_i = \begin{cases} P_i Q_i - cQ_i - wx_i Q_i & \text{if } x_i \geq x_i^* \\ P_i Q_i - cQ_i - wx_i Q - Q_i Q_v^* H(x_i, x_v^*) & \text{if } x_i < x_i^* \end{cases}$$

Firms can escape liability and minimise costs by choosing to meet the due standard, so that $x_i = x_i^*$. Then each firm's profit is:

$$\pi_i = P_i Q_i - cQ_i - wx_i^* Q_i$$

The zero profit condition then implies that:

$$P_i^{NR} = c + wx_i^* < c + wx_i^* + Q_v^* H(x_i^*, x_v^*) = P_i^*$$

But this implies that $Q_i^{NR} > Q_i^*$. Going back to industry *v*, this means that the original conjecture of the firms in that industry about firms in industry *i* could not have been correct. In other words, the negligence rule cannot produce efficient outcomes.

As in the analysis of the unilateral care model in a market setting, this conclusion once again suggests that traditional legal rules such as strict liability rule or a negligence rule are not efficient once a market setting is introduced. Under a negligence rule, firms in industry *i* can avoid liability by meeting the due standard of care, and this lowers marginal and average costs, forcing prices below efficient levels. The industry produces too much, even though all firms individually might have an incentive to take the appropriate per unit level of care.

5.5 Other legal rules in the bilateral care model

So far in our analysis of the bilateral care model, we have considered three rules: no liability, strict liability and a negligence rule that set the due standard of care for the injurer at the efficient level of care, $z = x_i^*$. Let us now consider three other institutional arrangements.

5.5.1 Strict liability with a defence of contributory negligence

The defence of *contributory negligence* allows the injurer to avoid liability (even if he failed to take any care) *as long as the* ***victim*** *fails to meet some due standard of care*. In other words, the rule is now that the injurer is liable for all damages, but only if the victim met a due standard of care (which the court must choose). Therefore, in contrast to the rule of strict liability that we studied in the previous lecture, there is no longer a guarantee that the victim will recover damages.

We will show that if the court sets the victims due standard at the efficient level x_v^*, then the injurer's best response is to choose $x = x_i^*$. Conversely, since the injurer chooses x_i^*, the victim's best response is to choose x_v^*. Hence, the rule of strict liability with a defence of contributory negligence that is set at x_v^*, induces efficient behaviour.

To see this, suppose that the injurer chooses a level of $x = x_i^*$. Then, if the due standard is set at x_v^*, the victim's costs will be:

$$\text{Victim's costs} = \begin{cases} w_v x_v & \text{if } x_v \geq x_v^* \text{ (meet or exceed the due standard)} \\ w_v x_v + H(x_i^*, x_v) & \text{if } x_v < x_v^* \text{(fail to meet the due standard)} \end{cases}$$

The victim's choice problem is therefore similar to the injurer's choice problem under a simple negligence rule in which $z = x_i^*$. We know that the solution to this problem is x_v^*. Thus, the victim's best response to x_i^* under this legal rule is x_v^*.

Now, consider the injurer's choice problem. In general, if the court sets the due standard for the victim at z_v, the injurer's costs will be:

$$\text{Injurer's costs} = \begin{cases} w_i x_i & \text{if } x_v > z_v \\ w_i x_i + H(x_i x_v) & \text{if } x_v \geq z_v \end{cases} \tag{5.5}$$

Now, suppose that the court sets the due standard for the victim at the efficient level, and suppose that the victim chooses $x_v = x_v^*$. Since the victim is taking adequate care, the injurer will be liable for damages. Therefore, the injurer's choice problem is:

$$\min_{x_i \geq 0} w_i x_i + H(x_i, x_v^*)$$

The solution to this problem by the injurer is x_i^*, the efficient level of care. Thus, in a non-market setting, x_i^* is a best response to x_v^*, and x_v^* is a best response to x_i^*. This means that (x_i^*, x_v^*) is a Nash equilibrium when the rule is strict liability with a defence of contributory negligence (and assuming that the court has chosen the appropriate due standard). Therefore, in the bilateral care model, a rule of strict liability with a defence of contributory negligence in which is efficient.

How does this rule operate in a market setting? Consider the model developed in section 5.4, where we assume that the marginal costs of care are identical in each industry and are equal to w. Suppose that firms in industry i take the efficient level of care, and that industry production is Q_i. Then, the profits of firms in industry v will be:

$$\pi_v = \begin{cases} P_v Q_v - cQ_v - wx_v Q_v & \text{if } x_v \geq x_v \\ P_v Q_v - cQ_v - wx_v Q - Q_v Q_i H(x_i^*, x_v) & \text{if } x_v < x_v^* \end{cases} \tag{5.6}$$

Firms in industry v can avoid liability by choosing the efficient level of care. Since they no longer face the full marginal social costs of their actions, there will be excessive production of good v. Similarly, since $Q_v > Q_v^*$, firms in industry i now face excessively high marginal costs, and will produce too little. Again, the legal rule of strict liability with a defence of contributory negligence does not produce efficient outcomes.

5.5.2 Application: The bilateral care model when there is no distinction between injurers and victims

In most bilateral activity situations, there is no clear distinction between injurers and victims because both parties involved in the accident suffer losses. This section illustrates the usefulness of the rule of strict liability with a defence of contributory negligence by considering the analysis of Arlen (1990), who examines the efficiency of various legal rules in a "double harm" setting.

Consider the bilateral model of accident law, but now assume that both injurers *and* victims suffer damage when an accident occurs (in other words, there is no real distinction between injurers and victims). Specifically, suppose that if an accident occurs, the 'injurer' suffers harm of h_i, and the 'victim' suffers harm of $h_v > 0$. Let x_i and x_v be the levels of care taken by the injurer and the victim. The probability of an accident given these levels of care is $\rho(x_i, x_v)$, which has the same properties that we have previously assumed. Let the marginal costs of care be w_i and w_v. Assume both parties are risk neutral.

Aggregate expected social costs are now:

$$w_i x_i + w_v x_v + \rho(x_i, x_v)(h_i + h_v) \tag{5.7}$$

And the two first-order conditions which characterise the efficient levels of care are:

$$w_i = -\frac{\partial \rho}{\partial x_i}(x_i^*, x_v^*)(h_i + h_v) \tag{5.8}$$

$$w_v = -\frac{\partial \rho}{\partial x_v}(x_i^*, x_v^*)(h_i + h_v) \tag{5.9}$$

Consider a rule of no liability, where damaged parties are never compensated for any losses. This rule does not induce efficient behaviour. To see this, note that under a no liability rule, for any combination of care levels, the injurer's marginal benefit of care is:

$$-\frac{\partial \rho}{\partial x_i}(x_i, x_v)h_i < -\frac{\partial \rho}{\partial x_i}(x_i, x_v)(h_i + h_v) \tag{5.10}$$

where the right-hand side of (5.10) is the social marginal benefit of the injurer's care. So, for any level of care taken by the victim, the injurer will choose an inefficiently low level of care, since he fails to fully internalise the social benefits of care. The same reasoning applies to the victim. As a result, the Nash equilibrium under this legal rule results in *both* parties taking an inefficiently low level of care.

A rule of strict liability – where damaged parties are always compensated for all losses that occur as a result of an accident – produces a similar outcome. To see this, note that under a strict liability rule, for any combination of care levels, the injurer's marginal benefit of care is:

$$-\frac{\partial \rho}{\partial x_i}(x_i, x_v)h_v < -\frac{\partial \rho}{\partial x_i}(x_i, x_v)(h_i + h_v)$$

where once again the right-hand side is the social marginal benefit of the injurer's care. So, once again, for any level of care taken by the victim, the injurer will choose an inefficiently low level of care, since he again fails to fully internalise the social benefits of care. The same reasoning applies to the victim and the Nash equilibrium results in both parties taking an inefficiently low level of care.

Which legal rules are efficient in this situation? Consider a rule of *strict liability with a defence of contributory negligence*, which states that each party must compensate the other for harm incurred, *unless* the party meets some due standard of care. This requires the court to set a due standard of care (z_i, z_v) for each party. Suppose that these due standards are set at the efficient levels, so $(z_i, z_v) = (x_i^*, x_v^*)$. Let's check if the efficient outcome is a Nash equilibrium. Suppose that the victim meets his due standard of care, so $x_v = x_v^*$. Since he has met his due standard, he does not have to compensate the injurer. Hence the injurer's expected costs are:

$$\begin{cases} w_i x_i + \rho(x_i, x_v^*) h_i & \text{if } x_i \geq x_i^* \\ w_i x_i + \rho(x_i, x_v^*)(h_i + h_v) & \text{if } x_i < x_i^* \end{cases}$$

The legal rule creates an upward 'jump' of $\rho(x_i, x_v^*)h_v$ in the injurer's expected cost function at the point x_i^*. To avoid these additional costs the injurer chooses $x_i = x_i^*$. In other words, if the victim is expected to behave efficiently, the best response of the injurer is to also behave efficiently. And since the parties are essentially symmetric under this legal rule, a similar line of reasoning applies to the victim: if the injurer is expected to behave efficiently, the best response of the victim is to also behave efficiently. Hence the efficient outcome (x_i^*, x_v^*) is a Nash equilibrium (it is also the only equilibrium). When both parties can take care and both can be harmed as a result of an accident, then the rule of strict liability with a defence of contributory negligence produces efficient outcomes.

5.5.3 Comparative negligence

As we have seen so far, liability rules can be regarded as cost-allocation rules between injurers and victims. A rule of *comparative negligence* allocates the cost of harm between the parties *in proportion to the contribution of negligence to the accident*. For example, if the victim's negligence is 20 per cent responsible for the accidental harm, then the victim may only recover 80 per cent of damages from the injurer.

This rule requires the court to:

1. Define a due standard for the injurer, z_i.
2. Define a due standard for the victim, z_v.
3. Compare the actual levels of care, x_i and x_v, with the due standards z_i and z_v.
4. Compute the percentage contribution of each party's negligence to the accident.

Let $b(x_i, x_v)$ be the 'blame function': percentage contribution of damages borne by the injurer when the injurer takes care x_i and the victim takes care of x_v. Then, we have:

$$b(x_i, x_v) = \frac{i\text{'s due standard} - i\text{'s actual care}}{(i\text{'s due standard} - i\text{'s actual care}) + (v\text{'s due standard} - v\text{'s actual care})}$$
$$= \frac{z_i - x_i}{(z_i - x_i) + (z_v - x_v)}$$

When both parties meet their due standards, this blame function is not defined. To deal with this case, let:

$$b(x_i, x_v) = \begin{cases} 0 & \text{if } x_i \geq z_i \\ \dfrac{z_i - x_i}{(z_i - x_i) + (z_v - x_v)} & \text{if } x_i < z_i \text{ and } x_v < z_v \\ 1 & \text{if } x_i < z_i \text{ and } x_v \geq z_v \end{cases} \tag{5.11}$$

It is straightforward to show that if the due standards of care are set at the efficient levels, then the Nash equilibrium under this legal rule involves both parties choosing the efficient level of care, with injurers avoiding liability and harm falling on the victim. In a non-market setting, a comparative negligence rule is efficient.

What about comparative negligence in a market setting? Since injurers avoid liability, they do not face the full social marginal costs of their actions, and so produce an inefficiently high amount, $Q_i^{CN} > Q_i^*$.

On the other hand, firms in industry v will have marginal and average costs of:

$$c + wx_v + Q_i^{CN} H(x_i, x_v^*) \tag{5.12}$$

To minimise these costs, each firm in industry v will choose care up to the point where:

$$w = -Q_i^{CN} \frac{\partial H(x_i^*, x_v)}{\partial x_v} \tag{5.13}$$

Since $Q_i^{CN} > Q_i^*$, firms in industry v will choose a level of care that is inefficiently high. This will mean that $Q_v^{CN} < Q_v^*$.

5.6 Notes

There is a vast literature on the economics of accident law. The literature on the bilateral care model begins with Brown (1973). Shavell (1987) and Landes and Posner (1987) are thorough book-length treatments of both the unilateral and bilateral care models.

5.7 Exercises

1. Suppose that A drives his truck at a speed of 80 km/hr, and B drives his car at a speed of 70 km/hr. A and B nearly collide, and B is forced to take evasive action. B crashes into a tree and his car (worth $10,000) is written off. B sues A for these damages. A sustains no damages.

   Consider the following six legal rules:

   - Strict Liability for Truck Drivers
   - No Liability
   - Negligence Rule for Truck Drivers
   - Strict Liability with a Defence of Contributory Negligence
   - Negligence Rule with a Defence of Contributory Negligence
   - Comparative Negligence

   Who is liable, and how are damages allocated under each of these rules? How would your answers change if the due standard for the injurer and the victim is 50km/hr? 70km/hr?
2. Consider the table below, which lists the levels of care, costs of care, and so on, for the injurer and a victim in a simple accident law game.

Levels of care		Cost of care		Expected damage	Total costs
Injurer	**Victim**	**Injurer**	**Victim**		
None	None	0	0	30	
None	Care	0	4	24	
Care	None	6	0	20	
Care	Care	6	4	12	

   (a) Complete the missing cells of the table suppose that there is a rule of **strict liability**. Write down the payoff matrix of the players under this legal rule. What is the Nash equilibrium in this game? Is the legal rule efficient? Give a brief economic explanation.

   (b) Now suppose that there is a rule of **no liability**. Write down the payoff matrix of the players under this legal rule. What is the Nash equilibrium in this game? Is the legal rule efficient? Give a brief economic explanation.

   (c) Now suppose that there is a **negligence rule**, which says that the injurer will be obligated to pay damages if he chooses {None}, but will not be held liable if he chooses {Care}. Write down the payoff matrix of the players under this legal rule. What is the Nash equilibrium in this game? Is the legal rule efficient? Give a brief economic explanation.

   (d) Now suppose that the legal rule is **strict liability with a defence of contributory negligence**, which states that the injurer is *always* obligated to pay all of the victim's damages, *except* if the victim is *contributorily negligent* (i.e. if the victim chooses {None}), in which case the injurer does not have to pay damages. Write down the payoff matrix of the players under this legal rule. What is the Nash equilibrium in this game? Is the legal rule efficient? Give a brief economic explanation.

(e) Now suppose that the legal rule is a **negligence rule with a defence of contributory negligence**, which states that if the injurer is negligent (i.e. if the injurer chooses {None}), he must pay the victim's damages, *except* if the victim is *contributorily negligent* (i.e. if the victim chooses {None}), in which case the injurer does not have to pay damages. Write down the payoff matrix of the players under this legal rule. What is the Nash equilibrium in this game? Is the legal rule efficient? Give a brief economic explanation.

3. In Chapter 4 we examined situations instances involving compensating victims for accidental harm, where injurers were wealth constrained – the injurer's total assets are less than the damage that they might actually cause. Suppose that the injurer has assets of $a > 0$, but that $a < h$, where h is the damage caused to victims. Consider the bilateral care model of accidents studied in this chapter, and consider the following legal rules:

   - No liability
   - Strict liability
   - Negligence Rule
   - Strict Liability with a Defence of Contributory Negligence
   - Negligence Rule with a Defence of Contributory Negligence
   - Comparative Negligence

   Which of these legal rules can induce both injurers and victims to take an efficient amount of care when injurers are wealth constrained?

4. The *Hand rule* for determining negligence was formulated by Judge Learned Hand in the 1947 case of *US* v. *Carroll Towing Company*. Let B be the burden (or cost) of the untaken precaution, P be the probability of an accident given that the precaution was not taken, and L be the injury (damage) from the accident. Using these variables, the Hand rule for determining negligence is that an individual is negligent if $B < PL$.

   Using the bilateral model of accident law, critically examine the Hand rule. Does the rule induce injurers and victims to take the efficient level of care? If so, explain why. If not, formulate a different version of the Hand rule which leads to efficient outcomes.

6

Markets for Potentially Harmful Goods – The Economics of Product Liability Rules

6.1 Introduction

In the previous chapter we examined situations where the parties undertaking care and incurring harm were 'economic strangers' in the following important sense: there was no existing economic relationship between the parties when they chose their levels of care, or when accidents occurred.

But in a market economy this is by no means the most common situation in which accidental harm occurs. In many situations, the injurer and the victim have engaged in one or more economic transactions before harm occurs. Many such situations are governed by *product liability rules*. Specifically, product liability laws determine the allocation of damages in situations where firms sell defective or potentially dangerous products to consumers (or downstream producers) in exchange for a monetary payment or a price, and where either firms or consumers (or both) can take care to alter the probability of an accident occurring.

There is a critical difference between this situation and the class of situations examined in the previous chapter: in the situations examined in this chapter, the parties *voluntarily* enter into an economic transaction before the accidental harm occurs. This means that the expected costs of harm and levels of care can potentially be anticipated and incorporated into the original terms of exchange. Further, expected harm will potentially affect both the demand and supply side of the market as producer costs and consumer willingness to pay may both be affected. Since market prices may adjust in response to consumers' marginal willingness to pay and producers' marginal opportunity costs – both of which will in general depend on the costs of care and allocation of damages – the incorporation of harm and the costs of care into market prices and quantities may occur even in the absence of formal bargaining between the parties. This means that there are certain situations in which the legal rule may again be irrelevant for both production and efficiency. However, *in contrast to the Coase Theorem this irrelevance result holds even in the absence of direct bargaining between the parties.*

It turns out that in these situations, under certain assumptions, legal rules are again irrelevant for market efficiency, even though producers and consumers interact anonymously on markets and no direct bargaining takes place. One of the main reasons for this irrelevance result is that competition and the desire to exploit gains from trade provide powerful incentives for producers and consumers to do certain things, even when the law does not compel them to do so. This is a very strong but very important result, and like the Coase Theorem it holds only under some circumstances. The interesting issue is analysing exactly which situations it holds and does not hold, and the implications that this has for the design of legal rules and economic policy more generally.

This chapter is structured as follows. Section 6.2 characterises the conditions for economic efficiency when firms produce goods that can potentially harm the individuals who purchase those goods. Section 6.3 focuses on the key issue of consumer perceptions of harm, and presents a simple framework for modelling the effects of consumer misperceptions. Section 6.4 puts these two pieces of the puzzle together and studies the efficiency properties of legal rules in competitive markets for goods that are potentially harmful to consumers. Section 6.5 extends this analysis to imperfectly competitive market settings. Section 6.6 studies a particular application: employment law and the economics of workplace safety regulations.

6.2 Efficiency when goods are potentially harmful

Consider a market for a good that is potentially harmful to consumers. Suppose any positive level of care can be chosen by the injurer, which in this case is the firm that is selling the good to the consumers, who are also victims in this setup. We will assume that all firms are identical. Let the total expected harm to consumers be equal to $nqH(x)$ where q is the quantity produced by each firm, x is the level of care taken by each firm, and $H(x)$ is the expected harm per unit of the good that is consumed. Let each firm's cost function be equal to $C(q)$. Finally, let each firm's per unit cost of care be equal to w. Total welfare is given by:

$$W = u(nq) - nC(q) - nq[wx + H(x)]$$

Welfare maximisation now requires three conditions. First, for a given number of (identical) firms, it must not be possible to increase welfare by having each firm produce more. This means that:

$$\frac{\partial W}{\partial n} = n^*u'(n^*q^*) - n^*\,[wx^* + H(x^*)] - n^*C'(q^*) = 0$$

or:

$$u'(n^*q^*) = wx^* + H(x^*) + C'(q^*) \tag{6.1}$$

Equation (6.1) states that consumption benefits from consuming the last unit of the good must equal the full marginal costs of consumption, where those costs now include the marginal expected harm that occurs as a result of consuming the good, as well as the cost of care. Notice that this condition implies that consumers should consume less of the good than they would if the good was harmless.

Second, for a given quantity, it must not be possible to increase welfare by changing the number of firms. This means that:

$$\frac{\partial W}{\partial n} = q^*u'(n^*q^*) - q^*\,[wx^* + H(x^*)] + C(q^*)$$

or:

$$u'(n^*q^*) = wx^* + H(x^*) + \frac{C(q^*)}{q^*} \tag{6.2}$$

Equation (6.2) states that the marginal consumption benefits must also equal *average* expected costs, where these costs again include the expected harm that occurs as a result of consuming the good. Since the consumer equates marginal benefits with price P, welfare maximisation again requires price = marginal cost = average cost.

Finally, efficiency requires that it must not be possible to increase welfare by altering the level of care:

$$\frac{\partial W}{\partial x} = -n^*q^*\,[w + H'(x^*)] = 0$$

or:

$$w = -H'(x^*) \tag{6.3}$$

Equation (6.3) states that for the last unit of care that is provided, the reduction in expected harm (which is the marginal benefit of care) should be equal to the marginal cost providing that last unit of care.

6.3 Consumer misperceptions of harm

In the analysis that follows, consumer perceptions regarding the extent of expected harm that is embodied in the good will play a key role. In our setup, perceptions of expected harm depend on:

- Consumer perceptions of $\rho(x)$, the probability that the good will actually cause harm; and
- Consumer perceptions of H, the harm that the good will actually cause if accidental damage occurs.

Depending on the legal rule that is in place, consumers who underestimate harm will behave very differently than those who overestimate harm. We summarise these perceptions by a single parameter, $\lambda \geq 0$. If the expected harm per unit of the good consumed is $H(x)$, then the consumer's perception or estimate of the expected harm is defined to be $\lambda H(x)$. Thus, if $\lambda = 1$, the consumer perceives or estimates the expected harm accurately and does not have any misperceptions. On the other hand, if $0 \leq \lambda < 1$ then the consumer *underperceives* or underestimates the expected harm that consumption of the good will cause. For example, if $\lambda = 0$ the consumer regards the good as being perfectly safe. This perception could indeed turn out to be correct, but, statistically speaking, it is a biased estimate of the true expected harm.

Finally, if $\lambda > 1$, then consumers *overperceive* or overestimate the expected harm from consumption of the good. Again, *ex post*, this perception could turn out to be correct, but statistically it is biased.

6.4 Product liability rules in perfectly competitive markets

This section examines the welfare consequences of various product liability rules in a competitive market setting. We consider three rules: strict liability, no liability and a negligence rule. We focus on the long-run, where firms can freely enter and exit the market and where firms can vary all inputs.

6.4.1.1 Strict liability

Under a rule of strict liability, firms must compensate consumers for all losses. This means that risk-neutral consumers treat the good as if it was perfectly harmless (since they are fully compensated for any harm that occurs), and that producers factor in all expected harm into their cost base. Since consumers regard the good as harmless, the consumer demand curve is:

$$P = u'(Q)$$

Note that consumer perceptions of harm do not enter into the demand curve. Since consumers are risk neutral and are fully compensated for all harm under the strict liability rule, their perceptions of the expected harm are irrelevant for demand.

Since firms must fully compensate consumers, each firm's profit is equal to $Pq - q[wx + H(x)] - C(q)$. Each price-taking profit-maximising firm will produce at the point where price equals marginal cost, so:

$$P_{SL}(x) = wx + H(x) + C'(q_{SL}).$$

Furthermore, for any q, under a strict liability rule, firms are faced with the full social costs of their actions. Therefore they will minimise the costs of care by equating the marginal benefits of care (the reduction in damages that they must pay consumers) with the marginal costs, so that:

$$w = -H'(x_{SL})$$

This is identical to equation (6.3), so $x_{SL} = x^*$. In a long-run competitive equilibrium, firms enter (or exit) the industry until profits are driven zero. For each firm, the average cost is:

$$P_{SL} = AC_{SL} = wx^* + H(x^*) + \frac{C(q_{SL})}{q_{SL}}$$

What quantity is produced by each firm in a long-run competitive equilibrium? It is the quantity that minimises average cost. But the quantity that minimises $\frac{C(q)}{q}$ also minimises $\frac{C(q)}{q} + wx^* + H(x^*)$. Therefore, under our assumptions, the quantity that minimises average costs is the same as if the good was not harmful. Therefore $q_{SL} = q^*$. In other words, under a strict liability rule the marginal cost curve and average cost curves are vertical, parallel translations of the original cost curves.

Figure 6.4.1 plots the marginal and average cost curves (MC_0, AC_0) for a harmless good, as well as the long-run supply curve (LRS_0) when the good is harmless. The diagram also plots the same (higher) curves under a strict liability rule when the good is potentially harmful. Notice that irrespective of consumers' estimates of the harm of the good, the demand curve under a strict liability does not shift, since consumers are assumed to be risk neutral and under this legal rule they are fully compensated for any losses.

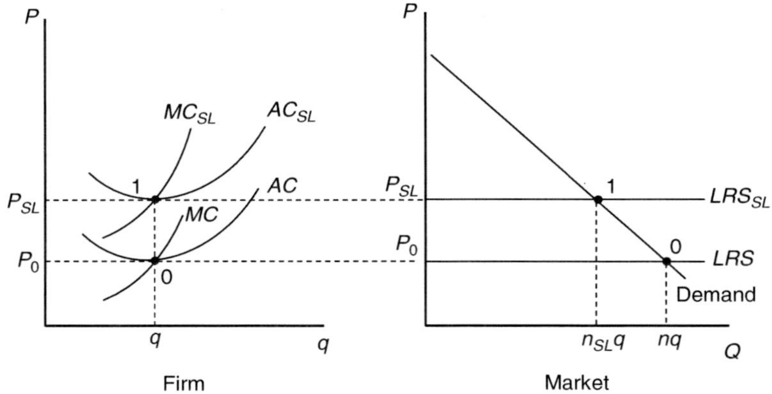

Figure 6.4.1 Competitive equilibrium under strict liability

In addition to producing at a point where price equals marginal cost, firms earn zero profits, so we also have $P_{SL} = AC_{SL} = wx^* + H(x^*) + \frac{C(q^*)}{q^*}$. Thus, price equals full average cost. But once again, since marginal cost also equals price, which in turn is equal to average cost, we must have marginal cost equal to average cost. This again occurs at the minimum of the average cost curve, which now includes the cost of care and the expected harm. The long-run competitive equilibrium is shown in Figure 6.4.1. The long-run market supply curve is flat and is equal to the minimum of the average cost curve.

The strict liability rule produces an efficient outcome. In the long run, each firm produces the same quantity that it did when the good was harmless, but there are fewer firms in the industry. The aggregate market quantity is lower, and consumers of the good bear the entire incidence of the harmfulness of the good. Compared to a harmless good, prices are higher by $wx^* + H(x^*)$, so the competitive price under strict liability is:

$$P_{SL} = C'(q^*) + wx^* + H(x^*) = \frac{C(q^*)}{q^*} + wx^* + H(x^*)$$

6.4.1.2 *No liability*

Under a rule of no liability, firms do not have to compensate consumers for any losses that are incurred when the good is consumed.

Assuming that consumers can observe the level of care that is provided, risk-neutral consumers reduce their marginal willingness to pay by the perceived marginal expected harm:

$$P(x) = u'(nq) - \lambda H(x)$$

Note that the price that consumers are willing to pay is a function of the level of care provided by firms, as well as the perception parameter λ. Notice that we have written the demand curve as a function of x. This is deliberate: even if consumers cannot perfectly perceive harm, an increase in x will increase their marginal willingness to pay for the good, and so also shift the demand curve.

Each producer's profit is equal to $P(x)q - qwx - C(q)$, and so for any number of firms, each price-taking profit-maximising firm chooses q by equating price with marginal cost. Therefore:

$$P(x) = wx + C'(q).$$

In a long-run equilibrium we have

$$P(x) = wx + \frac{C(q)}{q}$$

Once again, the quantity that minimises $\frac{C(q)}{q}$ will also minimise $wx + \frac{C(q)}{q}$. In other words, $q_{NL} = q^*$.

What level of care will firms provide? Since firms are not obligated to take care, it is tempting to conclude that they will choose $x = 0$. However, in general this conclusion is incorrect. To see why, suppose that $\lambda = 1$ and consider a candidate long-run equilibrium in which each firm provides an inefficiently low level of care, $x < x^*$. Each firm continues to produce q^* units since the minimum of the average cost curve still occurs at q^*. The market price in this candidate equilibrium is:

$$P(x) = wx + \frac{C(q^*)}{q^*}$$

and consumers' perceived net benefit is:

$$u(nq^*) - nq^*H(x) - Pnq^*$$

This situation cannot be sustained as a competitive equilibrium. To see why, suppose that all firms chose a slightly higher level of care, x', for all units supplied, with $x < x' < x^*$. This increases each firm's average cost and marginal cost. Suppose that each firm continued to supply

q^* units, but that each of them charged a price which was greater than their new average costs. Since we have assumed that $\lambda = 1$ here, consumers can perfectly observe this new higher level of care. For each unit of the good they are willing to pay $H(x) - H(x') > 0$ for such a change, since this is the reduction in expected harm per unit of the good.

But the increase in cost per unit from providing the higher level of care is $w(x' - x) < H(x) - H(x')$, where the inequality holds as long as $x < x' < x^*$. This means that there is a price that each firm could charge which would more than cover the increase in cost from greater care, and the price increase would be *less* than the consumer increase in willingness to pay. In other words, starting from a position where $x < x^*$, all firms could make a profit by providing a greater level of care than the initial level x. In other words, even though firms are not legally obligated to take greater care, the profit motive would drive them to do so.

Moreover, if $\lambda = 1$ and since x above was arbitrary, such a profit opportunity always exists as long as $x < x^*$. The gain to consumers (that is, their willingness to pay) for an additional unit of care per good is $-H'(x)$. The marginal cost to producers is w. Hence, no further profit opportunities will exist when:

$$-H'(x) = w$$

But this is just the same condition as the efficiency condition in equation (6.3). *In other words, in contrast to the results in Chapter 4, if $\lambda = 1$ the no liability rule is efficient.*

Since profits get bid down to zero in a competitive equilibrium, the price under a rule of no liability when $\lambda = 1$ is:

$$P_{NL} = \frac{C(q^*)}{q^*} + wx^* \tag{6.4}$$

which is lower than the price under strict liability. A legal rule of no liability produces the same level of care, output and welfare as a rule of strict liability and is efficient because the market price adjusts in response to all of the costs and benefits that are incurred by each party. With a rule of strict liability, consumers are fully insured against and potential risks, but this simply drives up the costs of firms and is reflected in a higher price for the good. With a no liability rule, consumers bear the full costs of all accidents, which lowers their marginal willingness to pay for the good. However, firms are forced to charge a lower price under competitive conditions since damages no longer form part of their cost base.

The effect of each legal rule on the market outcome is shown in Figure 6.4.2.

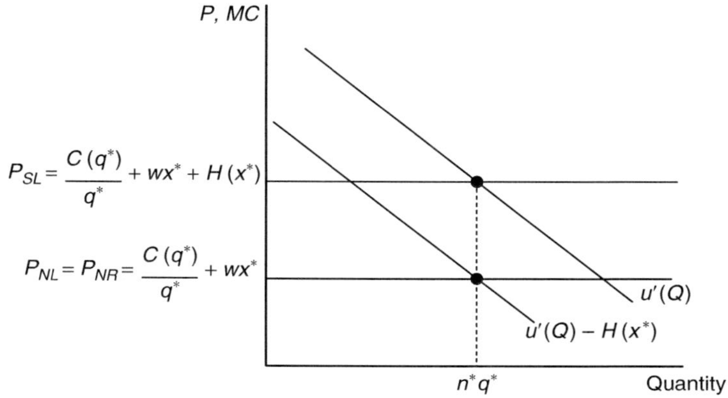

Figure 6.4.2 Equilibrium under no liability

If consumers misperceive the harmfulness of the product, then the previous result breaks down. To see why, note that if $\lambda \neq 1$, the consumer's willingness to pay for a change in the level of care provided by firms, x, is $-\lambda H'(x) \neq -H'(x)$. Firms still have an incentive to provide *some* care under a no liability rule (unless $\lambda = 0$), but their incentives no longer align exactly with efficient incentives.

Suppose, for example, that consumers underestimate the expected harmfulness of the product, so $\lambda < 1$. Then in the competitive equilibrium firms will provide care up to the point where consumer *perceived* marginal willingness to pay equals the marginal cost of care, so that:

$$-\lambda H'(x_{NL}^{\lambda}) = w$$

in the equilibrium, where x_{NL}^{λ} is the equilibrium level of care. But $\lambda < 1$, so:

$$-H'(x^*) = w = -\lambda H'(x_{NL}^{\lambda}) < -H'(x_{NL}^{\lambda})$$

This series of equalities and inequalities shows that the actual marginal benefit of care at the equilibrium, x_{NL}^{λ}, exceeds the marginal benefit at x^*, which implies that $x_{NL}^{\lambda} < x^*$. In other words, in the competitive equilibrium, firms underprovide care. In the limit, if consumers completely misperceive the product's harm, then $x_{NL}^{\lambda} = 0$, and no care would be provided.

On the other hand, if consumers *overestimate* the harmfulness of the product (so $\lambda > 1$), then the above argument is reversed. In the competitive equilibrium firms will still provide care up to the point where consumer marginal willingness to pay, so that:

$$-\lambda H'(x^{\lambda}) = w$$

But now $\lambda > 1$, so:

$$-H'(x^*) = w = -\lambda H'(x^{\lambda}) > -H'(x^{\lambda})$$

The actual marginal benefit of care at x^{λ} is less than the marginal benefit at x^*, which implies that $x^{\lambda} > x^*$, and firms overprovide care. The reason is straightforward: consumers believe that the good is very dangerous, and are willing to pay a relatively high amount at the margin, $-\lambda H'(x) > -H'(x)$ for firms to reduce care. Firms are willing to provide care as long as there is a profit opportunity for doing so, which is the case as long as $-\lambda H'(x) > w$. This provides firms with an incentive for overprovision of care.

The aggregate competitive equilibrium quantity under no liability when $\lambda < 1$ is greater than the efficient level, and when $\lambda > 1$ it is inefficiently low. To see this, note that each firm produces the same output, q_0, but that the number of firms in the industry varies with λ. To see how n changes with λ, note that the competitive equilibrium quantity is determined where the demand curve (which is determined by consumer misperceptions) meets the long-run market supply curve, or where:

$$u'[n(\lambda)q^*] - \lambda H[x(\lambda)] = \frac{C(q^*)}{q^*} + wx(\lambda) \tag{6.5}$$

Taking the total derivative yields:

$$\frac{dn}{d\lambda} = \frac{x'(\lambda)[w + \lambda H'(x(\lambda))] + H(x(\lambda))}{u''(nq^*)q^*} = \frac{H(x(\lambda))}{u''(nq^*)q^*} < 0$$

where we have used the fact that $w + \lambda H'(x(\lambda)) = 0$ in the competitive equilibrium. Total welfare is:

$$W = u[n(\lambda)q^*] - n(\lambda)C(q^*) - n(\lambda)q^*[wx(\lambda) + H(x(\lambda))] \tag{6.6}$$

As shown in the Appendix, the change in welfare with respect to λ has the following pattern:

$$\frac{dW}{d\lambda}\begin{cases} > 0 & \text{if } \lambda < 1 \\ = 0 & \text{if } \lambda = 1 \\ < 0 & \text{if } \lambda > 1 \end{cases}$$

In other words, under a no liability rule, welfare is at a maximum when consumers accurately perceive risk, and then falls away as consumers either underestimate or overestimate risk.

To summarise, in cases where there are consumer misperceptions and $\lambda \neq 1$, there will be a welfare loss which consists of two parts:

- First, there is a *price effect*: firms' marginal and average costs (and therefore the market price) are either inefficiently low (in the case where $\lambda < 1$) or inefficiently high (in the case where $\lambda > 1$). Since price equals marginal and average costs, this means that even if consumers could accurately perceive risk, they would consume either too many units of the good (in the case where $\lambda < 1$) or two few units of the good (in the case where $\lambda > 1$).
- Second, there is a *harm misperception effect*: there is a welfare loss because consumers incorrectly estimate the expected harm in each unit of the good, leading them to consume the wrong amount of the good for the level of care that is provided in equilibrium. In the case where $\lambda < 1$, this effect induces consumers to consume too many units, and in the case where $\lambda < 1$ it induces them to consume too little.

In other words, both effects tend to reinforce one another.

6.4.1.3 A negligence rule

Now suppose that firms in the industry face a negligence rule. Suppose that the due standard of care is set at the efficient level x^*. If firms meet the due standard of care, then consumers will bear all of the costs of any harm from consumption of the good. This will affect their willingness to pay for the good. On the other hand, if firms do not meet the due standard of care, then firms will be liable for any harm – and, once again, this will affect consumer demand. Thus, the consumer demand curve under a negligence rule is:

$$P = \begin{cases} u'(nq)q - \lambda H(x) & \text{if } x \geq x^* \\ u'(nq) & \text{if } x < x^* \end{cases}$$

Thus, producer profits are:

$$\pi = \begin{cases} u'(nq)q - \lambda H(x)q - qwx - C(q) & \text{if } x \geq x^* \\ u'(nq)q - qwx - qH(x) - C(q) & \text{if } x < x^* \end{cases} \tag{6.7}$$

There are three cases to consider, depending on the direction of consumer misperceptions. The outcome depends on the function $wx + \lambda H(x)$ for different values of λ. This function is shown in Figure 6.4.3.

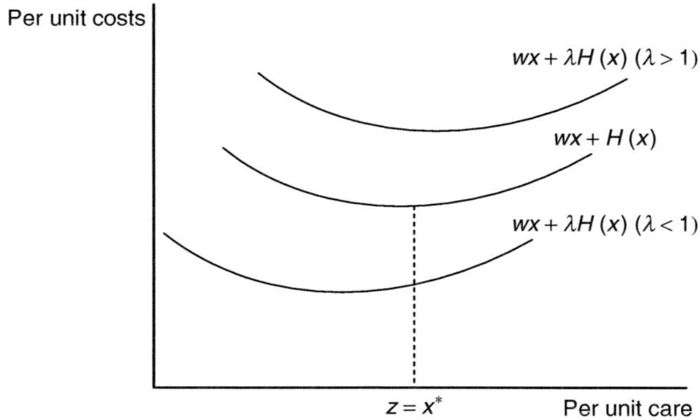

Figure 6.4.3 Equilibrium under a negligence rule

6.4.1.3.1 No consumer misperceptions ($\lambda = 1$). In this case, from equation (6.7) each firm's profit is:

$$\pi = u'(nq)q - qwx - qH(x) - C(q)$$

irrespective of the level of care. For any quantity, each firm maximises its profits by choosing $x = x^*$. Each firm therefore avoids liability and has costs of $qwx^* + C(q)$. Consumer demand is:

$$P = u'(nq) - H(x^*)$$

This is identical to the outcome under a no liability rule when $\lambda = 1$. The market price again is equal to each firm's marginal cost, so that:

$$P_{NR} = \frac{C(q^*)}{q^*} + wx^*$$

and again we have $Q_{NR} = Q_{SL} = Q_{NL} = Q^*$.

This result – the irrelevance of the legal rule for efficiency – has some interesting implications for policy analysis. For example, consider the following policy intervention. Suppose that the legal rule is a no liability rule, and suppose that consumers correctly perceive risk. Suppose that the government is considering placing a per unit tax of t on purchases of the dangerous good. Assuming that consumers correctly perceive the risks involved in consuming the dangerous good, what would be the welfare effects of this tax?

In the above model, a tax on the good drives a wedge between consumer marginal willingness to pay and production costs. But under a no liability rule, consumers *already* have a reduced their marginal willingness to pay by $H(x^*)$, since under a no liability rule they must bear the costs of any harm that the good causes. Since consumers already perceive the risks correctly and since under a no liability rule firms already provide the efficient level of care, an additional tax creates a deadweight loss, just as it does when the good is not dangerous. Once a legal rule is in place and prices can adjust to fully reflect any damage that the good may cause, *there is no role for further interventions*.

A possible case for intervention may arise if firms have some market power, or if consumers do not correctly perceive risks. However, a tax may not be the most appropriate intervention in these instances. Instead, more appropriate policies might involve lowering barriers to entry, or simply informing consumers of the true nature of the product's risks.

6.4.1.3.2 Consumers underestimate expected harm ($\lambda < 1$). In this case, each firm's profit is as in equation (6.7). For any quantity, each firm maximises its profits by choosing $x = x^*$. Each firm therefore avoids liability and has costs of $qwx^* + C(q)$. In a long-run equilibrium, average costs are again minimised at q^*. Consumer demand is:

$$P = u'(nq) - \lambda H(x^*)$$

Since $\lambda < 1$, the consumer demand curve is to the right of the demand curve for which $\lambda = 1$. In other words, because consumers underperceive risk, they demand too much of the good relative to the harm that it creates. Therefore, the demand curve meets the long-run supply curve at the point where:

$$u'(nq^*) - \lambda H(x^*) = wx^* + C(q^*)$$

This implies that $n_{NR} > n^*$. When consumers underestimate the expected harm of the product, there will be too many firms in the industry, and consumers consume too many units of the good. Welfare is lower than in the case where we have a negligence rule and $\lambda = 1$, or where there is a strict liability rule and $\lambda < 1$.

6.4.1.3.3 Consumers overestimate expected harm ($\lambda > 1$). In this case, each firm's profit is as in equation (6.7). Now, however, firms have very different incentives from the case where $\lambda < 1$. If firms choose to meet the due standard of care, consumers will bear all of the losses, and they will reduce demand by an inefficiently high amount $\lambda H(x)$, since they overperceive risk. But if firms do not meet the due standard of care, they will be found negligent and this will only cost them $H(x) < \lambda H(x)$. Therefore, each firm is better off not meeting the due standard of care and being found negligent.

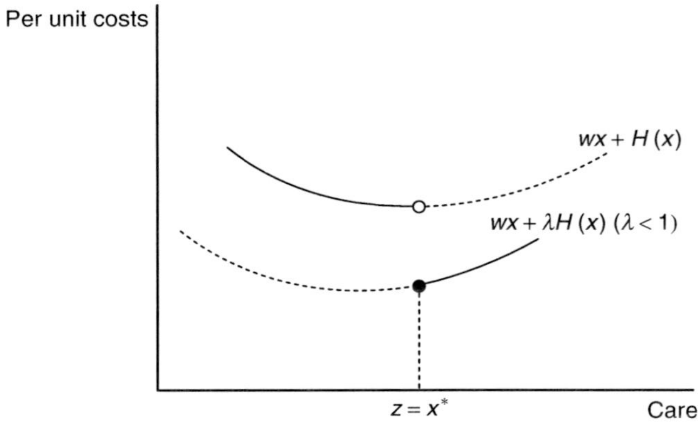

Figure 6.4.4 Equilibrium under a negligence rule when consumers underestimate harm

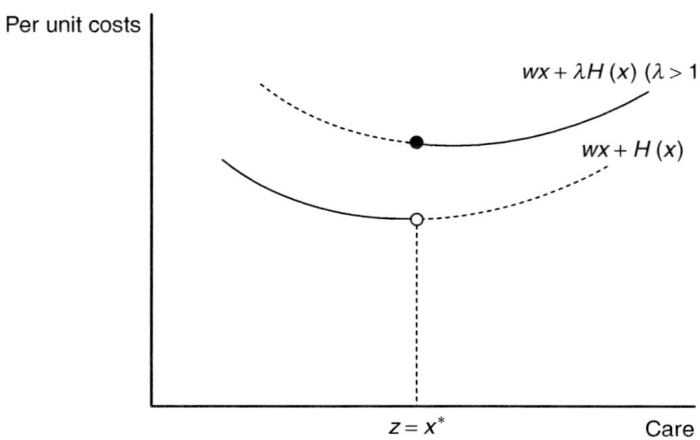

Figure 6.4.5 Equilibrium under a negligence rule when consumers overestimate harm

The profit-maximising choice of x is therefore to provide a level of care that is just slightly below x^*. Let this level be x^{oo}. By providing this level of care, each firm incurs liability for consumer harm and has costs of $qwx^{oo} + C(q) + qH(x^{oo})$. The consumer demand curve is:

$$P = u'(nq)$$

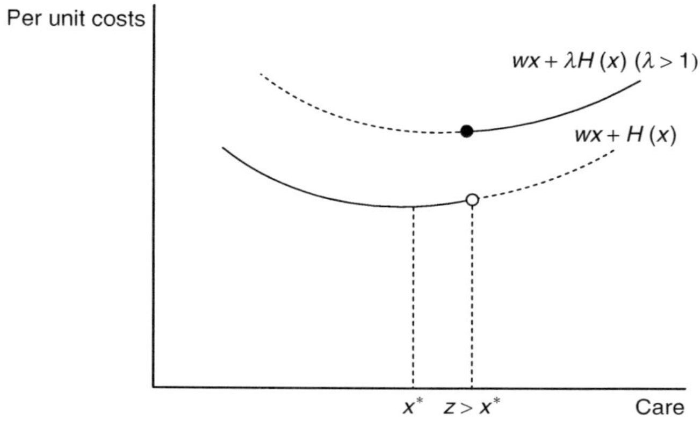

Figure 6.4.6 Equilibrium under a second-best negligence rule when consumers overestimate harm

This is almost identical to the outcome under strict liability, apart from the fact that the level of care x^{oo} is slightly less than the efficient level x^*.

There are alternative second-best negligence rules which would induce firms to choose $x = x^*$ when $\lambda > 1$.

As Figure 6.4.6 makes clear, if the due standard is set slightly higher than x^*, then profits will be:

$$\pi = \begin{cases} u'(nq)q - \lambda H(x)q - qwx - C(q) & \text{if } x \geq z \\ u'(nq)q - qwx - qH(x) - C(q) & \text{if } x < z \end{cases}$$

and firms can minimise costs by choosing x^* (and will again be found negligent). This outcome is efficient, since consumers' misperceptions will not enter the demand curve (they will be compensated for losses) and firms will provide the efficient level of care.

6.5 Product liability rules in imperfectly competitive markets: The case of Cournot oligopoly

This section considers product liability rules when markets are imperfectly competitive. The analysis focuses on the Cournot model of oligopoly. To simplify matters, we assume that all firms are identical with constant marginal costs, so $C(q) = cq$ for each firm.

6.5.1 Strict liability

Under strict liability, consumers are fully compensated for all harm. Therefore, the consumer demand curve is:

$$P(Q) = u'(Q)$$

Note again that consumer perceptions do not enter into the demand curve. Since consumers are fully compensated for all harm under the strict liability rule, their perceptions of the expected harm are irrelevant. Since firms must fully compensate consumers, each firm's profit is equal to:

$$\{P(Q) - [wx_i + H(x_i)] - c\}q_i \tag{6.8}$$

where x_i is the level of care chosen by firm i. Firms can minimise costs by choosing $x = x^*$. Therefore, each firm's profits are:

$$\pi_i = P(Q)q_i - cq_i - [wx^* + H(x^*)]q_i$$

In the Cournot model, each firm chooses its quantity, taking the choices of other firms as given. The first-order condition is:

$$P'(Q_{SL})q_{SL} + P(Q_{SL}) = c + wx^* + H(x^*)$$

Adding up across all n firms yields:

$$P'(Q_{SL})Q_{SL} + nP(Q_{SL}) = n[c + wx^* + H(x^*)] \tag{6.9}$$

or:

$$P_{SL} = \frac{\varepsilon}{\frac{1}{n}+\varepsilon}[c + wx^* + H(x^*)]$$

where ε is the elasticity of demand. Since $\frac{\varepsilon}{\frac{1}{n}+\varepsilon} > 1$, this price will be higher than the efficient price, which is $c + wx^* + H(x^*)$. Thus, market quantity will be inefficiently low, with the inefficiency declining with the number of firms. As in Chapter 4, the extent of price overshifting onto consumers depends on the extent to which the elasticity of ded changes as we move along the demand curve.

6.5.2 A no liability rule

Under a no liability rule, the demand curve facing each firm is:

$$P(Q,x_i) = u'(Q) - \lambda H(x_i)$$

and so each firm's profits are:

$$\pi_i = [P - wx_i - c_i]q_i = [u'(Q) - \lambda H(x_i) - wx_i - c_i]q_i$$

Each firm can maximise its profits by choosing x_i to minimise $wx_i + \lambda H(x_i)$. Firms will therefore choose a level of care, x_{NL}, which satisfies:

$$x_{NL} \begin{cases} < x^* & \text{if } \lambda < 1 \\ = x^* & \text{if } \lambda = 1 \\ > x^* & \text{if } \lambda > 1 \end{cases}$$

which is the same result as we had under perfect competition. This means that:

$$wx_{NL} + H(x_{NL}) \begin{cases} < wx^* + H(x^*) & \text{if } \lambda < 1 \\ = wx^* + H(x^*) & \text{if } \lambda = 1 \\ > wx^* + H(x^*) & \text{if } \lambda > 1 \end{cases} \tag{6.10}$$

Each firm's profits are:

$$\pi_i = [u'(Q) - \lambda H(x_{NL}) - wx_{NL} - c]q_i$$

Each firm again chooses its quantity, taking the choices of other firms as given. The first-order condition is:

$$u''(Q_{NL})q_{NL} + u'(Q_{NL}) = c + wx_{NL} + \lambda H(x_{NL})$$

Adding up across all n firms yields:

$$u''(Q_{NL})Q_{NL} + nu'(Q_{NL}) = n[c + wx_{NL} + \lambda H(x_{NL})] \tag{6.11}$$

The left-hand side is the same expression as the left-hand side of equation (6.9), evaluated at Q_{NL} rather than Q_{SL}. It is the sum of the individual marginal revenues of each firm. The right-hand side is the number of firms (n) multiplied by the sum of the marginal production costs, the cost of care, and the perceived harm to consumers. If $\lambda < 1$, then according to (6.10), $wx_{NL} + \lambda H(x_{NL}) < wx^* + H(x^*)$, and we must have:

$$u''(Q_{NL})Q_{NL} + nu'(Q_{NL}) < u''(Q_{SL})Q_{SL} + nu'(Q_{SL}) \tag{6.12}$$

We have assumed that $u''(Q) < 0$, but have said nothing about the sign of, $u'''(Q)$, which is the second derivative of the demand function. Let's consider the linear demand function, $P = a - Q$. If the demand function is linear, then $u'''(Q) = 0$, and the derivative of the function $f(Q) = u''(Q)Q + nu'(Q)$ is $f'(Q) = u'''(Q)Q + u''(Q) + nu''(Q) = u''(Q) + nu''(Q) < 0$, and so (6.12) implies that $Q_{NL} > Q_{SL}$. This is also true as long as $u'''(Q) < 0$, and may even be true if $u'''(Q) > 0$, as long as this is not 'too positive'.

On the other hand, if $\lambda > 1$, then according to (6.10), $wx_{NL} + \lambda H(x_{NL}) > wx^* + H(x^*)$, and $Q_{NL} < Q_{SL}$. Finally, if $\lambda = 1$, then $wx_{NL} + H(x_{NL}) = wx^* + H(x^*)$, and $Q_{NL} = Q_{SL}$.

Intuitively, under a no liability rule, firms provide care as long as consumer marginal willingness to pay [which is $-\lambda H'(x)$] exceeds the marginal cost of care w. Accordingly, if consumers underperceive risk, then firms will underprovide care, which drives down their per unit costs and induces them to produce more than they would under strict liability. If consumers overperceive risk, then firms will overprovide care, driving up their per unit costs and inducing them to produce less than they would under strict liability.

6.5.3 A negligence rule

Now suppose that each firm faces a negligence rule. Suppose that the due standard of care is set at the efficient level, x^*. The consumer demand curve is:

$$P = \begin{cases} u'(Q) - \lambda H(x_i) & \text{if } x_i \geq x^* \\ u'(Q) & \text{if } x_i < x^* \end{cases}$$

and each firm's profits are:

$$\pi = \begin{cases} u'(Q)q_i - \lambda H(x)q_i - q_i w x_i - c q_i & \textit{if } x_i - x^* \\ u'(Q)q_i - q_i w x - H(x_i)q_i - c q_i & \textit{if } x_i < x^* \end{cases} \tag{6.13}$$

As with the perfectly competitive market, there are again three cases to consider, depending on the direction of consumer misperceptions. For the same reasons, We again get the same three results:

- No misperceptions ($\lambda = 1$): $x_i = x^*$, which is the same outcome as the no liability rule when $\lambda = 1$.
- Consumers' underperceptions ($\lambda < 1$): $x_i = x^*$, which is the same outcome as the no liability rule when $\lambda = 1$.
- Consumers' overperceptions ($\lambda > 1$): $x_i \approx x^*$, with $x_i < x^*$.

Again, in the case of consumer overperceptions, there are alternative rules which would induce firms to choose $x = x^*$ when $\lambda > 1$ (that is, set the due standard slightly higher than x^*).

Consider in detail the case where consumers underperceive risk. Then the profit of each firm is:

$$\pi_i = u'(Q)q_i - \lambda H(x^*)q_i - q_i w x^* - c q_i$$

Each firm again chooses its quantity, taking the choices of other firms as given. The first-order condition is:

$$u''(Q_{NR})q_{NR} + u'(Q_{NR}) = c + wx^* + \lambda H(x^*)$$

Adding up across all n firms yields:

$$u''(Q_{NR})Q_{NR} + nu'(Q_{NR}) = n\ [c + wx^* + \lambda H(x^*)] \tag{6.14}$$

The left-hand side is again the same expression as the left-hand side of equation (6.9), evaluated at Q_{NR} rather than Q_{SL}. The right-hand side is the same as (6.9), except that we have $\lambda H(x^*)$ [$< H(x^*)$] rather than $H(x^*)$. This means that:

$$u''(Q_{NR})Q_{NR} + nu'(Q_{NR}) < u''(Q_{SL})Q_{SL} + nu'(Q_{SL}) \tag{6.15}$$

which, if the demand curve is linear or if $u'''(Q) < 0$ (or if $u'''(Q)$ is not too positive), again implies $Q_{NR} > Q_{SL}$. On the other hand, when consumers underperceive risk, the right-hand side of (6.14) is greater than the right-hand side of (6.11) [since x_{NL} minimises $wx + \lambda H(x)$]. Therefore, if consumers underperceive risk and demand curves are linear, we have:

$$Q_{SL} < Q_{NR} < Q_{NL}$$

If on the other hand consumers overperceive risk, then under a no liability rule firms will oversupply care, and consumer demand will be

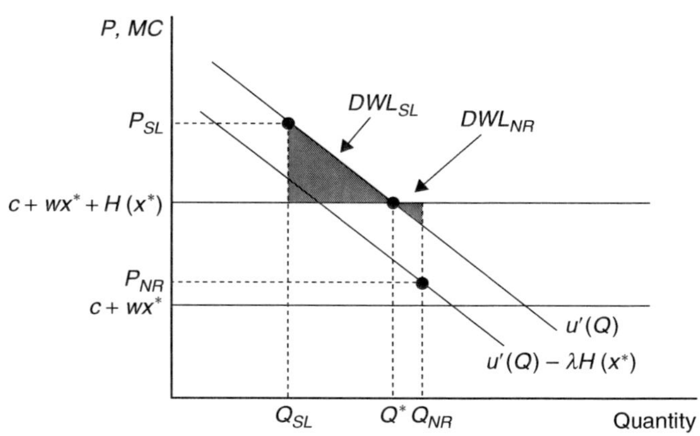

Figure 6.5.1 Cournot equilibrium under various product liability rules when consumers underperceive risk

lower than it should be. Hence in this case we will have $Q_{NL} < Q_{SL}$. Under a negligence rule, on the other hand, firms can be induced to choose the efficient level of care, but they will not be found negligent and therefore all losses are borne by consumers. These consumers overestimate harm, so consumer demand will again be less than what it should be. Thus, in the case where $\lambda > 1$, the previous ranking is reversed and we have $Q_{SL} > Q_{NR} > Q_{NL}$.

6.5.4 Welfare analysis

In the case of linear demand curves, welfare analysis in the Cournot model is straightforward, and simply requires computation of the sum of the consumer surplus and producer profits. To see how the efficiency of different rules can be compared, suppose that consumers underperceive risk. Let us compare a rule of strict liability and a negligence rule. If we take the linear demand function $u'(Q) = P = a - Q$ and plug $u''(Q) = -1$ into equations (6.9), (6.11) and (6.14), we get:

$$Q_{SL} = \frac{n}{n+1}[a - H(x^*) - wx^* - c] = \frac{n}{n+1}Q^* \tag{6.16}$$

and

$$\begin{aligned} Q_{NR} &= \frac{n}{n+1}[a - \lambda H(x^*) - wx^* - c] \\ &= \frac{n}{n+1}Q^* + \frac{n}{n+1}(1-\lambda)H(x^*) \end{aligned} \tag{6.17}$$

where Q^* is the efficient quantity. Since firms choose the efficient level of care under each legal rule, the welfare loss under each legal rule is simply the usual deadweight loss triangle of Cournot oligopoly, of Cournot oligopoly as shown in Figure 6.5.1. The first thing to notice is that the negligence rule may actually be efficient here, despite firms having market power and despite consumers not being able to accurately perceive risk. This happens if $Q_{NR} = Q^*$, which is true if:

$$Q^* = \frac{n}{n+1}Q^* + \frac{n}{n+1}(1-\lambda)H(x^*)$$

or:

$$HHI = \frac{(1-\lambda)\ H(x^*)}{Q^*} \tag{6.18}$$

where HHI is the *Herfindahl–Hirschman concentration index*, which is defined as $HHI = \sum_{i=1}^{n} s_i^2$, and in this case is simply equal to:

$$HHI = \sum_{i=1}^{n} s_i^2 = \sum_{i=1}^{n} \left(\frac{q_i}{Q} \right)^2 = \sum_{i=1}^{n} \left(\frac{Q/n}{Q} \right)^2 = \frac{1}{n} \tag{6.19}$$

The HHI is often used a measure of the degree of market power in the industry (although, as we show in Chapter 10, there are several problems with this interpretation). When markets are imperfectly competitive, there are two opposing welfare effects of a negligence rule when consumers underperceive risk. The first is the standard welfare loss from Cournot oligopoly, which is the *output-reducing effect* and is more severe, the fewer firms there are in the industry. The second is the *output-enhancing effect,* which in the absence of market power would result in an inefficiently *high* level of output and depends on the extent to which consumers underperceive risk. In equation (6.18), these two opposing (and otherwise welfare-reducing effects) offset each other exactly.

Another way to understand the effects of a negligence rule is to investigate what happens to welfare when there is a slight change in consumer misperceptions. Welfare under a negligence rule is (assuming a linear demand curve):

$$\begin{aligned} W(\lambda) = CS_{NR} + \pi_{NR} &= aQ_{NR}(\lambda) - \frac{1}{2}[Q_{NR}(\lambda)]^2 - \lambda H(x^*) - PQ_{NR} \\ &+ [P - c - wx^*]Q_{NR}(\lambda) \\ &= [a - c - H(x^*) - wx^*]Q_{NR}(\lambda) - \frac{1}{2}[Q_{NR}(\lambda)]^2 \end{aligned}$$

Under a negligence rule, the change in welfare when λ changes by a small amount is therefore equal to:

$$W'(\lambda) = [a - c - H(x^*) - wx^*]\frac{dQ_{NR}}{d\lambda} - \frac{dQ_{NR}}{d\lambda}Q_{NR}$$

Since $\frac{dQ_{NR}}{d\lambda} < 0$, this is positive as long as:

$$a - Q_{NR} < c + H(x^*) + wx^* \tag{6.20}$$

This expression has a very intuitive economic explanation. From equation (6.17), we know under a negligence rule that if λ rises, Q_{NR} falls. Equation (6.20) simply says that this reduction in quantity will be welfare improving if $a - Q_{NR}$ (which is the marginal consumption benefit of the last unit consumed), is less than the marginal social cost of that unit, which is $c + H(x^*) + wx^*$. Thus, a rise in welfare as a result of λ rising can only occur if the quantity that is produced under a negligence rule exceeds the efficient quantity.

More generally, the total welfare loss under a negligence rule can be lower or higher than the welfare loss under a strict liability rule. The triangle deadweight loss from a rule of strict liability is:

$$DWL_{SL} = \frac{1}{2}(Q^{*} - Q_{SL})^{2} = \frac{1}{2}\left(Q^{*} - \frac{n}{n+1}Q^{*}\right)^{2} = \frac{1}{2}\frac{(Q^{*})^{2}}{(n+1)^{2}} \qquad (6.21)$$

whereas the triangle deadweight loss from a negligence rule is:

$$DWL_{NR} = \frac{1}{2}(Q^{*} - Q_{NR})^{2} = \frac{1}{2}\left(Q^{*} - \frac{n}{n+1}Q^{*} - \frac{n}{n+1}(1-\lambda)H(x^{*})\right)^{2} \qquad (6.22)$$

A strict liability rule is preferable if:

$$DWL_{SL} < DWL_{NR} \Leftrightarrow HHI < \frac{(1-\lambda)H(x^{*})}{2Q^{*}} \qquad (6.23)$$

As the number of firms grows large, output increases and the left-hand side of this inequality grows smaller. Thus as the industry becomes less concentrated the inequality in (6.23) is more likely to be satisfied. Intuitively, when (6.23) holds the output-reducing effect is dominated by the output-enhancing effect, and a rule of strict liability is efficient. Moreover, as market concentration falls, the welfare loss from a strict liability rule falls, and the welfare loss from a negligence rule rises as output grows larger and exceeds the efficient quantity by an ever greater.

On the other hand, as market power increases and the number of firms declines, it is less likely that the inequality in (6.23) holds, and so more likely that a negligence rule becomes efficient. As market concentration rises, the welfare loss from underperception of risk and overconsumption becomes dominated by the output reducing effect under the negligence rule.

6.6 Application: Employment law

We can also interpret the model of product liability in the context of labour markets and employment regulation. In the context of employment law, workers are now suppliers of the product (labour services) and firms are the "consumers". Suppose that there are L identical workers (where we normalise so that $L = 1$), each with a reservation wage of $\overline{\omega}$. Each worker supplies either one unit of labour, or none. Workers have no bargaining power: they must accept the wage that is offered to them.

Firms are all identical and earn profits of $R-\bar{\omega}$ from employing a worker (where R is the firm's revenue), and nothing if they do not. Firms maximise their profits. A competitive equilibrium in this situation is where each firm maximises its profits, and workers choose to work at the firm which offers them the highest wage.

Suppose first that jobs are completely safe – workplace accidents do not occur. In the competitive equilibrium, firms offer workers a wage of $\bar{\omega}$, which workers accept. Welfare is $R-\bar{\omega}$.

Now suppose that jobs are unsafe. The key modification that we now introduce into our previous model of product liability law is to assume that *both* workers and firms can affect the expected level of harm to workers.

To this end, suppose that for each unit of labour that a worker supplies, there is expected marginal harm of $H(x_i, x_v)$, where x_i is the level of care per unit of labour provided by firms, and x_v is the level of care per unit of labour provided by employees. Let w_i and w_v be the marginal costs of care for employers and workers.

The efficient levels of care here are characterised by the usual marginal conditions: care should be provided by both parties up to the point where the marginal benefit per unit of care supplied equals the marginal cost. This means that:

$$w_i = -\frac{\partial H(x_i^* x_v^*)}{\partial x_i}$$

and

$$w_v = -\frac{\partial H(x_i^* x_v^*)}{\partial x_v}$$

We will assume that at these efficient levels of care, it is still efficient for firms to hire all of the workers, so that

$$R-\bar{\omega}-[w_i x_i^* + w_v x_v^* + H(x_i^* x_v^*)] > 0$$

Let us now examine legal rules in this setting. First, note that if workers and firms can negotiate *directly* over the level of care that each provided, then using Coasean-type reasoning, *any* legal rule will be efficient. However, in the absence of the usual Coasean preconditions, legal rules will matter for efficiency. The easiest way to see this is to analyse three different legal rules.

6.6.1.1 *A no liability rule*

Suppose, then, that direct negotiations over care are not possible. We will assume throughout the analysis that the level of care taken by firms is observable and can form part of an employment contract, but that the level of care taken by workers (which occurs subsequent to the contract being agreed to) is not.

First, suppose that a rule of no liability is in place, so that employees must bear the full costs of any accident. Note that for *any* level of care provided by firms under a no liability rule, workers will be induced to supply the level of care that minimises $w_v x_v + H(x_i, x_v)$. The reason for this is straightforward: having chosen their level of care, firms will – in order to minimise their wage bill of $\overline{\omega} + w_v x_v + H(x_i, x_v)$ – offer the wage that makes these costs as small as possible. Workers are free to choose any level of care that they wish, but having observed the level of care and the wage that firms are offering, they will choose to supply the level that minimises $\overline{\omega} + w_v x_v + H(x_i, x_v)$, since this gives them the highest net benefit at the wage that has been offered to them. Any other level of care would leave them out of pocket, since under a no liability rule it is workers who bear the costs of any accident.

Will employers take any care under this legal rule? Suppose that they do not take any care. We will show that this cannot occur in a competitive equilibrium.

To see this, note that for any wage $\overline{\omega}$, in this section in the absence of any care that is taken by employers, workers would need to be given a wage of at least:

$$\omega^0 = \overline{\omega} + w_v x_v^0 + H(0, x_v^0) \tag{6.24}$$

in order to be willing to supply labour, where x_v^0 minimises $w_v x_v + H(0, x_v)$. Since workers' cost of care is $w_v x_v^0$ and their expected harm is $H(0, x_v^0)$, they will not be willing to work unless (6.24) is satisfied.

So, suppose that firms take no care and pay this wage. Then all workers accept and the firm's profits are:

$$R - [\overline{\omega} + w_v x_v^0 + H(0, x_v)]$$

which we assume to be non-negative. Is this situation sustainable as an equilibrium? No. Suppose that a 'rogue' firm offered a lower wage of $\omega^* < \omega^0$ in exchange for a commitment to supply the efficient level of care, x_i^*, and where

$$\omega^* = \bar{\omega} + w_v x_v^* + H(x_i^*, x_v^*)$$

This rogue firm's costs are:

$$\omega^* + w_i x_i^*$$

and so it will make greater profits from undertaking this strategy as long as:

$$\omega^* + w_i x_i^* < \omega^0 \tag{6.25}$$

On the other hand, workers will be no worse off under this wage, since:

$$\omega^* - w_v x_v^* - H(x_i^*, x_v^*) = \bar{\omega} \tag{6.26}$$

Is a wage-care combination that satisfies (6.25) and (6.26) possible? If it is, then the rogue firm will earn higher profits than all of its competitors and leave workers as well off as they were with the other firms. Now since (x_i^*, x_v^*) is efficient, we know that:

$$w_i x_i^* + w_v x_v^* + H(x_i^*, x_v^*) < w_v x_v^0 + H(0, x_v^0) \tag{6.27}$$

If the 'rogue' firm offers the worker the wage ω^*, it will leave workers no worse off, but the increase in profit to the 'rogue' firm will be:

$$\omega^0 - (\omega^* + w_i x_i^*) = \bar{\omega} + w_v x_v^0 + H(0, x_v^0) - [\bar{\omega} + w_v x_v^* + H(x_i^*, x_v^*) + w_i x_i^*] > 0$$

Where the last inequality follows from (6.27). Therefore, a situation where firms supply no care cannot be an equilibrium.

But this reasoning applies to any positive level of care, with $x_i \neq x_i^*$, which means that the only competitive equilibrium under a no liability rule is where both firms and workers supply the efficient level of care. To check that this really is a competitive equilibrium, note that in such an equilibrium, firms will offer a wage of:

$$\omega^* = \bar{\omega} + w_v x_v^* + H(x_i^*, x_v^*)$$

At this wage, workers will voluntarily choose to supply x_v^* units of care, even though firms cannot monitor or observe the level of care taken by workers. And, beginning from this equilibrium, there is no combination of care and wages that a 'rogue' firm could offer that would increase profits and be accepted by workers. Hence it is the only competitive equilibrium.

6.6.2 Strict liability

The situation is quite different under a strict liability rule. In this case, firms are liable for all harm that workers incur in the workplace. But if firms cannot observe workers' care levels, then the previous reasoning breaks down.

To see this, suppose that firms choose the efficient level of care, and that they want to induce workers to also choose x_v^*, the workers' efficient level of care. Note that under a strict liability rule, firms certainly have an incentive to try to do: under a strict liability rule it is firms that bear the costs of harm to workers if an accident occurs.

Suppose that firms offer workers a wage of

$$\omega = \overline{\omega} + w_v x_v^* \tag{6.28}$$

As much as firms would like it to be the case, this will simply not induce workers to choose the efficient level of care. The reason is straightforward: worker care is unobservable and non-contractible, and so a rational worker will simply pocket the wage in (6.28) and supply no care, so $x_v = 0$. This happens because workers are compensated for all harm under a strict liability rule – there is no benefit to the worker taking any care, even if they are paid to do so.

Hence, under a rule of strict liability, firms will offer a wage of $\overline{\omega}$, and will incur total costs of

$$\overline{\omega} + w_i x_i^0 + H(x_i^0, 0)$$

This is the unique competitive equilibrium here, and so the rule of strict liability is not efficient.

6.6.3 Strict liability with a defence of contributory negligence

Finally, let us consider a rule of strict liability with a defence of contributory negligence. Suppose that the due standard of care for workers is $z_v = x_v^*$, and suppose that firms offer the following wage and care combination:

$$\omega_{SLDCN}^* = \overline{\omega} + w_v x_v^* \tag{6.29}$$

This wage–care combination will induce workers to behave efficiently, and this is the unique competitive equilibrium. The reason for this is straightforward: under this legal rule, firms are liable for the costs of accidents *unless* workers behave negligently. Thus, if workers are offered the wage–care combination in (6.29) and choose a level of care that is *less* than the efficient level, they will bear the costs of any accidents and will therefore receive less than their reservation wage in expectation. In other words, when faced with the wage–care combination in (6.29) under this legal rule, worker net benefits are maximised by them choosing the efficient level of care. And, since firms are liable for costs once workers behave efficiently, it is also in firms' interests to minimise these costs, and so firms too behave efficiently.

In other words, for any other wage–care combination that is offered, a 'rogue' firm can always offer the wage–care combination in (6.29) and make higher profits. Furthermore, the only wage–care combination where such profit-boosting behaviour is *not* possible is precisely the combination in (6.29). Hence (6.29) is the unique competitive equilibrium under this legal rule, which means that it produces efficient outcomes.

6.7 Notes

The basic insight of the analysis in this chapter – that changes in consumer willingness to pay for quality will induce firms to offer greater quality levels – is due to Rosen (1974), who examines product quality and variety in competitive markets. The analysis of product liability rules in Cournot oligopoly follows Polinksy and Rogerson (1983), although they do not consider the case where consumers overestimate expected harm. The condition for the superiority of the negligence rule in equation (6.23) is stated by Polinksy and Rogerson (1983), although the proof provided here which directly compares triangle deadweight losses, is to my knowledge, new. Spulber (1989) contains an excellent analysis of product liability rules.

6.8 Appendix

This appendix shows how welfare changes in a competitive market under a no liability rule when consumer perceptions of risk, λ, change. Welfare is given by equation (6.6):

$$W = u[n(\lambda)q_0] - n(\lambda)C(q_0) - n(\lambda)q_0[wx(\lambda) + H(x(\lambda))]$$

The change in welfare as λ changes is:

$$\frac{dW}{d\lambda} = n'(\lambda)\left\{u'[n(\lambda)q_0]q_0 - C(q_0) - q_0[wx(\lambda) + H(x(\lambda))]\right\} - n(\lambda)q_0x'(\lambda)[w + H'(x)]$$

This expression has two components. Let us consider the first. The term $n'(\lambda)$ is negative. The term $u'[n(\lambda)q_0]q_0 - C(q_0) - q_0[wx(\lambda) + H(x(\lambda))]$ is the difference between marginal social consumption benefits and marginal social costs. It is negative when $\lambda < 1$ (since consumers purchase too many units of the good in that case) and positive when $\lambda > 1$ (since consumers consume too few units in that case). The product of these two terms together is therefore positive if $\lambda < 1$, and negative if $\lambda > 1$.

The next term, $-n(\lambda)q_0x'(\lambda)[w + H'(x)]$, is the change in the social costs of care as λ changes. The term $x'(\lambda)$ is positive. The term $w + H'(x)$ is negative when $\lambda < 1$ (since care is underprovided in this case), and is positive when $\lambda > 1$ (since in that case care is overprovided). Hence the term $-n(\lambda)q_0x'(\lambda)[w + H'(x)]$ is positive if $\lambda < 1$, and negative if $\lambda > 1$.

Thus, the two components of $\frac{dW}{d\lambda}$ have the same sign, and so $\frac{dW}{d\lambda}$ is positive if $\lambda < 1$, and negative if $\lambda > 1$.

6.9 Exercises

1. Suppose there is a single monopoly firm that produces a single good, Q. The ordinary demand curve for this good is:

$$Q = 1 - P$$

where P is the price of the good and Q is the quantity demanded. Suppose that marginal costs of production are constant and equal to $c = 0$.

(a) What is the Pareto-optimal price and quantity? How much profit does the firm earn if it charges this price?

Now suppose that the good is potentially harmful to consumers. Let $0 < l < 1$ be the consumer's expected dollar loss per unit of the good consumed. The firm can completely eliminate these losses by taking care when it produces each unit of the good. The firm's per-unit cost of care is $k < l$. Consumers are assumed to be unable to take care, but can perfectly observe the firm's choice of care.

(b) Is it efficient for the firm to take care? Explain.

Now consider the following legal rules:

- No Liability
- Strict Liability
- Negligence Rule where the due standard of care is the efficient level of care.

Suppose that the firm acts as a monopolist.

(c) For each legal rule, compute the firm's profits when it takes care and when it does not take care. Does the monopolist always choose the efficient level of care? Which legal rule maximises aggregate welfare? Which legal rule does the firm prefer? Which legal rule do consumers prefer?

(d) Suppose that when implementing the negligence rule in part (b), the court makes a mistake and sets the due standard of care *below* the efficient level of care. Does your answer in part (b) change?

(e) Would your answers in parts (a) and (b) change if $k > l$?

Now suppose that consumers misperceive the losses that are associated with consuming the potentially harmful good. Specifically, if the actual expected losses are $l > 0$, the consumer perceives these as $(1 - \alpha)l$. Here,

$0 \leq \alpha \leq 1$ is the degree of the consumer's misperception. If $\alpha = 0$ then the consumer correctly perceives the potential losses that might be incurred, and if $\alpha = 1$ then the consumer completely misperceives the potential losses.

Consider again the following legal rules:

- No Liability
- Strict Liability
- Negligence Rule where the due standard of care is the efficient level of care.

Suppose again that the firm acts as a monopolist.

(f) For each legal rule and for any level of α, compute the firm's profits when it takes care and when it does not. Does the monopolist always choose the efficient level of care? Which legal rule maximises aggregate welfare? Which legal rule does the firm prefer? Which legal rule do consumers prefer?

(g) Now suppose that there are now two firms in the industry, labelled A and B. They act as Cournot duopolists, choosing quantities Q and Q (and levels of care) to maximise their own profits, taking the quantity choice and choice of care of the other firms as given.

Consider the following legal rules:

- No Liability
- Strict Liability
- Negligence Rule where the due standard of care is the efficient level of care.

(h) For each legal rule and for any level of α, find the Cournot equilibrium choice of quantities and care levels. Do the firms always choose the efficient level of care? Which legal rule maximises aggregate welfare? Which legal rule do the firms prefer? Which legal rule do consumers prefer?

7
The Economics of Property Rights

7.1 Introduction

This chapter examines one of the most important institutions in market economies: private property rights. Private ownership of property rights over an asset typically consists of a 'bundle' of rights, which usually include:

1. The right to ***use*** the asset;
2. The right to ***exclude*** others from using the asset; and
3. The right to ***dispose*** of the asset.

Legal rules governing private property are designed primarily to resolve conflicts between individuals who – for one reason or another – have overlapping property rights along one or more of these dimensions. This chapter examines the economics of all three features of property rights and how legal institutions and rules governing usage, exclusion and disposal can affect the efficiency of resource allocation. In particular, the analysis focuses on the broad economic issues relating to overlapping usage rights, overlapping exclusion rights, and overlapping disposal rights.

The first key insight regarding private usage and exclusion rights is the phenomenon of the *twin tragedies*: the tragedy of the *commons*, and the tragedy of the *anticommons*. Both overlapping usage rights *and* overlapping exclusion rights (as opposed to single user rights and single exclusion rights) can lead to resource misallocation and reduce economic well-being. Moreover, the extent of the economic waste increases as the number of users or excluders increases. We also show in this chapter that overlapping disposal rights can lead to similar inefficiencies.

The role of an efficient legal system is to design rules to minimise the likelihood of these phenomena occurring and, in so doing, minimise resource misallocation and economic waste, and maximise net economic benefits. However, even if individuals enjoy non-overlapping usage, exclusion and disposal rights over an economic resource, other kinds of efficiency losses are possible. Most importantly, property rights may be ill defined and/or insecure. Insecure property rights create incentives for *rent-seeking activity*, which is the devotion of valuable economic resources to transferring or appropriating existing resources (and preventing such transfers and appropriation from occurring), as opposed to using resources for productive purposes and adding economic value. Empirically, in some economies the efficiency losses associated with insecure property rights may dwarf the efficiency costs associated with overlapping usage, exclusion and disposal rights.

Finally, the chapter discusses some economic aspects of intellectual property rights. In particular, we use second-best welfare analysis to analyse the optimal length of a patent, which is a temporary monopoly right over a piece of intellectual property. The chapter is structured as follows. Section 7.2 examines the difference between property rights and liability rules using the concept of transaction costs. Section 7.3 examines the economic costs that are associated with overlapping usage, exclusion and disposal rights to property. Section 7.4 develops a simple model of insecure property rights, and studies the economic costs that are associated with insecure title. Section 7.5 turns to the economics of intellectual property rights, illustrating some of the main issues by looking at the costs and benefits of patent law.

7.2 Property rights versus liability rules

A property right endows the owner with the right to use, exclude or dispose of an economic asset. A *liability rule*, on the other hand, does *not* create a right to exclude another from using a resource. Instead, as we have seen in Chapter 4, a liability rule creates a right to claim *damages* for certain *injuries* to a resource. That is, liability rules state the conditions under which the 'injurer' is legally obligated to make a monetary transfer to the 'victim'.

Often property rights and liability rules coexist on the same economic asset. For example, on the one hand, individual A may enjoy a property right over a car – individual B cannot transfer the right to use the car the car from A simply by taking it and then paying compensation for damages to A in court. On the other hand, although A's right to the car may be absolute against attempted takings by private individuals, it may only be a qualified right against the government, which may be legally able take A's car for public use, subject only to having to pay individual A a 'fair' value for the car. Thus A may enjoy a property right against B, but may only enjoy a liability rule against the government.

How should we distinguish between property rights and liability rules? One useful way is to distinguish the two by referring to the legal remedy that is available to a prospective or actual victim. This is done as follows:

- If a party has a right to enjoin (prevent) the injury-causing conduct, then the person can be said to have a property right, since the threat of the injunction should deter a potential injurer from seeking to appropriate the right without negotiating with the owner and obtaining the owner's consent.
- If a party only has a right to compensatory damages, then he is only protected by a liability rule, because anyone who is prepared to pay the cost of injury to the victim will not be deterred from inflicting damage, and will not bother to negotiate with the owner and obtain the owner's consent.

The key distinction is in terms of *consent* or *voluntary transactions*. Because accidents are usually only *probabilistic* externalities, torts and liability rules involve *non-voluntary* transfers of wealth between victims and injurers. In other words, in certain circumstances a liability rule allows resources to be transferred from the victim to the injurer (or vice versa) without the victim's (or injurer's) *consent*.

On the other hand, the transfer of a property right *requires the owner's consent to the transfer*; this requirement prevents one person from taking something belonging to another, even if it is shown that the thing is worth more to him than the owner. In other words, property rights channel transactions away from the legal system and into the market (voluntary transactions), whereas liability rules allow transactions to be made via the legal system, bypassing markets.

Ideally, which factors should determine whether a person should hold a property right or a liability rule? The classic answer to this question can be found by analysing *transaction costs*. When the costs of arranging voluntary transactions are low enough, then the property right approach is economically preferable to the liability rule approach, because, in general, markets are a more reliable register of values than the legal system. On the other hand, when transaction costs are high enough, the property right approach is inferior, because the requirement of consent and voluntary transfer will prevent resources from being shifted to their most valuable uses. *In an efficient legal system, property rights will be used in settings of relatively low transaction costs, and liability rules will be used in settings of relatively high transaction costs.*

The transaction cost analysis of property rights versus liability rules is best illustrated by returning to the framework studied in Chapter 4.

Consider Figure 7.2.1. In this figure the amount of production (and pollution) is measured from right to left, beginning at the point O_F, which is the factory's origin.

Suppose that the residents enjoy a property right over clean air, which means that the factory cannot produce without first obtaining the residents' explicit consent, irrespective of how much the factory is willing to compensate the residents. The starting point for any negotiations is therefore O_F. In the absence of transaction costs the outcome under a property right would be Q_{LR}, where all possible gains from trade (A + B + C + D) are exhausted.

However, if there are transaction costs equal to $\$t$ per unit traded, then the outcome under a property right is Q_{PR}, where the marginal gains from trade are equal to the marginal transaction costs. This is not only inefficient in the usual sense (resulting in a welfare loss of A), but because of the transaction costs that the parties incur, the gains from trade are only C + D. The area B is not gained by the parties as a result of the costs of transacting. A property right here results in welfare gains of C + D relative to the no-trade situation.

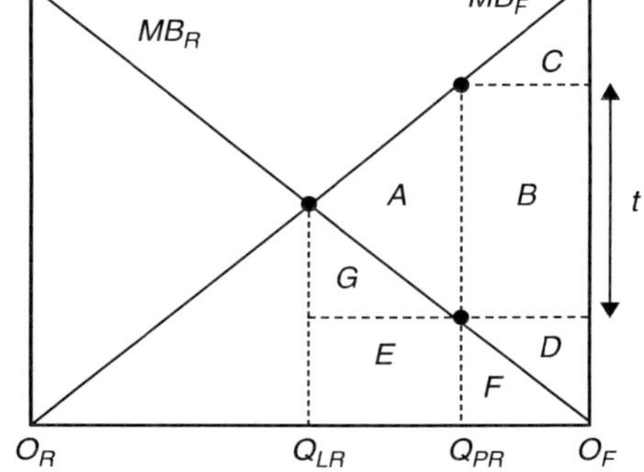

Figure 7.2.1 Property rights and transaction costs

On the other hand, if the residents only enjoy a liability rule, they must be compensated for damages from pollution – but if damages are computed accurately and fully compensate them for harm, then this will leave them no better off nor worse off than they were before the factory emitted any smoke. The factory would produce smoke up to the point at which their marginal benefit equals the marginal compensation paid to the residents. This occurs at point Q_{LR}. The factory would pay the residents the loss in benefits, which is E + F + G, and the residents would remain no worse off, whilst the factory would gain (A + B + C + D + E + F + G), for a net gain of (A + B + C + D).

Naturally, the residents prefer the property right to the liability rule, since even in a world of high transaction costs the former arrangement gives them a net gain of C, whereas the liability rule gives them a net gain of zero. Conversely, the factory would prefer a liability rule, since this gives them a net gain of (A + B + C + D), whereas the property right in a world of high transaction costs gives them a net gain of D.

7.2.1.1 *When are liability rules inferior to property rights?*

The preceding analysis showed that from an efficiency point of view, the liability rule is superior. But does the analysis necessarily imply that a liability rule is *always* superior to a property right?: after all, even in the case of zero transaction costs, both give the same outcome in the above situation. So why would a property right *ever* be preferable? One possible reason for preferring a property right when transaction costs are small is that courts may underestimate the entitlement holder's true valuation of the activity, instead preferring some measure of market value rather than personal subjective value.

Consider, for example, Figure 7.2.2. Suppose that a court estimates that the market marginal value of the residents' right to clean air is *v*, and under a liability rule awards them compensation on this basis. Then the factory will produce excessively, at $Q'_{LR} > Q_{LR}$. The factory will gain A + B + C + D + E + F + G + H + I and pay compensation (D + E + F + H), for a net gain of (A + B + C + G + I). The residents will be compensated (D + E + F + H), but will lose E + F + G + H + I + J, for a net gain of D – (G + I + J).

The overall welfare gain (relative to the initial situation of no trade) is A + B + C + D – J. The welfare loss from excessive production of the factory is J. Thus, for sufficiently small transaction costs and a sufficiently severe underestimation of the subjective value that the residents place on clean air, a property right may be preferable to a liability rule.

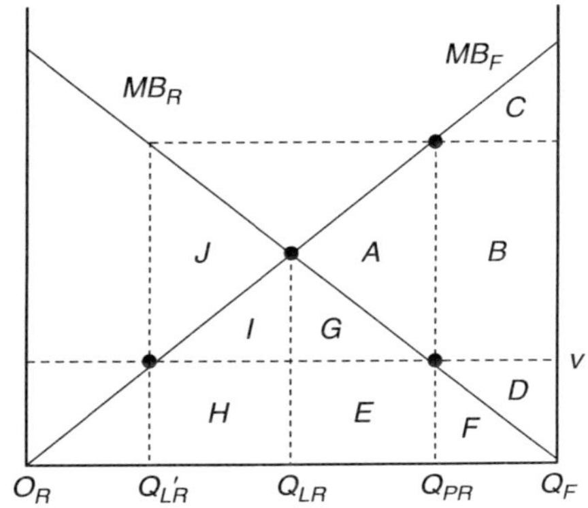

Figure 7.2.2 Liability rules and transaction costs

7.3 Overlapping and conflicting property rights

Property rights and property law play a key role in facilitating the creation of economic value. One key function of private property rights is the creation of incentives for internalising both positive and negative externalities. This privatisation of social costs and benefits reduces opportunities for – and incentives for – free-riding. This free-riding can manifest itself in very different ways. This section examines the most well-known benefit of private property rights: the virtues of single versus multiple usage and exclusion rights.

The key economic issues involved in overlapping or multiple usage and exclusion rights are best illustrated by the following simple example. Consider an economic asset, from which a valuable but depletable resource can be extracted. The asset replenishes itself in each period, but the extent of replenishment depends on the amount that is depleted in each period. The *sustainable* aggregate benefit of extraction is defined to be the (constant) aggregate benefit that can be obtained each year into the indefinite future.

Suppose that there are a large number of identical downstream firms which may extract the resource and use it as an input into production. To simplify matters, suppose that each firm either extracts one unit of the resource, or none. Let N denote the number of firms extracting at each point in time. This number N will be determined endogenously by the institutional arrangements that are in place.

Individual and aggregate extraction costs are normalised to zero. The individual and aggregate benefits of extraction vary with the number

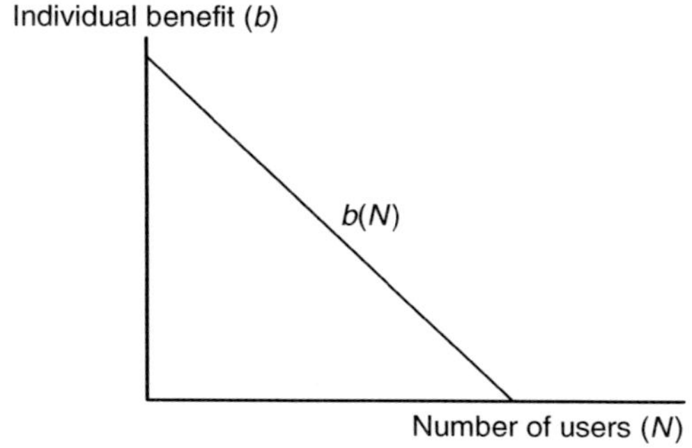

Figure 7.3.1 Individual benefits

of firms using the asset. The individual benefit in each period to each firm using the asset is $b(N)$, with $b(N) \geq 0$, $b'(N) < 0$ and $b''(N) \leq 0$. Individual benefits as a function of N are shown in Figure 7.3.1. These properties of the individual benefit function reflect the assumption that the individual benefit to each firm of using the asset is decreasing in the number of firms. This negative congestion-type externality could occur for a number of reasons. For instance, as more firms extract the resource, the likelihood of each firm being able to extract resources with an acceptably high quality could decline. Alternatively, in the more general case where there are positive extraction costs, for a given level of resource quality, per unit extraction costs could rise with the number for firms.

The aggregate benefit is:

$$B(N) = Nb(N)$$

At first, as more firms extract the resource, $B(N)$ rises with N, so the social marginal net benefit $B'(N) = b(N) + Nb'(N) > 0$ for some $N > 0$.

However, as the number of firms N rises, at some point the sustainable benefit begins to decline, and thus the net present value of aggregate benefits also declines. This happens because the change in the marginal social benefit is:

$$B''(N) = 2b'(N) + b''(N) < 0$$

Since there is a level of N where $b(N)=0$ [and so $B(N)=0$ as well], there must a point where we reach the maximum sustainable benefits of extraction, which we denote by B^*. Let N^* be the number of firms at which the maximum sustainable aggregate benefits of extraction are reached. That is,

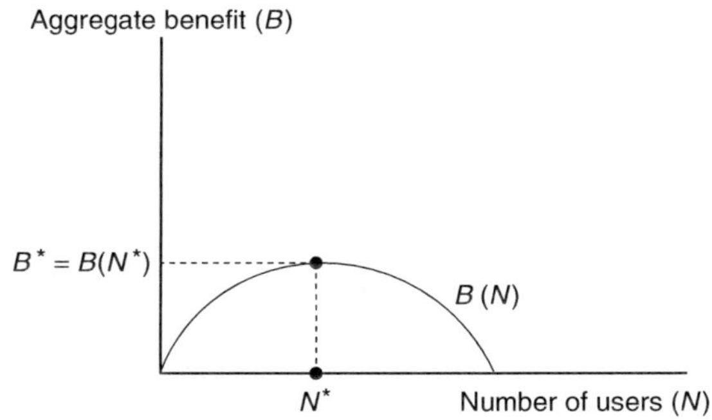

Figure 7.3.2 Aggregate benefits

$B^* = B(N^*)$, with $B'(N^*) = 0$, $B'(N) > 0$ for $N < N^*$ and $B'(N) < 0$ for $N > N^*$. This is shown in Figure 7.3.2.

The economic question surrounding legal rules governing usage rights here is straightforward: what is the legal rule which provides incentives for the maximum sustainable aggregate benefits to be achieved? Consider the following three legal rules:

1. **Open access with overlapping usage rights:** Under this arrangement, there are no restrictions on the usage rights of any firm.
2. **Private ownership with a single excluder:** Under this arrangement, there is a single owner who can charge users a price P for the right to extract the resource, and who can also exclude those who do not pay this fee.
3. **Private ownership with multiple excluders.** Under this arrangement, there are n > 1 upstream owners indexed by $i = 1,\ldots,n$ *each* of whom is permitted to charge users a price P_i for the right of downstream firms to extract the resource. Further, any one of the upstream owners can exclude a user who does not pay the fee P_i. Thus, each downstream firm must pay a total fee of $P = \sum_{i=1}^{n} P_i$, which is the sum of the individual fees charged by each owner.

7.3.2 Open access with overlapping usage rights

Under the open access legal rule, in deciding whether to exploit the resource or not, each downstream firm compares its marginal private benefit of extraction with its private marginal cost. Under open access, the private marginal cost is assumed to be zero, and for any number

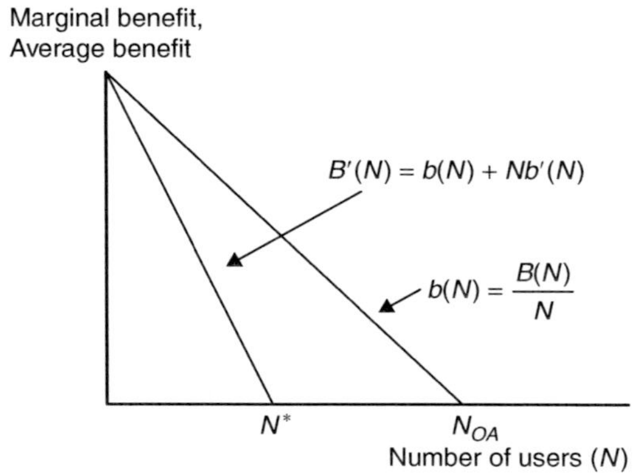

Figure 7.3.3 Marginal and average benefits

of users N, the net private benefit accruing to each user is simply the aggregate net benefit divided by N:

$$b(N) = AB = \frac{B(N)}{N}$$

This is positive but declining with N. Each downstream firm either extracts one unit, or none. Each downstream firm will therefore find extraction worthwhile as long as:

$$b(N) = AB > 0 \Leftrightarrow \frac{B(N)}{N} > 0 \Leftrightarrow B(N) > 0$$

Thus, individual firms would continue to choose to extract the resource until the individual (and therefore total) benefits are driven down to *zero*. In other words, under an open access regime with overlapping usage rights the sustainable level of extraction yields individual and aggregate benefits of zero:

$$b(N_{OA}) = B(N_{OA}) = 0$$

Under an open access rule, these are the benefits that are enjoyed each period into the indefinite future. The resource is depleted to the point where the sustainable individual, average and total benefits are zero. The welfare loss from this legal rule is the difference between the extraction level that yields the maximum sustainable aggregate benefits and the open access benefits:

$$\text{Welfare Loss} = B(N^*) - B(N_{OA}) = B(N^*) - 0 = B(N^*)$$

The source of this inefficiency is quite clear. The marginal social benefit at any N is $B'(N)$, whereas the marginal *private* benefit at any N is the average benefit $b(N) = B(N)/N$. Since $B(N)/N$ is positive but declining, this means that:

$$\frac{d}{dN}\left[\frac{B(N)}{N}\right] = \frac{B'(N)N - B(N)}{N^2} < 0$$

which means that $B'(N) < B(N)/N$. That is, the marginal social benefit is less than the marginal private benefit, but individual firms ignore the former and only take into account the latter, and so the resource is inefficiently overexploited.

Figure 7.3.4 shades in the loss that is incurred when $N_{OA} > N^*$ firms use the asset. This loss is incurred because for each firm that exceeds N^*, the marginal social cost of extraction (which is zero) exceeds the marginal social benefit of extraction (which is negative for $N > N^*$). The benefits up to N^* and the costs from N^* to N_{OA} offset each other exactly, and so total benefits under the open access regime are zero.

Since marginal private benefits exceed marginal social benefits under the open access regime, each user imposes an unpriced negative externality on the other users. For any N the value of this externality is equal to:

$$\frac{B(N)}{N} - B'(N)$$

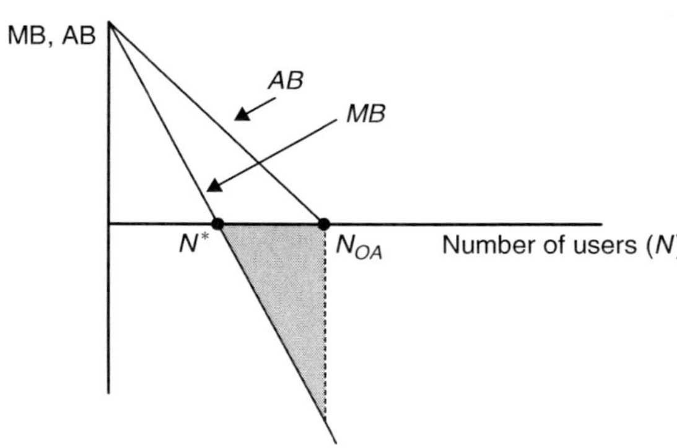

Figure 7.3.4 The welfare loss from an open access regime

This leads to overexploitation of the resource. The lesson is that 'communalising' property encourages social waste – it tends to encourage people to use goods and services in a way which takes no account of the possible negative effects of their use on others. This is the well-known resource overexploitation or 'tragedy of the commons' problem, which economists as far back as Hume (1739) have noted. By encouraging overuse, legal regimes which communalise property encourage people to continually exploit others. This is ultimately destructive of economic cooperation and sustainable participation in groups.

Note that if the number of firms using the resource could somehow be restricted (say, by direct regulation or legal fiat) or if there was a tax on usage, then this could reduce the welfare loss. Thus, one view of this situation is that it is competition and the unfettered pursuit of profit (combined with an absence of appropriate taxation) in the downstream market that is the source of the problem here, and that regulation and/or taxation is the solution. But this view is obviously incorrect. The actual economic problem, as we will see, is that the legal rule is inappropriate. More specifically, as we will now show, the source of the problem lies in overlapping usage rights.

7.3.2 Private ownership with a single, non-overlapping exclusion right

Under this legal rule, there is a single individual owner of the upstream owner (or group of owners who act as a single owner). The upstream owner can charge users a price P for the right to extract the resource, and can exclude those who do not pay this fee.

Let N be the number of users that the owner allows to exploit the resource. Each individual downstream firm once again compares its marginal private benefit with private marginal cost. For any N, the marginal private benefit accruing to each downstream firm is again simply the individual benefit $b(N)$, which is equal to the average benefit:

$$b(N) = AB = \frac{B(N)}{N}$$

We again assume that this is positive but declining with N. Once again, the average benefit curve is the aggregate demand curve or willingness to pay curve for usage rights. That is, the aggregate demand curve is:

$$P(N) = b(N) = \frac{B(N)}{N}$$

The upstream owner's revenue (and profit) from selling usage rights is:

$$P(N) \times N = \frac{B(N)}{N} \times N = B(N)$$

Choosing the number of users to maximise this profit yields:

$$P'(N^\circ)N^\circ + P(N^\circ) = 0 \Leftrightarrow B'(N^\circ) = 0$$

But since we also have $B'(N^*) = 0$, this means that $N^\circ = N^*$. The profit-maximising outcome under single ownership is also the efficient outcome, which maximises the sustainable benefits of extraction.

Why is private ownership efficient here? As we showed in the previous section, under the open access rule, each user imposes an unpriced negative externality on the other users and this led to overexploitation. Under private ownership with non-overlapping exclusion rights, however, overexploitation reduces the upstream owner's profit. The pursuit of profit induces the owner to set a usage fee of:

$$P(N^\circ) = \frac{B(N^*)}{N^*} = \frac{B(N^*)}{N^*} - B'(N^*)$$

which is *exactly* equal to the external cost (which was previously unpriced), evaluated at the efficient N. The usage fee is exactly equal to the efficient Pigouvian tax. Each downstream user pays a fee so that the revenue gain to the upstream owner just offsets the loss to the upstream owner from allowing another user to enter. In other words, the external effect still exists, but it is no longer Pareto relevant: the single upstream owner completely internalises it and it is now priced efficiently. In this instance, the 'invisible hand' and the pursuit of profit combined with an appropriate legal rule solves the tragedy of the commons. This shows that it is not competition and the unfettered pursuit of profit per se that are the sources of the original efficiency. The source of the problem lies in overlapping usage rights.

7.3.3 Private ownership with overlapping exclusion rights

The previous section showed that a single upstream profit-maximising owner with the right to exclude produced an efficient outcome. Now consider a slightly different legal rule: there are now multiple upstream owners, each of whom can charge downstream users a price P_i for the right to extract the resource. Each owner can exclude those who do not pay this fee. Let us analyse the incentive and efficiency effects of this legal rule. Each user once again compares his marginal private benefit with his private marginal cost. Each user will again find extraction worthwhile as long as:

$$b(N) - P = AB - P > 0$$

where now $P = \sum_{i=1}^{n} P_i$. The inverse aggregate demand curve is now:

$$P = \sum_{i=1}^{n} P_i = b(N) = \frac{B(N)}{N}$$

We can also write this demand curve as $N = N(P)$. Now each upstream owner's revenue (and profit) from selling usage rights depends on the price charged by other owners:

$$\pi_i = P_i \times N(P) = P_i N\left(\sum_{i=1}^{n} P_i\right) \quad \text{for each } i$$

Let us compute the Nash equilibrium configuration of prices. Choosing the price to maximise this profit, taking the other owners' prices as given, yields:

$$\frac{\partial \pi_i}{\partial P_i} = N\left(\sum_{i=1}^{n} P_i\right) + P_i N'\left(\sum_{i=1}^{n} P_i\right) = 0 \quad \text{for each } i$$

Since this holds for each owner i, we can add up over all n upstream owners to get:

$$nN + PN'(P) = 0$$

But

$$N'(P) = \frac{1}{P'(N)} = \frac{1}{\frac{d}{dN}\left[\frac{B(N)}{N}\right]} = \frac{N^2}{B'(N)N - B(N)}$$

Therefore, letting $N^{\circ\circ}$ be the number of users under this legal regime, we have:

$$nN^{oo} + \frac{B(N^{oo})}{N^{oo}} \frac{(N^{oo})^2}{B'(N^{oo})N^{oo} - B(N^{oo})} = 0 \tag{7.1}$$

So:

$$B'(N^{oo}) = \frac{B(N^{oo})}{N^{oo}}\left[\frac{n-1}{n}\right] > 0$$

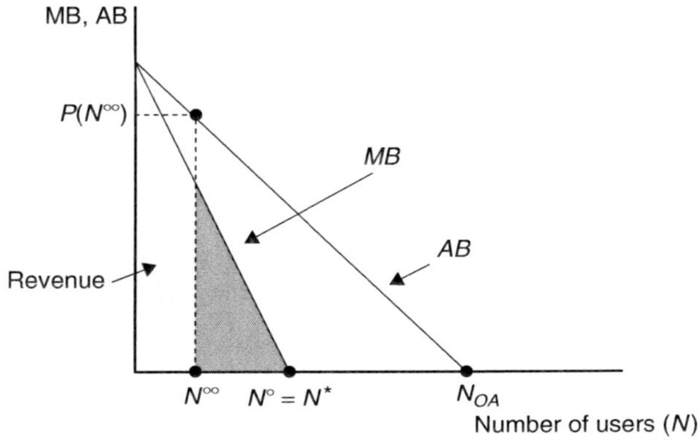

Figure 7.3.5 The tragedy of the anticommons

Where the inequality follows from the fact that both sides cannot be equal to zero (otherwise the first order condition for profit maximisation would be violated). But since at $N^{\circ\circ}$ we have $B'(N^{\circ\circ}) > 0$, this means that $N^{\circ\circ} < N^*$. There is *underexploitation* of the resource. The welfare loss is shown as the shaded area in Figure 7.3.5.

Why is private upstream ownership with multiple excluders inefficient? The reason is straightforward and again involves externalities: if owner *i* reduces his price (whilst other owners hold their price fixed), this reduces the aggregate price faced by downstream firms. This increases the number of downstream users (that is, the aggregate quantity demanded). Thus, as a result of owner *i*'s price reduction, all other owner/excluders enjoy a revenue increase – but without having to increase their own prices. In other words, each price reduction by *i* imposes an external benefit on the other owner/excluders.

Conversely, each price *increase* by *i* reduces the revenue of other owners and imposes a negative externality on them. Since each owner's price reduction imposes an uncompensated positive externality, there will be too few price reductions from an efficiency point of view. Alternatively, since each owner's price increase imposes an uncompensated negative externality on other owners, there will be too many price increases. For both reasons, prices will be too high from an efficiency point of view.

Note also that the inefficiency gets worse as number of excluders rises. Differentiating the first order condition for profit maximisation with respect to n yields.

$$nN'(P)P'(n) + N + P'(n)N'(P) + PN''(P)\,P'(n) = 0$$

So:

$$P'(n) = \frac{-N}{(n+1)N'(P) + PN''(P)} > 0$$

The aggregate price increases as the number of upstream excluders increases. In the limit, as the number of excluders goes to infinity, we have:

$$\lim_{n\to\infty} B'(N^{oo}) = B'(0)$$

and $B(N^{\circ\circ})$ approaches 0. As the number of excluders becomes very large, the number of downstream users N approaches zero and the total price P approaches $B'(0)$, gradually choking off all downstream demand. Aggregate benefits also approach zero. In other words, in the limit, the welfare loss in this equilibrium approaches the *same* welfare loss that occurs under the open access legal regime examined earlier.

One solution to this underexploitation problem is for the multiple excluders to try to collude to keep each of their prices at a level that encourages the efficient number of entrants. This would require setting prices so that:

$$\sum_{i=1}^{n} P_i = \frac{B(N^*)}{N^*}$$

so that, once again, the aggregate entry price is equal to the external cost at the optimum. However, even if such an agreement was reached, it would not be stable against cheating: if each excluder believes that the others will stick to the terms of the agreement, each will still have an incentive to increase their price in order to increase their own revenue at the expense of others losing revenue. Thus, each excluder still has an incentive to impose a negative external cost on the others by increasing their individual price.

The above analysis illustrates the symmetric nature of the welfare losses associated with multiple usage rights and multiple exclusion rights. Although economists have long analysed and been concerned with the tragedy of the commons, the welfare losses associated with overlapping exclusion rights and the anticommons can be just as serious – perhaps more so, depending on the situation.

7.3.4 Overlapping disposal rights

The previous section showed how welfare losses can occur as a result of overlapping or multiple usage and exclusion rights. But even if these problems can be avoided, welfare losses can also occur as a result of overlapping *disposal* rights to an asset.

7.3.4.1 A large number of atomistic owners with overlapping disposal rights

We view disposal rights as the right to transfer control of the resource to another party. To understand the nature of overlapping disposal rights, let us consider an example from corporate law. Suppose that there is an asset that is owned by a very large number of small or 'atomistic' shareholders, each of whom owns a very small fraction of the asset. The shareholders supply capital but do not have the skills or expertise to manage the asset, so they employ a manager. The manager charges the optimal usage price as discussed above, and so maximises the benefits of the asset's sustainable extraction rate and the asset's economic value, given his skills and expertise. Suppose the current (market) price of a share is P_S, and the market value of the asset is $B(N^*)$.

Suppose that there is a 'raider' who has superior management skills who would fire the current management team and increase the value of each share to $V > P_S$, which they could do if they owned at least 50 per cent of the shares. Suppose that the raider offers a price per share of P_R, where $P_S < P_R < V$. Efficiency dictates that the raider acquire the shares, since the value of the asset increases as a result of this transaction.

Shareholders have a simple decision here: they can either tender (that is, sell) their shares to the raider, or not. Because there are many individual shareholders, each shareholder's tender decision has a minuscule effect on the likelihood of the takeover bid succeeding. In other words, the probability of a shareholder being *pivotal* and affecting the outcome is negligible.

Under these conditions, consider the payoff to each very small shareholder from tendering (selling) his shares to the raider. Suppose that a shareholder believes that the takeover will succeed. The payoff from tendering shares is then P_R, but the payoff from not tendering is $V > P_R$. Thus the shareholder would not tender his shares. But this means that no shareholders will tender. Grossman and Hart (1980) therefore argue that the takeover bid will fail, and the potential welfare gain of $V - P$ will not be realised. The reason for this inefficiency is straightforward: each shareholder has a negligible effect on the probability that the takeover will succeed, so each has an incentive to free ride on the success of the takeover. The takeover will only succeed if $P_R > V$, which would result in a loss to the raider.

Why does this inefficiency occur? The reason is the overlapping disposal rights of shareholders, combined with the legal rule which states that the raider must acquire at least 50 per cent of the shares before he can take control. These institutional arrangements around control rights and disposal mean that each shareholder exerts an uncompensated economic benefit on his fellow shareholders if he tenders his shares. Since the benefit is uncompensated, private marginal benefit of tendering is less than the social marginal benefit of tendering. There is an incentive for free-riding. As the number of shareholders rises, the incentive for free-riding becomes greater.

7.3.4.2 Two owners with overlapping disposal rights

The conclusions of Grossman and Hart seem to be intuitively attractive but they have been challenged in an important paper by Bagnoli and Lipman (1988). To understand their criticism, we analyse the case of a small number of non-atomistic shareholders. To see how numbers matter, note that the problem associated with overlapping disposal rights does not arise if there is only a single shareholder, and is also not a problem with two shareholders if one of them is sufficiently large. To see the latter result, suppose that there are two shareholders, labelled A and B. Suppose that the fraction of shares owned by B is $s_B > 1/2$. Then the payoffs from tendering and not tendering can be illustrated in the payoff matrix in Table 7.3.1.

Since $P_R > P_S$ shareholder B has a dominant strategy here: to tender his shares. Since A knows this, A can free ride, not tender, and obtain V once the takeover is completed. The Nash equilibrium is therefore for B to tender and A not to tender. But since $s_B > 1/2$, this means that the takeover succeeds. The increase in economic value is realised and there is no efficiency loss. B is always *pivotal* in this example – his action always determines the outcome of the tender offer.

7.3.4.3 Three shareholders with overlapping disposal rights

In the preceding example there was a pure strategy Nash equilibrium in which the raider's takeover successfully went ahead because one

Table 7.3.1 The payoff matrix in the tender offer game with two shareholders

		Shareholder B	
		Tender	**Don't Tender**
Shareholder A	**Tender**	(P_R, P_R)	(P_R, P_S)
	Don't Tender	(V, P_R)	(P_S, P_S)

shareholder was sufficiently large as to always be *pivotal*: B's action determined whether or not the takeover was successful. The situation with three or more shareholders is more complicated, however, because shareholders are usually only pivotal in some situations.

Consider, for example, the case of three shareholders (A, B and C), each of whom owns one share. The raider must obtain two shares to take control. We consider symmetric mixed strategy Nash equilibria. Suppose that each shareholder tenders their shares with probability ρ. For each shareholder to be willing to randomise in this way, the expected payoff from tendering to be equal to the expected payoff from not tendering. The expected payoff from tendering a share is P_R. The expected payoff from not tendering a share is equal to

$$\Pr(\text{Tender Offer is Successful}) \times V + \Pr(\text{Tender Offer is Unsuccessful}) \times P_S$$
$$= \rho^2 V + [(1-\rho)^2 + 2\rho(1-\rho)]P_S$$

Thus, if the raider has offered P_R, for the mixed strategy to be an equilibrium, the two pure strategies must be equally desirable, and we must have:

$$P_R = \rho^2 V + [(1-\rho)^2 + 2\rho(1-\rho)]P_S \tag{7.2}$$

The right-hand side is a continuous function of ρ. If $\rho = 0$, then the right-hand side is equal to P_S, whereas if $\rho = 1$, the right-hand side is equal to V. Thus, by the intermediate value theorem, for any P_R there exists a value of ρ (which we denote by ρ^*) such that equality holds in equation (7.2). Moreover, the derivative of the right-hand side with respect to ρ is:

$$2\rho V - 2(1-\rho)P_S + 2P_S - 4\rho P_S = 2\rho(V - P_S)$$

which is positive if $V > P_S$. Thus, the number ρ^* is unique. The second derivative of the right-hand side is also positive, so the equation in (7.2) is an increasing, convex function of ρ. Thus, we have the situation shown in Figure 7.3.6.

For any P_R, there is a symmetric mixed strategy Nash equilibrium in which each shareholder tenders his shares with probability ρ^*, where this is the solution to:

$$P_R(\rho^*) = (\rho^*)^2 V + [(1-\rho^*)^2 + 2\rho^* (1-\rho^*)]P_S .$$

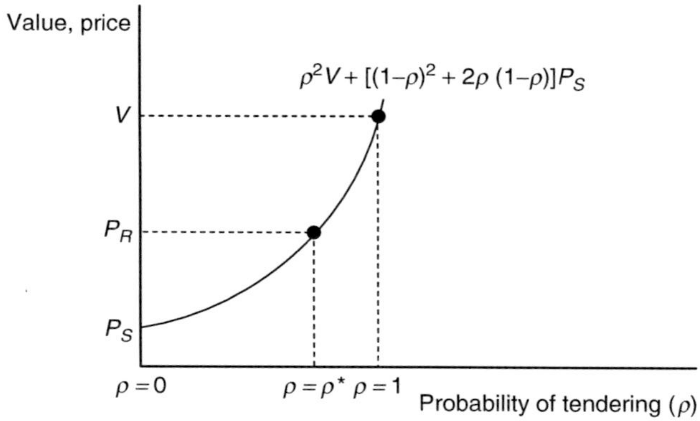

Figure 7.3.6 The expected payoff to an individual shareholder

In such an equilibrium, for any offer $P_R(\rho)$, the raider's expected profit is:

Expected Value of Shares if Tender Offer is Successful
+ Expected Value of Shares if Tender Offer is Unsuccessful
– Expected cost of acquiring shares

$$= \rho^3 3V + 3\rho^2(1-\rho)2V + 3\rho(1-\rho)^2 P_S - 3\rho P_R$$

Plugging in the value of P_R from above gives us the raider's expected profit:

$$6\rho^2(1-\rho)(V - P_S) \tag{7.3}$$

Thus, to maximise its expected profit, the raider should choose $\rho^* = \frac{2}{3}$. Notice also that the probability that a particular shareholder will be pivotal is $\rho^2(1-\rho)$. Thus, another interpretation of equation (7.3) is that the raider chooses a price that maximises the probability that each shareholder is pivotal. The expected profit as a function of ρ is shown in Figure 7.3.7.

In this equilibrium, the raider proposes a price of $P_R^* = \frac{4}{9}V + [(1-\rho)^2 + 2\rho(1-\rho)]P_S$, which gives an expected profit of $\frac{8}{9}(V - P_S)$. Thus, the raider expects to capture almost all of the economic value created by the takeover.

Note, however, that in this equilibrium there is some chance that the takeover will not succeed, even though it is efficient for the takeover to occur. The fact that it is not certain that the transaction will occur and

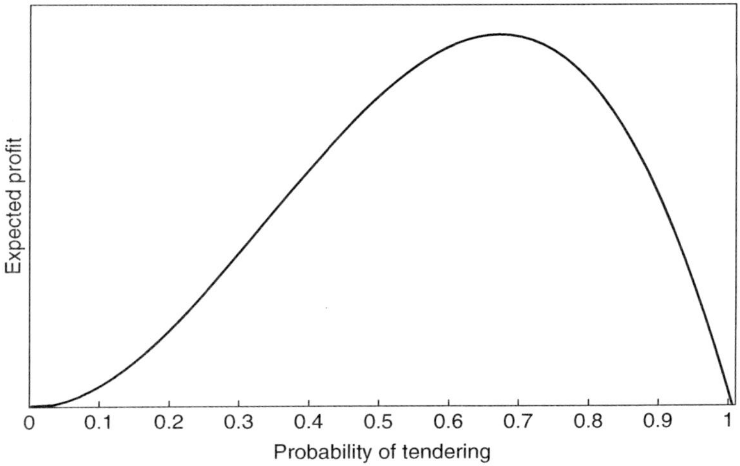

Figure 7.3.7 The expected payoff to the raider

resources move from low- to high-valued uses occurs as a result of the existence of an externality between shareholders. When a shareholder is pivotal and decides to tender his shares, he exerts an uncompensated economic benefit on his fellow shareholders. Thus, there is an incentive for free-riding. As the number of shareholders rises, the incentive for free-riding becomes greater, and the likelihood of a successful takeover declines.

7.4 The economics of insecure property rights

The preceding analysis shows that overlapping usage, exclusion and disposal rights can distort economic incentives. However, even if these problems do not exist, there may be more serious sources of inefficiency. Poorly defined and/or weakly enforced private property rights encourage *rent-seeking activities*: the wasteful use of resources to try to influence the distribution of wealth, rather than the creation of wealth. This section examines the costs of insecure property rights. The main conclusion is that when property rights are insecure, there are potentially three separate costs:

- **Rent-seeking costs:** The costs of devoting resources to securing property rights, rather than using them to produce valuable goods and services.

- **The costs of "winner take all" conflict:** In a winner take all conflict over property rights, the resources of the 'loser' of the contest are rendered valueless.
- **The costs of autarky:** Even if parties agree to split the insecure resource according to their winning probabilities, this may not be Pareto optimal, and conflict precludes trade that would exploit these possible gains.

7.4.1 A model of insecure property rights

To illustrate the main ideas, consider the following model, which is similar to that developed by Skaperdas and Syropoulos (1996). There are two individuals, 1 and 2, and two scarce inputs into production: labour (L) and land (T). The production function for each individual is:

$$Y_i = L_i + \frac{1}{\alpha} T_i^{\alpha} \tag{7.4}$$

where T_i is the amount of land that individual i employs, and L_i is the amount of labour that *i* employs, and $0 < \alpha < 1$ is a productivity parameter. Suppose that individuals each begin with R_i units of labour, which is secure.

7.4.1.1 Secure property rights to land

If property rights over land are fully secure, then labour is fully employed in productive activities, and each individual's production is:

$$Y_i = R_i + \frac{1}{\alpha} T_i^{\alpha}$$

where $0 < \alpha < 1$. The Pareto-optimal allocations of land and labour solve:

$$\max_{T_1, R_1} Y_1 = R_1 + \frac{1}{\alpha} T_1^{\alpha}$$

subject to:

$$R_2 + \frac{1}{\alpha} T_2^{\alpha} \geq Y_2$$

and the aggregate resource constraints $T_1 + T_2 = T$ and $R_1 + R_2 = R$. The solution is the set of points where:

$$T_1 = T_2 = \frac{T}{2}$$

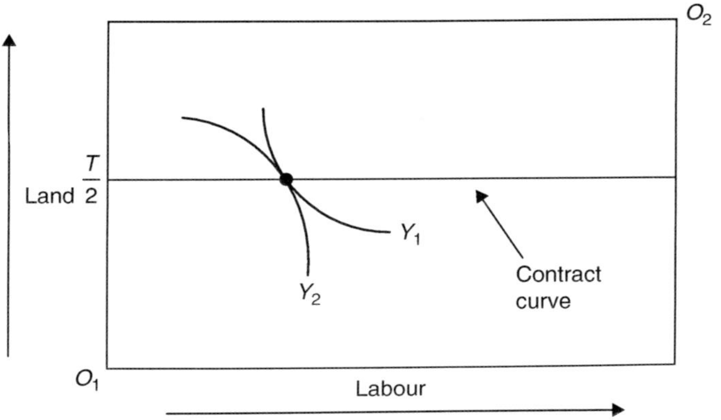

Figure 7.4.1 The contract curve

This is the horizontal line of the Edgeworth Box, as shown in Figure 7.4.1.

Aggregate production for this efficiently organised economy satisfies:

$$Y_1 + Y_2 = R + \frac{2}{\alpha}\left(\frac{T}{2}\right)^{\alpha} = R_1 + R_2 + \frac{2}{\alpha}\left(\frac{T}{2}\right)^{\alpha}$$

7.4.1.2 *Insecure property rights to land*

Now consider what may occur if private property rights over land are insecure. Suppose that there are overlapping claims to T, and both individuals devote resources to clarify and enforce their claims over it. Let the resources devoted to clarifying property rights be G_1 and G_2. Individuals engage in costly conflict over land. There is a probability ρ that individual 1 will, as a result of this conflict, ultimately gain the right to the land, where:

$$\rho(G_1, G_2) = \begin{cases} \dfrac{\varphi G_1}{\varphi G_1 + (1-\varphi)G_2} & \text{if } G_1 + G_2 > 0 \\ \varphi & \text{otherwise} \end{cases}$$

Here φ (where $0 < \varphi < 1$) is a measure of the relative security of individual 1's right to the land. If $\varphi = 0$, for example, then individual 1 has perfectly secure property rights to the land. If $\varphi = 0$, then individual 2 has perfectly secure property rights to the land. Any value of φ in between these two values represents a situation with insecure property rights.

Note that holding the choice of G by individual 2 fixed, a higher G for individual 1 increases the probability that they will prevail in the conflict. However, this comes at a cost, because individual 1 will then have less labour available for production should he win the conflict over land.

If 1 loses the conflict and 2 wins, then 1 has no land and can only produce with the labour that he has left over. Therefore, individual 1's expected benefits are:

$$B_1 = \rho\left(L_1 + \frac{T^\alpha}{\alpha}\right) + (1-\rho)L_1 = \frac{\varphi G_1}{\varphi G_1 + (1-\varphi)G_2}\frac{T^\alpha}{\alpha} + L_1$$

and for individual 2 we have:

$$B_2 = (1-\rho)\left(L_2 + \frac{T^\alpha}{\alpha}\right) + \rho L_2 = \frac{(1-\varphi)G_2}{\varphi G_1 + (1-\varphi)G_2}\frac{T^\alpha}{\alpha} + L_2$$

and where the constraint on labour for each party is:

$$L_i + G_i = R_i$$

The first-order conditions are:

$$\frac{\partial B_1}{\partial G_1} = \frac{\varphi(1-\varphi)G_2}{[\varphi G_1 + (1-\varphi)G_2]^2}\frac{T^\alpha}{\alpha} - 1 = 0 \qquad (7.5)$$

For individual 1, and

$$\frac{\partial B_2}{\partial G_2} = \frac{\varphi(1-\varphi)G_1}{[\varphi G_1 + (1-\varphi)G_2]^2}\frac{T^\alpha}{\alpha} - 1 = 0$$

The first term in each of these equations is the marginal benefit of an additional unit of G, given the choice of the other individual. The second term (–1) is the opportunity cost of a unit of G. Individuals simply take the level of G of the other party as given and choose G up to the point where expected marginal benefit equals marginal cost. There is a unique symmetric Nash equilibrium in which each party chooses the same amount of G. That is, in equilibrium, $G_1^* = G_2^* = G^*$. Plugging this in to equation (7.5) yields:

$$G^* = \varphi(1-\varphi)\frac{T^\alpha}{\alpha}$$

so that $L_i = R_i - G^* = R_i - \varphi(1-\varphi)\frac{T^\alpha}{\alpha}$. The equilibrium expected benefits here are:

$$B_1 = \varphi\frac{T^\alpha}{\alpha} + R_1 - \varphi(1-\varphi)\frac{T^\alpha}{\alpha} = \varphi^2\frac{T^\alpha}{\alpha} + R_1 \qquad (7.6)$$

and:

$$B_2 = (1-\varphi)\frac{T^\alpha}{\alpha} + R_2 - \varphi(1-\varphi)\frac{T^\alpha}{\alpha} = (1-\varphi)^2\frac{T^\alpha}{\alpha} + R_2 \qquad (7.7)$$

Thus, *ex ante*, the aggregate production possibilities frontier when there are insecure property rights satisfies:

$$B_1 + B_2 = [\varphi^2 + (1-\varphi)^2]\frac{T^\alpha}{\alpha} + R_1 + R_2 < \alpha\left(\frac{T}{2}\right)^\alpha + R_1 + R_2 \qquad (7.8)$$

7.4.1.2.1 The costs of insecure property rights. We can now examine the welfare losses from insecure property rights. The first cost is the *ex ante* loss in welfare which comes about because the Edgeworth Box has shrunk as a result of resources being devoted to distribution rather than production. This welfare loss here is equal to the sum of the G_1^* and G_2^*, which is $2G^* = 2\varphi(1-\varphi)\frac{T^\alpha}{\alpha}$. These are the *rent-seeking costs* due to insecure property rights, and they are illustrated in Figure 7.4.2, where the dashed box is the old Edgeworth Box, and the solid box is the new Edgeworth Box. Investing in G shrinks the box horizontally, reducing the 'size of the pie'.

The second class of costs comes about because after conflict occurs only one of the parties will end up with the land, whereas efficiency dictates that the land be shared equally between the parties. To isolate this cost, suppose that after the parties chose their G's, they agreed to split the land according to their equilibrium win probabilities, which are φ and $1 - \varphi$. Then aggregate production would be equal to:

$$B_1' + B_2' = \frac{(\varphi T)^\alpha}{\alpha} + \frac{[(1-\varphi)T]^\alpha}{\alpha} + R - 2\varphi(1-\varphi)\frac{T^\alpha}{\alpha}$$

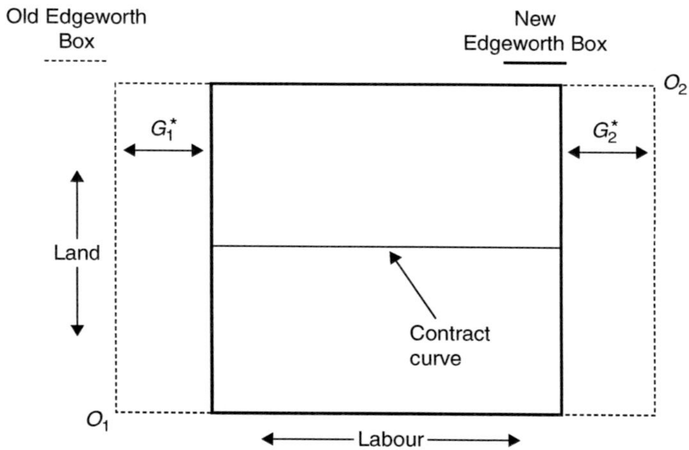

Figure 7.4.2 Rent-seeking costs shrink the Edgeworth Box

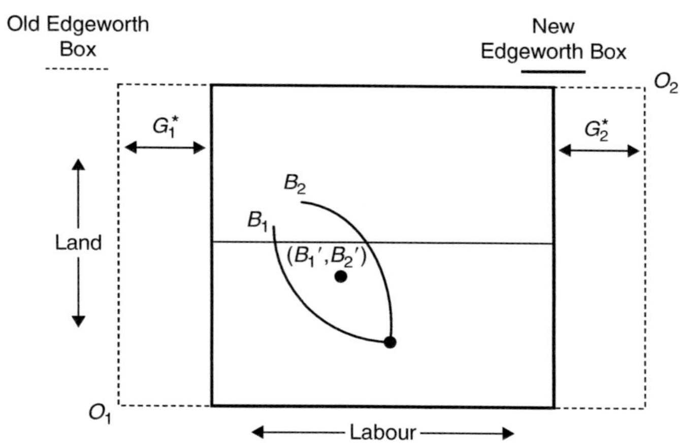

Figure 7.4.3 The cost of "winner takes all" conflict

To compare this with the *ex ante* benefits if such a split did not occur, we need to show that $\frac{(\varphi T)^{\alpha}}{\alpha} \geq \varphi \frac{T^{\alpha}}{\alpha}$, or that: $\varphi^{\alpha} \geq \varphi$. But this is always true if $0 < \varphi < 1$ and $0 < \alpha < 1$. These costs are illustrated in Figure 7.4.3, where the expected benefits in the absence of the split are B_1 and B_2 whereas after the split they are B_1' and B_2'. Notice that B_1' and B_2' need not be on the contract curve.

The final class of costs come about because even if the parties split land according to their win probabilities φ and $1-\varphi$, this is not generally Pareto optimal. Efficiency here requires the split to be equal, whereas φ and $1-\varphi$ will not, in general, be equal to one half. These are the costs of not being able to exchange land and labour when property rights over the former are insecure.

7.5 The economics of intellectual property rights

The analysis in section 8.3 showed that overlapping usage rights led to an inefficient overexploitation of a scarce resource. This outcome occurred because the resource was assumed to be *rivalrous in consumption*: one individual's consumption of the resource reduced the amount that was available for consumption by others. The solution to this is reality of rivalrous consumption was to have a single excluder charge a usage fee, which internalised the externalities flowing between multiple users. Hence the strong link between private property rights and economic efficiency.

In the absence of rivalry in consumption, overlapping usage rights do not create an overuse problem. Since one person's use does not reduce the amount that is available to others, this means that no negative externality is created by multiple usage and so there is nothing for an excluder to price. In fact, in the absence of consumption rivalry, it would be *inefficient* not to permit multiple users of a good that already exists to exploit it without any restrictions. It also follows that allowing multiple, overlapping excluders would be inappropriate.

Many new inventions, ideas or other forms of intellectual property possess exactly these kinds of characteristics: they are cheap to reproduce, and unlike land and other forms of property, they are not scarce or rivalrous in the short run, once they have been produced.

However, note the important qualification here: we have only talked about the short run, once a good has already been produced. What if the product does not yet exist? It is all too obvious that good ideas are hard to come by. Thus, although many inventions are costless to reproduce, they are certainly costly to produce in the first instance. In other words, the first unit of production may have very large, upfront, sunk cost, with subsequent units having low or zero marginal costs.

What would be the consequence of allowing multiple, overlapping users in this case? If an inventor is not able to exclude, he is not able to charge a price; and if he cannot charge a price, he cannot earn revenue; and if he cannot earn revenue, he cannot make a profit, and will have no incentive to produce in the first place.

In other words, there is a dilemma here: even though it is efficient not to exclude users once the good is produced, the good may not be produced unless exclusion is possible. Therefore, overlapping usage rights, whilst perhaps efficient in this situation in a static sense, are unlikely to be efficient in a broader, dynamic sense. But on the other hand, permanent single exclusion rights cannot be efficient in a broader dynamic sense either – investors will certainly produce many inventions, if they enjoyed permanent exclusion rights, but they would then only be made available to an inefficiently low number of consumers, at a price that is too high.

This is a classic problem of second-best policy analysis. In the absence of the constraint that inventors require adequate compensation to produce new ideas or inventions, the first-best rule is to allow overlapping usage rights. But clearly the constraint cannot be ignored. Once we introduce this important constraint into the analysis, the first best rule is no longer appropriate.

The solution to this problem is to grant the inventor an *intellectual property right,* which is a hybrid property right of sorts. It is a mix of a rule of a single excluder and a regime of overlapping users. From an efficiency point of view, the idea of an intellectual property right is to allow inventors to *temporarily* exclude other users (thus ensuring that they will at least be partially compensated for their efforts), but to eventually allow others the right to use the new technology without paying the inventor.

7.5.1 A simple model of intellectual property rights

This section considers these issues in more detail by analysing a model of innovation in which spending on research and development by a firm results in that firm being able to lower its marginal cost of production. We assume, however, the new innovation, once produced, can be easily copied by other firms (in the real world this need not always be the case). We also assume that firms sell their goods on a competitive market, so allowing other firms to copy the innovation drives down prices and benefits consumers. However, if firms could copy the innovation as soon as it becomes public, then the innovating firm would be unable to capture the full private benefits of its invention.

A *patent* confers a temporary monopoly right on the innovating producer, allowing it to produce the good at the lower marginal cost for a particular period of time. The idea is to allow the firm to capture some economic profits temporarily (for the length of the patent), which cover the sunk cost of innovation and thereby inducing the firm to innovate in the first place. Then, after the term of the patent has expired, the firm's competitors to gain access to the new technology and drive down prices, thus benefiting consumers. The optimal patent length balances these two opposing objectives.

Consider a competitive market for a single good. Consumer benefits of the good are equal to B, suppose that the current market price of the good is P, which is equal to marginal cost in the industry. Suppose that there is a sunk, upfront cost of $K > 0$, which is the cost of innovation. Innovation drives the marginal production cost to zero. Thus, in a competitive market in which all firms had access to the new technology, price would be driven to zero. At the new lower price, we assume that additional consumers enter the market. Thus, in addition to existing consumers enjoying the benefits of the good at a lower price, there are additional consumers who now consume the good but who previously did not.

Finally, we assume that benefits that are to be received in the future (and costs that are to be incurred in the future) are discounted at the common discount rate $r > 0$, with continuous compounding. Thus, the value today of a dollar to be received at time T in the future is e^{-rT}.

7.5.2 Welfare

In the absence of the new invention, total welfare is the present value of the sum over time of the difference between consumer benefits and producer costs:

$$W_0 = \int_0^\infty (B - P) e^{-rs} ds \tag{7.9}$$

On the other hand, if there is an invention which is granted a patent of length T welfare is:

$$W_1 = -K + \int_0^T (B - P)\, e^{-rs} ds + \int_0^T Pe^{-rs}\, ds + \int_T^\infty (B + \Delta B) e^{-rs} ds \tag{7.10}$$

where ΔB are the benefits accruing to new consumers who consume the good at the new lower price.

The first term in (7.10) is the cost of the new invention. The second term is the present value of the surplus that consumers continue to enjoy during the life of the patent. The third term is the present value of the firm's profit as a result of being able to sell the good at (just below) the current market price P but produce at a marginal cost of zero during the life of the patent. The final term is the present value of consumer benefits from being able to consume the good at a price of zero once the patent has expired.

Equation (7.10) can be simplified to:

$$W_1 = -K + \int_0^\infty Be^{-rs}ds + \int_T^\infty \Delta B e^{-rs}ds \tag{7.11}$$

New inventions are not always welfare-improving, even if they make consumers better off – innovation only improves welfare if its benefits exceed its costs. Therefore, welfare is higher from the invention only if:

$$\int_0^\infty (B-P)e^{-rs}ds < -K + \int_0^\infty Be^{-rs}ds + \int_0^\infty \Delta Be^{-rs}ds$$

or if:

$$K < \int_0^\infty Pe^{-rs}ds + \int_T^\infty \Delta B e^{-rs}ds \tag{7.12}$$

Equation (7.12) states that for a patent of length T it is efficient for the invention to take place if the present value of the sunk costs is less than the present value of the reduction in marginal production costs, plus the present value of additional consumption benefits. The sum on the right-hand side is therefore a measure of the benefits of innovation, whereas the term on the left-hand side is the cost of innovation. For the remainder of this section, we assume that there is a positive value T such that the condition in (7.12) holds.

7.5.2.1 *The optimal length of a patent*

Now consider the problem of designing an appropriate intellectual property rights regime. The critical policy variable in this set-up is the choice of the patent length, T. A moment's reflection reveals that in this set-up, a patent length of $T = 0$ is not efficient: if $T = 0$, then the inventor will be unable to recover his fixed costs K and will not innovate. On the other hand, a patent length of $T = \infty$ is also clearly not optimal, since that would involve consumers receiving no additional consumption benefits, with $\int_T^\infty \Delta Be^{-rs}ds \to 0$ as $T \to \infty$, and so the innovation would be pointless from a benefit point of view.

Therefore, as a general rule, the optimal patent length is positive and finite. The optimal length is found by solving:

$$\max_T -K + \int_0^\infty Be^{-rs}ds + \int_0^\infty \Delta Be^{-rs}ds \text{ subject to } K \le \int_0^T Pe^{-rs}ds \tag{7.13}$$

The first term in (7.13) is the expression for total welfare in (7.11). The constraint in (7.13) is the break-even constraint for the producer – for the invention to be produced, the producer must be compensated an amount that is at least equal to his sunk costs, so that he at least breaks even.

Since the objective function is decreasing in T and since the constraint is increasing in T, the optimal patent length here involves setting T so that the producer just breaks even. Therefore the optimal patent length T^* satisfies:

$$K = \int_0^{T^*} Pe^{-rs} ds \tag{7.14}$$

or:

$$K = \frac{P}{r}(1 - e^{-rT^*})$$

so that the optimal patent length is:

$$T^* = -\frac{1}{r}\log\left(1 - \frac{rK}{P}\right) \tag{7.15}$$

The determination of the optimal patent length in this model is illustrated in Figure 7.5.1. The curve $\dfrac{B + \Delta Be^{-rT}}{r}$ is the present value of the gains to consumers from innovation. It is maximised at $T = 0$, which is the first-best optimum. However, at $T = 0$, the innovator would make a loss and would therefore not innovate, and there would be no welfare gain. The curve $\dfrac{P}{r}(1 - e^{-rT}) - K$ is the second-best constraint, and is the net present value of the innovator's profit stream. Setting T so that profits are zero maximises welfare subject to the second-best constraint holding, and gives the optimal patent length $T^* = -\dfrac{1}{r}\log\left(1 - \dfrac{rK}{P}\right)$.

Given a patent length of T^*, the level of welfare is:

$$W_1^* = -\int_0^{T^*} Pe^{-rs} ds + \int_0^{\infty} Be^{-rs} ds + \int_{T^*}^{\infty} \Delta Be^{-rs} ds \tag{7.16}$$

and the incremental welfare gain from innovation is:

$$\begin{aligned} W_1^* - W_0 &= -\int_0^{T^*} Pe^{-rs} ds + \int_0^{\infty} Be^{-rs} ds + \int_{T^*}^{\infty} \Delta Be^{-rs} ds - \left[\int_0^{\infty} (B - P)e^{-rs} ds\right] \\ &= \int_{T^*}^{\infty} (\Delta B + P)e^{-rs} ds \end{aligned} \tag{7.17}$$

It is straightforward to show both analytically and diagrammatically (using Figure 7.5.1 and 7.5.2 below) that in this model, all else being equal:

- The optimal patent length is increasing in K. If it is more costly for the firm to invent, it will need to be compensated with higher

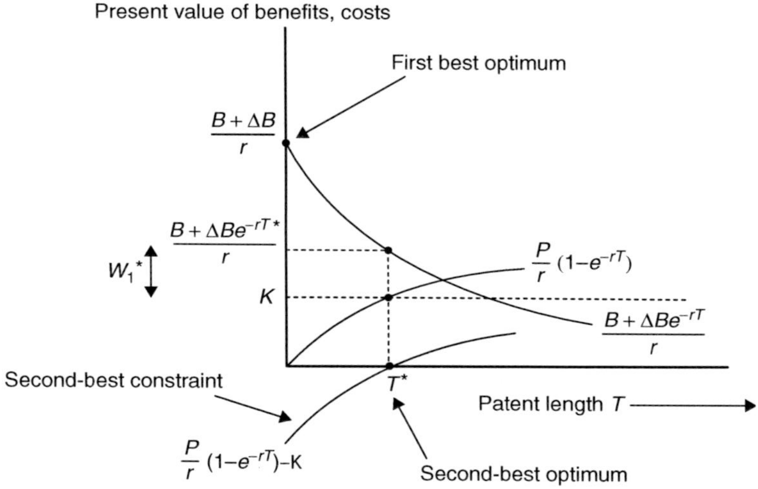

Figure 7.5.1 The optimal patent length

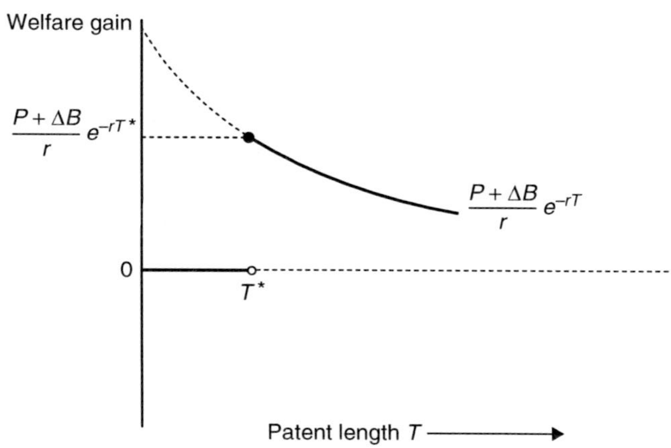

Figure 7.5.2 The welfare gain from the optimally designed patent length

revenues in present value terms for a fixed P, the only way that this can happen is if T rises. A rise in K also reduces the welfare gain from innovation, even if the patent length is adjusted optimally.

- The optimal patent length is decreasing in P. If the original price of the good is higher, then for a given cost of inventing, the firm does not need as long a patent length in order to cover its costs. Thus it is efficient to have a lower T in this case. A higher P also increases the welfare gain from innovation when the optimal patent length is chosen.
- The optimal patent length is increasing in r. If r rises, then for any initial price P and any given patent length T, the present value of the revenue earned by the innovator falls, and research and development costs will not be fully recovered. The only way that revenues can be restored to previous levels (in present value terms) is if the patent length rises. A rise in r also reduces the welfare gain from innovation, even when the patent length is adjusted optimally.

7.6 Notes

The literature on the economics of property rights is vast. Alchian (1965) and Alchian and Demsetz (1973) are classic contributions. The classic article on the symmetry between the costs of the commons and the anticommons is Buchanan and Yoon (2000). Heller (2008) is a book-length treatment of the tragedy of the anticommons which contains many illustrative examples.

Grossman and Hart (1980) analyse the free-rider problem in corporate takeovers. Bagnoli and Lipman (1988) show that the Grossman and Hart result does not obtain if there is a finite number of identical shareholders. The analysis in the text draws on their treatment. Palfrey and Rosenthal (1984) is the classic article on discrete public good contribution games.

The analysis of the costs of insecure property rights follows Skaperdas and Syropoulos (1996). Grossman (2001) contains a similar analysis with more than two parties. The analysis of the economics of patents in this chapter is inspired by Chapter 5 of Nordhaus (1969). Landes and Posner (2003) is a book-length treatment on the economics of intellectual property rights. Watt (2000) is a book-length treatment of the economics of copyright.

7.7 Exercises

1. (The Unscrupulous Diners) Another example of overlapping usage rights occurs when a group of diners jointly enjoys a meal at a restaurant, and there is an explicit restaurant policy that the bill cannot be split. Alternatively, there is often an unspoken agreement or convention (or even an explicit agreement among diners) that the table's bill will be split equally.

Gneezy et al. (2004) perform a series of actual restaurant experiments to examine this problem. They observed and manipulated conditions for several groups of six diners at a popular dining establishment. When asked to choose, prior to ordering, whether to split the bill or pay individually, 80 per cent choose the latter. That is, individuals preferred the environment with private property rights and without externalities. However, in the presence of externalities, they nevertheless take advantage of others. When the bill was split, the group spent more.

Consider a simple example of the split bill problem. Suppose that there are two diners at a lunch (A and B). When A is making his order, he knows that each additional dollar of spending will be subsidised by B, and vice versa. Note here that the benefit of an additional dollar of spending on individual item is privatised, but the cost is socialised: the private cost to each individual diner of their last dollar of spending is only \$0.50, but the joint cost is \$1.00. Thus, each additional dollar of spending by A imposes a negative external cost on B. Alternatively, each *reduction* in spending by A creates a *positive* external benefit on B (his portion of the bill is now reduced by \$0.50 without having to do anything).

Suppose that each diner can order a main meal and a dessert. The price of a main meal is \$10, and the individual benefit is \$12. The price of a dessert is also \$10, but the individual benefit is only \$6.

(a) Is it efficient for the diners to order dessert?
(b) Write down the payoff matrix for the unscrupulous diner game when the bill is split. Find the Nash equilibrium. Show that the diners will overeat. If the diners get a zero benefit from not going to dinner together, show that if the bill is split they are better off not going to dinner at all.
(c) Now assume that the diners agree not to split the bill. Repeat part (b). Show that the diners do not overeat and that there are positive individual and aggregate benefits from dining.
(d) Why would a restaurant insist on a rule of 'no split bills'?

2. This question considers the framework introduced in Chapter 3 in a world with insecure property rights, and follows Robson and Skaperdas (2008). Consider an economy with two agents, 1 and 2. Agents own an initial amount of money (m) and can make payments to each other, but the total amount of money available in the economy remains constant. Each agent likes money, so utility functions are increasing in m.

   Agent 1 undertakes an activity, x, which pleases agent 1, but makes his neighbour, agent 2, unhappy (for example, playing loud music). In other words, agent 1's utility function increases with x but agent 2's utility function decreases with x. There is a limit on x (say, 24 hours per day). Denote this limit by $\overline{x}$.

   There are two legal regimes, labelled I and II. In regime I, agent 1 is legally entitled to play loud music all day and agent 2 must pay agent 1 to get a specified number of hours without noise. In regime II, agent 1 must obtain, in exchange for a money payment, agent 2's permission to play a specified positive number of hours of loud music.

   (a) Represent this economy in an Edgeworth box diagram under two legal regimes. Illustrate the competitive equilibrium allocations of money and playing of loud music, and the competitive equilibrium price ratio in the two legal regimes. Are the competitive equilibrium allocations Pareto optimal? Explain. Is it necessarily the case that in the competitive equilibrium, agent 1 always chooses to play the same amount of loud music? Explain, with reference to the efficiency version and the invariance version of the Coase Theorem.

(b) Now suppose that small transactions costs drive a wedge between the marginal rates of substitution of the agents. In other words, in a competitive equilibrium, marginal rates of substitution need not be equal, even though no gains from trade may exist. What effect will these small transactions costs have on the competitive equilibrium allocations? Explain, with reference to the Coase Theorem.

(c) Now suppose that transactions costs are again zero, but suppose legal rights regarding the production of loud noise must are *insecure*, and must be clarified by a court or some other recognised tribunal which makes binding decisions. The agents can use their initial allocations of money to influence the court's decision on which legal regime prevails.

Suppose that the court's decision depends on the *relative* of quantity of money devoted to influence activities by each agent. For any pair (m_1, m_2) of expenditures on influence activities, let $p(m_1, m_2)$ be the probability that the court will decide that regime I prevails, and let $1 - p(m_1, m_2)$ be the probability that the court will decide that regime II prevails, with $0 < p(m_1, m_2) < 1$, and $\frac{\partial p}{\partial m_1} > 0, \frac{\partial^2 p}{\partial m_1^2} < 0, \frac{\partial p}{\partial m_2} < 0, \frac{\partial^2 p}{\partial m_2^2} > 0$. What implications do these insecure legal rights have for the final production of loud music? Can the invariance version of the Coase Theorem still hold, even though initial legal rights are insecure or not well defined?

8
Contract Law and Markets

8.1 Introduction

In Chapter 3 we examined situations in which transactions costs were low. We focused on the ability of parties to bargain around legal rules, which rendered those rules irrelevant for efficiency and, in certain cases, also irrelevant for production decisions (although not irrelevant for the distribution of wealth). In these situations, we assumed that a body of contract law or rules was in place, so that any agreements between the parties were enforceable and were in fact enforced. Under these assumptions, the efficiency properties of economic outcomes are not so much reliant on the nature of legal rules as they are on the existence of *some* legal framework and some set of rules, as well as a set of rules regarding contracts.

In the second class of situations (Chapters 4 and 5), we examined settings where bargaining was prohibitively expensive. In these situations, the efficiency of economic outcomes was heavily reliant on the design of the legal rules which governed those outcomes. Some rules yielded efficient outcomes, and some did not. If transaction costs are high and legal errors are made, then the analysis in Chapters 4 and 5 suggests that there could be significant efficiency consequences. Since no bargaining was assumed to take place in Chapters 4 and 5, contract law was irrelevant.

Chapter 6 examined an intermediate class of situations, where consumers could (perhaps imperfectly) assess the attributes of the good before they purchased it. Under a no liability rule, we saw that if consumers' perceptions of the harmfulness of the good are accurate, then the pursuit of profit and the forces of competition induce firms in competitive markets to provide the efficient level of care, even though the legal rule does not oblige them to do so.

This chapter brings these separate strands together and examines situations where transaction costs are sufficiently low for parties to engage in some contracting over outcomes, but where such contracting may be *incomplete* because transaction costs, while low, are not zero. In these situations, contracts may not be self-enforcing and may not completely specify what will occur in certain circumstances. The possibility of opportunistic behaviour and the lack of a complete contingent contract creates a potential role for a body legal rules – contract law – to determine what should happen when breaches of contract occur, and what compensation for breach of contract should be paid. These rules in turn create incentives for parties to act in certain ways.

The chapter is structured as follows. Section 8.2 presents a simple framework for assessing the incentives and welfare effects of breaches of contract by buyers and sellers in a competitive market setting. Section 8.3, which is based on the insights of Klein and Leffler (1981), studies the incentives for sellers and buyers to breach their contractual obligations if they are involved in a long-lived economic relationship, when there are no formal punishments for such breaches. Section 8.4 develops a model of damages for breach of contract which mirrors the approach to accident law taken in Chapters 6 and 7. The analysis shows that a negligence-type rule for breaches of contract induces both buyers and sellers to fully internalise the social costs of their actions and behave efficiently.

8.2 Breach of contract in competitive markets

We first examine the effect of the possibility of breaches of contract on market outcomes, assuming that there are no damage measures for breach of contract in place. Consider a competitive market for a good. The marginal cost of production is $c>0$. The marginal benefits of consumption are $u'(Q)$. The efficient outcome in this market is at Q^*, where marginal benefit equals marginal cost:

$$u'(Q^*) = c$$

The competitive equilibrium market price is $P^* = c$.

8.2.1 Breaches of contract by buyers

Now consider the same market, but suppose that contractual agreements are not perfectly enforced. Goods are exchanged by means of a contractual arrangement whereby sellers and buyers agree on a price P, sellers then deliver the good, and then after receiving the good, buyers pay the agreed price. However, suppose for goods that are sold, sellers expect that a fraction ρ of buyers will breach their contractual obligations and refuse to pay the agreed price (alternatively, sellers expect that each buyer will breach the contract and only pay $(1 - \rho)P$ instead of the agreed price). This means that if the agreed price is P°, each seller's expected marginal revenue is:

$$(1-\rho)P^\circ$$

where P° is the equilibrium market price in the absence of perfectly enforced contracts. Sellers will produce up until the point where expected marginal revenue equals marginal cost, so in the competitive equilibrium, we have:

$$(1-\rho)P^\circ = c$$

or:

$$P^\circ = \frac{c}{(1-\rho)} \tag{8.1}$$

In this equilibrium, marginal costs are "grossed up" by (1 minus) the probability that buyers will actually pay the full price, and these grossed up costs are incorporated into the equilibrium market price.

To compute the *ex ante* welfare loss from imperfectly enforced contracts, note that some buyers in this market breach their contract and do not pay the full market price (that is, a fraction ρ of them) but still receive the good. Therefore, in this equilibrium, the net benefits to buyers are:

$$u(Q^\circ) - P^\circ Q^\circ + \rho P^\circ Q^\circ = u(Q^\circ) - (1-\rho)P^\circ Q^\circ$$

On the other hand, seller profits are:

$$0 = \pi = (1-\rho)P^\circ Q^\circ - cQ^\circ$$

Hence, total welfare is:

$$W^\circ(\rho) = CS + \pi = u(Q^\circ) - (1-\rho)P^\circ Q^\circ + 0 = u(Q^\circ) - cQ^\circ$$

Since total welfare in the presence of fully enforced contractual agreements is $W^* = u(Q^*) - cQ^*$, the welfare loss from imperfectly enforced contracts is:

$$\Delta W = u(Q^*) - cQ^* - [u(Q^\circ) - cQ^\circ] \tag{8.2}$$

This is the shaded area in Figure 8.2.1. Note that in this example, where the long-run market supply curve is perfectly elastic, the incidence of the

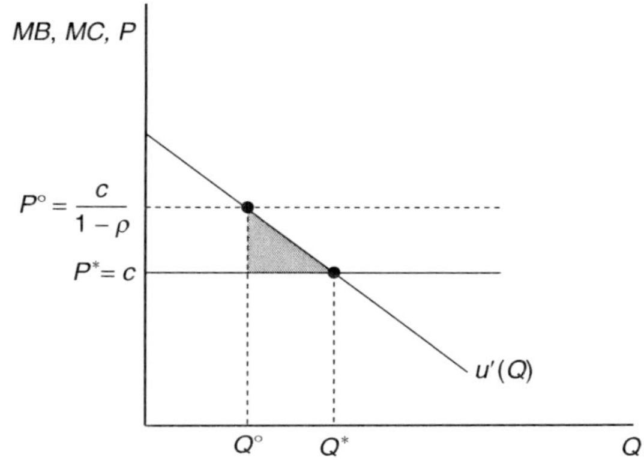

Figure 8.2.1 Competitive equilibrium in a market with imperfectly enforced contracts

costs of imperfectly enforced contracts falls entirely on buyers. We can also compute the welfare gain from a marginal improvement in contract enforcement, by computing $dW^\circ/d\rho$. We have:

$$W^{\circ\prime}(\rho) = u'(Q^\circ)Q'(P^\circ)\frac{dP^\circ}{d\rho} - cQ'(P^\circ)\frac{dP^\circ}{d\rho}$$

$$= Q'(P^\circ)\frac{c}{(1-\rho)^2}[u'(Q^\circ) - c] < 0 \qquad (8.3)$$

Since the triangle welfare loss is greater if the demand curve is more elastic, this also means that the welfare gain from improvements in contract enforcement arrangements is higher if the demand curve is more elastic.

8.2.2 Breaches of contract by sellers

Now consider the same market again, but suppose that contractual agreements are not honoured by sellers. Goods are again assumed to be exchanged by means of a contractual arrangement whereby sellers and buyers agree on a price P – but now buyers pay this price first, and after receiving this payment, sellers deliver the good. However, suppose for goods that are sold, sellers do not deliver a fraction ρ of them. In other words, some sellers will breach their contractual obligations and refuse to deliver the good. Suppose that firms agree to supply

Q° goods at a price of P. Then the total quantity that will actually be supplied is:

$$Q' = (1 - \rho)Q^\circ$$

and total revenue is:

$$PQ^\circ$$

The marginal cost of supplying goods that have been contracted for delivery does not change. Imposing a zero profit condition in this market means that total revenue must equal total cost:

$$PQ^\circ = cQ'$$

which means that:

$$\frac{P}{1-\rho}Q' = cQ'$$

or:

$$P = (1 - \rho)c$$

Buyers believe that they will receive Q° units, but actually only receive $Q' < Q^\circ$ units. The additional revenue is pocketed by sellers. In the absence of any other market adjustment, this would mean that sellers would earn positive economic profits. But these positive profits cannot persist in a competitive equilibrium, and so firms compete those profits away by bidding down the price below marginal cost.

Assuming that buyers do not correctly anticipate that contracts will not be honoured and do not adjust their behaviour in response to the possibility of a breach of contract, there will be a welfare loss as a result of firms breaching their obligations. This comes about because buyers believe that they will receive benefits from the goods that they have paid for, but do not in fact receive those benefits. At the price of $P = (1-\rho)c$, buyers are willing to purchase up to the point where $u'(Q) = P = (1 - \rho)c$. They therefore believe that they will obtain benefits of $u(Q^\circ)$. However, buyers only actually obtain $Q' = (1 - \rho)Q^\circ$ units of the good, and so only actually obtain benefits of $u(Q') = u\,[(1 - \rho)Q^\circ]$.

Buyers therefore pay D for some units of the good that do not end up being delivered, and enjoy total benefits of A + B + C. On the other side of the market, sellers incur costs of B + C. In aggregate, there is a welfare loss of F which is the shaded triangle in Figure 8.2.2.

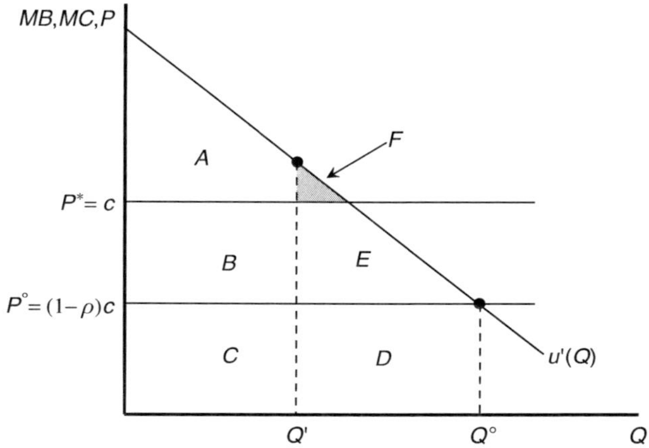

Figure 8.2.2 The welfare effects of breaches of contract by sellers

8.3 Market forces, reputation, and contractual performance

In the previous section we examined a situation where sellers breached their contractual obligations by failing to deliver the good. But contractual obligations can also be breached in other ways. For example, sellers can promise to deliver a high-quality good (which has been purchased at a high price) but instead deliver a low-quality good. Klein and Leffler (1981) examine this situation and show that under certain circumstances, market forces and the pursuit of long-run profits can induce firms to deliver high-quality goods when they have promised to do so, even though there is no legal obligation for them to do so.

The basic idea of their analysis is as follows. Suppose that there is a good that comes in two kinds of quality: high and low. Consumers have unit demands and will purchase as long as their valuations for the good exceed the price that they pay. Similarly, producers will supply the good as long as the price received is at least as large as the production costs. The gains from trade are maximised when the high-quality good is produced and consumed.

Consumers can only ascertain the quality of the good after they have purchased it. Alternatively, the pre-purchase costs of quality verification are sufficiently high to exceed the gains from trade.

We assume that the benefits to consumers of the high- and low-quality good are B_H and B_L respectively, and that production costs are c_H and c_L. Finally, suppose that firms are price takers and that there are two possible market prices, P_H and P_L that they can charge. We assume that $B_H > B_L$, $c_H > c_L$, $P_H > P_L$, and that $B_H - c_H > B_L - c_L$.

There are several possible outcomes that could occur in this market. If consumers decide to pay a high price and firms deliver the high-quality good at this price, then consumer net benefits are $B_H - P_H$ and producer profits are $P_H - c_H$. On the other hand, a firm could decide to pocket the high price and deliver the low-quality good, in which case consumer net benefits are $B_L - P_H$ and producer profits are $P_H - c_L$. The other configurations and decisions are shown in the payoff matrix in Table 8.3.1.

This game is straightforward to analyse. Since $c_L < c_H$, it is a dominant strategy for the producer to choose to produce the low-quality good. And since the producer has this dominant strategy, the consumer will only choose to pay the higher price if $P_H < P_L$ which we assumed did not hold. Therefore, the unique Nash equilibrium of this one-shot game is for the producer to produce a good of low quality, and for the consumer to purchase the low-quality good at a low price. This equilibrium is inefficient.

Now suppose that there is the opportunity of a long-lived economic relationship between buyers and sellers, so that the game above is repeated an infinite number of times. Suppose that consumers adopt the following decision rule: pay a high price as long as the good consumed in the previous period was of high quality; otherwise never again pay the high price.

We will show that if the firm adopts a strategy of producing a high-quality good as long as the consumer pays a high price, then this combination of strategies can be sustained as a subgame perfect equilibrium of the infinitely repeated game. Consider the strategy of the producer. The payoff from producing a low-quality good in the current period is:

$$B^{\text{Producer}}_{\text{Cheat}} = P_H - c_L + \delta(P_L - c_L) + \delta^2(P_L - c_L) + \delta^3(P_L - c_L) + \cdots$$

$$= P_H - c_L + \frac{\delta}{1-\delta}(P_L - c_L)$$

Table 8.3.1 The payoff matrix in the Klein–Leffler model

		Producer	
		High Quality	**Low Quality**
Consumer	**High Price**	$(B_H - P_H, P_H - c_H)$	$(B_L - P_H, P_H - c_L)$
	Low Price	$(B_H - P_L, P_L - c_H)$	$(B_L - P_L, P_L - c_L)$

On the other hand, suppose that the producer decides not to cheat. Then his payoff is:

$$B^{\text{Producer}}_{\text{Don t Cheat}} = P_H - c_H + \delta(P_H - c_H) + \delta^2(P_H - c_H) + \delta^3(P_H - c_H) + \cdots$$
$$= \frac{1}{1-\delta}(P_H - c_H)$$

Thus the producer will decide not to cheat if:

$$B^{\text{Producer}}_{\text{Don t Cheat}} \geq B^{\text{Producer}}_{\text{Cheat}} \Leftrightarrow \delta \geq \frac{c_H - c_L}{P_H - P_L} \tag{8.4}$$

A similar set of calculations for the consumer show that consumers will pay the high price as long as:

$$B^{\text{Consumer}}_{\text{Don't Cheat}} \geq B^{\text{Consumer}}_{\text{Cheat}} \Leftrightarrow \delta \geq \frac{P_H - P_L}{B_H - B_L} \tag{8.5}$$

If $B_H - B_L > c_H - c_L$ then there exists a $\delta < 1$ such that it is subgame perfect equilibrium for the efficient outcome to occur in every period (note, however, that there are also many other equilibria).

To see this, suppose that $B_H - B_L > c_H - c_L$. Let $P_H = \frac{B_H + c_H}{2}$ and $P_L = \frac{B_L + c_L}{2}$. Then:

$$\frac{P_H - P_L}{B_H - B_L} = \frac{1}{2} + \frac{1}{2}\frac{c_H - c_L}{B_H - B_L} > \frac{2(c_H - c_L)}{(c_H - c_L) + (B_H - B_L)} = \frac{c_H - c_L}{P_H - P_L} \tag{8.6}$$

so setting $\delta = \frac{1}{2} + \frac{1}{2}\frac{c_H - c_L}{B_H - B_L} + \varepsilon$ where $\varepsilon > 0$ is a small positive number, will give us the required result. The intuition behind this result is as follows. If the common discount factor is sufficiently large, then both parties value the future highly enough to be willing to give up the (relatively high) current (but one-off) benefits of breaching their contractual obligations, plus the (relatively low) gains from low-quality trades, in exchange for obtaining an continued stream of (slightly lower) payoffs from fulfilling their contractual obligations. The key insight is that it is possible for such behaviour to be sustained in the absence of formal rules around contractual performance and damage measures for breach of contract.

8.4 Damage measures for breach of contract

Despite the results of Klein and Leffler, buyers and sellers do breach contractual agreements, and there is a well-developed body of legal rules pertaining to contractual agreements. In this section we examine how parties who are harmed by such breaches of contract ('victims' of breaches of contract) should be compensated, and whether measures that are frequently employed by courts induce efficient behaviour.

Consider the following situation. There are two parties: a buyer (B) and a seller (S). They sign an agreement or contract which specifies that S deliver a good, in exchange for a payment P. This payment is paid up front by B. After the contract is signed, the parties expect that the seller will produce the good and will deliver it at some future date.

In general, the purpose of enforceable agreements between firms or individuals is to provide an environment in which the parties to the agreement can take certain economic investments or actions, based on the expectation or knowledge that the terms of the agreement will carried out. To allow for this possibility, suppose that the buyer makes a *reliance investment* of x_B at a marginal cost of w_B. The value of performance to the buyer is $V(x_B)$, with $V'(x_B) > 0$ and $V''(x_B) < 0$. For example, suppose that based on the expectation that the seller will deliver the good, the buyer purchases other goods that are complementary and which enhance the value of the good which the seller is supposed to deliver.

The seller can take actions to increase the probability that he will be able to perform the contract, and reduce the probability that he will not be able to perform. Suppose that the seller takes an action x_S, with a marginal cost of w_S which increases the probability that the seller will be able to deliver the good.

If all possible contingencies or states of the world could be anticipated costlessly and with complete certainty, parties to a contract could simply write down these contingencies in the contract and specify what happens in each state of the world. Such an agreement is called a *fully contingent* contract.

However, future states of the world are not known with certainty, and circumstances will arise in which one of the parties no longer values performance of the contract under the original terms. When such circumstances are not anticipated by either party, disputes arise. Contract law provides rules for resolving such disputes.

The probability of breach is assumed to be $\rho(x_S)$, and the probability of performance is $1 - \rho(x_S)$. We assume that $\rho'(x_S) < 0$, and $\rho''(x_S) > 0$. Thus, x_S here can be thought of as the seller's *precaution* or *care* to ensure that he puts himself in a position to perform the contract. The situation is therefore exactly analogous to the bilateral model of accident law that was examined in Chapter 6. We assume that the level of care taken by the seller is *non-contractible,* and that no renegotiation is possible. These are important assumptions.

Ideally, as discussed above, the parties would like to specify a *price schedule,* which would give a different price for every possible level of care that the seller could take. We assume that the parties *cannot* write such contracts here, because it is too costly for them to do so. On the other hand, we also assume that agreements are enforceable in a court of law, and that the buyer is awarded damages in the event of a breach. In the event of a breach of the contract by the seller, the court awards damages of d to the buyer, which are meant to compensate the buyer for the harm caused by the breach. In principle, d could depend on the actions taken by both the buyer and the seller as well as the price, so we write:

$$d = d\ (x_S, x_B, P)$$

Suppose that both parties know that if the contract is breached, damages of d will be awarded. To summarise, the sequence of events is as follows:

- The parties sign a contract and specify the delivery price P. The buyer pays this price to the seller.
- The buyer makes a reliance investment of $x_B > 0$, at a cost of $w_B x_B$.
- The seller takes an action $x_S > 0$, at a cost of $w_S x_S$, which affects the likelihood that the contract is performed.
- Given x_S, the seller is either able to perform the contract (which happens with probability $1 - \rho(x_S)$, or cannot perform, in which case he breaches the contract, which happens with probability $\rho(x_S)$.
- If the seller breaches, the buyer files a lawsuit at no cost.
- The court awards damages of d.

Throughout the analysis we assume that the parties are risk neutral. The expected benefit of the contract to the buyer is then:

$$B_B = -P + [1 - \rho(x_S)]V(x_B) + \rho(x_S)d - w_B x_B \tag{8.7}$$

and the expected benefit of the contract to the seller is:

$$B_S = P - \rho(x_S)d - w_S x_S \tag{8.8}$$

Adding these two gives the joint expected benefits of the contract:

$$B = (x_S, x_B) = B_B + B_S$$
$$= -P + [1 - \rho(x_S)]V(x_B) + \rho(x_S)d - w_B x_B + P - \rho(x_S)d - w_S x_S$$
$$= [1 - \rho(x_S)]V(x_B) - w_B x_B - w_S x_S \tag{8.9}$$

Note that under the assumption of risk neutrality, neither the price nor the damage measure enter this expression, since both are simply a transfer between the seller and the buyer.

8.4.1 Efficiency

The set-up is very similar to the bilateral model of accidents that we examined in Chapter 5. Efficiency requires that the following two conditions hold:

- The buyer should invest in reliance up to the point where the marginal benefit of reliance equals the marginal cost; and
- The seller should invest in precaution up to the point where the marginal benefit of precaution equal the marginal cost.

Therefore, at the optimum (x_S^*, x_B^*) we have:

$$[1 - \rho(x_S^*)]V'(x_B^*) = w_B \tag{8.10}$$

and:

$$-\rho'(x_S^*)]V(x_B^*) = w_S \tag{8.11}$$

Note first a key point: in most cases it will be efficient for the seller to breach the contract with some positive probability. Note also what the first of these conditions states. Under conditions of complete certainty, the buyer would invest in reliance up the point where the marginal value of reliance, $V'(x_B)$, was equal to marginal cost, w_B. Call this level x_B°. Condition (8.10) above states that where there is some possibility that the contract may be breached, the buyer should invest up to the point where the discounted marginal value of reliance equals its marginal cost, where the value is discounted by the probability that the contract will be performed. Thus, we have:

$$V'(x_B^*) = \frac{w_B}{1 - \rho(x_S^*)} > w_B = V'(x_B^\circ) \tag{8.12}$$

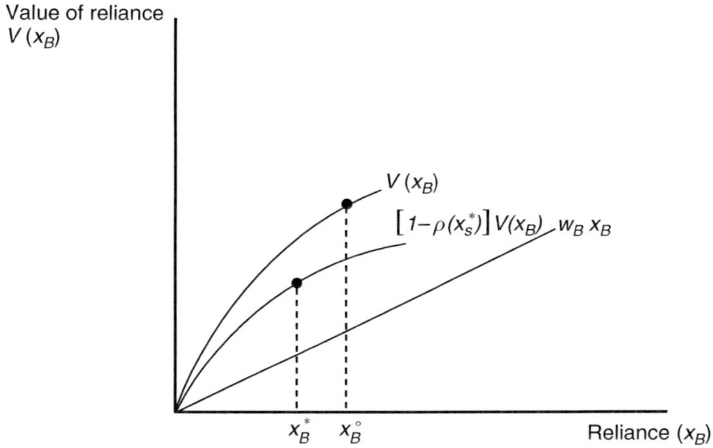

Figure 8.4.1 Efficient reliance by the buyer

and since $V()$ is concave, this implies that $x_B^* < x_B^\circ$. The efficient level of reliance investment is less than that which would be chosen under conditions of complete certainty.

8.4.2 Expectation damages

We can now examine the efficiency properties of various damage measures for breach of contract, beginning with expectation damages. In the event of the contract being breached, expectation damages put the buyer of the good or service in the same position that they would have been in had the contract been performed. In our example, the buyer has already prepaid the purchase price and has also invested in reliance. Hence, these are both sunk costs at the time the seller breaches or performs the contract. For any x_B, the buyer expects to receive $V(x_B)$ if the contract is performed. This means that for any x_B, expectation damages here are:

$$d^E = V(x_B)$$

Note that the level of damages depends on the level of reliance taken by the buyer.

8.4.2.1 The seller's behaviour

Suppose that the parties know that expectation damages will be awarded in the event of a breach. The expected value of the contract to the seller is:

$$B_S = P - \rho(x_S)d^E - w_S x_S = P - \rho(x_S)V(x_B) - w_S x_S$$

For any x_B, the seller will choose precaution up to the point where private marginal benefit equals private marginal cost:

$$-\rho'(x_S^E)V(x_B) = w_S \tag{8.13}$$

But note that this expression is the same as the efficiency condition for efficient precaution as outlined earlier in (8.11). In other words, *expectation damages induce efficient behaviour by the seller.*

8.4.2.2 *The buyer's behaviour*

Given that the buyer is fully compensated under the expectation damages rule, the expected value of the contract to the buyer under expectation damages is:

$$\begin{aligned} B_B &= -P + [1-\rho(x_S)]V(x_B) + \rho(x_S)V(x_B) - w_B x_B \\ &= -P + V(x_B) - w_B x_B \end{aligned} \tag{8.14}$$

For any x_B, the seller will choose precaution up to the point where private marginal benefit equals private marginal cost. But note that the above expression is independent of the probability $\rho(x_s)$. The buyer has a dominant strategy – to choose x_B so that:

$$V'(x_B^E) = w_B \tag{8.15}$$

which is satisfied at the point $x_B^E = x_B^\circ > x_B^*$. Under expectations damages, the buyer overinvests in reliance.

8.4.2.3 *Equilibrium*

Given the behaviour of the buyer, the seller's choice of care will then satisfy:

$$-\rho'(x_S^E)V(x_B^E) = w_S \tag{8.16}$$

Since $V(x_B^E) > V(x_B^*)$ and the right-hand side is equal to w_S, it must be the case that on the left-hand side we have:

$$-\rho'(x_S^E) < -\rho'(x_S^*)$$

so:

$$\rho'(x_S^E) > -\rho'(x_S^*) \tag{8.17}$$

Since $\rho'(x_S)$ is negative, and since $\rho''(x_S) > 0$, this means that $x_S^E > x_S^*$. The seller invests in the optimal amount of care given the level of reliance, but since the buyer overinvests in reliance, the seller also overinvests in care from an efficiency point of view.

This result is exactly analogous to the rule of strict liability in the bilateral model of accident law. Since expectation damages fully insure the "victim" of the breach (the buyer), the buyer underinvests in care (overinvests in reliance), and the "injurer" (the seller) overinvests in care.

8.4.3 Reliance damages

Reliance damages put the buyer in the same position as they would have been had the contract not been entered into. If we assume that the buyer had initial benefits of zero, this means that the reliance measure simply returns the initial price and the buyer's reliance investment $w_B x_B$. This means that:

$$d^{\text{Reliance}} = P + w_B x_B$$

Note that the level of damages again depends on the level of reliance taken by the buyer.

8.4.3.1 The seller's behaviour

Suppose that the parties know that reliance damages remedy will be awarded to the buyer in the event of a breach. The expected value of the contract to the seller is:

$$B_S = P - \rho(x_S) d^{\text{Reliance}} - w_S x_S = P - \rho(x_S)(P + w_B x_B) - w_S x_S \qquad (8.18)$$

For any x_B, the seller will choose precaution up to the point where private marginal benefit equals private marginal cost:

$$-\rho'(x_S^{\text{Reliance}})[P + w_B x_B] = w_S$$

Since the buyer would never enter into the contract if the price paid plus the cost of reliance exceeded the value of the reliance, we must have $P + w_B x_B < V(x_B)$. This then means that:

$$w_S = -\rho'(x_S^{\text{Reliance}})[P + w_B x_B] < -\rho'(x_S^{\text{Reliance}}) V(x_B) \qquad (8.19)$$

For any x_B. In particular, the inequality in (8.19) must hold for $x_B = x_B^*$. This means that:

$$-\rho'(x_S^*) V(x_B^*) = w_S = -\rho'(x_S^{\text{Reliance}})[P + w_B x_B] < -\rho'(x_S^{\text{Reliance}}) V(x_B^*) \qquad (8.20)$$

so that

$$-\rho'(x_S^*) < -\rho'(x_S^{\text{Reliance}})$$

and so

$$\rho'(x_S^*) > \rho'(x_S^{\text{Reliance}}) \tag{8.21}$$

Once again, since $\rho'(x_S)$ is negative, and since $\rho''(x_S) > 0$, this means that $x_S^{\text{Reliance}} < x_S^*$. The seller *underinvests* in precaution (alternatively, the seller breaches the contract too frequently, compared to the efficient breach frequency). Intuitively, since $P + w_B x_B < V(x_B)$, under reliance damages the seller is not faced with the full social costs of his breach decision, and he breaches too often.

8.4.3.2 The buyer's behaviour

The expected value of the contract to the buyer under reliance damages is:

$$\begin{aligned} B_B &= -P + [1 - \rho(x_S)]V(x_B) + \rho(x_S)d^{\text{Reliance}} - w_B x_B \\ &= -P + [1 - \rho(x_S)]V(x_B) + \rho(x_S)[P + w_B x_B] - w_B x_B \\ &= [1 - p(x_S)][V(x_B) - P - w_B x_B] \end{aligned}$$

Maximising this is equivalent to maximising:

$$V(x_B) - P - w_B x_B$$

As a result, the buyer again chooses an inefficiently high level of reliance. Because $w_B x_B$ is returned to the buyer in the event of a breach, the buyer ignores the loss of $w_B x_B$ in the event of non-performance. This results in overinvestment.

8.4.4 Restitution damages

Under restitution damages, the seller returns any payments that have been made to him by the buyer. Since we have assumed that the buyer paid the price up front, this means that:

$$d^{\text{Rest}} = P$$

Note that the level of damages does not depend on the level of reliance taken by the buyer.

8.4.4.1 The seller's behaviour

Suppose that the parties know that restitution damages will be awarded. The expected value of the contract to the seller is:

$$B_S = P - \rho(x_S)d^{\text{Rest}} - w_S x_S = P - \rho(x_S)P - w_S x_S$$

The seller will choose precaution up to the point where private marginal benefit equals private marginal cost:

$$-\rho'(x_S^{\text{Rest}})P = w_S$$

Since the buyer would never enter into the contract if the price paid plus the cost of reliance exceeded the value of the reliance, we must have $P < V(x_B)$ for all x_B. This then means that:

$$-\rho'(x_S^*)V(x_B^*) = w_S = -\rho'(x_S^{\text{Rest}})P < -\rho'(x_S^{\text{Rest}})V(x_B^*)$$

And so

$$\rho'(x_S^{\text{Rest}}) < \rho'(x_S^*)$$

Since $\rho'(x_S)$ is negative, and since $\rho''(x_S) > 0$, this means that $x_S^{\text{Rest}} < x_S^*$, which means that the seller again underinvests in precaution (and so breaches the contract too frequently, compared to the efficient breach frequency).

8.4.4.2 The buyer's behaviour

The expected benefit of the contract to the buyer is now:

$$\begin{aligned} B_B &= -P + [1 - \rho(x_S)]V(x_B) + (x_S)d^{\text{Rest}} - w_B x_B \\ &= -P + [1 - \rho(x_S)]V(x_B) + \rho(x_S)P - w_B x_B \end{aligned}$$

Now the buyer's first-order condition is:

$$[1 - \rho(x_S)]V'(x_B) = w_B$$

Note that this means that given the seller's investment in care, the buyer actually invests efficiently. However, given that the seller underinvests in care, the buyer will also underinvest in reliance.

8.4.5 The rule in *Hadley* v. *Baxendale*

The main conclusion of the previous section is that *none of the three damage measures are able to achieve efficiency in both the level of care and the reliance investment.* The results are summarised in Table 8.4.1.

Table 8.4.1 The effects of different damage measures for breach of contract

Damage measure	Buyer	Seller
Expectation damages	Over-reliance	Efficient, given reliance, but since buyer overinvests in reliance, this means that care is inefficiently high.
Reliance damages	Over-reliance	Inefficiently low.
Restitution damages	Under-reliance	Inefficiently low

As discussed earlier, the model that we have developed in this section is similar to the basic bilateral accident model developed in Chapter 5, and yet all of the damage measures we have examined so far fail the efficiency test. The reason is that none of them replicate or approximate the efficient rules we examined in the accident law setting. The expectation measure shows promise – it induces efficient behaviour by the seller – but ultimately fails because the buyer is fully insured against all risk and so there is a moral hazard problem with this measure.

Drawing on the lessons from Chapter 5, it is reasonable to expect that some kind of due standard or negligence rule might perform well in the contract law setting. Let us investigate such a rule, which is known in the literature as the rule in *Hadley* v. *Baxendale*, after the legal case in which it was (with suitable interpretation from economists!) first proposed.[1]

Suppose that courts award expectation damages to buyers, but only to the extent that such expectation damages are "reasonable". In particular, suppose that the court knows the efficient level of reliance, x_B^*, and suppose that it implements a rule which awards the buyer $V(x_B^*)$ in the event of a breach, irrespective of the actual level of reliance investment that the buyer has made. Let us investigate the behaviour of the parties under this rule.

8.4.5.1 *The seller's behaviour*

Suppose that the parties know that expectation damages of $V(x_B^*)$ will be awarded. The expected value of the contract to the seller is:

$$B_S = P - \rho(x_S)V(x_B^*) - w_S x_S$$

For any x_B, the seller will choose precaution up to the point where private marginal benefit equals private marginal cost:

$$-\rho'(x_S^E)V(x_B^*) = w_S$$

But note that this expression is the same as the efficiency condition for efficient precaution as outlined earlier in (8.11). In other words, reasonable expectation damages of $V(x_B^*)$ induce efficient behaviour by the seller.

8.4.5.2 *The buyer's behaviour*

Given that the buyer is compensated an amount of $V(x_B^*)$ irrespective of the level of reliance that he actually chooses, the expected value of the contract to the buyer under expectation damages is:

$$B_B = -P + [1 - \rho(x_S)]V(x_B) + \rho(x_S)V(x_B^*) - w_B x_B \tag{8.22}$$

For any x_S, the buyer will choose precaution up to the point where private marginal benefit equals private marginal cost. But note now that in contrast to equation (8.14), the expression (8.22) depends on the probability $\rho(x_S)$. The buyer's optimal choice of reliance now satifies:

$$[1-\rho(x_S)]V'(x_B^E) = w_B \tag{8.23}$$

8.4.5.3 Equilibrium

Given that the seller chooses $x_S^E = x_S^*$ the buyer's reliance satisfies:

$$[1-\rho(x_S^*)]V'(x_B^*) = w_B \tag{8.24}$$

and so both the buyer and the seller behave efficiently. This result is exactly analogous to a rule of strict liability with a defence of contributory negligence in the bilateral model of accident law, where the due standard of care is chosen to be the efficient level of care. These expectation damages insure the 'victim' of the breach (the buyer) only to the extent that he behaves reasonably. Moreover, the buyer cannot influence these damages by his choice of reliance, so that there is no moral hazard issue. On the other side of the contract, the seller faces the full social costs of his actions, where those social costs are computed at the efficient point. Hence it is as if the seller effectively faces an efficient Pigouvian tax under this rule.

8.5 Notes

There is a large literature on the economics of contract law. This chapter has covered the basics. Shavell (1980) and Rogerson (1984) are the classic papers analysing the economic effects of damage measures for breach of contract. The presentation of the economics of damage measures in this chapter draws on the framework of Benoit and Kornhauser (2002). Klein and Leffler (1981) examine the incentives to provide high-quality goods in a competitive market setting in the absence of damage measures for breach of contract. Pashigian (1998) contains a useful summary of the Klein–Leffler model.

8.6 Exercises

1. A buyer and a seller are contemplating signing a contract for the delivery of a good. They agree on a price of $P > 0$ for the good. The seller does not know what his costs will be, although he does know the likelihood with which various costs will occur. The table below lists the possible costs for the seller and the probability with which they arise.

Cost	Probability
20	$\frac{1}{3}$
50	$\frac{1}{3}$
90	$\frac{1}{3}$

Suppose that, after the contract is signed, the buyer can make a reliance investment decision. If the buyer invests $r_L = 4$ and the contract is performed, then the buyer receives a return of $V_L = 47$. If the buyer invests $r_H = 20$ and the contract is performed, then the buyer receives a return of $V_H = 80$.

(a) Briefly explain the concept of an *efficient breach* of contract. If the buyer invests $r_L = 4$, how frequently should the seller breach the contract, assuming he behaves efficiently? If the buyer invests $r_H = 20$, how often should the seller breach, assuming he behaves efficiently? Assuming the seller behaves efficiently, what is the joint expected value of the contract if the buyer invests $r_L = 4$? Assuming the seller behaves efficiently, what is the joint expected value of the contract if the buyer invests $r_H = 20$? Assuming the seller behaves efficiently, what is the efficient level of reliance investment by the buyer?

(b) Define and briefly explain the remedies of *expectation damages*, *reliance damages* and *restitution damages* in contract law. Taking the reliance investment by the buyer as given, which of these damage measures induce efficient breach decisions in the above setting? Explain.

(c) Suppose that in the above example, the parties know that in the event of a breach by the seller, the court will award *expectation damages* to the buyer. Under this legal rule, in the above example, will the buyer choose the efficient level of reliance investment? How does the buyer's reliance decision depend on the price, *p*? What is the joint value of the contract under expectation damages? If the parties know that in the event of a breach by the seller, the court will award expectation damages to the buyer, what range of prices must *p* lie between for them to even agree to sign a contract?

2. Suppose there is a single monopoly firm that produces a single good, *Q*. The ordinary demand curve for this good is:

$$Q = 1 - P$$

where *P* is the price of the good and *Q* is the quantity demanded. Suppose that marginal costs of production are constant and equal to $c = 0$.

(a) What is the Pareto-optimal price and quantity? How much profit does the firm earn if it charges this price?

Now suppose that the good is potentially harmful to consumers. Let $0 < l < 1$ be the consumer's expected dollar loss per unit of the good consumed. The firm can completely eliminate these losses by taking care when it produces each unit of the good. The firm's per-unit cost of care is $k < l$. Consumers are assumed to be unable to take care, and cannot observe the firm's choice of care before they purchase the product.

(b) Is it efficient for the firm to take care?

(c) Suppose that there is a no liability rule in place, but that the firm and the consumer are engaged in a long-lasting commercial relationship which starts at time $t = 0$ and lasts into the indefinite future (that is, forever).

In each period, consumers purchase a quantity of the good and must consume it; the good is non-durable. In each period the firm can choose to produce safe goods or potentially harmful goods. The problem for consumers is that they cannot observe the level of care taken by the firm in that period until *after* they have purchased the good (the good is an experience good).

Assume that the firm can now offer the consumer a *warranty* in each period, which is just a costless written assurance by the firm that the good is safe and will not harm them. If such a warranty is provided at $t = 0$, then the consumer believes the firm and their demand curve for the good in period $t = 0$ is:

$$Q = 1 - P$$

If the firm does provide a warranty, it has two choices at time $t = 0$:

- **Take Care:** The firm can honour its warranty and take care, incurring a per-unit cost of $k > 0$. It can still act like a monopolist and choose whatever price it wishes. If the firm honours its warranty, then it builds up its *reputation*: if it again provides a warranty in the next period ($t = 1$), then consumers will again believe them and will again have the same demand curve, $Q = 1 - P$.
- **Don't Take Care:** The firm breaks the commitment made in its warranty and does not take care, and so does not incur the per-unit cost of $k > 0$. It can still act like a monopolist and choose whatever price it wishes. Consumers must consume the potentially dangerous good and cannot sue for damages or breach of contract. If the firm chooses this strategy and fails to take care after it has provided a warranty to do so, then its reputation is immediately destroyed: consumers *never* believe them again, and the demand curve for *all* subsequent periods ($t = 1, 2, 3,\ldots$) is:

$$Q = 1 - P - l$$

irrespective of whether the firm provides a warranty or not in those subsequent periods.

You may again assume that $k < l$. The firm discounts future profits at the rate $0 < \delta < 1$ (this means that the firm is indifferent between receiving \$$\delta$ today and \$1 tomorrow).

(d) At time $t = 0$, what is the discounted present value of the firm's profits if it provides a warranty, acts as a monopolist and follows the **Take Care** strategy? What is the net present value of the consumer surplus if the firm chooses this strategy?

(e) At time $t = 0$, what is the discounted present value of the firm's profits if it provides a warranty, acts as a monopolist and follows the **Don't Take Care** strategy? What is the net present value of the consumer surplus if the firm chooses this strategy?

(f) Which strategy maximises the net present value of aggregate welfare? Explain.

Consider the following statement:

'If the firm is sufficiently patient (if δ is sufficiently high), then it will choose the strategy that maximises the net present value of aggregate welfare.'

(g) Is the statement True, False or Uncertain? If the statement is true, find the level of δ that makes the firm indifferent between the two strategies. If the statement is false or uncertain, explain why.

3. (An application to employment contracts). Unfair dismissal laws impose fines on employers for firing workers in certain circumstances, and in some circumstances prevent employers from firing workers altogether. This question asks you to consider the efficiency properties of some common law alternatives to unfair dismissal laws.

Suppose that an employer and a worker are contemplating signing a contract for the completion of a task by the worker at some point in the future. They agree on a wage $w > 0$ that the employer will pay the worker if the task is carried out. The employer has the option of firing the worker, in which case the task is not carried out and the wage is not paid.

After the employment contract is signed, the worker makes some reliance investment of $r > 0$ (for example, he may move cities in order to take up the new job). If he is not dismissed, the value of this reliance investment is $V(r) > 0$, where $V'(r) > 0$ and $V''(r) < 0$. If he is dismissed, the value of this reliance investment is zero.

In this setting, assume that performance of the contract is the choice of the employer. He can either *perform* the contract by having the worker to carry out the task and pay him the agreed wage, or he can *breach* the contract by dismissing (firing) the worker before the task is carried out, and refuse to pay the worker the agreed wage.

The problem for the parties is that neither the employer nor the worker know exactly how good the worker will be at the task. Let ρ be the employer's possible profit level (not including the wage payment w) when the worker completes the task. The parties regard ρ as a random variable which can take on n different values, with probabilities $\rho_i = \Pr(\pi = \pi_i)$, where $0 < \rho_i < 1$ and $\sum_i \rho_i = 1$.

The true value of ρ is not revealed until after the contract is signed and the worker makes his reliance investment. For example, the worker could turn out to be extremely good, implying a high value of ρ for the employer. In such a case, the employer would not want to fire the worker and would be happy to get ρ in return for paying the worker the agreed wage of w.

On the other hand, the worker might reveal himself to be a complete disaster at the job, implying a low or even a negative value of ρ for the employer. In such a case, the employer may want to fire the worker instead of receiving a low value of ρ and paying the worker the agreed wage of w.

(a) In this context, explain what a *complete employment contract* would look like. Why might the parties not be able to (or not wish to) sign a complete employment contract?

For the remaining parts of this question, assume that complete employment contracts cannot be signed.

(b) In this setting, it is ever efficient for the employer to dismiss the worker? From an efficiency point of view, how frequently should the employer dismiss the worker? Explain.

(c) Assuming the employer dismisses the worker only when it is efficient to do so, what is the efficient level of reliance investment by the worker?
(d) Recall the three damage measures for breach of contract that we studied in this chapter. Apply these damage measures to this employment contract setting. Which of these legal rules induce the employer to make efficient dismissals? Which of these legal rules induce the worker to make efficient reliance investment decisions?
(e) Explain, with reference to the rule in *Hadley* v. *Baxendale*, how you would design efficient unfair dismissal laws. What should be the appropriate goal of such laws – higher employment levels, higher wages, higher profits, or something else? What sort of information would you need to design such laws?

9

Crime, Punishment and Deterrence – Markets for Illegal Activities and the Economics of Public Law Enforcement

9.1 Introduction

In previous chapters we examined legal rules that govern private harms and breaches of private agreements. This chapter analyses markets for illegal activities, which are thought to generate a more widely dispersed kind of social harm and which, in general, cannot be perfectly detected or enforced.

Individuals face two kinds of costs when contemplating whether to commit an illegal act: the cost of the activity itself, and the expected punishment that they may face. The economic approach to crime treats the expected punishment as a 'price' which individuals take into account when choosing whether to commit a crime. In modern economies punishments usually take the form of monetary fines or imprisonment terms. But there are also other types of punishment, including social norms and community 'shaming' or stigmas attached to certain kinds of behaviour.

This chapter introduces a simple analytical framework to examine the incentive effects of monetary fines and imprisonment terms. Efficient deterrence and enforcement policy is examined as a standard cost–benefit problem. Within this structure we also examine two kinds of legal rules: strict criminal liability and fault-based criminal liability.

The chapter is structured as follows. Section 9.2 introduces the basic approach to crime and punishment that is used throughout the chapter, and examines the welfare effects of fines, imprisonment and enforcement activities. Section 9.3 applies this approach to markets for illegal activities, and considers several applications, including evasion of specific taxes. Section 9.4 examines the issue of plea bargaining, whilst section 9.5 analyses the economics of organised crime.

9.2 The economic approach to crime: A general analytical framework

This section develops a simple analytical framework for examining some of the economic issues that arise in the analysis of crime and punishment. Suppose that there is some activity, the level of which is denoted by x, which causes uncompensated harm to others. We will refer to x as the 'crime rate', although the analysis can be applied to any activity which the state deems illegal. Individuals benefit privately from this activity, and this benefit is denoted by $B(x)$ with $B'(x) \geq 0$ and $B''(x) < 0$. We assume that the individual has a privately optimal level of illegal activity, denoted by x°, which is where $B'(x^{\circ}) = 0$.

Let $H(x)$ be the aggregate external harm caused by the activity x. We assume that these external costs are increasing and that marginal costs are non-decreasing, so $H'(x) > 0$ and $H''(x) \geq 0$. In the absence of enforcement costs or compliance costs, the efficient level of illegal activity maximises $W = B(x) - H(x)$. We assume that there is a unique efficient level of illegal activity x^*, where x^* satisfies $B'(x^*) = H'(x^*)$.

There are several important points to note here. First, the benefits that accrue to the individual are included in the aggregate measure of welfare. To not include them would risk assuming the economic issue away and would ignore the private incentives of individuals to engage in illegal activity – if individuals do not gain some benefit from committing illegal acts, why do they commit them? Secondly, even if enforcement is not costless, the efficient level of illegal activity is generally *not* zero, although our specification certainly allows this a possibility (rather than imposing it).

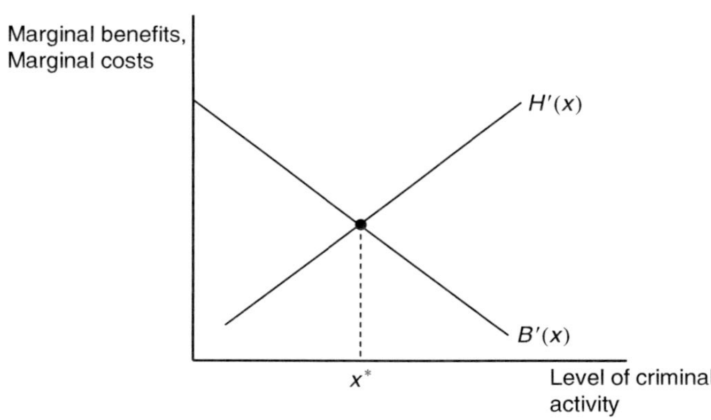

Figure 9.2.1 The efficient level of illegal activity

9.2.1 Deterring illegal activity with monetary fines

The basic assumption is that the individual's choice of x leads to negative external harm. The economic approach to crime draws on the standard Pigouvian approach to the problem of negative externalities, with some slight modifications. Consider first a legal rule of *strict liability* for illegal acts: the individual is punished for any level of x that they choose. An alternative rule (which we examine further below) is one of *fault-based liability*, where the individual is only punished if the level of activity that they choose exceeds some predetermined level, say $\bar{x}$. This is analytically similar to the negligence rules we examined in Chapters 4, 5 and 6, and we examine it further below.

Suppose that there is some probability ρ that the individual will be caught and fined when they commit the illegal activity. Let the resource cost of achieving this probability be $C(\rho)$, with $C'(\rho) > 0$ and $C''(\rho) \geq 0$. These are *enforcement costs*. For the moment we assume that the probability of detection is fixed at some level $\bar{\rho}$ and therefore enforcement costs are fixed at $\bar{C} = C(\bar{\rho})$. Including enforcement costs, total welfare is now:

$$W = B(x) - H(x) - \bar{C} \tag{9.1}$$

Let us consider a system of fines that are designed to deter illegal activity. The analysis again emphasises the importance of marginal incentives, rather than total incentives. Let the size of the *marginal* or per unit fine be equal to $f > 0$. Thus, if an individual commits a level of criminal activity equal to x, he will face a fine of $fx > 0$ with probability $\bar{\rho}$, and no fine with probability $1 - \bar{\rho}$.

Note that the marginal fine f here does not explicitly include the benefits obtained by the individual. The reason for this assumption is straightforward: for some crimes (such as financial crime) it may be possible to force the criminal to return some or all of the gains that he obtains from crime. But for others (such as murder) this will simply not be possible, since most or all of the criminal's benefit could be non-pecuniary.

Finally, we allow for the possibility that a system of fines may be costly to administer in total (with total costs of $K > 0$), but that the *marginal* cost of administering fines is zero (this assumption is relaxed later). There are now two questions of interest:

1. How does the individual react to different levels of f? (The positive question)
2. What is the efficient marginal fine? (The normative question).

9.2.1.1 *Criminal behaviour*

We will assume that the individual is risk-neutral, and therefore acts as if he is maximising his expected net benefits, solving:

$$\max_{x\geq 0} B(x) - \bar{\rho}fx - (1-\bar{\rho})0 = B(x) - \bar{\rho}fx \tag{9.2}$$

The individual optimises by setting x equal to x_c, where x_c solves $B'(x_c) = \bar{\rho}f$. That is, the individual engages in illegal activity up until the point where his marginal benefit equals the 'price' of the activity, where the price is the expected *marginal* fine. This gives us the following 'demand curve' for illegal activity:

$$x_c = x(\bar{\rho}f) \equiv B'^{-1}(\bar{\rho}f) \tag{9.3}$$

with

$$\frac{dx_c}{df} = x'(\bar{\rho}f) = \frac{d}{df}B'^{-1}(\bar{\rho}f) = \frac{1}{\frac{d}{df}B'(\bar{\rho}f)} = \frac{1}{\bar{\rho}B''(f)} < 0$$

and where the second last equality follows from the inverse function theorem, and the last inequality follows from the assumption that $B'' < 0$.

The 'demand curve' for illegal activity is downward sloping as a function of the 'price' $\bar{\rho}f$. This is the *deterrence hypothesis*: a higher expected marginal punishment reduces the individual's crime rate. Note that the deterrence hypothesis by itself says nothing about the *magnitude* of the deterrence effect. That depends on the slope of the demand curve or the *elasticity of the demand for crime with respect to the expected marginal punishment*. We will examine this elasticity below.

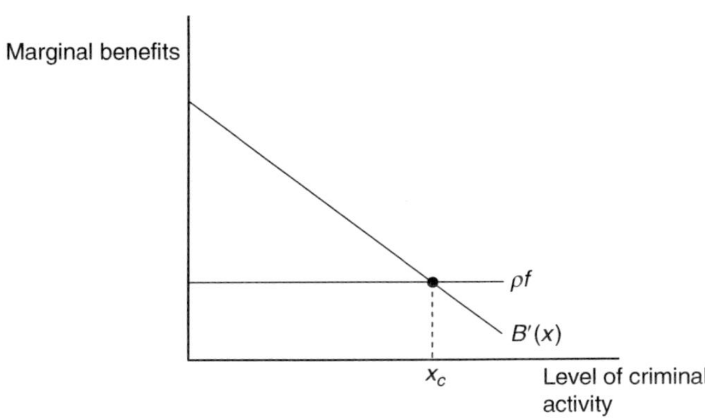

Figure 9.2.2 Individual behaviour in response to a fine

9.2.1.2 Efficient fines

The optimal fine maximises welfare, W. Remember, however, that any choice of fine will flow through into individual behaviour according to equation (9.3) above. The enforcement authority cannot control illegal activity directly – it can only do so indirectly, through its choice of the fine. What level of f maximises welfare? We assume that revenue is received by the government on behalf of the taxpayer and returned to them in a lump-sum fashion, and that the system of fines is costless to administer *at the margin*. Thus, at the margin, fines are assumed to be pure wealth transfers from criminals to the rest of society. This assumption regarding punishments can be relaxed, and we do so below.

Using the economic intuition of the Pigouvian approach, we can test the following 'guess'. Recall that the Pigouvian approach sets a tax of t^*, where this satisfies:

$$t^* = H'(x^*)$$

Thus, economic intuition leads us to the conjecture that if we follow this approach and set the marginal fine f so that $\bar{p}f = H'(x^*)$, the individual will, in accordance with the standard Pigouvian rule, fully internalise the external costs of his actions and choose the efficient rate of illegal activity.

This guess turns out to be correct. To see this, note that with a fine of $\bar{p}f$, expected welfare is the sum of the individual's net benefit and the net benefit to the rest of society, both of which include the expected revenue from the fine:

$$W(f) = B(x) - \bar{p}fx + \bar{p}fx - H(x) - \bar{C}$$

$$= B(x) - H(x) - \bar{C} \qquad (9.4)$$

where for any fine, the criminal will choose $x_c = x(\bar{p}f)$, and where, without loss of generality, we have set the costs of administering the system of fines at $K = 0$. Note that society gains the fine f only when a crime is actually detected (which happens with probability $\bar{p}$), but the social harm H occurs whether the crime is detected or not. Plugging $x_c = x(\bar{p}f)$ into (9.4) yields:

$$W(f) = B[x(\bar{p}f)] - H[x(\bar{p}f)] - C(\bar{p})$$

Choosing the marginal fine f to maximise welfare yields the first-order condition:

$$\frac{dB[x(\bar{\rho}f^*)]}{dx}\frac{dx}{d(\bar{\rho}f^*)}\bar{\rho} = \frac{dH[x(\bar{\rho}f^*)]}{dx}\frac{dx}{d(\bar{\rho}f^*)}\bar{\rho} \tag{9.5}$$

The first term in (9.5) is the marginal change in the individual's benefits when his choice of illegal activity changes. The second term on the left-hand side tells us how responsive illegal activity is to an increase in the expected fine. The third term, $\bar{\rho}$, is the marginal change in the expected fine as f changes. Multiplied together, these terms give the individual's expected marginal loss when the fine increases by a small amount. It is the expected marginal social cost of increasing f.

The first term on the right-hand side of (9.5) is the marginal social harm of illegal activity. The second term is again just a measure of the responsiveness of illegal activity with respect to an increase in the fine. The third term, $\bar{\rho}$, is again the marginal change in the expected fine as f changes. These three terms multiplied together give the expected marginal change in harm when the fine increases by a small amount. In other words, it is the expected marginal social cost of increasing f.

The optimal fine balances out marginal social costs and benefits. Cancelling terms, we get:

$$\frac{dB[x(\bar{\rho}f^*)]}{dx} = \frac{dH[x(\bar{\rho}f^*)]}{dx} \tag{9.6}$$

This can be simplified by noting from the individual's behaviour that:

$$\frac{dB[x(\bar{\rho}f^*)]}{dx} = \bar{\rho}f^*$$

and so the condition in equation (9.6) becomes:

$$\bar{\rho}f^* = \frac{dH[x(\bar{\rho}f^*)]}{dx} \tag{9.7}$$

These two conditions verify that the Pigouvian intuition explored earlier is correct. First, since equation (9.6) has marginal benefits equal to marginal harm, this verifies that it is possible to design a system of fines such that the individual chooses the efficient level of illegal activity. Secondly, equation (9.7) confirms that the efficient solution is to set the expected marginal fine (which in expected terms is equivalent to a

Pigouvian tax here) equal to the marginal external harm evaluated at the optimal rate of illegal activity. Dividing both sides of (9.7) by $\bar{\rho}$ yields:

$$f^* = \frac{\frac{dH[x(\bar{\rho}f^*)]}{dx}}{\bar{\rho}} \tag{9.8}$$

This is a fundamental equation in the economic approach to crime, punishment and illegal activity. It states that for a fixed probability of detection, the welfare-maximising fine f^* is equal to the discounted value of marginal harm at the efficient level of x, where the discount rate is the probability of detection $\bar{\rho}$.

There are several points worth noting here:

1. This result was obtained under the assumption of risk-neutral behaviour on the part of the individual. Different attitudes towards risk will, in general, lead to a different result.
2. The optimal fine is higher, the smaller is the probability of detection and the higher is the marginal harm at the optimum.
3. Since $\bar{\rho} < 1$, the efficient marginal fine will *exceed* the marginal harm created by the illegal activity at the optimum. In a world of imperfect detection, it is simply not good enough to fine individuals an amount that is equal to the marginal external harm. To do so would lead to an inefficiently low expected punishment and in inefficiently high level of illegal activity – indeed, the crime rate would be massively high relative to the efficient level if $\bar{\rho}$ is close to zero. Thus, for example, punishment schemes which simply force individuals to return stolen goods or repay amounts of money that they have stolen – without any other punishment – are probably doomed to fail from an efficiency point of view. A similar conclusion holds for 'restorative justice' programmes, which effectively set the 'fine' equal to the marginal social harm that is created. If $\bar{\rho} < 1$ this kind of scheme will tend to encourage inefficiently high rates of illegal activity, since the expected punishment will be far too low from an efficiency point of view.
4. Finally, we have fixed the probability of detection at $\bar{\rho}$. But since fines are assumed to be pure transfers from individuals to the rest of society, and since individuals only cares about the expected fine, *and* since $\bar{\rho} > 0$ means that $C(\bar{\rho}) > 0$, it may be possible to improve upon this solution.

To expand upon the last point, note that for any ρ, efficiency requires that:

$$\rho f^* = \frac{dH[x(\rho f^*)]}{dx} \tag{9.9}$$

But a risk-neutral individual's choice of x only depends on ρf^*, not f^* by itself. Thus, with the individual assumed to be risk-neutral, it is possible to decrease ρ and increase f^* and equation (9.9) would still hold, with the criminal continuing to choose x^*. Since the individual's expected benefit and the external harm remain unchanged, the welfare gain from doing this is:

$$dW = -C'(\rho)d\rho \tag{9.10}$$

which is positive if $d\rho < 0$. Thus, if increasing the probability of detection is costly and fines are costless to administer at the margin, then the optimal enforcement policy is to keep increasing f and keep reducing ρ so that equation (9.9) still holds, and to keep doing so until $\rho \approx 0$. Once this is achieved, welfare is equal to:

$$W = B(x^*) - H(x^*) - C(\rho) \approx B(x^*) - H(x^*) - C(0)$$

which is the highest level of welfare that can be obtained, given that enforcement is costly. If there are no fixed enforcement costs, then $C(0) = 0$, and $W \approx B(x^*) - H(x^*)$ when the efficient fine is chosen.

9.2.2 Optimal enforcement when fines cannot be increased without limit

The prescription for deterring crime in (9.8) is simple but far from adequate. It is usually the case that fines *cannot* be increased without limit. If individuals are wealth constrained for example, then increasing the fine above their wealth level will have *no* additional deterrence effect, since there is no additional financial liability for the individual in the event that they are caught. Indeed, this is exactly analogous to the judgement proof problem in accident law we examined in earlier chapters. So setting the fine at 'the highest level possible' usually involves choosing f to be some maximal level, say f_m.

Let us assume, then, that this has been done, and analyse the choice of ρ. The criminal's choice of x still obeys:

$$B'(x) = \rho f_m$$

The key lesson that emerges is since increasing ρ is costly, it may no longer be optimal to choose ρ in such a way that $\rho f_m = H'(x^*)$. To see this, note that fines are still a transfer between individuals and society and are costless to administer at the margin, so social welfare can still be written as:

$$W = B(x) - H(x) - C(\rho) \tag{9.11}$$

With f fixed at f_m, an increase in ρ certainly has an additional deterrence effect by increasing the 'price' that individuals face for engaging in illegal activity, but this now comes at a social cost. The optimal ρ balances out these benefits and costs. Since the criminal's choice of crime obeys $W = B'(x) = \rho f_m$, we can write $x_c = x_c(\rho f_m)$, and so:

$$W = B\{x_c[\rho f_m]\} - H\{x_c[\rho f_m]\} - C(\rho)$$

The first-order condition for the efficient choice of ρ is:

$$B'(x_c) = \frac{dx_c}{d(\rho^* f_m)} f_m - H'(x_c)\frac{dx_c}{d(\rho^* f_m)} f_m - C'(\rho^*) = 0 \qquad (9.12)$$

or:

$$\underbrace{-B'(x_c)\frac{dx_c}{d(\rho^* f_m)} f_m + C'(\rho^*)}_{MSC} = \underbrace{-H'(x_c)\frac{dx_c}{d(\rho^* f_m)} f_m}_{MSB} \qquad (9.13)$$

The first term on the left-hand side of (9.13) is the individual's marginal benefit of illegal activity. The second term on the left-hand side of (9.13) is a measure of the responsiveness of illegal activity with respect to an increase in the probability of detection. The third term is the marginal change in the expected fine when the probability of detection ρ changes. The product of these three terms is the change in the individual's expected benefit when ρ increases. Finally, the fourth term on the left-hand side of (9.13) is the marginal cost of increasing ρ, and depends on the technology of enforcement. The left-hand side of (9.13) is therefore a measure of the marginal social cost (MSC) of increasing ρ. It is the sum of the decline in the expected welfare of those who engage in illegal behaviour, plus the additional cost due to the increase in ρ.

The first term on the right-hand side of (9.13) is the marginal social harm from illegal activity. The second term on the left-hand side of (9.13) is once again a measure of the responsiveness of illegal activity with respect to an increase in the expected fine. The third term is the marginal change in the expected fine when the probability of detection ρ changes. The right-hand side is therefore a measure of the marginal social benefit (MSB) of increasing ρ. It is the marginal reduction in social harm that comes about when ρ changes. The rule in (9.13) just says that if increasing the fine is no longer possible, resources should be spent on enforcement activity until the marginal social costs are equal to the marginal social benefits.

We can simplify this expression further by utilising the concept of elasticity. Let $\varepsilon = \frac{dx_c}{d(\rho f_m)} \frac{\rho f_m}{x_c}$ be the *elasticity of the crime rate with respect to the expected marginal fine*. Rearranging the efficiency condition in equation (9.13), we get:

$$\varepsilon[B'(x_c) - H'(x_c)] = \frac{\rho C'(\rho^*)}{x_c} \tag{9.14}$$

Since the marginal costs of enforcement are assumed to be positive and since we will no longer have $\rho \approx 0$, the right-hand side is positive. Thus, the left-hand side must also be positive, since the two sides are equal. The term $\varepsilon = \frac{dx_c}{d(\rho f_m)} \frac{\rho f_m}{x_c}$ is a measure of the responsiveness of the individual's demand curve to changes in the 'price' that is faced, and is negative, since the demand curve for illegal activity slopes downwards. This means that we must have:

$$B'(x_c) - H'(x_c) < 0$$

or:

$$B'(x_c) < H'(x_c)$$

But since we still have $B'(x_c) = \rho^* f_m$, this means that, at the optimal ρ^*, we must have:

$$\rho^* f_m < H'(x_c)$$

If it is costly to increase ρ and fines cannot be increased any further, it is no longer efficient to set $H'(x_c) = \rho^* f_m$. Since marginal benefits of crime are less than the marginal social harm, it must be the case that the crime rate is higher here than was suggested by equation (9.9). In other words, the standard Pigouvian result breaks down under these conditions, and some degree of *underdeterrence* is optimal. The extent of the underdeterrence depends on the marginal costs of enforcement – the higher they are, the more efficient is a higher crime rate.

9.2.3 The effects of legal errors

The previous analysis assumed that if an individual did not commit an illegal act, they would not be liable for punishment. But courts and juries are not perfect, and sometimes make incorrect decisions.

Let us consider a criminal justice system which operates with errors. Specifically, consider the following kinds of errors:

- Type I error: a person who does not commit a crime is found guilty.
- Type II error: a person who does commit a crime is found not guilty.

Let e_1 be the probability of a type I error, and let e_2 be the probability of a type II error. We continue to assume that individuals are risk-neutral. For simplicity, we assume that the individual now has two choices with respect to criminal activity: he can either commit a crime (from which he receives a benefit B), or he can choose not to commit a crime, in which case he receives nothing. If the probability of detection and the fine are fixed at ρ and f, what is the effect of type I and type II errors on the incentive to commit crime?

If an individual commits a crime, let us assume that he is still arrested with probability ρ, but now there is a possibility that he will not be fined. This means that his expected benefit from committing crime is:

$$\begin{aligned}&\rho(1-e_2)[B-f]+\rho e_2 B+(1-\rho)B\\&=B-\rho(1-e_2)f\end{aligned}$$

Notice that if $e_2=0$ (that is, no type II errors occur), then this collapses to $B-\rho f$, which is the discrete version of the expression that we derived earlier in equation (9.2). On the other hand, if the individual does not commit any crime, the expected benefit is:

$$-\rho e_1 f$$

Notice that if $e_1=0$ (that is, no type I errors occur), then this collapses to 0. Thus, expected net benefits the net gain from committing a crime is:

$$\begin{aligned}&B-\rho(1-e_2)f-(-\rho e_1 f)\\&=B-\rho(1-e_2)f+\rho e_1 f\\&=B-\rho(1-e_1-e_2)f\end{aligned}$$

This is increasing in both e_1 and e_2. In other words, *both types of errors create a greater incentive for risk-neutral individuals to commit crime.* Intuitively, on the one hand, a higher e_2 means that individuals who would have committed crime in any case now have a greater incentive to do so, since there is a possibility that they will be found not guilty when they in fact committed the crime. On the other hand, a higher e_1 means that individuals who might *not* have committed crime now have an incentive to do so, since there is a possibility that they will be found not guilty even when they in fact do not commit crime.

9.2.4 Efficient imprisonment

In the previous section we analysed a setting in which fines could be increased without limit, and also situations in which that assumption did not hold, where fines could not increase above some maximal level f_m. In some situations fines may not be available at all, or may be used in conjunction with imprisonment terms. This section therefore examines the economics of imprisonment. The critical difference between our analysis of fines and imprisonment is that we will assume that imprisoning individuals uses up economic resources at the margin, whereas in the case of fines we assumed that there were no marginal administration costs. The analysis in this section therefore applies to any punishment which is costly to administer at the margin.

To simplify the analysis, we will assume throughout this section that the marginal social harm from crime is constant, so that $H(x) = hx$.

Let:

- t be the marginal imprisonment term: that is, the length of imprisonment imposed per unit of illegal activity. Thus, if an individual commits illegal activity at a rate of x and is caught, he faces a punishment of tx.
- $\alpha > 0$ be the marginal social cost of imprisoning a convicted individual for one unit of time. Thus, if an individual commits illegal activity of x, and is caught, the resource costs of imposing this punishment are αtx.
- $l > 0$ be the subjective disutility or loss to the individual per unit of time of imprisonment. Thus, if an individual commits illegal activity of x and is caught, the subjective disutility costs to the individual are ltx.

Let us examine the efficient choice of marginal imprisonment term, t. To illustrate the nature of the trade-offs involved, we assume that $f = 0$ and that ρ is fixed at $\bar{\rho}$. The individual's expected payoff from engaging in criminal activity of x is:

$$B(x) - \bar{\rho}ltx$$

The individual engages in illegal activity up to the point where marginal benefits equal expected marginal costs:

$$B'(x_c) = \bar{\rho}lt$$

So we can write the individual's 'demand curve' as:

$$x_c = x_c(\bar{\rho}lt) \qquad (9.15)$$

where again the demand curve slopes downwards. For any imprisonment term *t*, the individual's choice of activity must satisfy this equation. When this level of illegal activity is chosen, the individual's net welfare is:

$$B(x_c) - \bar{\rho}ltx_c$$

Unlike fines, imprisonment is not purely a transfer between individuals and the rest of society. Imprisonment creates social costs of its own. These costs, however, are only incurred if the individual is caught and punished (which happens with probability $\bar{\rho}$). In other words, if the level of illegal activity is x_c, then expected social harm is equal to:

$$hx_c + \bar{\rho}\alpha tx_c$$

Thus, aggregate expected social welfare is now:

$$\begin{aligned} W &= B(x_c) - \bar{\rho}ltx_c - (hx_c + \bar{\rho}\alpha tx_c) - C(\bar{\rho}) \\ &= B(x_c) - x_c\left[h + \bar{\rho}t(l+\alpha)\right] - C(\bar{\rho}) \end{aligned}$$

Once again, since $x_c = x_c(\bar{\rho}lt)$, we can write:

$$W = B\left[x_c(\bar{\rho}lt)\right] - x_c(\bar{\rho}lt)\left[h + \bar{\rho}t(l+\alpha)\right] - C(\bar{\rho}) \qquad (9.16)$$

A marginal increase in the marginal imprisonment term *t* now has three separate welfare effects. Two are marginal effects, and one is an *inframarginal* effect. The marginal effects are as follows:

- A marginal increase in *t* reduces the level of illegal activity by raising the expected 'price'. This reduces the welfare of individuals who undertake the illegal activity, and is a welfare loss.
- Because it reduces illegal activity, the marginal increase in *t* reduces the social harm caused by crime. And since illegal activity falls, this saves on imprisonment costs for those illegal activities which no longer occur because the individual is deterred from committing them. This is a welfare gain.

These changes only occur at the margin. The inframarginal effect is as follows:

- The increase in *t* makes prison sentences longer. This reduces the expected welfare of criminals and has a social cost because prisons are costly to run. These costs must be incurred with probability $\bar{\rho}$, on those illegal activities which are *not* deterred (that is, all level of criminal activity for which $x < x_c$). These are the *inframarginal* illegal activities – all those activities which are not deterred by a small change in *t*. This too is a welfare loss.

The optimal imprisonment term balances out these welfare gains and losses. Differentiating W with respect to t and setting the result equal to zero, we get:

$$B'(x_c)\left[\frac{dx_c}{d(\bar{\rho}lt^*)}\bar{\rho}l\right]-\left[\frac{dx_c}{d(\bar{\rho}lt^*)}\bar{\rho}l\right][h+\bar{\rho}t^*(l+\alpha)]-x_c\bar{\rho}(l+\alpha)=0$$

or:

$$\left[\frac{dx_c}{d(\bar{\rho}lt^*)}\bar{\rho}l\right](B'(x_c)-\bar{\rho}t^*l)-\left[\frac{dx_c}{d(\bar{\rho}lt^*)}\bar{\rho}l\right](h+\bar{\rho}t^*\alpha)=x_c\bar{\rho}(l+\alpha) \quad (9.17)$$

But we know that for any t, the individual's behaviour satisfies:

$$B'(x_c)=\bar{\rho}tl$$

Thus, the first term on the left-hand side of (9.17) is zero, and we are left with:

$$-\left[\frac{dx_c}{d(\bar{\rho}lt^*)}\bar{\rho}l\right](h+\bar{\rho}t^*\alpha)=x_c\bar{\rho}(l+\alpha) \quad (9.18)$$

We can simplify equation (9.18) further by again utilising the concept of elasticity. Let $\varepsilon=\frac{dx_c}{d(\bar{\rho}lt^*)}\frac{\bar{\rho}lt^*}{x_c}$ now be the elasticity of the crime rate with respect to the expected marginal imprisonment term. Then multiplying both sides of equation (9.18) by t^*/x_c gives:

$$-\varepsilon(h+\bar{\rho}t^*\alpha)=t^*\bar{\rho}(l+\alpha) \quad (9.19)$$

and so the efficient expected marginal imprisonment length satisfies:

$$\bar{\rho}t^*=\frac{-\varepsilon h}{l+\alpha(1+\varepsilon)} \quad (9.20)$$

Suppose that the elasticity of demand is constant. There are several important conclusions to draw from the results in equations (9.19) and (9.20):

- The expected marginal punishment is increasing in h, the marginal social harm of crime. Illegal activities that are more harmful *at the margin* should receive higher expected *marginal* punishments.
- The expected marginal punishment is decreasing in l, the individual's subjective marginal disutility costs of imprisonment. Individuals who have a higher *marginal* disutility of being punished should receive lower expected marginal punishments. The reason is obvious: the more an individual dislikes prison, the more likely a shorter sentence

will deter them from committing a desired level of illegal activity, and shorter sentences reduce the costs to society of imprisoning criminals.

- The expected marginal punishment may be increasing or decreasing in α, the marginal resource costs of imprisonment per unit of time. The sign depends on whether the demand for illegal activity is elastic or inelastic. Why do we get this result? Go back to equation (9.19), which has marginal benefits of changing the expected punishment on the left-hand side, and marginal social costs on the right-hand side. Note that α enters both sides. Now suppose that α rises. Then welfare must fall. But the welfare loss can be partially mitigated by changing the expected marginal imprisonment term. Equation (9.19) indicates that when α rises both the marginal benefits and marginal costs of changing $\bar{p}t$ rise. But if demand for illegal activity is elastic (i.e. if $\varepsilon < -1$) then the marginal costs (the left-hand side) rise by more than the marginal benefits (the right-hand side). The only way that equality can be maintained between the two sides is if $\bar{p}t^*$ falls. In these circumstances, the efficient response to an increase in the marginal costs of imprisonment is to reduce the marginal expected imprisonment term (and hence allow the crime rate x to rise). On the other hand, if the demand for illegal activity is inelastic (i.e. if $\varepsilon > -1$), then when α rises, the marginal costs of expected imprisonment rise by less than the marginal benefit, and the efficient response is to *increase* the expected marginal imprisonment term, thus *reducing* the crime rate.
- The expected marginal punishment is increasing in ε, the elasticity of the crime rate with respect to the expected marginal punishment. Remember that $\varepsilon < 0$, so this means that individuals whose behaviour is less (more) responsive to the expected marginal punishment require higher (lower) expected *marginal* punishments in order to deter them in an efficient manner.

The efficient rate of illegal activity when these additional costs of improsonment are taken into account may be higher or lower than that obtained when only fines were available and could be increased without limit. To see this, note that equation (9.19) implies that:

$$-(\varepsilon+1)(h+\bar{p}t^*\alpha) = t^*\bar{p}l - h \tag{9.21}$$

But the right-hand side of equation (9.21) is equal to $B'(x_c) - H'(x_c)$, which was equal to zero when fines could be increased without limit. The left-hand side of (9.21) can be positive or negative, depending on the elasticity of the crime rate with respect to the expected punishment. It is positive if $\varepsilon < -1$ (that is, if demand is elastic). In this case, we must have $B'(x_c) > h$ which implies that the crime rate is lower than the rate implied in equation (9.9). On the other hand, if $\varepsilon > -1$ (that is, if demand is inelastic), then $B'(x_c) < h$ which implies that the crime rate is higher than the rate implied in equation (9.9).

9.2.4.1 Optimal enforcement with imprisonment terms

What is the appropriate role of enforcement activities when fines are not available and only costly imprisonment terms can be used as a deterrence device? Do we get a similar result to the one we obtained in equation (9.9) (namely, that the marginal expected imprisonment term t should be increased by as much as possible)? To answer this question, suppose that t is fixed, but that ρ can be varied. Welfare is:

$$W = B[x_c(\rho lt)] - x_c\,(\rho lt)[h + \rho t(l + \alpha)] - C(\rho)$$

At the optimum, the change in welfare with respect to ρ is:

$$\frac{\partial W}{\partial \rho} = \frac{dB}{dx_c}\frac{dx_c}{d(\rho lt)}lt - \frac{dx_c}{d(\rho lt)}lt[h + \rho t(l+\alpha)] - x_c t(l+\alpha) - C'(\rho) = 0 \qquad (9.22)$$

Once again, noting that $\frac{dB}{dx_c} = \rho lt$, equation (9.22) can be written as:

$$-\frac{dx_c}{d(\rho lt)}lt[h + \rho t\alpha] = C'(\rho) + x_c t(l + \rho) \qquad (9.23)$$

The first term on the left-hand side is the marginal change in the crime rate when the expected marginal punishment rises, and the second term is the change in the expected punishment as ρ rises. Together, the product of these two terms equals the change in the crime rate when ρ rises. The term in square brackets is the marginal social cost of illegal activity, and when the illegal activity falls these costs are not incurred. The term is the sum of two effects: the reduction in social harm h and the reduction in expected punishment costs, $\rho t\alpha$. Hence, the left-hand side is the marginal social benefit of increasing enforcement activities.

The right-hand side is the marginal social cost of increasing ρ and is the sum of two terms. The first term is the marginal resource cost of increasing enforcement activity. The second term involves an infra-marginal resource cost: it is the product of $x_c t$, which is simply the *total* time spent in prison when the crime rate is x_c, and $(l + \alpha)$, which is the per unit social costs of imprisonment. Thus, $x_c t(l + \alpha)$ is the total social cost of imprisonment for those who continue to engage in illegal activity. When ρ rises, some individuals will be undeterred and will continue to commit crime. The term $x_c t(l + \alpha)$ is the change in the social cost of punishing them when ρ is increased.

Using our definition of elasticity, we can express equation (9.23) as:

$$-\varepsilon[h+\rho t\alpha]=\frac{\rho C'(\rho)}{x_c}+\rho t(l+\alpha) \qquad (9.24)$$

But we also know from our analysis of the optimal marginal imprisonment length that for any ρ, we have:

$$-\varepsilon(h+\rho t^*\alpha)=t^*\rho(l+\alpha) \qquad (9.25)$$

These two equations together imply that:

$$\frac{\rho^* C'(\rho^*)}{x_c}=0$$

which in turn implies that $\rho^*=0$. Thus, as we had with a fine, when ρ can be changed and t can be increased without limit, it is once again optimal to set the marginal punishment at a very high level, and ρ at a very low level, as long as the expected punishment is adjusted to satisfy:

$$t\rho=\frac{-\varepsilon h}{l+\alpha(1+\varepsilon)} \qquad (9.26)$$

The reason for this result is straightforward: the criminal's behaviour depends solely on the expected punishment $t\rho$. The resource costs of imprisonment also only depend on $t\rho$. On the other hand, the resource costs of enforcement depend only on ρ. Thus, for any expected marginal punishment, it is always possible to hold $t\rho$ fixed (and therefore hold the crime rate and the social costs of crime fixed) and increase welfare by increasing t and lowering ρ, thereby reducing enforcement costs.

9.2.5 Optimal enforcement when imprisonment terms cannot be increased without limit

Finally, suppose that t cannot be increased without limit, so that there is a maximum marginal imprisonment length t, which we denote by t_m. Then applying equation (9.24) yields:

$$-\varepsilon[h+\rho^* t_m\alpha]=\frac{\rho^* C'(\rho^*)}{x_c}+\rho^* t_m(l+\alpha) \qquad (9.27)$$

or

$$-\varepsilon[h+\rho^* t_m\alpha]-\rho^* t_m(l+\alpha)=\frac{\rho^* C'(\rho^*)}{x_c}$$

The left-hand side is the difference between the marginal benefits and marginal costs of increasing ρt when t can be increased without limit. Since the right-hand side is positive, this difference is also positive, implying an expected marginal punishment that is less than that implied by equation (9.26). Hence, the level of illegal activity must be higher. In other words, when t cannot be increased without limit and enforcement is costly, we again get the result that some degree of underdeterrence is optimal, relative to the case where t can be increased without limit.

9.2.6 Fault-based criminal liability

For some illegal activities, punishments are not meted out unless the illegal activity exceeds some threshold level. For example, in many jurisdictions it is not illegal to have a low positive blood alcohol level whilst driving, but it does become illegal if that level increases above some minimum threshold. This is an example of a fault-based criminal liability rule. Under such a rule, the government defines some threshold level of activity $\bar{x}$, and punishes acts which meet or exceed $\bar{x}$ but not those which do not. Such rules very much resemble the negligence rule we examined in Chapters 4 and 5.

The previous analytical framework can easily be extended to a fault-based liability regime. Consider, for example, the case of fines. Let ρ be the probability of detection and let f be the fine that is imposed (imprisonment terms are examined below). The individual's expected net benefits are now:

$$\begin{cases} B(x) & \text{if } x \leq \bar{x} \\ B(x) - \rho f x & \text{if } x > \bar{x} \end{cases}$$

How does the individual respond to such a rule? First, since the individual is not punished for illegal activities for which $x \leq \bar{x}$, the individual will commit those acts, irrespective of the level of the expected marginal fine. Secondly, for activities for which $x > \bar{x}$, if the expected marginal fine is below $B'(\bar{x})$, then even though the individual is at risk of being found criminally liable for these activities they will still commit those acts for which $B'(x) > \rho f$, since marginal benefits exceed marginal expected costs. Hence, the individual's choice of illegal activity is:

$$x_c = \hat{x}$$

where $\hat{x} = \min\{\bar{x}, \rho f\}$.

What is the efficient threshold and fine? Recall that the efficient level of illegal activity is x^*, where the marginal benefits of illegal activity equal the marginal social costs. Therefore, if the threshold is set at $\bar{x} = x^*$ and the expected marginal fine is at least as large as $\rho f = H'(x^*)$ (with ρ again as small as possible), then the individual will choose to commit $x_c = x^*$, the efficient level of crime. Moreover, since the individual does not choose $x > x^*$, no fine is actually levied, and no punishment actually occurs.

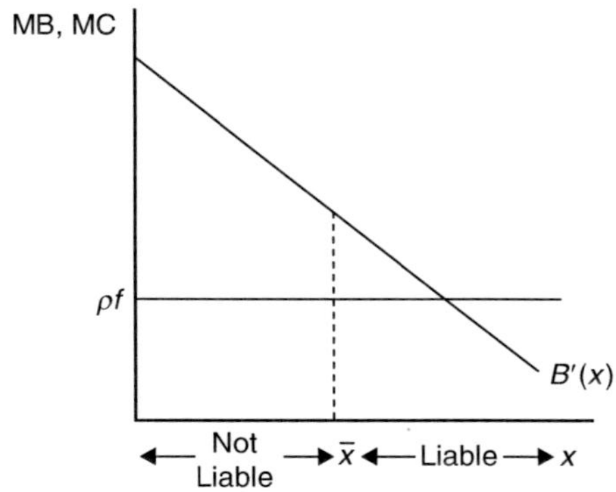

Figure 9.2.3 Fault-based criminal liability

This last result is particularly interesting in the case of imprisonment. If fines are not available and if the threshold is set at $\bar{x} = x^*$ and the expected marginal imprisonment term is at least as large as $\rho t = H'(x^*)$ with ρ again as small as possible), then the individual will choose $x_c = x^*$, the efficient level of illegal activity. Moreover, since the individual does not choose $x > x^*$, *no punishment actually occurs*. Thus, in the case of imprisonment terms and an optimally chosen criminal liability threshold, no social costs of imprisonment are incurred, and individuals do not bear any costs of going to prison. Assuming that the threshold is chosen appropriately and assuming both fines and imprisonment can be increased without limit, welfare under both fines and imprisonment is equal to $W^* = B(x^*) - H(x^*)$. In this case, imprisonment is equivalent to a system of monetary fines.

9.3 Markets for illegal goods

So far in this chapter we have considered situations in which an activity is deemed illegal but where there is no market for the good or activity under consideration. But many illegal goods and services (such as drugs, weapons, gambling, prostitution, and abortion) take place in market settings, with producers, consumers and market prices. This section extends the basic principles of the analysis in the earlier part of the chapter to deal with illegal markets.[1]

Suppose that there is a good whose marginal and average production cost is constant and equal to $c > 0$ for each firm in the industry. Since all firms are alike and since marginal costs are constant, we can treat firms in the industry as a single price-taking firm with output of Q and the same cost function. Suppose that it is illegal to supply the good. Let ρ be the probability that a producer is caught selling the good. Let us assume that the producer faces two kinds of punishment. If a producer is caught, production is confiscated and destroyed, *and* a fine of $\$f$ per unit of the good is also imposed. The two questions of interest are:

1. How will participants in this market behave? and
2. What is the efficient ρ and f?

9.3.1 Competitive markets for illegal goods and services

We first consider a perfectly competitive market for the good. Suppose that firms are risk neutral. Let the competitive equilibrium price be P^*. In a competitive equilibrium, producers supply the good up to the point where the expected market price that they receive (which in a perfectly competitive market is equal to their expected marginal revenue) equals their expected marginal cost.

A producer's expected revenue from supplying one unit of the good (that is, their expected marginal revenue) is equal to $(1-\rho)P^*$, whilst expected unit costs are equal to $c + \rho f$. Therefore, equating the expressions for expected marginal revenue and marginal cost above allows us to solve for the market-clearing price:

$$P^* = \frac{c+\rho f}{1-\rho} \tag{9.28}$$

The equilibrium market price is increasing in the fine and increasing in ρ, the probability of detection. Following Becker et al. (2006), it is useful to work with the *odds ratio*, which is the ratio of the probability of being detected to the probability of not being detected:

$$\theta \equiv \frac{\rho}{1-\rho}$$

Note that $1+\theta = \dfrac{1}{1-\rho}$. We can then write the competitive equilibrium market price as:

$$P^* = (1 + \theta)\, c + \theta f = c + \theta c + \theta f \tag{9.29}$$

The amount $\theta(c+f) = P^* - c$ is the expected marginal economic value of the goods that are confiscated, and is equal to the excess of price over production cost. Thus the competitive equilibrium market price is equal to the marginal cost of production, plus a term that reflects the expected value of goods that are confiscated.

Even though price exceeds production cost, firms earn zero expected profits in this market – the excess of price over cost compensates them for the additional loss to them that is associated with the possibility or risk that their goods will be confiscated and destroyed, resulting in a loss of revenue.

Specifying a demand curve allows us to pin down the equilibrium quantity. For example, suppose that the demand curve is:

$$Q_D = a - P$$

Then the equilibrium quantity is:

$$Q_D = a - c - \theta(c + f)$$

The market quantity is decreasing in ρ and f. For a given probability of detection and fine, the extent of the reduction in quantity depends on the elasticity of demand.

9.3.1.1 *Welfare analysis*

Welfare analysis of crime and punishment in a market setting is straightforward. Suppose that the total private benefits from consumption of the good are:

$$B = B(Q)$$

The inverse demand for the good is given by

$$B'(Q) = P \tag{9.30}$$

Suppose also that consumption leads to social external harm of:

$$H(Q) = hQ$$

Let us find the efficient quantity. Total welfare is given by:

$$W = B(Q) - hQ - cQ$$

The efficient level of consumption and production is where marginal social benefits equal marginal social costs, or where:

$$B'(Q^*) = c + h.$$

In a free market, however, production and consumption would occur at $Q^\circ > Q^*$, where Q° satisfies:

$$B'(Q^\circ) = c$$

The free market outcome here is not efficient.

9.3.1.2 *Efficient fines*

Suppose that in an effort to reduce consumption towards the efficient level, authorities make production and sales of the good illegal. Suppose first that if illegal activity is detected, no goods are confiscated, but a fine is imposed on producers. Suppose that revenue from the fine is returned to consumers in a lump-sum fashion. Let the enforcement costs be $C(\rho)$, and suppose initially that ρ is fixed. Since no goods are confiscated, marginal revenue for each firm is simply equal to the market price, and so equation (9.28) indicates that the equilibrium market price will be $P^* = c + \rho f$. Since the market price depends on ρ and f, it will also be the case that the equilibrium market quantity will also depend on f. Welfare is equal to:

$$\begin{aligned} W(f) &= B[Q(f)] - hQ(f) - (c + \rho f)Q(f) + \rho f Q - C(\rho) \\ &= B[Q(f)] - hQ(f) - cQ(f) - C(\rho) \end{aligned} \tag{9.31}$$

The optimal fine can be found by taking the derivative of equation (9.31) and setting it to zero, which gives:

$$W'(f) = \frac{dB}{dQ}\frac{dQ}{df} - \frac{dQ}{df}(h + c) = 0 \tag{9.32}$$

Hence, given a fixed ρ, the efficient fine equates marginal private consumption benefits with marginal social costs. But from the demand curve in equation (9.30), these marginal consumption benefits are equal to the market price, and so from equation (9.32) we get:

$$c + \rho f^* = c + h$$

or:

$$\rho f^* = h \tag{9.33}$$

As in our earlier analysis, the efficient expected fine is equal to the marginal external harm.

What if ρ can be varied and the per unit fine f can be increased without limit? Since increasing ρ is costly whereas increasing f is not, it is possible to increase f and reduce ρ whilst keeping the expected fine constant, but also improving welfare by reducing enforcement costs. In the limit, if f can be increased without limit, welfare is:

$$W = B(Q^*) - hQ^* - cQ^*$$

This is a similar conclusion to the one we previously derived for fines. If the fine can be increased without limit and firms are risk neutral, the efficient deterrence policy involves setting f as high as possible and ρ as low as possible, whilst keeping $\rho f^* = h$.

But what if f cannot be increased without limit? Suppose that there is a maximal fine in place, so that $f = f_{m^*}$. Welfare is now:

$$W(\rho) = B[Q(\rho)] - hQ(\rho) - cQ(\rho) - C(\rho) \tag{9.34}$$

and the optimal ρ satisfies:

$$W'(\rho^*) = B'(Q)Q'(\rho^*) - hQ'(\rho^*) - cQ'(\rho^*) - C'(\rho^*) = 0$$

So that:

$$[B'(Q) - h - c]Q'(\rho^*) = [P - h - c]Q'(P)P'(\rho^*)$$
$$= [P - h - c]\varepsilon^D \frac{Q}{P} f_m = C'(\rho)$$

where ε^D is the elasticity of demand for the good. The right-hand side is positive, so the left-hand side must be as well. But since we have assumed that the demand for the good is a downward-sloping function of price, this implies that:

$$P < c + h$$

If increasing fines without limit is not possible, some degree of underdeterrence is optimal. This is similar to the result we had in section 9.2.2.

9.3.1.3 *Efficient confiscation*

Suppose now that in addition to levying a fine, the government can confiscate illegally produced goods. The economic value of the goods that are confiscated is P. Since there is a probability ρ that a unit of the good will be confiscated, the expected value of a confiscated good is ρP. Since these goods are destroyed, this is a social cost. The per unit opportunity cost of the resources that are used to produce the goods is c. Therefore the per unit social cost of each unit that is produced is:

$$c + \rho P$$

But we also know that:

$$(1 - \rho)P = c + \rho f$$

This implies that:

$$\rho P = P - c - \rho f$$

Therefore the social cost of each unit that is produced is:

$$c + \rho P = c + P - c - \rho f = P - \rho f$$

Since the fine revenue is returned in a lump-sum fashion to consumers, total welfare when goods are confiscated is:

$$W = B(Q) - hQ - (P - \rho f)Q + \rho fQ - C(\rho) = B(Q) - hQ - PQ - C(\rho)$$

It may seem slightly strange that the price P enters negatively into the expression for welfare here. Ordinarily, P is a transfer from consumers to producers. It enters here, however, because of the fact that goods are confiscated and destroyed.

What is the optimal enforcement policy in this case? The change in welfare with respect to ρ is:

$$\frac{dW}{d\rho} = B'(Q)Q'(\rho) - hQ'(\rho) - PQ'(\rho) - QP'(\rho) - C'(\rho)$$

Now $Q'(\rho) = \dfrac{dQ}{dP}\dfrac{dP}{d\rho}$ so we get:

$$\begin{aligned}\frac{dW}{d\rho} &= [B'(Q) - h]Q'(\rho) - [PQ'(P) + Q]P'(\rho) - C'(\rho) \\ &= [B'(Q) - h]Q'(\rho) - Q[1 + \varepsilon^D]P'(\rho) - C'(\rho) \qquad (9.35)\end{aligned}$$

If demand for the good is inelastic (so that $1 + \varepsilon^D > 0$), and if $B'(Q) > h$, then this expression is negative. In this case, it can *never* be efficient to have $\rho > 0$. This implies that if the external harm from consumption of the good is sufficiently low, no goods should be confiscated. Instead, if fines can be increased without limit, then the optimal policy is to not confiscate any goods, set $\rho \approx 0$, and set f very high, so that $\rho f = h$.

On the other hand, if demand for the good is elastic, or if $B'(Q) < h$, then the expression in (9.35) may be positive for some positive values of ρ. If fines cannot be increased without limit, then the optimal enforcement policy ρ^* obeys:

$$[B'(Q) - h]Q'(\rho^*) - Q[1 + \varepsilon^D]P'(\rho^*) = C'(\rho^*)$$

The right-hand side is the marginal resource cost of increasing enforcement. The left-hand side is the marginal benefit of increasing enforcement, and is comprised of two parts. The term $[B'(Q) - h]Q'(\rho^*)$ is the marginal welfare gain that comes about as consumption is reduced and there is less external harm. If the external harm h is sufficiently high, this term is positive. The term $-Q[1 + \varepsilon^D]P'(\rho^*)$ is the change in the resource costs as fewer goods are produced and confiscated. When demand is elastic (so that $1 + \varepsilon^D < 0$), this term is also positive, so resource costs decline as ρ rises.

9.3.2 Application of the market approach: The economics of evasion of a specific tax

The model developed in this chapter has a wide variety of applications, including to markets for drugs, prostitution, and other illegal activities.

The approach can also be applied to public finance issues, such as optimal taxation in a setting where taxes can be evaded. Consider a firm in a competitive market which sells products at the market price P. Suppose that sales of the product are subject to a specific tax of t. Consider the firm's decision to conceal sales. The advantage to the firm of concealing sales is that any tax paid to the firm becomes part of its revenue base, instead of having to be paid to the tax authority. Thus, concealment increases the firm's revenues.

Concealment is directly costly for the firm. Suppose that the firm is risk neutral. Let ρ be the probability that the firm is detected. The firm declares a fraction s of its sales for tax purposes, and $c(.)$ is the marginal cost of concealing sales, which in general is a function of the fraction of sales that are concealed. Suppose that the firm faces a fine of f per dollar of tax evaded (which we assume includes the tax that is owed, so $f > 1$). Finally, let C be the firm's constant marginal production cost.

In a competitive market, expected marginal revenue equals expected marginal cost. Therefore we must have:

$$P = C + c(1 - s) + ts + \rho(1 - s)tf \tag{9.36}$$

Under perfect competition, firms compete by pushing down the costs on the right-hand side of (9.36), until the marginal loss to the firm is equal to the marginal gain:

$$-c'(1 - s) + t - \rho tf = 0$$

or:

$$c'(1-s) = t(1 - \rho f) \tag{9.37}$$

Since the left-hand side is positive, the equality will only hold at an interior point if $\rho f \leq 1$. If $\rho f > 1$ then $s = 1$ and there is no underreporting, since doing so would increase the expected tax liability per unit sold of the firm. Notice that the optimal decision to evade is independent of other variables in the model, and depends only on the probability of detection, the fine, and the tax rate.

We now investigate the effect of tax increase on the consumer price. Suppose that the tax rate changes by an amount dt. Then, differentiating (9.36) with respect to t, we can see that the market price changes by:

$$\begin{aligned}\frac{dP}{dt} &= -\,c'(1-s)\frac{ds}{dt} + s + t\frac{ds}{dt} + \rho f\left[(1-s) - t\frac{ds}{dt}\right]\\ &= \frac{ds}{dt}[t(1-\rho f) - c'(1-s)] + s + \rho f(1-s)\\ &= s + \rho f(1-s)\end{aligned}$$

where the second last equality follows from the fact that $c'(1-s) = t(1-\rho f)$ in equilibrium. Since $s < 1$ and $\rho f < 1$, it follows that:

$$0 < \frac{dP}{dt} < 1 \tag{9.38}$$

Note the contrast with the standard incidence result in the absence of tax evasion, which states that $\frac{dP}{dt} = 1$.

9.4 Plea bargaining and the costs of trial

In the previous sections we assumed that once offenders were caught, they were automatically convicted. But criminal trials are a costly and uncertain process. In this section we investigate the effects of prosecution and defence costs on illegal activity. Suppose that if an individual is caught (which still happens with some probability ρ) there is a marginal cost of prosecution that is equal to $a > 0$. In addition, suppose that there is a marginal cost to the individual of going to trial of $b > 0$. Once the individual is caught, the outcome of the trial is certain: he will be punished and fined an amount f per unit of illegal activity in which he has engaged. Assume that ρ is fixed. If the individual commits illegal activity of x, his net expected benefit is:

$$B(x) - \rho(f + b)x$$

The individual's optimal level of illegal activity satisfies:

$$B'(x_c) - \rho(f + b) \tag{9.39}$$

Welfare is now:

$$W = B(x) - \rho(a + b)x - hx \tag{9.40}$$

where we have omitted the costs of detection and enforcement, which are assumed to be fixed. The efficient level of crime now satisfies:

$$B'(x^*) = \rho(a + b) + h \tag{9.41}$$

and the expression for welfare in (9.40) is maximised. To induce the individual to choose this efficient level of illegal activity, we simply set the expected fine in (9.39) to be equal to the marginal cost of illegal activity on the right-hand side of (9.41), which gives:

$$\rho(f + b) = \rho(a + b) + h$$

or:

$$f = a + \frac{h}{\rho} \tag{9.42}$$

The enforcement authority should set the fine equal to the costs of prosecution, plus the discounted value of the marginal social harm, where the discount rate is the probability of the individual being caught. Note that at this fine, the level of illegal activity is *lower* than if prosecution and defence costs were zero, since $B'(x^*) = \rho(a+b)+h > h$. However, if ρ can be varied and fines can be increased without limit, it is again possible to have $\rho \approx 0$, in which case we would have $\rho(a+b) \approx 0$ and it would be possible to increase the level of illegal activity, avoid legal costs and increase welfare, so that we again have $B'(x^*) = h$.

However, even if ρ cannot be reduced to close to zero, there is another way that the costs of going to trial for both the prosecutor and the defendant could be avoided: plea bargaining. Suppose that ρ is fixed and that setting $\rho(a+b) \approx 0$ is not possible. Under the rule in (9.42) once individuals are caught, they face costs of:

$$f + b = a + \frac{h}{\rho} + b \tag{9.43}$$

On the other hand, the prosecutor's expected net benefit of going to trial is:

$$a + \frac{h}{\rho} - a = \frac{h}{\rho} \tag{9.44}$$

Notice that the incidence of trial costs falls completely on the criminal. At the welfare optimum, the expected trial costs are fully incorporated into the fine, which is paid by the criminal.

Suppose that the prosecutor makes an offer to the individual to accept a fine of F, instead of going to trial. Then for this fine to be acceptable to both parties, it must satisfy:

$$\frac{h}{\rho} \leq F \leq a + \frac{h}{\rho} + b \tag{9.45}$$

Such a plea bargain fine always exists, since $a + b > 0$, and the gains from plea bargaining are the total costs of not going to trial. Suppose that the parties split these gains equally. Then the prosecutor receives revenue of:

$$\frac{h}{\rho} + \frac{a+b}{2}$$

and the individual faces costs of:

$$a + \frac{h}{\rho} + b - \frac{a+b}{2} = \frac{h}{\rho} + \frac{a+b}{2}$$

Note that the fine that the criminal accepts could be under a plea bargain could be *higher* than what he would have to pay in the absence of plea bargaining. Indeed, with the split the surplus rule, this happens if $b > a$. Intuitively, the criminal is willing to pay a higher monetary fine if the costs of trial that he would otherwise face are sufficiently high.

Are there any social gains from plea bargaining? With plea bargaining, the individual's level of illegal activity now obeys:

$$B'(x_{PB}) = \rho\left[\frac{a+b}{2} + \frac{h}{\rho}\right] \tag{9.46}$$

which *exceeds* the level of illegal activity in (9.41). Intuitively, the lower 'price' of committing illegal activity results in an increase in those activities. This higher crime rate is part of the social cost of plea bargaining.

However, plea bargaining also provides a social benefit, since the costs of going to trial by both criminals and prosecutors are now not actually incurred. The 'price' that the criminal faces is now a pure wealth transfer, and this transfer and its receipt by the prosecutor involve no use of real resources. Social welfare is therefore equal to:

$$W_{PB} = B(x_{PB}) - hx_{PB}$$

where x_c obeys the expression in (9.46) above. The difference between the two measures of welfare is:

$$W_{PB} - W^* = B(x_{PB}) - hx_{PB} - [B(x^*) - \rho(a+b)x^* - hx]$$

which is always positive, as shown in Figure 9.4.1. The triangle labelled W^* in Figure 9.4.1 is the level of welfare when trials are costly and fines are levied optimally. If plea bargaining occurs, the individual accepts the offer of a fine which reduces his total expected cost of committing

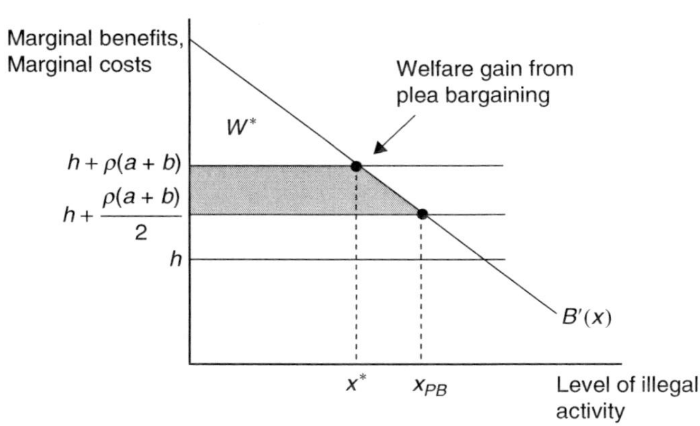

Figure 9.4.1 The costs and benefits of plea bargaining

illegal activity, which therefore provides an incentive to increases illegal activity. However, at x^*, the marginal social benefit of increasing illegal activity is $\rho(a+b)+h$, whereas the marginal social cost in the presence of plea bargaining is only h. Since marginal benefits exceed marginal costs, it is efficient to have the crime rate increase – but only if the costs of trial can be avoided. This is exactly what plea bargaining achieves.

9.4.1 Plea bargaining and the prisoner's dilemma

The prisoner's dilemma has been widely cited as an illustration of how individual incentives and external effects can lead to socially undesirable outcomes. But this is a very narrow view of the prisoner's dilemma. Under certain circumstances, prisoner-dilemma-like situations can also lead to efficient outcomes and be a source of welfare efficiency. Indeed, the original story from which the prisoner's dilemma derives its name is one of success and an efficient outcome for the prosecutor – not the failure and the socially undesirable outcome that is emphasised so often.

To see this, suppose that there are two criminals who have committed a crime and have been charged by the prosecutor. The prisoners both know that they are guilty of the crime, as does the prosecutor. However, the goal of the prosecutor is to have them confess to the crime, so that a costly trial is avoided. The prosecutor's problem is to design a mechanism or incentive scheme in which it is in *both* criminals' individual self-interests to confess, and that they voluntarily do so – even though they would both be better off if they did not confess.

This is a simple problem in mechanism design, which has a very simple solution. Suppose that the prosecutor announces a menu of fines. First, if both prisoners confess, the fine is f_{cc}. Second, if one prisoner confesses and the other does not, then the fines are f_{cd} and f_{dc} respectively, where $f_{dc} > f_{cc}$. Finally, if both fail to confess, they will each face a fine of f_{dd}, where $f_{dd} > f_{cd}$. In addition, it is assumed that the prisoners' most preferable outcome is for them to both not confess, so we further assume that $f_{dd} > f_{cc}$. The payoff matrix of this game is shown in Table 9.4.1.

Table 9.4.1 The payoff matrix for the prisoner's dilemma

		Prisoner 2	
		Confess	**Don't Confess**
Prisoner 1	**Confess**	$(-f_{cc}, -f_{cc})$	$(-f_{cd}, -f_{dc})$
	Don't Confess	$(-f_{dc}, -f_{cd})$	$(-f_{dd}, -f_{dd})$

As is well known, the dominant strategy equilibrium in this situation is for both prisoners to confess, and the outcome is that they both face a higher fine than they would have if they had both not confessed. That is certainly a bad outcome for the prisoners. But from a broader social welfare perspective, this is exactly the outcome that the prosecutor desires. Both prisoners confess and an unnecessary, costly trial is avoided. In this broader sense, the equilibrium of the prisoner's dilemma leads to an efficient outcome.

9.5 The economics of organised crime

The framework developed in this Chapter can also be applied to the analysis of organised crime. Schelling (1967) is one of the earliest economic examinations of organised crime in the literature. He argues that criminal activity is 'organised' if it has a hierarchical structure, entails a common use of legal and financial advice, common communication methods, and common methods of contract enforcement. In other words, the defining characteristic of organised crime is collusion and implicit agreement among criminals.

9.5.1 Taxation, black markets, and organised crime

Why does organised crime exist and prosper? One possible reason is excessively high taxation. This section develops a simple model to illustrate the effect that taxation of legal goods can have on the incentives to supply goods illegally.

Suppose that there is a single good that is produced in the legal and illegal sectors. Each good is of the same quality, and sells at the same price. Consumers cannot tell the difference between the two types of good. Taxes are only paid on legally produced goods. Suppose that, initially, there is a zero tax rate on legally produced goods. Let the consumer price be P. The supply curves in the legal (L) and illegal (I) sectors are:

$$Q_L^S = Q_L^S(P)$$

$$Q_I^S = Q_I^S(P)$$

The demand curve is:

$$Q^D = Q^D(P)$$

Initially, in the absence of taxation, we have:

$$Q_L^S(P) + Q_I^S(P) = Q^D(P)$$

Now suppose that a tax is imposed on the production of legal goods. We then have:

$$Q_L^S[P(t)-t]+Q_I^S[P(t)]=Q^D[P(t)] \tag{9.47}$$

We can now investigate the effect of a change in taxation on overall production, as well as production in each sector. Totally differentiating (9.47) with respect to *t* yields:

$$\frac{dQ_L^S}{d[P(t)-t]}[P'(t)-1]dt+\frac{dQ_I^S}{dP}[P'(t)]dt=\frac{dQ^D}{dP}[P'(t)]dt \tag{9.48}$$

Rearranging this yields:

$$P'(t)=\frac{\dfrac{dQ_L^S}{d[P(t)-t]}}{\dfrac{dQ_L^S}{d[P(t)-t]}+\dfrac{dQ_I^S}{dP}-\dfrac{dQ^D}{dP}}=\frac{+}{+++}>0 \tag{9.49}$$

The expression in (9.49) simply states that the price paid by consumers rises with the tax on legally produced goods. Hence $\frac{dQ^D}{dt}=\frac{dQ^D}{dP}\frac{dP}{dt}<0$, and quantity demanded for the good falls. We also have:

$$\frac{dQ_I^S}{dt}=\frac{dQ_I^S}{dP}\frac{dP}{dt}>0$$

and:

$$\frac{dQ_L^S}{dt}\frac{dQ_L^S}{dP}\left(\frac{dP}{dt}-1\right)=\frac{dQ_L^S}{dP}\frac{-\dfrac{dQ_I^S}{dP}+\dfrac{dQ^D}{dP}}{\dfrac{dQ_L^S}{d[P(t)-t]}+\dfrac{dQ_I^S}{dP}-\dfrac{dQ^D}{dP}}=+\frac{-}{+++}<0$$

When a tax is placed on legally produced goods, the quantity supplied of illegally produced goods rises, and the quantity supplied of legally produced goods falls. Overall, however, demand falls – but not by as much as it would in the absence of illegal activity. As the tax rises, the legal sector contracts and the illegal sector expands.

9.5.2 The monopoly criminal enterprise

The earlier analysis in this chapter examined the production, exchange and consumption of illegal goods and services in a competitive market. We now modify this analysis by examining a monopoly supplier of illegal goods and services. The analysis may also apply to a situation in which oligopolistic suppliers collude and act as a monopoly criminal enterprise or loose network of criminal gangs. Hence, the model can be regarded as a preliminary look at some of the issues involved in the examination of the economics of organised crime.

Consider a monopoly supplier of an illegal good who faces a demand curve of

$$P(Q) = B'(Q) \tag{9.50}$$

Suppose again that consumption leads to social external harm of:

$$H(Q) = hQ$$

Suppose that the good is confiscated with probability ρ, and that a per unit fine of f is also levied in the event that illegal production is detected. The monopolist's expected total revenue from supplying the good is equal to $TR = (1 - \rho)P(Q)Q$, whilst expected total costs are equal to $TC = (c + \rho f)Q$. Therefore, the monopolist's profits are:

$$\pi = (1 - \rho)P(Q)Q - (c + \rho f)Q \tag{9.51}$$

Equating marginal revenue with marginal cost gives us:

$$MR(Q^M) = P'(Q^M)Q^M + P(Q^M) = \frac{c + \rho f}{1 - \rho} \tag{9.52}$$

or:

$$P^M = \frac{\varepsilon}{1 + \varepsilon} \frac{c + \rho f}{1 - \rho} \tag{9.53}$$

In a market for an illegal good, the monopoly price exceeds the competitive price by a mark-up that depends on the elasticity of demand. This is exactly the same outcome as if the good was legal. All else being equal, if efficient consumption is the goal, then the enforcement authorities will need to impose a fine that is *lower* in the monopoly industry than that which would be imposed under perfect competition. Indeed, with a monopoly supplier, a *subsidy* may be needed to ensure efficiency. Intuitively, since the monopolist wants to reduce output in any case, the Pigouvian tax needed to internalise any external costs is smaller than it would be under perfect competition. If, in the absence of confiscation and a fine, the monopolist would maximise profits by restricting output to a level that was *below* the efficient level, then making production of the good is completely unnecessary, and a subsidy is required.

The analysis seems to suggest that an industry for illegal goods and services which is operated by organised criminal enterprises, which erects barriers to entry to prevent competition, and which keeps prices high, may be preferable to an industry in which there is free entry and exit. But this conclusion neglects many of the costs associated with organised crime. Perhaps the most significant of these are the rent-seeking costs associated with securing and maintaining the monopoly criminal franchise. Whereas the rent-seeking costs used by existing and aspiring monopolists in markets for legal goods typically involve employing lobbyists and engaging in relatively harmless activities, the methods employed by criminal enterprises are not as benign, and typically involve extortion; blackmail; fraud; corruption of the police, the judiciary and government officials; theft; violence and murder. The direct costs of engaging in these activities, as well as the indirect or external costs, are likely to be significant.

These rent-seeking costs are not confined to existing criminal enterprises. Monopoly profits create an incentive for entry and may induce others to attempt to take over or extinguish the existing monopolist's operations. In a legal market this would be done by purchasing shares and putting together a takeover bid; but in illegal markets the only way that successful entry is possible is for entrants to gain a comparative advantage in violence. Hence the existence of monopoly rents provides both criminal enterprises and potential entrants with an incentive to invest in a wide range of illegal activities, which have their own direct and indirect social costs.

On the other hand, it is possible that the alternatives to organised crime – disorganised crime – may result in a greater degree of violence as competition between gangs or bosses increases. In addition, there may be economies of scale and scope in illegal activities. There are large fixed costs involved in corrupting public officials, training criminals, creating networks, and finding criminals who are sufficiently 'trustworthy' and skilful. Collusion between criminal gangs allows them to internalise many of the negative externalities that are associated with violence. In other words, the criminal organisation may have natural monopoly characteristics, and it may be efficient to only have one rather than many.

9.6 Notes

The classic paper on the economic approach to crime is Becker (1968). Useful summaries of the literature can be found in Polinsky and Shavell (2000) and Garoupa (1997). The analysis of fines and imprisonment in this chapter is based on the approach of Polinsky and Shavell (2000), whilst the analysis of markets for illegal activity draws on Becker, Murphy and Murphy (2006). Winter (2008) has a non-technical coverage of a wide variety of issues that arise in the economic analysis of crime. Eide (1994) is a useful summary of the empirical literature, and Bowmaker (2005) is an entertaining and thorough survey of many economic applications of the economic approach to crime, including markets for illegal drugs, prostitution, pornography, suicide, legal and illegal gambling, and abortion. Grossman and Katz (1983) study the economics of plea bargaining, but in a different setting from the one considered in this chapter. The model of indirect tax evasion explored in this Chapter draws on Cremer and Gahvari (1993). Schelling (1967) is one of the first economic analyses of organised crime. Skaperdas (2001) is a more recent treatment. Gambetta (1993) is a book-length examination of the mafia. Fiorentini and Peltzman (1995) contains many interesting papers on the economics of organised crime.

9.7 Exercises

1. Suppose that individuals are risk neutral and that the benefits from illegal activity (denoted by x) are:

$$B(x) = 5x - \frac{1}{2}x^2$$

Suppose that the marginal social harm per unit of criminal activity is $h = 2$. The resource cost of enforcement activity is:

$$C(\rho) = \frac{1}{2}\rho^2$$

where ρ is the probability of detection.

(a) For a given marginal fine f and a given probability of detection ρ, what level of illegal activity x will be chosen by individuals?

Suppose that the marginal fine f can be increased without limit.

(b) What is the optimal marginal fine? What is the optimal enforcement probability? What is the efficient level of illegal activity, and what is the level of total welfare at this level? What is the government's expected revenue?

(c) Now suppose that the fine cannot be increased without limit, and that the maximal fine is $F = 3$. Repeat part (a). What is the efficiency loss from not be able to increase the fine above $F = 3$?

(d) Now suppose that the maximal fine is $F = 4$. Repeat part (a). What happens to the crime rate compared to your answer in part (b)?

2. Suppose that individuals are risk neutral and that the marginal gains from illegal activity (denoted by x) are:

$$B'(x) = A^{\frac{1}{\varepsilon}} x^{-\frac{1}{\varepsilon}}$$

where A is a positive constant and $\varepsilon > 0$.

(a) What is the individual's 'demand curve' for illegal activity?

(b) What is the point elasticity of the level of illegal activity with respect to changes in the expected per unit punishment?

(c) Suppose that there is an imprisonment length of 1 year per unit of crime committed. Let the probability of detection equal 0.1, and suppose that each year in prison gives the individual disutility of \$40,000. What is the expected 'price' of each unit of crime committed? If $\varepsilon = 0.5$, what is the crime rate?

(d) Use the results from this chapter to derive the optimal imprisonment term as a function of the number you computed in part (b), the marginal harm h, the probability of detection ρ, the disutility of imprisonment l, and the costs of imprisonment α. How does the optimal imprisonment term t vary with each of these parameters? Explain.

3. Consider the market for marijuana. Suppose that there is a constant marginal production cost of $50 per kilogramme for growing marijuana and selling it to buyers. Suppose that the private benefit of marijuana consumption is:

$$B(Q) = 100Q - \frac{1}{2}Q^2$$

where Q is measured in kilogrammes. Suppose that the social external harm of marijuana consumption is:

$$H(Q) = 30Q$$

(a) What is the efficient level of marijuana consumption and production? What level of consumption and production would be produced by a completely free and competitive market for marijuana? Is the free market outcome efficient? If so, explain why. If not, compute the welfare loss.

Now suppose that supplying marijuana is illegal. If authorities find marijuana growing or in the hands of dealers, they seize the product and fine the supplier.

Let ρ be the probability that a supplier is caught, and let F be the per kilogramme fine that is levied. The competitive 'street price' of marijuana is P. The total resource cost of enforcing laws against the production and supply of marijuana is:

$$C(\rho) = \frac{1}{1-\rho}$$

(b) If supplying marijuana is illegal, what is a marijuana supplier's expected marginal cost? What is a marijuana supplier's expected marginal revenue? Find an expression for the competitive street price P in terms of the production cost, fine, and probability of detection. For any fine F and probability of detection p, what quantity will be consumed in the competitive equilibrium?

(c) If catching suppliers is costly and the fine F could be increased without limit, what is the efficient fine? What is the efficient probability of detection? With this combination of F and ρ, what is the street price of marijuana, what is the quantity that is produced, and what is the government's expected revenue?

(d) Now suppose that the fine cannot be increased without limit, and that the maximal fine is $F = 30$. What is the marginal welfare gain from increasing ρ? What is the marginal welfare cost of increasing ρ? Use these results to compute the efficient probability of detection, and find the efficient quantity. Show that when detection is costly and there is a maximal fine, the quantity computed in part (b) is no longer efficient. What is the welfare loss from not being able to increase the fine above $F = 30$?

(e) Now suppose that the maximal fine is $F = 40$. Repeat part (d). What happens to the quantity of marijuana consumption compared to your answer in part (d)? Explain.

4. This question follows on from Question 3 and uses the same model and parameters. Suppose that instead of there being a perfectly competitive market for marijuana, there is a monopoly marijuana firm, which is owned and run by organised crime bosses. All other assumptions remain the same.

(a) Suppose that selling marijuana is not illegal and that the monopolist must charge a single price per kilogramme. What is the monopolist's profit-maximising price? Is the monopoly outcome efficient? If so, explain why. If not, compute the welfare loss from monopoly.

(b) From an efficiency point of view, which is preferable: a free marijuana market or a monopoly supplier?

Now suppose that supplying marijuana is illegal. If authorities find marijuana growing or in the hands of dealers, they seize the product and fine the supplier.

Let r be the probability that a supplier is caught, and let F be the per kilogramme fine that is levied. The total resource cost of enforcing laws against the production and supply of marijuana is again:

$$C(\rho) = \frac{1}{1-\rho}$$

(c) If supplying marijuana is illegal, what is the monopolist's expected marginal cost? What is the monopolist's expected marginal revenue? Find an expression for the profit-maximising monopoly price in terms of its production cost, the fine, and the probability of detection. For any fine F and probability of detection ρ, what quantity will be sold by the monopolist?

(d) If detecting sales is costly and the fine F could be increased without limit, what is the efficient fine? What is the efficient probability of detection? With this combination of F and ρ, what is the street price of marijuana, what is the quantity that is produced, and what is the government's expected revenue? Is the expected fine with a monopoly supplier higher or lower than the expected fine under perfect competition?

5. Consider an economy in which all individuals have the following utility function over wealth:

$$u(w) = aw + bw^2$$

(a) For what values of b are individuals risk-neutral? For what values of b are individuals risk averse? For what values of b are individuals risk-loving?

Suppose that the individual's initial wealth is w_0, and suppose that the individual can take two possible actions: he can either commit a crime, or not commit a crime. If he commits a crime and is caught, he faces a fine of $f < w_0$. The gain from the criminal act is $g > 0$. Suppose that the probability of getting caught is ρ, where $0 < \rho < 1$.

(b) What is the individual's expected utility if he commits the crime? Does the expected utility of committing crime rise or fall with increases in b? Write down the condition under which an individual will decide to commit a crime.

(c) Given your answers in (a) and (b), if the government chooses a probability of detection ρ and a fine f, is this more likely to deter risk-averse individuals, risk-neutral individuals, or risk-loving individuals from committing crime?

Now suppose that the government can now alter ρ and f, but can only do so in such a way as to keep the expected punishment ρf constant.

(d) If the government raises ρ and lowers f (while keeping ρf constant), what happens to the expected value of the individual's wealth if he commits a crime? What happens to the variance of the individual's wealth if he commits a crime? Is the change to ρ and f more likely to deter risk-averse individuals, risk-neutral individuals, or risk-loving individuals from committing crime?

(e) If the government lowers ρ and raises f (while keeping ρf constant), what happens to the expected value of the individual's wealth if he commits a crime? What happens to the variance of the individual's wealth if he commits a crime? Is the change to p and f more likely to deter risk-averse individuals, risk-neutral individuals, or risk-loving individuals from committing crime?

10
Topics in Corporate Law and Competition Law

10.1 Introduction

One of the key insights of the Coase Theorem is that the inefficiencies and difficulties that are associated with uncompensated positive and negative external effects can be mitigated if parties are permitted to bargain. For firms, one extreme form of bargaining is to permanently internalise externalities by merging. This can happen through formal merger negotiations or via takeover bids. This chapter examines some of the economic issues that arise within firms in response to different legal rules, and when firms seek to internalise externalities by merging. The Chapter also studies a wide variety of economic issues that arise in corporate law and governance, and competition law.

Section 10.2 examines the effect of different legal rules on the incentives to merge. Section 10.3 studies the effect of various kinds of liability rules on managerial compensation arrangements. Sections 10.4 and 10.5 deal with takeovers and the dilution of shareholder rights, as well as corporate governance and the measurement of voting power when shareholders in a public company possess voting rights. Section 10.6 turns to competition law and examines the usefulness of standard measures of market concentration in assessing the desirability of merger activity. Section 10.7 uses the lessons from Chapter 9 to study the design of legal rules to deter collusive price-fixing behaviour between firms.

10.2 Liability rules and the gains from mergers and corporate takeovers

In many instances, the levels of care of more than one injurer may affect the probability of an accident and the extent of harm to victims.

For example, there may be two firms whose output together increases the probability of harm occurring to a victim. In this situation, there are multiple externalities: each firm's actions affect the victim, but the actions of each also affect the other. This section analyses the incentive and efficiency effects of various kinds of liability rules in these settings. As a by-product of the analysis, it is also possible to place a value on the gains from firms merging.

The model is a straightforward extension of the unilateral and bilateral care models of Chapters 4 and 5. Suppose that victims cannot take any care to avoid accidents, and suppose that there are two firms, labelled 1 and 2, who are potential injurers. The probability of accidental harm is:

$$\rho(x_1, x_2)$$

where x_1 is the level of care of firm 1, and x_2 is the level of care of firm 2. In what follows, let w_1 be the marginal cost of care for firm 1, let w_2 be the marginal cost of care for firm 2, and let $h > 0$ be the dollar value of damage to the victim if an accident occurs.

10.2.1 Strict liability

Consider first the following *strict liability rule*: irrespective of the level of care taken by firms 1 and 2, if there is an accident, firm 1 will be liable for a pre-specified fraction s_1 of the victim's losses, and firm 2 will be liable for a pre-specified fraction s_2 of the victim's losses, where $s_1 + s_2 = 1$.

Assuming that the firms cannot collude, does this rule induce either of the firms to take an efficient level of care? To answer this, we first need to work out the efficient levels of care. Expected total social costs are:

$$w_1x_1 + w_2x_2 + \rho(x_1, x_2)h$$

Social costs are minimised when, for both firms, the marginal cost of an extra unit of care is equal to the marginal benefit. So the efficient levels of care, x_1^* and x_2^*, must satisfy the following two marginal conditions:

$$w_1 = -\frac{\partial \rho(x_1^*, x_2^*)}{\partial x_1}h \quad \text{and} \quad w_2 = -\frac{\partial \rho(x_1^*, x_2^*)}{\partial x_2}h$$

We will assume that x_1^* and x_2^* are unique, so that:

$$w_1x_1^* + w_2x_2^* + \rho(x_1^*, x_2^*)h < w_1x_1 + w_2x_2 + \rho(x_1, x_2)h$$

for all $(x_1, x_2) \neq (x_1^*, x_2^*)$.

Now consider the strict liability rule. Firm 1's expected costs are:

$$w_1x_1 + s_1\rho(x_1, x_2)h$$

and firm 2's expected costs are:

$$w_2x_2 + s_2\rho(x_1, x_2)h$$

Firms choose x_1 and x_2 non-cooperatively, to minimise their own individual expected costs. The Nash equilibrium levels of care, (x_1°, x_2°) satisfy:

$$w_1 = -s_1 \frac{\partial\rho(x_1^\circ, x_2^\circ)h}{\partial x_1}$$

for firm 1, and:

$$w_2 = -s_2 \frac{\partial\rho(x_1^\circ, x_2^\circ)h}{\partial x_2}$$

To investigate the efficiency properties of this Nash equilibrium, suppose that $x_2^\circ = x_2^*$. Then firm 1 would face a private marginal benefit that is less than the social marginal benefit of its actions, since

$$s_1\rho(x_1, x_2^*)h < \rho(x_1, x_2^*)h$$

by virtue of the fact that $s_1 < 1$. Therefore, firm 1 would choose $x_1^\circ < x_1^*$. Hence x_1^* cannot be a best response to x_2^*. Similarly, x_2^* cannot be a best response to x_1^*. These two facts suggest that (x_1^*, x_2^*) is not a Nash equilibrium under this legal rule, so $(x_1^\circ, x_2^\circ) \neq (x_1^*, x_2^*)$ and so:

$$w_1x_1^\circ + w_2x_2^\circ + \rho(x_1^\circ, x_2^\circ)h > w_1x_1^* + w_2x_2^* + \rho(x_1^*, x_2^*)h$$

That is, (x_1°, x_2°) is not efficient.

10.2.1.1 The gains from merging under strict liability

Note that if firms were to merge, collude or act cooperatively, then they would jointly choose x_1 and x_2 to minimise their joint expected costs under the legal rule. Their joint costs under strict liability are:

$$\begin{aligned} &w_1x_1 + s_1.\rho(x_1, x_2)h + w_2x_2 + s_2.\rho(x_1, x_2)h \\ &= w_1x_1 + w_2x_2 + (s_1 + s_2).\rho(x_1, x_2)h \\ &= w_1x_1 + w_2x_2 + \rho(x_1, x_2)h \end{aligned}$$

since $s_1 + s_2 = 1$. Therefore, if the firms were to merge, the legal rule would effectively induce them to internalise all of the social costs of their actions. The gains from the merger would simply be:

$$w_1x_1^\circ + w_2x_2^\circ + \rho(x_1^\circ, x_2^\circ)h - [w_1x_1^* + w_2x_2^* + \rho(x_1^*, x_2^*)h] \qquad (10.1)$$

Another way of stating this result is that a rule of strict liability provides significant incentives for firms to merge. Alternatively, for mergers not to occur under this rule, transaction costs must be at least as large as the gains in (10.1).

10.2.2 A negligence rule

Now consider the following negligence rule: the court sets due standards of care, z_1 and z_2 for firms 1 and 2, and applies these due standards as follows:

- If a firm meets its due standard of care, it is not liable.
- If either firm is the only firm which does not meet its due standard of care, it will be held liable for the total amount of the victim's losses.
- If both firms do not meet their due standards of care, they will both be held liable for some pre-specified portion of the victim's losses, with firm 1 paying a fraction s_1 of the losses, and injurer 2 paying a fraction s_2 of losses, with $s_1 + s_2 = 1$.

Assuming that firms cannot collude among themselves, does this negligence rule induce either of the firms to take an efficient level of care? Assume that $z_1 = x_1^*$ and $z_2 = x_2^*$ are the due standards of care. First, note that no firm will choose a level of care that exceeds their due standard, since this simply adds extra costs of care without any offsetting benefit. Thus, the firms have only two classes of strategies: either meet the due standard (i.e. $x_i = x_i^*$) or not meet the due standard (i.e $x_i < x_i^*$). The individual payoffs from each strategy for each player depend on what the other player does. We can represent the players expected costs from these two classes of strategies in Table 10.2.1.

Let us find the Nash equilibria of this game (there may be more than one). Consider each of the cells in Table 10.2.1.

Table 10.2.1 Costs under a negligence rule

		Firm 2	
		Meet	Don't Meet
Firm 1	Meet	$(w_1x_1^*, w_2x_2^*)$	$[w_1x_1^*, w_2x_2 + \rho(x_1^*, x_2)h]$
	Don't Meet	$[w_1x_1 + \rho(x_1, x_2^*)h, w_2x_2^*]$	$[w_1x_1 + s_1\rho(x_1, x_2)h, w_2x_2 + s_2\rho(x_1, x_2)h]$

- {Meet, Meet} **is a Nash equilibrium.**

  To show this, we just need to show that {*Meet*} is a best response to {*Meet*} for each player. So, consider player 1, and suppose player 2 chooses {*Meet*}. Under the negligence rule, firm 2 does not have to compensate the victim, and we are effectively back in a unilateral care model, with $\rho(x_1)h = \rho(x_1, x_2^*)h$ and x_2^* fixed. Firm 1's cost function is:

$$1\text{'s expected costs} = \begin{cases} w_1x_1^* & \text{if } x_1 = x_1^* \\ w_1x_1 + \rho(x_1, x_2^*)h & \text{if } x_1 < x_1^* \end{cases}$$

  Since x_1^* minimises $w_1x_1 + \rho(x_1, x_2^*)h$, setting the due standard at x_1^* creates a jump in 1's cost function at exactly the right place, and his costs are minimised by choosing $x_1 = x_1^*$.

  Thus, x_1^* is a best response to x_2^*. Similarly, it is straightforward to show using the same kind of reasoning, that x_2^* is a best response to x_2^*. Thus, {Meet, Meet} is a Nash equilibrium.

- {Meet, Don't Meet} **and** {Don't Meet, Meet} **are not Nash equilibria.**

  Suppose they were. Then this would imply, for example, that {Don't Meet} would be a best response to {Meet}. But this contradicts the result we just established – that {Meet} was the unique best response to {Meet}. So {Meet, Don't Meet} and {Don't Meet, Meet} cannot be Nash equilibria.

- {Don't Meet, Don't Meet} **is not a Nash equilibrium.**

  If {Don't Meet, Don't Meet} is a Nash equilibrium, this would mean that {Don't Meet} would be a best response to {Don't Meet} for each player. This would require:

$$w_1x_1 + s_1\rho(x_1, x_2)h < w_1x_1^* \tag{10.2}$$

for firm 1 and:

$$w_2x_2 + s_2\rho(x_1, x_2)h < w_2x_2^* \tag{10.3}$$

for firm 2. Adding these two conditions yields:

$$w_1x_1 + s_1\rho(x_1, x_2)h + w_2x_2 + s_2\rho(x_1, x_2)h < w_1x_1^* + w_2x_2^* \tag{10.4}$$

So if {Don't Meet, Don't Meet} is a Nash equilibrium, the condition in (10.4) must hold. Since $s_1 + s_2 = 1$, the condition is equivalent to the existence of an x_1 and an x_2, with $x_1 \neq x_1^*$ and $x_2 \neq x_2^*$, and with:

$$w_1x_1 + w_2x_2 + \rho(x_1, x_2)h < w_1x_1^* + wx_2^* \tag{10.5}$$

But $w_1x_1^* + w_2x_2^* < w_1x_1^* + w_2x_2^* + \rho(x_1^*, x_2^*)h$, so if equation (10.5) were to hold, it must also be true that if {Don't Meet, Don't Meet} is a Nash equilibrium, there must exist x_1 and x_2, with $x_1 \neq x_1^*$ and $x_2 \neq x_2^*$, such that

$$w_1x_1 + w_2x_2 + \rho(x_1, x_2)h < w_1x_1^* + w_2x_2^* + \rho(x_1^*, x_2^*)h$$

But this cannot be true, since (x_1^*, x_2^*) minimises $w_1x_1 + w_2x_2 + \rho(x_1, x_2)h$. Thus, {Don't Meet, Don't Meet} cannot possibly be a Nash equilibrium.

We can also say something about the incentives for mergers and the likelihood of mergers under this legal rule. Since this legal rule induces efficient outcomes, there would be no gains to the firms if they merged. Together with the conclusions regarding strict liability, we can conclude that mergers should be more likely under a strict liability rule than in the presence of a negligence rule.

10.3 Vicarious liability, managerial compensation and the manager–shareholder relationship

Chapters 4 and 5 discussed the judgement proof problem – if an individual or a firm does not have sufficient assets to pay for accidental harm, then both strict liability and the negligence rule will, with some exceptions, fail to induce efficient behaviour by the injurer. The judgement proof problem may occur in a wide variety of situations, including in corporate law. For example, a manager who is employed by shareholder and runs the day-to-day operations of the firm may take actions on the firm's behalf that cause harm to a victim, but for which the manager, if he were held personally liable for the harm, would not have sufficient assets to compensate the victim.

If the harm exceeds the manager's wealth, then the analysis of Chapter 4 suggests that this will lead, in general, to the manager having poor incentives to take care. But can this inefficient arrangement be improved upon? *Vicarious liability* is one way of addressing the judgement proof problem. Vicarious liability occurs when liability for damages is imposed on one party for losses caused by another party. This situation arises in many applications, including between shareholders and managers; construction companies and subcontractors; and between firms and employees. This section analyses a simple model of vicarious liability and applies it to the shareholder/manager relationship. We assume that there are three parties:

- A victim (v), who is harmed by an employee of the company if an accident occurs, but who cannot himself take care.

- An employee of a company (for example, a manager) who can take care of x_i to reduce the probability of an accident.
- A principal, who owns the assets of the company and employs the manager and pays him a wage of W. The wage can be structured in such a way as to depend on the level of care (if care is observable). Alternatively, if the manager's level of care is not observable, the wage can be structured in such a way as to depend on whether an accident occurs or not.

We consider a principal–agent contracting framework in which there are two possible outcomes: an accident either occurs, or does not. We assume that the manager (the agent) takes an action (care) that can be directly observed by the shareholders (the principal). We assume that both parties are risk neutral.

The shareholders are the owners of the firm's assets, and these exceed the harm to the victim. On the other hand, The manager does not have a sufficiently high level of assets to cover the victim's damages. The shareholders contract with the manager for the performance of some service. Let:

W_n = wage if harm does not occur
W_h = wage if harm occurs
$\overline{W}$ = the manager's reservation utility

Throughout the analysis we will assume that:

$$W_n + a < h \tag{10.6}$$

where a is the level of the manager's assets.

10.3.1 Strict liability

Consider first a legal rule of strict liability without vicarious liability: this means that the manager must personally pay for the harm that his lack of care may cause. The goal of the shareholders is to design a contract to minimise their expected payment to the manager. On the other hand, the manager will want a sufficiently high wage to compensate him for the cost of care and the possibility that he will lose all of his assets if an accident occurs.

Shareholders are assumed to be able to observe the level of care taken by the manager. They want to design a contract which solves:

$$\min_{W_n, W_h, x_i} \; [1-\rho(x_i)]W_n + \rho(x_i)\, W_h \tag{10.7}$$

subject to

$$[1-\rho(x_i)][a+W_n]+\rho(x_i)[(a+W_h)-(a+W_h)]-x_i \geq \overline{W}$$

or:

$$[1-\rho(x_i)][a+W_n]-x_i \geq \overline{W}$$

Since the shareholders would not want to have W_n larger than it needs to be, they will set W_n so that:

$$\overline{W}=[1-\rho(x_i)][a+W_n]-x_i$$

or:

$$W_n=\frac{\overline{W}+x_i}{1-\rho(x_i)}-a \tag{10.8}$$

Substituting this into the shareholder's objective function yields:

$$\min_{W_h, x_i} \overline{W}+x_i-a+\rho(x_i)(a+W_h) \tag{10.9}$$

Since these costs are increasing in W_h, the principal should set $W_h = 0$ for any level of care taken by the manager. Then the shareholders solve:

$$\min_{x_i} \overline{W}+x_i-a+\rho(x_i)a \tag{10.10}$$

This states that the level of care that the shareholders would the manager want to take is exactly the same level of care that the manager himself wants to take. Moreover, since $a < h$, this level of care will be inefficiently low.

To implement this outcome, let x_i° minimise the shareholders' expected costs in (10.10), and define:

$$V_S^{\circ}=\min_{x_i} \overline{W}+x_i-a+\rho(x_i)a=\overline{W}+x_i^{\circ}-a+\rho(x_i^{\circ})a \tag{10.11}$$

Then, since $W_h = 0$, by equation (10.7) this must also be the manager's expected wage. Therefore we need to design the wage so that:

$$V_S^{\circ}=[1-\rho(x_i)]W_n \tag{10.12}$$

This is straightforward to do. Just rearrange (10.12) and let the compensation scheme be:

$$W_n(x_i) = \frac{V_S^\circ}{1-\rho(x_i)} = \frac{\overline{W} + x_i^\circ - a + \rho(x_i^\circ)a}{1-\rho(x_i)} \tag{10.13}$$

If the manager chooses $x_i = x_i^\circ$, then the shareholders will pay out an expected amount of V_S°. So let us examine the manager's incentives under this compensation scheme. The manager's expected utility is:

$$\begin{aligned}[1-\rho(x_i)][a+W_n]-x_i &= [1-\rho(x_i)]\left[a+\frac{\overline{W}+x_i^\circ-a+\rho(x_i^\circ)a}{1-\rho(x_i)}\right]-x_i \\ &= a[1-\rho(x_i)]+\overline{W}+x_i^\circ-a+\rho(x_i^\circ)a-x_i \\ &= \overline{W}+x_i^\circ+\rho(x_i^\circ)a-x_i-\rho(x_i)a\end{aligned}$$

This attains a maximum of $\overline{W}$ at the point $x_i = x_i^\circ$. Thus the manager is incentivised to choose the level of care which the shareholders would like him to, and at this level of care the manager is just indifferent between accepting the compensation scheme and rejecting it.

The compensation scheme in (10.13) is decreasing and convex in the level of the manager's care. Thus the wage as a function of the level of the manager's care takes the shape illustrated in Figure 10.3.1.

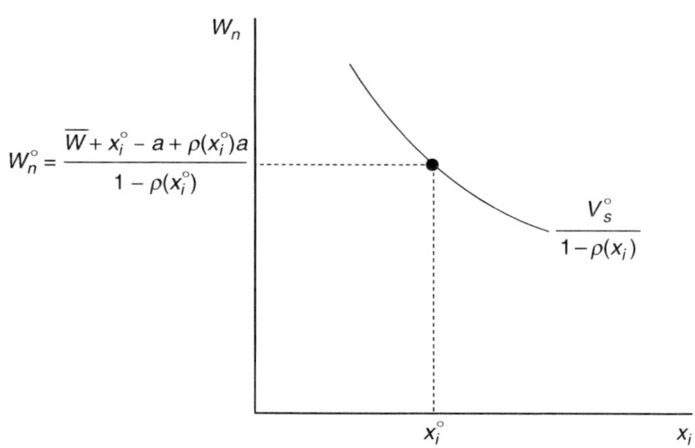

Figure 10.3.1 The compensation scheme under strict liability when care can be observed

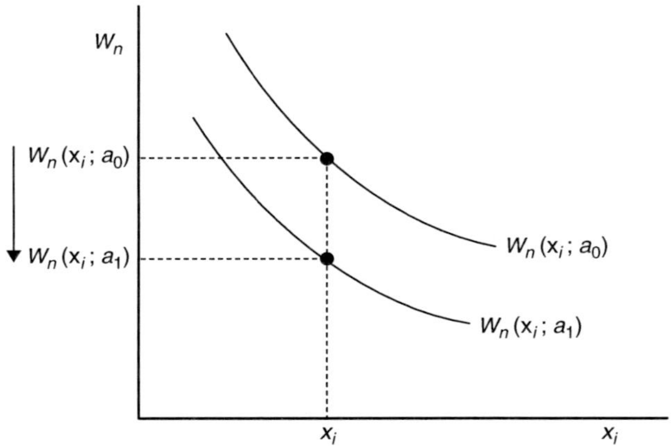

Figure 10.3.2 The shift in the compensation scheme when the manager's assets rise

If the manager's assets rise, we have:

$$\frac{dW_n}{da}(x_i) = \frac{\frac{dx_i^\circ}{da} - 1 + \rho'(x_i^\circ)\frac{dx_i^\circ}{da}a + \rho(x_i^\circ)}{1-\rho(x_i)} = \frac{\frac{dx_i^\circ}{da}[1+\rho'(x_i^\circ)a] + \rho(x_i^\circ) - 1}{1-\rho(x_i)}$$

$$= \frac{\rho(x_i^\circ) - 1}{1-\rho(x_i)} < 0$$

Thus, for each level of x_i, the wage if an accident does not occur is decreasing in the level of manager's assets. An increase in the manager's assets therefore shifts the compensation schedule downwards, as shown in Figure 10.3.2. This happens because the manager's expected payoff is increasing in his level of assets. If these assets increase then, for a fixed level of care, the shareholders can afford to pay the manager a lower wage if an accident does not occur, and still leave him indifferent between accepting and not accepting the remuneration package.

How does the compensation scheme change at the *optimal* wage? We have:

$$\frac{dW_n}{da}(x_i^\circ) = \frac{d}{da}\left[\frac{\overline{W} + x_i^\circ}{1-\rho(x_i^\circ)} - a\right] = \frac{\frac{dx_i^\circ}{da}[1-\rho(x_i^\circ)] + (\overline{W} + x_i^\circ)\rho'(x_i^\circ)\frac{dx_i^\circ}{da}}{[1-\rho(x_i)]^2} - 1$$

$$= \frac{dx_i^\circ}{da}\frac{[1-\rho(x_i^\circ)] + (\overline{W} + x_i^\circ)\rho(x_i^\circ)}{[1-\rho(x_i)]^2} - 1$$

Since $1+\rho'(x_i^\circ)a=0$ and since $\overline{W}+x_i^\circ>a$, we have $1+\rho'(x_i^\circ)(\overline{W}+x_i^\circ)<0$, and so:

$$\frac{dW_n}{da}(x_i^\circ)<0 \tag{10.14}$$

Intuitively, an increase in the manager's assets make him better off at the existing optimal wage: he will wish to take a higher level of care (which is costly), but this reduces the probability of an accident and if an accident does not occur he receives more wealth. If an accident does occur he receives nothing anyway. So overall, at the existing wage, he is better off. The shareholders can therefore afford to keep the manager at his reservation utility by reducing his wage. The compensation scheme shifts downwards for each level of care, and at the efficient level of care, the manager's wage is lower than it was when his assets were lower. This is shown in Figure 10.3.3.

10.3.2 Vicarious liability

Now suppose that shareholders of the company are held vicariously liable for the full amount of harm to the victim, *h*, which occurs as a result of the manager's lack of care. Under this legal rule, the objective of the shareholders is again to design a contract to minimise their total expected payment, which now incorporates payments to the manager and to the victim of the accident if it occurs.

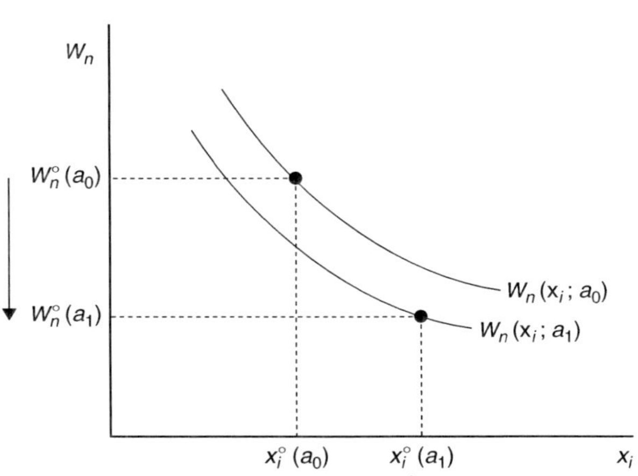

Figure 10.3.3 An increase in the manager's assets reduces the wage paid to him if an accident does not occur

We again assume that shareholders can observe the level of care taken by the manager. Then the wage that they pay the manager can be conditioned on the level of care. The shareholders' problem is to solve:

$$\min_{W_n, W_h, x_i} \; [1-\rho(x_i)]\, W_n + \rho(x_i)\,(W_h + h) \tag{10.15}$$

subject to:

$$a + [1-\rho(x_i)]\, W_n + \rho(x_i)\, W_h - x_i \geq \overline{W}$$

It is important to remember throughout the analysis that although shareholders can set x_i *indirectly* by developing a compensation scheme for the manager, they cannot choose x_i *directly*: the manager's level of care is chosen by him and him alone. The critical point is that the shareholders may be able to induce manager to choose the level of care that they desire, by creating appropriate incentives in the compensation scheme that the manager agrees to.

Since the shareholders would not want pay the manager more than they need to, they will again arrange payments so that in expectation, the manager (in expectation) receives his reservation wage:

$$a + [1-\rho(x_i)]\, W_n + \rho(x_i)\, W_h - x_i = \overline{W} \tag{10.16}$$

or:

$$\overline{W} + x_i - a = [1-\rho(x_i)]\, W_n + \rho(x_i)\, W_h \tag{10.17}$$

The manager's expected wage payment on the right-hand side of (10.17) is equal to his reservation wage, plus the level of care that he takes, less his assets. Note that the expected wage is increasing in the level of care chosen by the manager.

Shareholders are only interested in the level of care that makes them as well off as they can possibly be. Substituting (10.17) into (10.15) gives us the shareholder's new problem:

$$\min_{x_i} \; \overline{W} + x_i - a + \rho(x_i)h \tag{10.18}$$

Since this is equivalent to choosing x_i to minimise $x_i + \rho(x_i)h$, the solution to this problem is $x_i = x_i^*$, the efficient level of care. Thus, if the level of care can be observed by the shareholders and they are made vicariously liable for the harm caused by the manager's lack of care, then the shareholders end up fully internalising the external costs of the manager's lack of care indirectly, via the compensation scheme that is paid to the manager. Intuitively, under vicarious liability, the joint welfare of the shareholder and the manager depends on the costs of care and the expected damages inflicted on the victim by the manager, and so it is in mutual interests of both the shareholders and the manager to write contracts which make the sum of these two things as small as possible.

Once the shareholders have decided that they want the manager to choose a level of care that is equal to x_i^*, they must design a compensation scheme to incentivise the manager to actually choose this level of care. This can be done as follows. First, the let the wage in the event of an accident be zero. Next, let:

$$V_S^* = \min_{x_i} \overline{W} + x_i - a + \rho(x_i)h = \overline{W} + x_i^* - a + \rho(x_i^*)h \qquad (10.19)$$

be the total expected payment that the shareholders must make if the efficient level of care is taken by the manager. Finally, let the wage in the event of an accident be:

$$W_n(x_i) = \frac{V_S^* - \rho(x_i)h}{1 - \rho(x_i)} \qquad (10.20)$$

Then, for any x_i, the expected wage received by the manager is:

$$[1 - \rho(x_i)]W_n(x_i) = V_S^* - \rho(x_i)h = \overline{W} + x_i^* - a + \rho(x_i^*)h - \rho(x_i)h \qquad (10.21)$$

The manager's total expected wage, net of the expenditure that he takes on care, is:

$$\overline{W} + x_i^* - a + \rho(x_i^*)h - \rho(x_i)h - x_i \qquad (10.22)$$

Under the compensation scheme in (10.20) and (10.22), the manager's expected remuneration is maximised when he chooses the efficient level of care. Therefore, the compensation scheme induces the manager to behave efficiently, even though the manager's objective is to simply maximise his expected wage, less his expenditure on care, and even though under a rule of vicarious liability he faces *no* liability for the harm to victims that his lack of care may cause.

When the efficient level of care is chosen, the manager receives an expected wage that is equal to $\overline{W} - a + x_i^*$ which, if we subtract his expenditure on care, leaves him with $\overline{W} - a$ and makes him just indifferent between accepting the compensation scheme and not accepting. Given this level of care, the shareholders' expected wage payment to the manager is then:

$$V_S^* - \rho(x_i^*)h$$

and their total expected payment (including expected payments to victims as a result of the manager's lack of care) is:

$$\begin{aligned} V_S^* - \rho(x_i^*)h + \rho(x_i^*)h &= V_S^* \\ &= \overline{W} + x_i^* - a + \rho(x_i^*)h \end{aligned}$$

Thus, the compensation scheme in which the manager receives nothing if an accident occurs, and the payment in equation (10.20) if an accident does not occur, achieves the lowest possible expected payout for the shareholders, and induces the manager to choose the efficient level of care. Note that the shareholders' expected payout is a function of the reservation utility of the manager, his level of assets, the costs of care, and the expected harm to victims.

Recall from (10.20) that this managerial compensation scheme pays a wage of:

$$W_n(x_i) = \frac{V_S^* - \rho(x_i)h}{1 - \rho(x_i)}$$

if an accident does not occur. We have:

$$\frac{dW_n}{dx_i} = \frac{-\rho'(x_i)h[1-\rho(x_i)] + [V_S^* - \rho(x_i)h]\rho'(x_i)}{[1-\rho(x_i)]^2} = \frac{(V_S^* - h)\rho'(x_i)}{[1-\rho(x_i)]^2} > 0$$

where the last inequality follows from the fact that $V_S^* = [1 - \rho(x_i^*)]W_n + \rho(x_i^*)h < h$. We also have:

$$\frac{d^2W_n}{d(x_i)^2} = (V_S^* - h)\frac{\rho''(x_i)[1-\rho(x_i)]^2 + 2[\rho'(x_i)]^2[1-\rho(x_i)]}{[1-\rho(x_i)]^4} < 0$$

Thus, in contrast to the situation under strict liability, the wage if there is no accident is an *increasing* and concave function of the level of care taken by the manager. This is shown in Figure 10.3.4.

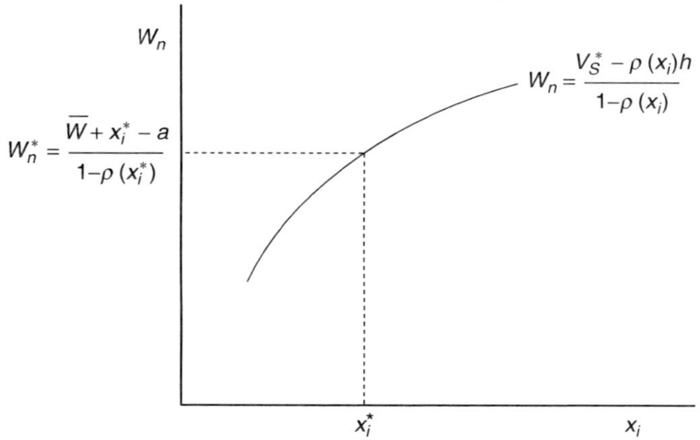

Figure 10.3.4 The wage paid to the manager if an accident does not occur under vicarious liability

It is worth considering the expected wage of this optimal compensation scheme in a little more detail. In equilibrium, the expected wage is equal to $\overline{W} + x_i^* - a$. Suppose that the level of harm rises. Then we know from the analysis in Chapter 4 that must x_i^* rise. Hence, *the manager's expected wage at the optimum level of care rises if the level of harm rises.*

On the other hand, what can we say about the *actual* wage, W_n? Choose any level of care, x_i. For this level of care, we have:

$$W_n(x_i) = \frac{V_S^* - \rho(x_i)h}{1 - \rho(x_i)}$$

Now

$$\frac{dW_n(x_i)}{dh} = \frac{\left[\frac{dV_S^*}{dh} - p'(x_i^*)\frac{dx_i^*}{dh}h - \rho(x_i)\right][1-\rho(x_i)] + [V_S^* - \rho(x_i)h]\rho'(x_i^*)\frac{dx_i^*}{dh}h}{[1-\rho(x_i)]^2}$$

$$= \frac{[\rho(x_i^*) - \rho(x_i)][1-\rho(x_i)] + [V_S^* - h]\rho'(x_i^*)\frac{dx_i^*}{dh}h}{[1-\rho(x_i)]^2} \qquad (10.23)$$

The first term in the numerator of (10.23) is positive (negative) if x_i exceeds (is less than) x_i^*. The last term is positive. Therefore $\frac{dW_n(x_i)}{dh} > 0$ for all $x_i \geq x_i^*$ and for some $x_i < x_i^*$ as well, as long as x_i is sufficiently close to x_i^*. The situation is shown in Figure 10.3.5. If the level of harm

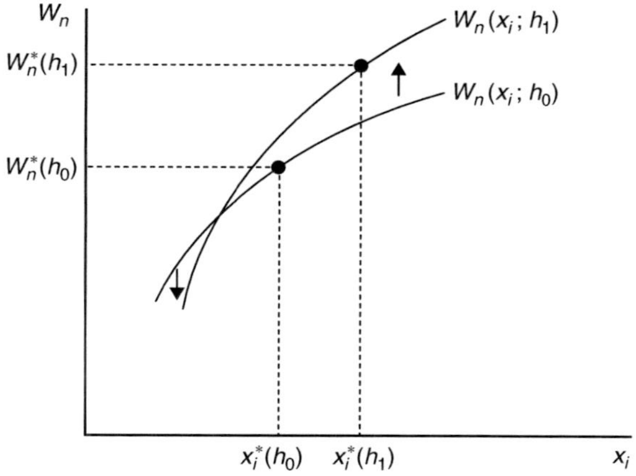

Figure 10.3.5 If the level of harm increases under vicarious liability, the wage paid to the manager when an accident does not occur must rise

rises, the shareholders – who are vicariously liable – would like the manager to take more care. The manager requires higher compensation to still find the contract acceptable.

Summarising our results:

- Under strict liability, the manager is induced to choose an inefficiently low level of care and receives his reservation utility in expected terms. Shareholders pay an expected amount of V_S°, which is given in equation (10.11).
- Under vicarious liability, the manager is induced to choose the efficient level of care and receives his reservation utility in expected terms. Shareholders pay an expected amount of $V_S^\star$, which is given in equation (10.19).

Since the shareholders are assumed to possess all of the bargaining power in this situation, the manager receives his reservation utility under either legal rule and is indifferent between the two schemes. However, note that comparing (10.11) and (10.19), we can see that a move from strict liability to shareholder liability will result in the shareholders paying out more in total (in expected terms), since:

$$V_S^\circ = \overline{W} + x_i^\circ - a + \rho(x_i^\circ)a < \overline{W} + x_i^\star - a + \rho(x_i^\star)h = V_S^\star$$

which follows from the fact that $x_i^\circ + \rho(x_i^\circ)a < x_i^\star + \rho(x_i^\star)h$ for any $a < h$.

Therefore, although vicarious liability results in an efficient allocation of resources (and improves the welfare of victims), shareholders are made worse off as a result of a move from strict liability to vicarious liability. The expected loss to shareholders is less than the expected gain to victims, and so from an overall efficiency point of view, vicarious liability is preferable to strict liability when managers have assets that are less than the harm that they cause.

10.4 Corporate takeovers and the dilution of shareholder property rights

In Chapter 7 we considered the problem of overlapping disposal rights in the context of corporate takeovers. One of the main conclusions there was that in contrast to the pessimistic result of Grossman and Hart (1980), there was a mixed strategy equilibrium in which a more efficient raider succeeded with some positive probability in taking over the corporation. Moreover, the equilibrium probability of a successful takeover turned out to be equal to the probability that each shareholder was pivotal. Finally, we showed that the raider's equilibrium expected profits depended positively on this probability, and so the raider's incentive was to maximise the probability that each shareholder would be pivotal.

More generally, suppose that there are N shareholders, each of whom holds one share. Suppose that the raider requires $K < N$ shares to be tendered to gain control of the company. Then the probability that an individual shareholder is pivotal is:

$$\frac{N!}{K!(N-K!}\rho^K(1-\rho)^{N-K} \tag{10.24}$$

Recall that for any N, the raider seeks to maximise this in any equilibrium. Hence the equilibrium probability that an individual shareholder will tender their shares is:

$$\arg\max_{\rho}\frac{N!}{K!(N-K!}\rho^K(1-\rho)^{N-K} = \frac{K}{N} \tag{10.25}$$

As an application of this result, recall that we provided an example in Chapter 7 with $N = 3$ shareholders and where the raider required that at least $K = 2$ two shareholders to tender in order to gain control. In that example, the equilibrium, profit-maximising probability of any individual shareholder tendering was $\rho = \frac{K}{N} = \frac{2}{3}$. Recall that this probability was indirectly chosen by the raider by designing the offer price P_R.

More generally, suppose that N is even and that the raider requires at least 50 per cent of the shares to gain control of the company, so that $K = \frac{N}{2}$. Then, according to the Bagnoli–Lipman result, the equilibrium probability of each individual shareholder tending is $\frac{N}{2N} = \frac{1}{2}$, and the probability that *at least* half of the shareholders tender their shares is:

$$\sum_{j=K}^{N} \binom{N}{K} \left(\frac{1}{2}\right)^{j} \left(\frac{1}{2}\right)^{N-j} = \sum_{j=N/2}^{N} \binom{N}{N/2} \left(\frac{1}{2}\right)^{j} \left(\frac{1}{2}\right)^{N-j}$$

Grossman and Hart (1980) argue that the free-rider problem can be overcome by *dilution* of shareholder rights. Dilution occurs when a raider reduces 'the value of post-raid company by a certain amount, which the raider is permitted to pay himself. For example, the raider can be allowed to pay himself a large salary or to issue a number of new shares to himself'.[1]

Their simple argument runs as follows. Let φ be the dilution factor, which the shareholders agree upon when the company's constitution is being drafted. Suppose that the raider makes a tender offer of $P_R > P_S$, and suppose that a representative shareholder believes that the raid will succeed. Recall that in the Grossman and Hart framework, this means that each shareholder had no incentives to tender their shares, preferring to free-ride on the actions of other shareholders. As a consequence, in the absence of dilution, the takeover will fail.

Now consider the effect of dilution in this situation. Each individual shareholder can either tender or not. If each shareholder continues to believe that the takeover will succeed, then each shareholder's payoff is:

$$= \begin{cases} P_R & \text{if a share is tendered} \\ V - \varphi & \text{if a share is not tendered} \end{cases} \tag{10.26}$$

Thus, if the dilution factor is sufficiently large, we will have $P_R \geq V - \varphi$, and the shareholder will tender his shares.

Let us see how dilution works in our example from Chapter 7, with three symmetric shareholders: A, B and C. Let the dilution factor be such that $P_R > V - \varphi$. Is there a pure strategy equilibrium in which all shareholders tender their shares? Suppose that shareholders A and B have tendered their shares. Then shareholder C's payoff is exactly as it is in equation (10.26), namely:

$$= \begin{cases} P_R & \text{if a share is tendered} \\ V - \varphi & \text{if a share is not tendered} \end{cases}$$

Thus, C will tender his share. Since all shareholders are alike here, this shows that if the dilution factor is sufficiently large, there is a pure strategy equilibrium in which *all* shareholders tender their shares. In this example, the voluntary dilution of property rights increases the probability that resources move from low- to high-valued uses.

10.5 Shareholder voting and corporate governance

Voting rights are an important part of corporate governance and legal arrangements applying to publicly held companies. Shareholders derive benefits from owning shares which have voting rights attached to them, since they can be used to influence decisions of the company and therefore increase the value of the firm. Shareholders can, in conjunction with monitoring the managers of the firm, use their voting rights to replace a poor management team. This section examines some economic aspects of shareholder voting rights.

10.5.1 One share/one value

One of the most important corporate governance arrangements involves the extent to which ownership of a company's shares allows the shareholder to vote on motions and influence the future direction of the company. Do these arrangements matter for efficiency? Why not, for example, allow different classes of shares, some of which entitle the owner to a share of the dividends where this entitlement differs from their entitlement to vote on motions?

Grossman and Hart (1988) argue that there is a good efficiency reason for the one share/one vote rule: it protects shareholder property rights. They develop their argument using the following example, which assumes that for one class of shares, the entitlement to the firm's dividends is not identical to the entitlement to vote. Suppose there are two classes of shares in a company:

- 'A' class shares: these have a claim to *all* of the voting rights but 50 per cent of the dividends;
- 'B' class shares: these have a claim to *no* voting rights and 50 per cent of the dividends.

The key point in this example is the discrepancy between voting rights and rights to the company's dividend stream: in other words, a departure from the one share/one vote legal arrangement. In particular, class A shares have 100 per cent of the voting rights but are entitled to only 50 per cent of the firm's dividends.

Let us see why this matters. Suppose that the total value of all shares is \$200 under the incumbent management team. In addition, suppose that there is a raider that wishes to take over the company, and that the value of the shares is only \$180 under the raider. Then clearly it would be inefficient for the takeover to proceed. Suppose, however, that the raider is the only party with significant *private benefits* of corporate control. We will see that the presence of these benefits, combined with an absence of a one share/one vote rule, can lead to an inefficient allocation of resources.

To see this, suppose that the raider makes an offer to buy class A shares for \$101. Then the owner of class A shares will certainly sell them, since if he does not, he will only receive \$100 if the raider fails, and \$90 if he succeeds. Thus, since the class A shares have 100 per cent of the voting rights attached to them, the raider will be able to assume control of the company. But this now imposes a negative externality on the owner of the Class B shares: his shares are now only worth \$90. The total value of the firm falls to 191. The raider's loss is \$11, but if his private benefits of control are (say) \$12, then he still gains.

To see how the one share/one vote rule matters here, let us change the example and move partially towards a one share/one vote arrangement. Suppose that class A shares have a claim to 75 per cent of the firm's dividends. These shares are therefore now worth \$150 ($= 0.75 \times$ \$200) under the incumbent. The raider's offer of \$101 for these shares would be rejected; indeed, the raider must now pay \$151 to gain the shares and gain control of the company. If this happened, then a negative external effect is still imposed on the owners of the class B shares – but the external cost is much smaller. The value of the class B shares now falls from \$50 to $0.25 \times$ \$180 = \$45, and the total value of the company only falls from \$200 to \$196 (= \$151 + \$45). The raider's loss is now higher, and is equal to \$151 – $0.75 \times$ \$180 = \$16. If the raider's private benefits of control are \$12, then he would not gain from purchasing these shares, and would therefore no longer attempt to gain control of the company.

This example illustrates the basic point that moving towards a one share/one vote corporate governance arrangement enhances the security of shareholder property rights by reducing the possibility of value-reducing takeovers. It also illustrates the basic idea that a misalignment of voting rights and rights to the company's dividend stream can lead to situations where one class of shareholders can impose a negative external cost on others.

10.5.2 Shareholder voting power

Are raw numbers of shares always the best indicator of the extent to which an individual can influence the outcome of a particular motion? To examine this question, we apply the tools of cooperative game theory that were introduced in Chapter 3, with only a few minor modifications. Suppose, for example, that a particular motion comes before shareholders. Then the motion will either pass or not pass (fail). If motions must pass by a strict majority of voting shares in favour, then (in the absence of abstentions) there are only two relevant kinds of coalitions that can form: those which can force a motion to pass (*winning coalitions*), and those which cannot (*losing coalitions*).

Consider the simplest case, where there are N shareholders, each of whom owns one share with voting rights. Without loss of generality, with transferable utility we can set $v(S) = 1$ if the coalition S is winning, and $v(S) = 0$ if S is not winning, so that:

$$v(S) = \begin{cases} 1 & \text{if } |S| > \dfrac{N}{2} \\ 0 & \text{if } |S| \leq \dfrac{N}{2} \end{cases} \tag{10.27}$$

The cooperative game described by the characteristic function in equation (10.27) is called a *simple majority game*.

As a complete model for analysing corporate voting, however, it is inadequate, because it does not allow for the possibility that shareholders may not hold the same number of shares. To allow for this possibility, we consider the notion of a *weighted majority game*, which consists of a set N of individuals, a collection of *weights* $\{w_i > 0 : i = 1, \ldots, N\}$ and a *quota* q. We represent a weighted majority game by:

$$[q; w_1, \ldots, w_N]$$

In this environment, a coalition S is winning if:

$$\sum_{i \in S} w_i \geq q$$

Setting $q = \frac{N}{2} + 1$ and $w_i = 1$ for all i gets us back to the situation in which each shareholder holds the same number of shares and there is simple majority rule.

If shareholder i owns w_i voting shares then we have a weighted majority game, and the characteristic function of the weighted majority game is:

$$v(S) = \begin{cases} 1 & \text{if} \sum_{i \in S} w_i \geq q \\ 0 & \text{if} \sum_{i \in S} w_i < q \end{cases}$$

How influential is an individual shareholder? As we saw in Chapter 7 and earlier in this chapter, the concept of 'pivotalness' is critical for examining the extent to which an individual shareholder's decision affects the outcome in any given situation.

This idea of pivotalness can be extended to the analysis of shareholder voting. The concept of a shareholder's *voting power* captures the likelihood that a shareholder will influence the outcome of a particular motion that will in turn affect the firm's future direction. If a shareholder can purchase shares which have voting rights attached to them and such a purchase will increase the shareholder's influence, then those shares may be more valuable to that particular shareholder. Hence there may be a close link between an individual shareholder's voting power and the value that they attach to shares – which means that voting power may, in some circumstances, influence the company's share price.

The motivation behind the concept of voting power can be illustrated using the following simple example. Suppose that a company has 36 voting shares, and three shareholders: A, B and C. Suppose that the distribution of shares is as in Table 10.5.1.

With 36 shares in total, to pass a motion would require a clear majority or 19 shares. Using our notation, the representation of this game is therefore:

$$[q; w_1, \ldots, w_N] = [19; 11, 17, 8]$$

Table 10.5.1 An example of shareholder voting

	A	B	C
Shares	11	17	8
Percentage of Shares	0.30556	0.47222	0.22222
Winning Coalitions	{*A*, *B*}	{*B*, *A*}	{*C*, *A*}
	{*A*, *C*}	{*B*, *C*}	{*C*, *B*}
Containing Shareholder *i*	{*A*, *B*, *C*}	{*A*, *B*, *C*}	{*A*, *B*, *C*}

This situation illustrates the basic point that using raw numbers of shares to determine voting power or influence is clearly inappropriate. If we just looked at the raw numbers of shares, it would seem reasonable to think that shareholder B, who holds 17 shares (or over 47 per cent of voting rights), should be more influential than each of the other two shareholders. However, this reasoning is incorrect: all of the winning coalitions in the above game require at least two of the shareholders. Therefore, no shareholder could be said to have more influence than the other in this situation. In this situation, any reasonable measure of voting power should have each shareholder having equal power or influence. Since raw percentages of shares do not have this property, they are unsuitable as a measure of voting power and shareholder influence.

The concept of *voting power* simply attempts to formalise this reality that raw numbers of shares are not always a reasonable indicator of how likely certain shareholder will be pivotal (in the sense that they can turn a losing coalition into a winning one). We now turn to three such measures that have been developed and used in the literature.

10.5.2.1 The Shapley–Shubik power index

Shapley and Shubik (1954) introduced an index for measuring an individual's voting power in a committee. They consider all $N!$ possible arrangements of voters. They view a voter's power as the a priori probability that he will be pivotal in some arrangement of voters. Pivotalness requires that:

- If every voter before shareholder i in the arrangement votes in favour of the motion, and if every voter after i in the arrangement votes against the motion, then the bill would fail; and
- If voter i and every voter before i in the arrangement votes in favour of the motion, and if every voter after i in the arrangement votes against the motion, then the motion would pass.

The *Shapley–Shubik power index* for voter i is simply the number of arrangements of voters in which voter i satisfies these two conditions, divided by the total number of arrangements of voters. It therefore assigns a shareholder the probability that he will cast the deciding vote if all arrangements of voters are equally likely. The expected frequency with which a shareholder is the pivot, over all possible alignments of the voters, is an indication of the shareholder's voting power.

Let us compute this measure of voting power. Consider all possible orderings of the N shareholders, and consider all the ways in which a winning coalition can be built up. There are $N!$ possible orderings of the shareholders. For each one of these orderings, some unique player will join a coalition and turn it from a losing coalition into a winning coalition. In other words, there will be a unique pivotal voter for each possible permutation of shareholders. The number of times that shareholder *i* is pivotal, divided by the total number of possible alignments, is shareholder *i*'s voting power. That is:

$$\phi_i^{SS} = \frac{\text{Number of arrangements in which shareholder } i \text{ is pivotal}}{N!}$$

where it is assumed that each of the $N!$ alignments is equally probable. If S is a winning coalition and $S-\{i\}$ is losing, then i is pivotal. Let $s = |S|$ be the size of coalition S. Given the size of S, the number of ways of arranging the previous $s-1$ voters is $(s-1)!$. Also, the number of ways in which the remaining $(N-s)$ shareholders can be arranged is $(N-s)!$. Therefore, given S, the total number of ways that voter i can be pivotal is simply:

$$(s-1)!(N-s)!$$

We therefore get:

$$\phi_i^{SS} = \frac{\sum_{S\,:i\text{ is pivotal}} (s-1)!(N-s)!}{N!}$$

(See, for example, Owen (1995, p. 265) or Felsenthal and Machover (1998, p. 197.)[2] To illustrate how to compute this index, let us go back and again consider the weighted majority game:

$$[19;\ 11,\ 17,\ 8]$$

The $3! = 6$ possible ways of arranging the shareholders are:

$$\begin{array}{ll} \{A,\underline{B},C\} & \{B,\underline{C},A\} \\ \{A,\underline{C},B\} & \{C,\underline{A},B\} \\ \{B,\underline{A},C\} & \{C,\underline{B},A\} \end{array}$$

where the pivotal shareholder in each arrangement is underlined. Therefore it is easy to see that:

$$\phi_i^{SS} = \frac{1}{3} \text{ for } i = A,\ B,\ C$$

10.5.2.2 *The Banzhaf power index*

Banzhaf's (1965) index is also concerned with the fraction of possibilities in which a voter is pivotal, but only considers the *combinations* of such possibilities, rather than *permutations*. In other words, Banzhaf's approach does not worry about the order in which voters are arranged. To distinguish between the Banzhaf approach and the Shapley–Shubik approach, consider any winning coalition $S \cup \{i\}$. If i leaves this group and S turns into a losing coalition, then i is said to be *critical* (the ways in which the coalition S can be arranged are ignored). The (*normalised*) *Banzhaf power index* of voter i is the number of coalitions in which i is critical, divided by the total number of all such coalitions in which some voter is critical. Mathematically, we have:

$$\phi_i^{Bz} = \frac{\theta_i}{\sum_{j=1}^{N} \theta_j}$$

where θ_i is the number of coalitions in which i is critical (also known as the number of *swings* for i). Returning to our previous example, the coalitions in which some player i is critical are $\{A,B\},\{B,C\}$ and $\{C,A\}$. Each shareholder is critical in two coalitions. Therefore, $\sum_{j=1}^{N} \theta_j = 6$ and we have:

$$\phi_i^{Bz} = \frac{1}{3} \quad \text{for } i = A, B, C$$

which, in this particular example, is the same as ϕ_i^{SS} (this need not always be the case).

10.5.2.3 *The Deegan–Packel power index*

Another index of voting power that has received some attention in the literature is that proposed by Deegan and Packel (1978). Their measure is based on the notion of *minimal winning coalitions* (MWCs), which are coalitions that become losing if *any* single voter is removed.[3] Following Riker's (1962) *size principle*, they argue that coalitions exceeding the minimal winning ones will not form (why bother recruiting more supporters if your coalition is already winning?) They also assume that each MWC is equally likely, and that members of MWCs split any gains equally.

These assumptions uniquely determine the following power index. Suppose that player i is a member of the minimal winning coalitions

$\{S_1, S_2, \ldots, S_{K_i}\}$, which have $s_1, s_2, \ldots, s_{K_i}$ members respectively. Then the *total Deegan–Packel (DP) power* of i is:

$$TDPP_i = \sum_{k=1}^{K_i} \frac{1}{s_{K_i}}$$

and the *Deegan–Packel power index* of i is:

$$\phi_i^{DP} \equiv \frac{TDPP_i}{\sum_{j=1}^{N} TDPP_j}$$

Returning to our example, note that the minimal winning coalitions are $\{A, B\}, \{B, C\}$, and $\{C, A\}$. Therefore,

$$TDPP_i = \frac{1}{2} + \frac{1}{2} = 1 \quad \text{for} \quad i = A, B, C$$

and so:

$$\phi_i^{DP} = \frac{1}{3} \quad \text{for} \quad i = A, B, C$$

which, once again, is the same as ϕ_i^{SS} and ϕ_i^{Bz} (again, this need not always be the case).

10.6 Corporate takeovers, welfare, and the measurement of market concentration

So far in this chapter we have examined the effect of legal rules on merger incentives, issues that arise in the design of managerial compensation in the context of accident law, as well as issues around the influence that shareholders can have on managerial decisions within publicly held companies. Another key set of legal issues that arise in the context of mergers and corporate takeovers are those that involve competition and market concentration, and the link between concentration and economic welfare.

Can we use measures of market share to estimate aggregate welfare in oligopolistic markets? Suppose, for example, that there are four firms in an industry. We can compute the market share of each firm i as:

$$s_i = \frac{q_i}{Q}$$

where $Q=\Sigma_{i=1}^{4} q_i$ is the aggregate market output. To make things concrete, suppose that we have:

$$\begin{aligned} s_1 &= 0.45 \\ s_2 &= 0.25 \\ s_3 &= 0.20 \\ s_4 &= 0.10 \end{aligned}$$

We could then plot these on a graph, with market share rank on the horizontal axis, and cumulative market share on the vertical axis, as in Figure 10.6.1.

In Figure 10.6.1, we have also plotted market share curve for a market with a large number of firms, in which all firms have an equal share. The flatter the line, the more equal are the market shares. In a perfectly competitive market, there would be many firms, each with a small market share. Such a graph could be used to examine the 'competitiveness' or degree of 'concentration' of a particular industry.

Alternatively, in an industry with $N > 2$ firms, we could compute the *Herfindahl–Hirschman index* (HHI) which was encountered in Chapter 5:

$$HHI = \sum_{i=1}^{N} s_i^2$$

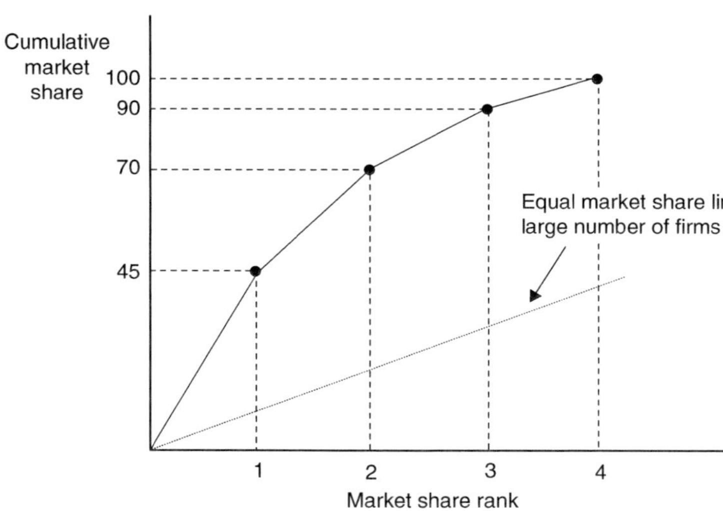

Figure 10.6.1 Market shares

where, again, $s_i = q_i / Q$. If a single firm in the industry is 'dominant' and has a very high market share, then the HHI is large (close to one). On the other hand, if no firm dominates, then each of the s_i are small, and so $\sum_{i=1}^{N} s_i^2$ would be close to zero. In general, $0 < HHI < 1$, with a lower value indicating a 'more competitive' market.

10.6.1 The link between market concentration and economic welfare

The HHI may be able to measure the 'competitiveness' of a market, but is it an appropriate measure of welfare?

To isolate the consequences of using concentration indices as a guide to policy, let us consider two markets, *X* and *Y*, with identical demand curves and an identical number of firms. The only difference between these markets is the cost structure of the firms. This difference in cost structure drives differences in market concentration. If industry *Y* has a higher measure of market concentration than industry *X*, is welfare lower in market *Y*?

To illustrate the main issues, consider the following constant elasticity of demand function:

$$Q(P) = AP^{-\varepsilon}$$

where $\varepsilon > 0$ is the absolute value of price elasticity of demand. There are *n* non-identical firms, indexed by $i = 1,\ldots,n$. Suppose that each firm has constant marginal costs of c_i. The marginal revenue of firm *i* is:

$$MR_i(q_i, \mathbf{q}_{-i}) = P\left(1 - \frac{s_i}{\varepsilon}\right) \tag{10.28}$$

where $s_i = \dfrac{q_i}{\sum_{i=1}^{n} q_i}$ is the equilibrium market share of firm *i*. In a Cournot equilibrium, firms set marginal revenue equal to marginal cost, so that:

$$P\left(1 - \frac{s_i}{\varepsilon}\right) = c_i \tag{10.29}$$

Summing over all *n* firms gives the equilibrium market price:

$$P^* = \frac{\bar{c}}{1 - \dfrac{1}{n\varepsilon}} \tag{10.30}$$

where $\bar{c} \equiv \frac{\sum_{i=1}^{n} c_i}{n}$ is the average marginal cost across all firms. Each firm's output, q_i is equal to:

$$q_i = A\varepsilon\left[1-\frac{c_i\left(1-\frac{1}{n\varepsilon}\right)}{\bar{c}}\right]\left[\frac{\bar{c}}{1-\frac{1}{n\varepsilon}}\right]^{-\varepsilon} \quad (10.31)$$

Firm *i*'s profits are:

$$\pi_i = A\varepsilon\left[\frac{\bar{c}}{1-\frac{1}{n\varepsilon}}\right]^{-\varepsilon}\left[\frac{\bar{c}}{1-\frac{1}{n\varepsilon}}-c_i\right]^2 \quad (10.32)$$

and consumer welfare is:

$$CS(P) = \int_{P^*}^{\infty} Q(P)dP = \int_{\frac{\bar{c}}{1-\frac{1}{n\varepsilon}}}^{\infty} AP^{-\varepsilon}dP$$
$$= \frac{1}{\varepsilon-1}\left(\frac{\bar{c}}{1-\frac{1}{n\varepsilon}}\right)^{1-\varepsilon} \quad (10.33)$$

The expression in equation (10.33) reveals an important result in this particular example: with constant marginal costs, and if the number of firms is also constant, then consumer welfare depends only on the *average* marginal cost, $\bar{c}$, and not on the *spread* of the marginal costs among these firms. Consumers are indifferent between a situation in which firm 1 was a low-cost firm and the remaining firms were high cost, or a situation in which firm 1 was a high-cost firm and the remaining firms had low costs, as long as $\sum_{i=1}^{n} c_i$ remained unchanged. This is just a special case of the more general problem analysed in Bergstrom and Varian (1985) who show that in certain cases equilibrium outcomes (that is, market price and quantity, private provision of public goods, and so on) in various strategic situations may be independent of the distribution of the characteristics across the participants.

On the other hand, industry profits *will* depend on the distribution of characteristics across firms. Note that firm *i*'s market share is:

$$s_i = \varepsilon\left[1-\frac{c_i}{\bar{c}}\left(1-\frac{1}{n\varepsilon}\right)\right]$$

and that total industry profits are:

$$\Pi = \sum_{i=1}^{n} \pi_i = A\varepsilon \left[\frac{\bar{c}}{1 - \frac{1}{n\varepsilon}} \right]^{-} \left\{ \sum_{i=1}^{n} \left[\frac{\bar{c}}{1 - \frac{1}{n\varepsilon}} - c_i \right]^2 \right\}$$

$$= \frac{PQ}{\varepsilon} \left[\sum_{i=1}^{n} s_i^{\,2} \right] \tag{10.34}$$

$$= \frac{PQ}{\varepsilon} HHI$$

where $HHI = \sum_{i=1}^{n} s_i^2$ is the Herfindahl–Hirschman concentration index defined earlier. Aggregate profits depend on the distribution of market shares, which (from the expression for s_i) themselves depend on the distribution of costs. Low- (high-)cost firms will have high (low) market share. Aggregate welfare is the sum of the consumer surplus and producer profits:

$$W = CS + \Pi = CS + \frac{PQ}{\varepsilon} HHI$$

$$= \frac{1}{\varepsilon - 1} \left(\frac{\bar{c}}{1 - \frac{1}{n\varepsilon}} \right)^{1-\varepsilon} + A\varepsilon \left[\frac{\bar{c}}{1 - \frac{1}{n\varepsilon}} \right]^{-\varepsilon} \left\{ \sum_{i=1}^{n} \left[\frac{\bar{c}}{1 - \frac{1}{n\varepsilon}} - c_i \right]^2 \right\} \tag{10.35}$$

10.6.1.1 Does welfare always fall when concentration rises?

Suppose that industry X has a lower measure of market concentration than industry Y. Let HHI_j be the concentration index in industry j, with $j = X,Y$, and assume that $HHI_X < HHI_Y$. Is welfare always higher in market X? *The answer is no.* To see this, suppose that the distribution of marginal costs in market X is $c_1, c_2, \ldots, c_n$, and that the cost structure in market Y is a *mean-preserving spread* of the cost structure in market X, so that the cost structure in market Y is $c_1 + h_1, c_2 + h_2, \ldots, c_n + h_n$, with $\sum_{i=1}^{n} h_i = 0$. Then $\bar{c}$ is unchanged, and by equations (10.30) and (10.33), we know that $Q_X = Q_Y, P_X = P_Y$, and $CS_X = CS_Y$. The concentration index in market Y is:

$$HHI_Y = \left\{ \sum_{i=1}^{n} \left[\frac{\bar{c}}{1 - \frac{1}{n\varepsilon}} - (c_i + h_i) \right]^2 \right\}$$

$$= \left\{ \sum_{i=1}^{n} \left[\frac{\overline{c}}{1 - \frac{1}{n\varepsilon}} - c_i \right]^2 \right\} + \left[2\sum_{i=1}^{n} c_i h_i + \sum_{i=1}^{n} h_i^2 \right]$$

$$= HHI_X + \left[2\sum_{i=1}^{n} c_i h_j + \sum_{i=1}^{n} h_i^2 \right]$$

where we have used the assumption that $\sum_{i=1}^{n} h_i = 0$. Since $\Pi_Y = \frac{PQ}{\varepsilon} HHI_Y$, we have:

$$\Pi_Y = \frac{PQ}{\varepsilon} . \left(HHI_X + 2\sum_{i=1}^{n} c_i h_i + \sum_{i=1}^{n} h_i^2 \right)$$

$$= \frac{PQ}{\varepsilon} HHI_X + \frac{PQ}{\varepsilon} \left(2\sum_{i=1}^{n} c_i h_i + \sum_{i=1}^{n} h_i^2 \right)$$

$$= \Pi_X + \frac{PQ}{\varepsilon} \left(2\sum_{i=1}^{n} c_i h_i + \sum_{i=1}^{n} h_i^2 \right)$$

This immediately gives us the following set of results. Suppose that the cost structure in industry *Y* is a mean-preserving spread of the cost structure in market *X*. Then:

1. If $2\sum_{i=1}^{n} c_i h_i + \sum_{i=1}^{n} h_i^2 > 0$, then $HHI_Y > HHI_X \Leftrightarrow \Pi_Y > \Pi_X \Leftrightarrow W_Y > W_X$.
2. If $2\sum_{i=1}^{n} c_i h_i$ is sufficiently negative so that $2\sum_{i=1}^{n} c_i h_i + \sum_{i=1}^{n} h_i^2 < 0$, then $HHI_Y < HHI_X \Leftrightarrow \Pi_Y < \Pi_X \Leftrightarrow W_Y < W_X$.

Suppose that the mean-preserving spread of costs is independent of the original cost structure, so that $\sum_{i=1}^{n} c_i h_i = 0$. If markets *X* and *Y* are identical in all respects except for their cost structures, and if the cost structure in market *Y* is an independent mean-preserving spread of the cost structure in market *X*, then case 1 above applies, and *both market concentration and welfare will be higher in market Y than they are in market X.*

This is exactly the opposite result than the one we would obtain if we relied on naïve intuition about the relationship between market concentration and welfare. Intuitively, the mean-preserving spread of costs keeps the average marginal cost (and therefore equilibrium price) the same, but results in a cost structure whose distribution has a larger number of lower-cost firms. The market share (and profits) of these low-cost firms increases by more than the decrease in the market share and profits of high-cost firms, and so both the market concentration measure and aggregate welfare must also both rise.

A higher concentration index is therefore neither a necessary nor a sufficient condition for aggregate welfare to be lower in an industry, even with the same number of firms and the same market demand.

10.7 Collusion and price fixing

10.7.1 Collusion in the Cournot model

In the earlier part of this chapter we showed how legal rules may provide firms with significant cost incentives to merge. But there may be other reasons for firms to merge. For example, firms may wish to collude in order to increase profits by raising their prices. One question that immediately arises is whether collusion is stable in the Cournot model. In this discussion, when we say *collusion* we mean an implicit or explicit agreement by the firms to restrict total market output to the monopoly level.

Consider the following simple example. Suppose that the demand curve is $Q = a–P$, and that there are two firms with identical marginal costs of c. Suppose that the two firms sign an agreement which stipulates that each of them will produce half of the monopoly level of output. In other words, suppose that they both agree to produce:

$$\frac{Q^M}{2} = \frac{a-c}{4}$$

This agreement maximises the joint industry profits, but is it strategically stable? The answer, in general is no. In other words, firm 1 will want to cheat on the collusive agreement (and so will firm 2). Therefore, *such collusive agreements are inherently unstable*. This conclusion makes the analysis and punishment of collusive activity somewhat problematic – standard economic theory suggests that collusive agreements will, as a general rule, be very difficult to sustain.

10.7.2 Efficient deterrence for price fixers and monopolists

The previous section argued that agreements to fix prices or quantities between Cournot duopolists (or oligopolists, for that matter) may be inherently unstable and therefore difficult to observe and enforce. Nevertheless, price fixing cartels do exist. How, then, should price fixing be punished? This section applies the framework of Chapter 9 to address this question.

To illustrate the main idea, suppose again that the demand curve is:

$$P = a - Q$$

We again assume that marginal costs are constant and equal to $c > 0$. The efficient quantity is $Q^* = a - c$. Now consider a price-fixing cartel, which somehow manages to reach a stable, enforceable agreement between its members to fix its price and quantity at the monopoly level. Thus, we assume that the members of the cartel basically act as a single, profit-maximising monopolist.

Under these circumstances, the cartel's profit is:

$$\pi(P) = (P - c)Q(P) = (P - c)(a - P) \tag{10.36}$$

At a price P, the consumer surplus is:

$$CS(P) = \frac{1}{2}[Q(P)]^2 = \frac{1}{2}(a - P)^2$$

Following the results from Chapter 9, the marginal damage or harm to consumers from a price increase is simply the change in consumer surplus as the price rises, which is equal to:

$$CS'(P) = -(a - P) = -Q \tag{10.37}$$

Thus we have a situation that is similar to the general set-up in Chapter 9: there is a party (a cartel) whose actions are inflicting 'harm' on another group, consumers. It is important to point out, however, that the analogy with the results in Chapter 9 only goes so far. Price fixing is not 'theft', since the transactions between consumers and producers are entirely voluntary. The 'harm' that is created when a cartel increases its price only becomes an issue for efficiency analysis when price increases above marginal cost, in which case there is an efficiency loss.

Nevertheless, the analytical approach in Chapter 9 is very useful here. In Chapter 9, the optimal punishment strategy involved setting the marginal expected fine ρf equal to the marginal social harm at the optimum. In this example, the marginal harm to consumers is the loss of consumer surplus, which is $Q = a - P$. At the optimum, $P = c$, so let us set the marginal expected fine equal to $\rho f = Q^* = a - c$. That is, suppose that the marginal fine is equal to

$$f^* = \frac{a-c}{\rho} = \frac{Q^*}{\rho} \tag{10.38}$$

Equation (10.38) states that the efficient marginal fine is equal to the efficient quantity, discounted by the probability of detection.

The first obvious question to address is: does this fine actually deter a cartel from price fixing? Remember that the fine here is a *marginal* fine: it is levied per unit of the harmful activity (which is the increase in the market price). Therefore, with this marginal fine in place, the cartel's expected profit is:

$$\begin{aligned} \mathrm{E}[\pi] &= (P-c)(a-P) - \rho f^* P \\ &= (P-c)(a-P) - \rho\frac{a-c}{\rho}P \\ &= (P-c)(a-P) - (a-c)P \\ &= -P^2 - ac + aP + cP - aP + cP \\ &= -P^2 - ac + 2cp \end{aligned} \tag{10.39}$$

The cartel chooses P to maximise this expression. The result is:

$$-2P + 2c = 0 \tag{10.40}$$

Solving this expression, we obtain the result that the cartel chooses $P = c$, which is the efficient outcome: the fine effectively deters price fixing.

Under this legal rule, the cartel's expected profit is:

$$\mathrm{E}[\pi] = -c^2 - ac + 2c^2 = c^2 - ac < 0 \tag{10.41}$$

and expected revenue from the fine is:

$$\rho f^* c = \rho\frac{a-c}{\rho}c = ac - c^2$$

With this fine in place, equation (10.41) indicates that the cartel earns negative profits, and so may be better off shutting down completely. This is inefficient. To avoid this occurring, we alter the marginal fine slightly so that it effectively also pays the cartel a total amount equal to $ac - c^2$. If this is done, the cartel's expected profit would become:

$$\begin{aligned} \mathbf{E}[\pi] &= (P-c)(a-P) - \rho f^{*}P + ac - c^2 \\ &= (P-c)(a-p)P - \rho\frac{a-c}{\rho}P + ac - c^2 \\ &= (P-c)(a-P) - (a-c)P + c(a-c) \\ &= (P-c)(a-P) - (a-c)(P-c) \\ &= (P-c)(a-P) - \rho\frac{(a-c)}{\rho}(P-c) \\ &= (P-c)(a-P) - \rho f^{*}(P-c) \end{aligned} \tag{10.42}$$

The optimal punishment scheme now involves imposing a total fine on the cartel that is equal to:

$$f^{*}(P-c) = \frac{(a-c)}{\rho}(P-c) = \frac{Q^{*}(P-c)}{\rho} \tag{10.43}$$

Equation (10.43) is very intuitive. It states that the total fine should be equal to the efficient quantity Q^* multiplied by the cartel's actual profit margin, discounted by the probability of detection. Note that the total fine is zero if the cartel prices at marginal cost. The rule in (10.43) therefore states that the total fine should be proportional to the cartel's 'overcharge' $P - c$, where the factor of proportionality is the

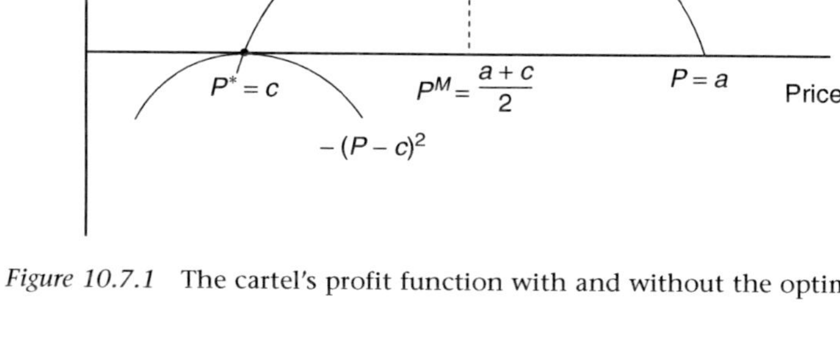

Figure 10.7.1 The cartel's profit function with and without the optimal fine

efficient quantity discounted by the probability of detection. With this rule in place, the cartel's expected profit is $\mathrm{E}[\pi] = -(P-c)^2$, which again induces the cartel to choose $P = c$, so that its expected profits are zero. The expected fine revenue is:

$$\rho f^*(P-c) = 0$$

and so there is no expected monetary gain to the enforcement authority from this system of fines.

Note that this rule does *not* set the fine equal to the *actual* profit of the cartel; nor does it consider the *actual* total harm to consumers when the cartel chooses a price of *P*. This happens for two reasons. First, since the probability of detection is lower than one, it is the expected fine that has the deterrence effect, not the fine itself. Second, a rule which focused on the actual harm to consumers (that is, the loss of consumer surplus at the cartel's price P, compared to the efficient outcome) would result in underdeterrence, because with a higher price, quantity is lower. Since the harm to consumers is the change in consumer surplus, and since the marginal change in consumer surplus is $-QdP$, setting a fine proportional to the actual quantity that is chosen will result in under deterrence, since when price exceeds marginal cost, $Q < Q^*$.

10.8 Notes

Easterbrook and Fishel (1991) is a thorough coverage of the economic structure of corporate law. Manne (1965) is a crucial first paper on mergers and the market for corporate control. Hart (1995) contains a useful discussion of voting structure in public companies. Lucas (1983) is an excellent introduction to weighted majority games and voting power. Teall (2007) contains a useful discussion and analysis of voting power and corporate governance issues. The link between concentration and welfare seems to be well known in the literature (see, for example, Shy 1996), but seems to have had little influence on the design of actual competition policies. Hylton (2003, Chapter 3) and Spulber (1989, Chapter 19) also analyse optimal enforcement and deterrence of anti-trust violations.

10.9 Exercises

1. Suppose that victims cannot take any care to avoid accidents, and suppose that there are two firms who are potential injurers, each of whom can take care. The following table describes the levels of care, costs of care, and expected damages.

Levels of care		Costs of care		Expected damage to victim	Total social costs
Firm 1	Firm 2	Firm 1	Firm 2		
None	None	0	0	30	
None	Care	0	4	24	
Care	None	6	0	20	
Care	Care	6	4	12	

(a) Compute the total social costs for each combination of levels of care. What is the efficient outcome here?

Consider the following *strict liability rule*: irrespective of the level of care taken by each firm, if there is an accident, firm 1 will be liable for a pre-specified fraction s_1 of the victim's losses, and firm 2 will be liable for a pre-specified fraction s_2 of the victim's losses, with $s_1 + s_2 = 1$.

(b) Suppose that the firms cannot collude amongst themselves. Write down the payoff matrix for the strategic game between firms 1 and 2. Does the strict liability rule outlined above induce both firms to behave efficiently? In other words, is the efficient outcome a Nash equilibrium?

(c) Is {None, None} a Nash equilibrium? If so, under what conditions? If not, why not?

(d) Is {Care, None} a Nash equilibrium? If so, under what conditions? If not, why not?

(e) Is {None, Care} a Nash equilibrium? If so, under what conditions? If not, why not?

(f) Does your answer in part (b) change if the firms can collude amongst themselves and jointly choose their levels of (for example, if the firms were to merge to form a single firm)? Explain.

Now consider the following *negligence rule*: the court first sets due standards of care, z_1 and z_2 for firms 1 and 2, and applies these due standards as follows:

- If a firm meets its due standard of care, it is not liable to pay any damages to the victim.
- If firm 1 is the only firm which does not meet its due standard of care, it will be held liable for the total amount of the victim's damages. Similarly, if firm 2 is the only firm which does not meet its due standard of care, it will be held liable for the total amount of the victim's damages.
- If both firms 1 and 2 do not meet their due standards of care, they will both be held liable for some pre-specified portion of the victim's damages, with firm 1 paying a fraction s_1 of the victim's damages, and firm 2 paying a fraction s_2 of the victim's damages, where again we have $s_1 + s_2 = 1$.

(g) Suppose that the due standards of care are set at the efficient levels for each firm. Repeat parts (b) to (f) above.

2. Consider the four-player weighted majority game:

$$[51; 40, 30, 20, 10]$$

   (a) In which coalition is player 1 pivotal?
   (b) Find the voting power of player 1, using the Shapley–Shubik index.
   (c) Repeat questions (a) and (b) for players 2, 3 and 4.
3. Price controls are a common form of regulation. Suppose there is a single firm that produces a single good, Q. The ordinary demand curve for this good is:

$$Q = 1 - P$$

   where P is the price of the good and x is the quantity demanded. Suppose that marginal costs of production are constant and equal to $c = 0$.
   (a) What is the efficient price and quantity? How much profit does the firm earn if it charges this price?
   (b) If the firm acts as a monopolist and chooses a single price to maximise its profits, what price would it select? What would its profits be in such a situation? What quantity would it produce? Who is harmed if the firm is allowed to act as an unregulated monopolist, and how much are they harmed?

   Now suppose you are advising the government on the design of a system of consumer protection laws to regulate prices. A firm is said to be a *price gouger* if it sets its price above its marginal cost. Let ρ be the (exogenous) probability that a price gouging firm will be prosecuted and found guilty by a court and punished.
   (c) Given ρ, design a system of fines that induces the firm to choose the efficient price and quantity. For example, you may recommend that the government should fine the firm according to the quantity it produces, the price it charges, its level of profits, revenue, or some combination of these variables (or none of them). The choice is up to you. You may assume that the firm is a risk-neutral expected profit maximiser. Carefully explain why your system of fines is optimal. Does your optimal fine depend on ρ? If your optimal fine is implemented and the firm correctly perceives ρ, will the firm ever price gouge?
   (d) Now suppose that the firm's marginal costs are constant and equal to ½, but that the government mistakenly believes that the firm's marginal costs are zero. If the government implements the scheme of fines you designed in question 1, what are the welfare consequences?
   (e) Now suppose that the firm's marginal costs are constant and equal to 0 (and the government knows this), but that the government does not know that the true demand curve is actually:

$$Q = 2 - P$$

   If the government implements the scheme of fines you found in question 1, what are the welfare consequences?
   (f) What can you conclude about the ability of governments to implement efficient price-gouging laws? Briefly discuss, with reference to your answers above.

11
Litigation, Settlement and the Market for Lawyers

11.1 Introduction

Chapter 3 examined situations in which parties to a dispute could potentially (if transaction costs were sufficiently low) negotiate over an economic outcome and, by doing so, exhaust all gains from trade. Moreover, under certain assumptions (for example, quasi-linearity of utility functions), the final outcome and the size of the aggregate gains from trade were independent of the initial allocation of property rights or legal rule than was in place. This is the essence of the Coase Theorem.

But how does this 'negotiation' or 'bargaining' process take place? And if parties *always* negotiate, why is it that even though the vast majority of disputes settle out of court, not all of them do? Haggling, threats, offers, counteroffers, proposals, objections, counterproposals, counterobjections are part and parcel of many economic transactions and most legal disputes. This chapter goes inside the 'black box' of the legal negotiation process and examines how bargaining rules and institutions may affect observed outcomes. The incentive to file lawsuits and settle out of court are also examined under various cost-allocation rules, with the English and American rules presented as special cases.

The chapter is structured as follows. Sections 11.2 and 11.3 study the two common approaches to bargaining that have been explored in the economic literature. Section 11.4 examines the economics of legal disputes and the gains from settling out of court, and explores some reasons why parties might go to court. Section 11.5 presents a general model of legal conflict which can be used to address a wide variety of questions around the economics of litigation. Section 11.6 applies this setup to the market for lawyers, and explores the efficiency properties of this market, assuming that legal services are demanded solely for the purposes of redistributing existing resources. Section 11.7 explores a related but slightly different set of issues: legal complexity and variability, but reaches similar conclusions to the analysis in section 11.6. Section 11.8 returns to the set of questions presented back in Chapter 1, and explores the final issue outlined there: the common law efficiency hypothesis.

11.2 Legal disputes and the influence of bargaining rules and institutions on economic outcomes

Up to this point we have largely ignored the issue of how parties involved in Coasean bargaining might actually split the gains from exchange, and how rules around bargaining might affect the distribution of the gains from trade. But bargaining norms, rules and institutions are an important part of the legal landscape, and can have a considerable influence on economic outcomes. Moreover, the way in which the gains from settlement are distributed can send an important signal to those who may be involved in legal disputes in the future. For example, if bargaining rules provide for generous settlement terms for plaintiffs, then, *ceteris paribus*, this increases the gains to plaintiffs from filing lawsuits.

There is a well-developed body of economic theory, known as *bargaining theory*, which examines these issues. There are two broad approaches to modelling bargaining norms and institutions:

1. The *non-cooperative bargaining* approach starts out with a set of 'rules of the game', under which offers and counteroffers can be made by parties, and derives the bargaining outcome as the equilibrium of a non-cooperative 'offer and acceptance' game.
2. The *axiomatic bargaining approach* posits a set of axioms or which are 'reasonable' for a bargaining solution to possess, and then attempts to characterise these axioms in terms of bargaining solutions.

There are significant analytical differences between the two approaches. Remarkably, however, it turns out that there are often very close links between the outcomes that each approach predicts.

11.2.1 Legal disputes and non-cooperative bargaining theory

The non-cooperative bargaining approach models a situation in which offers and counteroffers can be made, as they would be in a 'real world' bargaining situation between parties haggling with each other during a legal dispute. The standard non-cooperative setup is as follows.

Suppose that there are two parties to a legal dispute. Time is discrete, and is indexed by $t = 0,1,2,...,\infty$. The size of each time period (the time between offers and counteroffers) is denoted by $\Delta > 0$, which can be interpreted as the absolute size of the *frictions* in the bargaining process, or the time taken between each round of the bargaining process. As Δ approaches zero, these frictions disappear.

Bargaining proceeds as a game of alternating offers. To apply the framework, let us return to our earlier two-party example from Chapter 3, where the two parties are the factory (F) and the residents (R). The parties bargain over a surplus, which is the dollar value of the gains from trade. For convenience, we denote this surplus by $\pi > 0$. Dispute resolution is assumed to take place according to the following procedure. In even periods t = 0,2,4,...,∞ the factory makes an *offer* to the residents, where an offer is a proposal pair $(\pi_F, \pi - \pi_F)$ to share the gains from surplus. The residents R can either *accept* this offer, in which case the game ends; or they can *reject* F's offer, in which case the game moves to the next period. In odd periods $t = 1,3,5,...,\infty$ the roles of the players are reversed. If a player receives a share of the surplus x_i in period *t*, then the benefit from that share is:

$$u_i(x_i) = x_i e^{-r_i \Delta t} \tag{11.1}$$

where $r_i > 0$ is the *discount rate* of player *i*. Let $\delta_i \equiv e^{-r_i \Delta}$ be player *i*'s *discount factor*. This reflects the value that the party places on future dollars, relative to current dollars. A high discount factor (or a low discount rate) means that the party places a relatively high value today on dollars to be received in the future.

11.2.1.1 Non-cooperative bargaining when T is finite

To understand what will happen in this model of bargaining, consider the version of the game which has a finite terminal period, *T*, and suppose that the factory and the residents have identical discount factors, denoted by δ. Suppose that T is even. The game can be solved by backward induction. Suppose that the parties enter the final period, period *T*, with no agreement locked in. Then, since *T* is even, the factory has the right to make an offer in this final period. Since the game ends in period *T*, the factory's offer must be accepted by the residents. Thus the factory has all of the bargaining power, and would propose the split that is most advantageous to it, which is $\pi_F = \pi, \pi_R = 0$. Since this occurs in the final round, the offer must be accepted by the residents, since they have no choice according to the rules of the game.

Now roll back to period $T - 1$. The residents know that they must offer the factory at least $\delta\pi$, otherwise the factory will reject the offer and wait until the last period, where they receive π. Thus the residents offer $[\delta\pi,(1-\delta)\pi]$ and the factory accepts. Knowing this, and rolling back to period $T - 2$, the factory will know that the residents will only accept an offer at least as big as $\delta(1-\delta)\pi$. Thus the factory offers $\{[1-\delta(1-\delta)]\pi, \delta(1-\delta)\pi\}$ and this is accepted by the residents.

The pattern is now clear. In period 0, the factory gets to make an offer. It constructs an offer which gives the residents the discounted value of the payoff that they expect to get in the next period, which is:

$$(\delta - \delta^2 + \delta^3 - \delta^4 + \cdots + \delta^{T-1} - \delta^T)\pi \tag{11.2}$$

and it keeps for itself:

$$(1 - \delta + \delta^2 - \delta^3 + \delta^4 - \cdots - \delta^{T-1} + \delta^T)\pi \tag{11.3}$$

To express these formulae more compactly, note that:

$$S = 1 + \delta + \delta^2 + \delta^3 + \delta^4 + \cdots + \delta^{T-1} + \delta^T = \frac{1-\delta^{T-1}}{1-\delta},$$

Define $S_E = 1 + \delta^2 + \delta^4 + \cdots + \delta^T$ and $S_o = \delta + \delta^3 + \delta^5 + \cdots + \delta^{T-1}$. Then $S = S_E + S_O$. Finally, note that:

$$S_E = 1 + \delta^2 + \delta^4 + \cdots + \delta^T = 1 + \delta(\delta + \delta^3 + \cdots + \delta^{T-1}) = 1 + \delta S_O$$

and so:

$$S_0 = \frac{\delta - \delta^{T+1}}{(1-\delta)(1+\delta)} \quad \text{and} \quad S_E = 1 + \delta\frac{\delta - \delta^{T+1}}{(1-\delta)(1+\delta)} \tag{11.4}$$

Now the factory's payoff is:

$$(S_E - S_O)\pi = (1 + \delta S_O - S_O)\pi = [1 - (1-\delta)S_O]\pi = \left[1 - (1-\delta)\frac{\delta - \delta^{T+1}}{(1-\delta)(1+\delta)}\right]\pi$$

$$= \left[1 - \frac{\delta - \delta^{T+1}}{(1+\delta)}\right]\pi = \pi\frac{1+\delta^{T+1}}{1+\delta} \tag{11.5}$$

and the residents' payoff is:

$$\pi\left(1 - \frac{1+\delta^{T+1}}{1+\delta}\right) \tag{11.6}$$

Since these payoffs have been constructed in such a way that the factory and the residents are willing to accept these payoffs as soon as the game begins, *the equilibrium also involves both parties agreeing immediately.*

Even though the bargaining rules allow the parties to 'haggle', the parties do not actually do any haggling in equilibrium. This does *not* mean, however, that rules governing haggling do not matter. The fact that offers and counteroffers are permitted under the rules of the game, combined with the fact that both parties are impatient, leads to an equilibrium in which an offer is accepted immediately. But the payoffs in (11.5) and (11.6) obviously depend on the length of the bargaining process. For example, if the bargaining rules stipulated that the game must be a 'one-shot' offer and acceptance game, with no possibility of counteroffers, then the party that is allowed to make the initial offer will obtain the entire surplus. Clearly, then, bargaining institutions and rules matter for bargaining outcomes.

11.2.1.2 The role of bargaining rules in dispute resolution

In the non-cooperative setting described above there are at least two very real ways in which bargaining norms, rules or formal regulations that govern dispute resolution can affect the distribution of the parties' payoffs, and which will therefore alter incentives to sue and settle:

1. **The identity of the first mover:** In the equilibrium described above, the factory's payoff is $\pi\dfrac{1+\delta^{T+1}}{1+\delta}$, which is greater than the residents' payoff $\pi\left(1-\dfrac{1+\delta^{T+1}}{1+\delta}\right)$ as long as $\delta<1$. *If the parties are otherwise identical, the first mover always receives a higher payoff.*
2. **The number of rounds of offers and counteroffers that are permitted (the length of T):** Consider the extreme case where the residents are not permitted to make a counteroffer and *must* accept the factory's offer. Then clearly the residents will receive *no* surplus, which is the worst outcome for them. More generally, note that for $\delta<1$, we have:

$$\frac{d}{dT}\left(\pi\frac{1+\delta^{T+1}}{1+\delta}\right)=\pi\frac{1}{1+\delta}\frac{d}{dT}\delta^{T+1}=\pi\frac{1}{1+\delta}\text{In}\delta\times\delta^{T+1}<0$$

so that the factory's payoff is decreasing (and the residents payoff is increasing) in T. Even though the parties will reach agreement immediately, the factory (the first mover) prefers a bargaining rule which prevents a large number of counteroffers being made, whilst the second mover prefers that counteroffers be allowed for an indeterminate amount of time.

11.2.1.3 *Bargaining when T is infinite*

What about the situation in which there is no artificially imposed point in time for the bargaining to end? In other words, what happens as $T \to \infty$? One reasonable 'guess' is that the payoffs in the infinite horizon bargaining situation are the limits as $T \to \infty$ of the payoffs in the simpler case in which $T < \infty$. Since $\delta < 1$, the limit of $\pi \frac{1+\delta^{T+1}}{1+\delta}$ as $T \to \infty$ is $\frac{\pi}{1+\delta}$. The residents' payoff is whatever is left over, which is:

$$\lim_{X \to \infty} \pi \left(1 - \frac{1+\delta^{T+1}}{1+\delta} \right) = \frac{\delta \pi}{1+\delta} \tag{11.7}$$

Conveniently, this 'guess' turns out to be correct: the unique equilibrium payoffs of the infinite horizon version of this game are the limit of the equilibrium offers in the finite horizon game. Moreover, the unique equilibrium involves the residents immediately accepting the factory's offer. Again, since haggling is allowed and the parties are impatient, the factory's offer is immediately accepted.

11.2.1.4 *Non-cooperative bargaining without frictions: The split the surplus rule*

Recall that in the non-cooperative bargaining framework, if a player receives a share of the surplus x_i in period t, then the benefit from that share is:

$$u_i(x_i) = x_i e^{-r_i \Delta t}$$

where $d_i \equiv e^{-r_i \Delta}$ is party i's discount factor and $\Delta > 0$ is the absolute size of the frictions in the bargaining process. As frictions disappear, $\Delta \to 0$, which implies that:

$$\lim_{\Delta \to 0} d_i = \lim_{\Delta \to 0}{}^{-r_i \Delta} = \frac{1}{e^{r_i \times 0}} = 1$$

Applying the result in equation (11.7), this then implies that as bargaining becomes frictionless, the equilibrium shares of the parties converge to $\pi_F = \pi_R = \frac{\pi}{2}$. That is, if the parties have identical discount rates and if bargaining frictions are non-existent, the factory's first mover advantage disappears and the parties will 'split the surplus' equally. We will return to this result.

11.3 The axiomatic bargaining approach

The axiomatic approach to bargaining has developed alongside the non-cooperative approach, but it attacks the problem in a very different way. Instead of spelling out the rules of a bargaining situation or negotiation process and looking for equilibrium strategies and outcomes of a well-defined game, the axiomatic approach specifies a set of axioms or rules that a bargaining solution should obey, and then derives a formula or bargaining outcome which is logically equivalent to those rules.

In the axiomatic approach, a *two-person bargaining problem* consists of the following:

- A set of players (in our example, the factory and the residents);
- A set S of *possible agreements*, which the players can jointly implement should they reach agreement; and
- A unique *disagreement point* **D** which is the outcome if the players fail to reach an agreement. The disagreement point here is simply the utilities the factory and the residents would receive if they could not reach an agreement.

Let us again return to the example presented in Chapter 3. In that example the disagreement point depends on the initial assignment of legal or property rights. Assume that both parties have identical quasi-linear preferences. Let $Q_0 = \lambda\bar{Q}$ be the level of Q which the factory can produce without having to gain permission from the residents or pay compensation to them. The parameter $\lambda \in [0,1]$ here has a natural interpretation: it is an index of the factory's initial security of property rights. If $\lambda = 0$, then the factory must obtain the residents' permission to produce any units at all. If $\lambda = 1$, then the factory has the right to produce the maximum Q if it wishes. If $0 < \lambda < 1$, then the factory is entitled to produce $\lambda\bar{Q}$ without obtaining the residents' permission.

The *disagreement point* or *threat point* for the factory is:

$$d_F = \{\bar{M}_F, \lambda\bar{Q}\}$$

and for the residents it is:

$$d_R = \{\bar{M}_R, (\bar{Q} - \lambda\bar{Q})\} = \{\bar{M}_R, (1-\lambda)\bar{Q}\}$$

The benefits that they enjoy at this disagreement point are:

$$\mathbf{D} = \{\bar{u}_F \equiv \bar{M}_F + u(\lambda\bar{Q}), \bar{u}_R \equiv \bar{M}_R + u[(1-\lambda)\bar{Q}]\}$$

The set S of possible agreements here is simply the utility possibilities set: the combination of utilities or benefits such that the amount of money distributed between the parties is equal to the total amount of money available, and such that the production of Q is feasible:

$$S \equiv \{u_F, u_R : M_F + M_R = \bar{M} \text{ and } 0 \leq Q \leq \bar{Q}\}$$

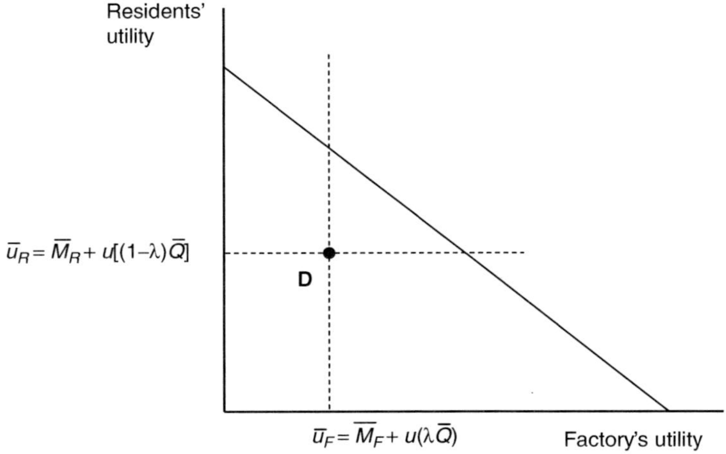

Figure 11.3.1 The set of possible agreements between the factory and the residents

The disagreement point **D** and the set of possible agreements S constitutes a *bargaining situation.*

A *bargaining solution* is simply an algorithm or set of rules that, for each bargaining situation (*S*, **D**), picks out a particular combination of utilities or benefits, denoted by *b*(*S*, **D**). For any given bargaining problem (*S*, **D**) the goal of bargaining theory is to write down a set of conditions or axioms which would seem 'natural' or 'reasonable' for a solution *b*(*S*, **D**) to satisfy, and then to discover whether these conditions are consistent with the requirement that the solution is unique in all situations. This is the motivation for *Nash's axioms*, which are loosely stated as follows:

- **Scale invariance:** Suppose that a bargaining solution is proposed. If there is a linear scaling up of each party's benefits, then the original bargaining solution should also be scaled up accordingly.
- **Symmetry:** If the parties are perfectly symmetric and have the same disagreement point and the same payoff possibilities, then they should receive the same final payoffs after bargaining.
- **Independence of irrelevant alternatives (IIA):** If the original bargaining solution proposes some outcome which lies within some smaller set of possible outcomes, then if we were to start from that smaller set of possible outcomes, the outcome proposed under that bargaining solution should remain unchanged. That is, removing 'irrelevant' alternatives should not change the bargaining outcome.
- **Efficiency:** The bargaining solution should not leave any gains from trade unexploited.

For the bargaining problem between the factory and the residents, the function defined by:

$$u^N(S,\mathbf{D}) \equiv \underset{u_F,u_R}{\operatorname{argmax}}\ (u_F - \bar{u}_F)(u_R - \bar{u}_R) \tag{11.8}$$

subject to

$$(u_F u_R) \in S \text{ and } (u_F, u_R) \geq (\bar{u}_F, \bar{u}_R) \tag{11.9}$$

is the unique bargaining solution that satisfies Nash's axioms. That is, Nash's axioms are logically equivalent to maximising the product of the parties' net benefits. This provides a mathematically convenient solution to bargaining problems in which Nash's axioms are appropriate.

As an example of this result in action, consider the simplest case where the factory and the residents are bargaining over a surplus of π dollars. Each of them starts out with zero dollars. The payoffs are π_F and π_R, with $\pi_F + \pi_R = \pi$. The Nash solution solves:

$$\underset{\pi_F,\pi_R}{\arg\max}(\pi_F - 0)(\pi_R - 0)$$

subject to $\pi_F + \pi_R = \pi$. Substituting this into the expression above yields:

$$\underset{\pi_F}{\arg\max}\,\pi_F(\pi - \pi_F)$$

The solution is

$$\pi_R^* = \pi_F^* = \frac{\pi}{2} \tag{11.10}$$

In other words, the parties split the surplus equally. More generally, if d_F is the disagreement point of the factory and d_R is the disagreement point of the residents, then the Nash solution solves:

$$\underset{\pi_F \geq d_F,\pi_R \geq d_R}{\arg\max}(\pi_F - d_F)(\pi_R - d_R)$$

subject to $\pi_F + \pi_R = \pi$. The solution is:

$$u_F = d_F + \frac{\pi - d_F - d_R}{2},\ u_R = d_R + \frac{\pi - d_F - d_R}{2} \tag{11.11}$$

Recall that in section 11.2.1.4 we showed that under the non-cooperative approach, as bargaining becomes frictionless, the equilibrium shares of the parties each converge to $\pi_F = \pi_R = \frac{\pi}{2}$. Thus, we have a remarkable feature of the cooperative Nash bargaining solution: it can also be justified within the framework of non-cooperative game theory. This is an important result, because it tells us when the use of the Nash solution is most appropriate. To wit, if the parties are assumed to have identical discount rates and if bargaining frictions are non-existent, the parties will 'split the surplus' in the non-cooperative approach, and so behave as if they are implementing Nash's axioms. Thus, the Nash solution can be justified as the limit of the non-cooperative subgame perfect outcome when there are good reasons to assume that the absolute magnitudes of frictions in the bargaining situation are very small, or small enough to be safely ignored.

11.3.1 Bargaining theory and rational threats

A further issue in bargaining is the source or interpretation of the disagreement point **D**, the point which the parties would fall back on if they fail to agree. In the context of law and economics, failing to reach agreement usually means going to trial. Each party's likelihood of success in court therefore determines the position of their disagreement point. In other words, in law and economics, the disagreement point is rarely fixed and exogenous.

To analyse this situation, Nash (1951) formulated the concept of *rational threats*. The basic idea of rational threats is as follows. Consider a situation where the disagreement point is variable, and can be influenced by the parties before they enter negotiations. That is, there are now two stages to the bargaining process:

- **Stage 1:** The parties engage in activities which influence their own disagreement point as well as that of their opponents.
- **Stage 2:** The parties begin from the disagreement points that emerge from stage 1, and bargain and reach an agreement according to the Nash solution.

To analyse this game, we need to first write down the payoffs and be explicit about the strategies of the parties. We will use the factory and the residents example again. Let the strategies in the first stage of the game be denoted by (s_F, s_R). The disagreement points of the factory is $d_F(s_F, s_R)$, and the disagreement point of the residents is $d_R(s_F, s_R)$. The payoffs in the final stage of the game are:

$$d_F(s_F, s_R) + \frac{\pi - d_F(s_F, s_R) - d_R(s_F, s_R)}{2} \qquad (11.12)$$

and

$$d_R(s_F, s_R) + \frac{\pi - d_F(s_F, s_R) - d_R(s_F, s_R)}{2} \qquad (11.13)$$

This is called a *rational threat game*. The model can be solved by simply finding the Nash equilibrium $(s_F^\star, s_R^\star)$ of the game in which the players have the payoffs in (11.12) and (11.13). This is a very natural way of modelling legal disputes in a more realistic setting, where players can employ lawyers and gather evidence before trial in order to influence their threat points at the negotiating table, and in doing so, make themselves better off.

11.3.2 Objections and counterobjections: The Nash approach as a model of haggling and dispute resolution

One possible criticism of the axiomatic bargaining approach is that the axioms are often too abstract or difficult to justify in terms of economic behaviour. Why is one particular set of axioms more acceptable or desirable than another, and why should parties in a bargaining situation obey them instead of another set of axioms? Fortunately, however, in the case of the Nash solution, there is an alternative, more direct and more intuitive approach to axiomatic bargaining, which yields very similar results.[1] Moreover, in the context of law and economics, the approach is a very natural one.

Let us sketch this approach. Suppose that the factory and the residents are in a legal dispute in which their disagreement points are assumed to be zero, and that there is a proposal on the table from the residents to share the gains from trade as follows:

$$(\pi_F^*, \pi - \pi_F^*)$$

An **objection** by the factory to any proposed agreement π_F^* is a pair (π_F, ρ) for which $\rho\pi_F > \pi_F^*$, where $0 < \rho < 1$. The interpretation of an objection is that by threatening to walk away from the bargaining table, the factory can cause negotiations to break down with probability $1 - \rho$, and if this were to occur the factory would receive nothing. However, if negotiations do not break down (which occurs with probability ρ) the factory will receive π_F. The expected value to the factory of this objection is therefore $\rho\pi_F$, which to be something that the factory wishes to raise, must be higher than the payoff that the factory would receive under the proposal π_F^* that is currently on the table. If the factory can find such a pair (π_F, ρ), then it is said to have an objection to π_F^*.

The residents are said to have a **counterobjection** to the factory's objection (π_F, ρ) if $\rho\pi_R^* \geq \pi_R$. The interpretation is that even in this new, risky situation that the factory has created by lodging an objection, the residents can profitably insist on the original proposal. If negotiations were to break down, the residents would also receive nothing, but if negotiations do not break down (which occurs with probability ρ) and the residents insist on the original proposal, then they will receive π_R^*. The expected value of this countergambit is therefore $\rho\pi_R^*$, which is higher than π_R, the payoff that the residents would receive under the objection conveyed by the factory. If the residents can find such a pair (π_R^*, ρ), then they are said to have a counterobjection to the factory's objection (π_F, ρ).

It turns out that the Nash solution described above can also be characterised as the set of all agreements such that the residents can counterobject to *every* objection of the factory, and the factory can counterobject to *every* objection by the residents. In other words, Nash's axioms, if we wish, can be dispensed with altogether and we can instead think about the proposed solution in terms of objections and counterobjections.

The requirement that every possible objection can be met with a counterobjection is a very restrictive requirement which narrows down the set of possible outcomes to a single point. Suppose, for example, that the disagreement point is (0,0), and that the players are negotiating over a surplus of $\pi = 1$. Then the point (½,½) is the only point at which the residents can counterobject to every objection of the factory, and the factory can counterobject to every objection by the residents.

To see the link between the Nash solution and the objection/counterobjection result, suppose that there is some other outcome which does not maximise the product of the parties' payoffs, but which, for every objection that the factory had, the residents could make a counterobjection. Let this solution be $(\pi, 1 - \pi)$, and suppose it does not maximise the product of the payoffs. We will show that this leads to a contradiction. Suppose that the factory objects to this outcome, nominating an alternative split, $\pi' > \pi$. Choose ρ arbitrarily, with the only restriction being that that $\rho > \frac{\pi}{\pi'}$. Then, by assumption, the residents have a counterobjection, so $\rho \geq \frac{1-\pi'}{1-\pi}$ as well. But this implies that $\frac{\pi}{\pi'} \geq \frac{1-\pi'}{1-\pi}$. If not (that is, if we instead had $\frac{\pi}{\pi'} < \frac{1-\pi'}{1-\pi}$) it would be possible to find a ρ which could be 'squeezed' in between $\frac{\pi}{\pi'}$ and $\frac{1-\pi'}{1-\pi}$, which would be an objection for the factory, but which would not allow the possibility of a counterobjection by the residents. But since $\frac{\pi}{\pi'} \geq \frac{1-\pi'}{1-\pi}$, and π' was chosen arbitrarily, this means that $\pi(1-\pi)$ must maximise the product of the parties' payoffs. We are therefore left with a contradiction, and it must therefore be the case that the Nash solution is the only outcome which has the property that for every objection that the factory can make, the residents can make a counterobjection.

11.4 Legal disputes and the gains from settling out of court

11.4.1 Litigation versus settlement as a bargaining situation

Let us return to the example from Chapter 3 involving the factory and the residents. We will use the bargaining framework outlined in the previous section in this chapter to illustrate the gains from settling out of court. Suppose that the factory's production of $\overline{Q}$ units is currently causing harm to the residents, but the residents enjoy a property right to clean air. That is, the residents have the legal right to prevent the factory from polluting, and so could enforce $Q = 0$ in a court of law and avoid the costs that they are currently incurring from the factory's production. To try to enforce this right, suppose that the residents file a lawsuit against the factory. The residents then become the *plaintiffs* and the factory becomes the *defendant* in this legal dispute. Suppose that the parties have identical quasi-linear preferences and that it is efficient for the factory to produce $Q^* = \overline{Q}/2$ units. Prior to trial, the parties may engage in pre-trial negotiation in the hope of arriving at a settlement which would result in the factory making a payment of $T \geq 0$ to the residents in exchange for the right to produce.

We assume that neither party knows the court's ruling with certainty. Remember that the factory's utility is increasing in Q, whereas the residents' utility is increasing in $\overline{Q} - Q$, the absence of production. Let ρ be the (commonly perceived) probability that the residents will win in court. If the residents win, they enjoy utility of $u(\overline{Q})$. On the other hand, if they lose, they receive nothing. If the factory wins, they receive $u(\overline{Q})$, but nothing if they lose. Finally, let:

C_R = the resident's (fixed) costs of going to trial
C_F = the factory's costs of going to trial
T = amount that defendant must plaintiff if they settle
N_R = the residents' costs of settling/negotiating
N_F = the factory perceived costs of settling/negotiating

There are only two states of the world here: the state of the world in which the residents wins, and the state of the world in which they lose. Notice also that the costs of going to trial and of settling are assumed to be fixed. Thus, the expected benefits for the residents from going to trial are:

$$\rho[U(\overline{Q}) - C_R] + (1 - \rho)[0 - C_R] = \rho u(\overline{Q}) - C_R$$

and the expected benefits for the factory are:

$$\rho[0 - C_F] + (1-\rho)[u(\overline{Q}) - C_F] \\ = (1-\rho)u(\overline{Q}) - C_F$$

On the other hand, suppose that the parties settle out of court. Let T be the transfer that the factory makes to the residents. When the parties settle, they agree that the factory should produce the efficient level of production. The payoff to the residents from settling out of court is:

$$T + u\left(\frac{\overline{Q}}{2}\right) - N_R$$

whereas the payoff to the factory from settling out of court is:

$$-T + u\left(\frac{\overline{Q}}{2}\right) - N_F$$

The residents will be willing to settle out of court as long as they gain from doing so, which requires:

$$T + u\left(\frac{\overline{Q}}{2}\right) - N_R > \rho u(\overline{Q}) - C_R$$

or:

$$T > \rho u(\overline{Q}) - (C_R - N_R) - u\left(\frac{\overline{Q}}{2}\right)$$

On the other hand, the factory will be willing to settle out of court as long as they gain from doing so, which requires:

$$-T + u\left(\frac{\overline{Q}}{2}\right) - N_F > (1-\rho)u(\overline{Q}) - C_F$$

or:

$$T < -(1-\rho)u(\overline{Q}) + (C_F - N_F) + u\left(\frac{\overline{Q}}{2}\right)$$

Thus, the gains from settlement will be positive as long as both inequalities are satisfied:

$$u\left(\frac{\overline{Q}}{2}\right) - (1-\rho)u(\overline{Q}) + (C_F - N_F) > \rho u(\overline{Q}) - (C_R - N_R) - u\left(\frac{\overline{Q}}{2}\right)$$

or:

$$2u\left(\frac{\overline{Q}}{2}\right) - N_F - N_R > u(\overline{Q}) - C_F - C_R \qquad (11.14)$$

The interpretation of this condition is straightforward. The left-hand side is the size of the joint surplus that is available to the parties if they negotiate out of court and agree to implement the efficient level of production. The right-hand side is the size of the joint surplus that is available to the parties if they go to court. The gains from settlement will be positive as long as the former exceeds the latter. Notice that in our formulation, since $\frac{\overline{Q}}{2}$ is the efficient outcome, $2u\left(\frac{\overline{Q}}{2}\right)$ must exceed $u(\overline{Q})$. Further, for each it is reasonable to assume that the costs of settling are less than the costs of going to court. Under these assumptions, equation (11.14) will always hold: *in this framework, if any agreements between the parties can be implemented, then the parties will never go to court, and trials will never be observed.*

11.4.2 Why go to court?

Whilst most legal disputes do settle out of court, we know that there are obviously exceptions to this: in the real world, legal trials do in fact occur. So why might parties go to court? Various explanations have been advanced in the literature.

11.4.2.1 Asymmetric information

One obvious answer is asymmetric information: if one party has very reliable information regarding the evidence that will be presented at trial that will help his case and the other does not, then they may both be willing to go to court. To see how asymmetric information can affect the likelihood of trial, suppose that there are two possible types of plaintiffs: those with a high probability of victory at trial ($\rho = \rho_h$) and those with a low probability of victory at trial ($\rho = \rho_l$), with $\rho_h > \rho_l$. A plaintiff knows his own probability of victory, so each type of plaintiff can compute his expected gain from going to trial. For convenience, we will assume that there are no costs involved in settling.

For each type of plaintiff, we can compute the expected gain from going to trial. For the high types, the expected value of going to trial is:

$$\rho_h u(\overline{Q}) - C_R$$

For the low types, the expected value of going to trial is:

$$\rho_l u(\overline{Q}) - C_R$$

Assume that defendants cannot observe the plaintiff's true type. The defendant only knows that in general there is a fraction θ of high types in the population, and a fraction $(1 - \theta)$ of low types in the population. If the defendant has incomplete information, he perceives the average plaintiff probability of victory to be $\bar{\rho} = \theta\rho_h + (1-\theta)\rho_l$. Suppose the defendant has incomplete information, and makes a settlement offer of $S > 0$ to the plaintiff, where this amount of money is comprised of a monetary transfer and the value of the efficient level of product to the plaintiff.

The maximum offer that the defendant would be willing to make to ensure that all types of plaintiffs accept the offer must satisfy:

$$S \geq \rho_h u(\overline{Q}) - C_R$$

So setting $S = S_h = \rho_h u(\overline{Q}) - C_R$ is the lowest offer the defendant could make to ensure settlement occurs. The defendant's expected net benefits under such a *pooling strategy* are $u(\overline{Q}) - [\rho_h u(\overline{Q}) - C_R] = (1 - \rho_h)u(\overline{Q}) + C_R$.

On the other hand, suppose the defendant follows a *separating strategy* and makes a settlement offer so that *only* low types would be willing to accept. Low types would be willing to accept as long as:

$$S \geq \rho_l u(\overline{Q}) - C_R$$

So setting

$$S = S_l = \rho_l u(\overline{Q}) - C_R \tag{11.15}$$

is the lowest offer the defendant could make to ensure settlement occurs only with the low-type plaintiffs. The defendant's expected costs of making such an offer are:

$$\begin{aligned} &\theta[(1-\rho_h)u(\overline{Q}) - C_F] + (1-\theta)\{u(\overline{Q}) - [\rho_l u(\overline{Q}) - C_R]\} \\ &= \theta[(1-\rho_h)u(\overline{Q}) - C_F] + (1-\theta)[(1-\rho_l)u(\overline{Q}) + C_R] \end{aligned} \tag{11.16}$$

Finally, suppose that the defendant makes a settlement offer so that *no* types of plaintiffs would be willing to accept. This is the *always go to trial* strategy. Setting $S = 0$ ensures that the case always goes to trial, and the defendant's expected net benefits of making such an offer are:

$$\theta[(1-\rho_h)u(\overline{Q}) - C_F] + (1-\theta)[(1-\rho_l)u(\overline{Q}) - C_F] \tag{11.17}$$

Which strategy should the defendant follow? The defendant should follow the strategy which involves the highest expected net benefits. Let us rank these strategies in order of their costs.

First, note that the always go to trial strategy is never the best option, since the expression in (11.16) always exceeds that in (11.17). The separating strategy will therefore have the highest net benefit of all three strategies if:

$$\theta[(1-\rho_h)u(\overline{Q})-C_F]+(1-\theta)[(1-\rho_l)u(\overline{Q})+C_R]>(1-\rho_h)u(\overline{Q})+C_R$$

or if:

$$\frac{\theta}{1-\theta}<\frac{(\rho_h-\rho_l)u(\overline{Q})}{C_F+C_R} \qquad (11.18)$$

If θ is sufficiently small, then there is a relatively low probability that the defendant faces a highquality plaintiff. This makes it more likely that the lefthand side of (11.18) is less than the righthand side, and makes the separating strategy more attractive. This means that when θ is sufficiently small, there will be a chance that cases will go to trial, since the offer in (11.15) will only be accepted by low types, and high types will want to go to trial.

On the other hand, if θ is sufficiently large, then there is a relatively high probability that the defendant faces a high-quality plaintiff. This makes it less likely that the left-hand side of (11.18) is less than the right-hand side, and makes the pooling strategy more attractive. In this case, the defendant will not allow any cases to go to trial.

11.4.2.2 Differing perceptions

Another very simple approach to addressing the question of why cases go to trial is to introduce the concept of *differing perceptions*. The basic idea in this approach is that parties may have different beliefs regarding the plaintiff's probability of success at trial, ρ. If these differences in perception are sufficiently large, then they can eliminate any expected gains from settling out of court.

To see how this can happen, suppose that the parties are alike except for their perceptions of the probability of the plaintiff's victory. Let us return to our example of the residents and the factory. Suppose that the expected benefit to the residents from going to trial is:

$$\rho_R u(\overline{Q})-C$$

and the expected benefits for the factory are:

$$(1-\rho_F)u(\overline{Q})-C$$

Where we have assumed that both parties face identical costs of going to trial ordinarily, in the absence of differing perceptions, we would have $\rho_R = \rho_F$. Suppose that the costs of negotiating a settlement out of court are zero. Then the payoff to the residents from settling out of court is:

$$T+u\left(\frac{\overline{Q}}{2}\right)$$

whereas the payoff to the factory from settling out of court is:

$$-T+u\left(\frac{\overline{Q}}{2}\right)$$

where again T is a transfer between the parties. The residents will be willing to settle out of court as long as they gain from doing so, which requires:

$$T+u\left(\frac{\overline{Q}}{2}\right)>\rho_R u(\overline{Q})-C$$

or:

$$T>\rho_R u(\overline{Q})-C-u\left(\frac{\overline{Q}}{2}\right)$$

On the other hand, the factory will be willing to settle out of court as long as they gain from doing so, which requires:

$$-T+u\left(\frac{\overline{Q}}{2}\right)>(1-\rho_F)u(\overline{Q})-C$$

or:

$$T<-(1-\rho_F)u(\overline{Q})+C+u\left(\frac{\overline{Q}}{2}\right)$$

Thus, the gains from settlement will be positive as long as both inequalities are satisfied, which requires:

$$u\left(\frac{\overline{Q}}{2}\right)-(1-\rho_F)u(\overline{Q})+C>\rho_R u(\overline{Q})-C-u\left(\frac{\overline{Q}}{2}\right)$$

or:

$$2\left[u\left(\frac{\overline{Q}}{2}\right)+C\right]>(\rho_R-\rho_F+1)u(\overline{Q}) \tag{11.19}$$

When there are identical perceptions, we have $\rho_R = \rho_F$ and the inequality in (11.19) must always be satisfied. However, when perceptions differ, it is no longer necessarily the case that (11.19) will hold. For example, suppose that $\rho_R = 0.9$, $\rho_F = 0.1$, the costs of going to trial for each party are $C = 0.1$, and that $u(Q) = \sqrt{Q}$. Let $\bar{Q} = 2$. Then the efficient production level is $Q^* = \frac{\bar{Q}}{2} = 1$. The left-hand side of (11.19) is equal to 2.2, whilst the right-hand side is equal to $\sqrt{2} < 2.2$ if there are common perceptions. However, if $\rho_R = 0.9$, and $\rho_F = 0.1$ the right-hand side is equal to $1.8 \times \sqrt{2} = 2.55 > 2.2$. Thus, differing perceptions can eliminate the possibility of efficiency-enhancing gains from trade, making it attractive for the parties to instead engage in costly conflict.

11.4.2.3 *Another reason why parties might prefer to go to court*

There are other reasons for why parties might go to trial, which involve neither differing perceptions nor asymmetric information. One possibility is to realise that the costs of trial and settling are not fixed as we have assumed above, but that they emerge endogenously as a result of the parties engaging in rational threats against each other. This means that it could be possible for at least one party, the costs of gearing up for trial and then negotiating – using the rational threat approach described earlier – may exceed the costs of the alternative strategy of 'burning the bridges' from the outset, cutting off the lines of communication, and simply committing to go to court no matter what.

Robson and Skaperdas (2008) develop a model which explores the circumstances under which this can occur. The basic idea is that at the outset of a legal dispute process, there are two strategic paths that each of the parties can choose to go down:

1. Gearing up for trial by employing costly mechanisms to influence disagreement points, but in the end settling out of court (the rational threat game); or
2. Commit to going to court no matter what.

The payoff structures in each of these strategic situations are very different. Hence, as a general rule, the payoffs and costs incurred by each party will be very different in each situation. Since out of court settlement involves implementing the efficient level of production, the size of the 'pie' is bigger – so, all else being equal, this is usually the preferred option for the reasons discussed above. However, because the expected joint gains from eventually settling are so high, this means that the expected gains from influencing one's disagreement point in the rational threat game are much higher as well – which means that one or both parties may be more willing to incur very high legal costs in order to secure the gains from exchange.

Once these costs are taken into account, the net gains from going down the rational threat route could easily be less than the net gains from going down the conflict route from the outset. Hence it may not only be individually rational for individuals at the outset to want to go to trial – *it may even be efficient*, because the costs of activities that influence disagreement points in the rational threat game are not incurred. In other words, even though the parties miss out on getting a share of a larger pie by committing to go to court, much of this pie may have been dissipated anyway in costly preparations for gearing up for going to court and then settling.

11.5 A general model of legal conflict: Legal expenditure as a rent-seeking game

The model of strategic evidence gathering in Chapter 2 can be generalised to analyse litigation expenditure and explore various issues such as the endogenous determination of costs and the effect of cost-shifting rules. We illustrate some of these issues by considering the evidence-gathering framework in Chapter 2, involving a plaintiff and a defendant.

Suppose that the total cost of producing evidence is $C_P\,(e_P)$ the plaintiff and $C_D\,(e_D)$ for the defendant. Suppose that the likelihood ratio is:

$$\frac{\rho(E\,|\,G)}{\rho(E\,|\,I)}=\frac{\rho(e_P,e_D\,|\,G)}{\rho(e_P,e_D\,|\,I)}\frac{f(e_P)}{g(e_D)}$$

Where $f(.)$ and g(.) are increasing, concave functions. Suppose that the judgement has a value of $\$J$ to the plaintiff, and the defendant stands to lose $\$J$ if the plaintiff is successful. If they are both risk neutral, then the expected net benefits to the plaintiff of going to trial are:

$$B_P=\frac{f(e_P)}{f(e_P)+g(e_D)}J-C_P(e_P)$$

and

$$B_D=-\frac{f(e_P)}{f(e_P)+g(e_D)}J-C_D(e_D)$$

for the defendant. In an interior Nash equilibrium, the necessary first-order conditions are:

$$\frac{f'(e_P)g(e_D)}{[f(e_P)+g(e_D)]^2}J = C_P'(e_P) \tag{11.20}$$

and:

$$\frac{f(e_P)\,g'(e_D)}{[f(e_P)+g(e_D)]^2}J = C_D'(e_D \tag{11.21}$$

One obvious implication of (11.20) and (11.21) is that if the parties have identical cost functions and evidence production functions, they will employ the same amount of effort in the legal battle.

11.5.1 Cost-shifting rules

The simple model of litigation spending can be used to analyse the effect of cost-shifting rules if parties go to trial. A cost-shifting or fee-shifting arrangement simply specifies who pays which costs, depending on the result of the trial. There are two main cost-shifting systems that have been analysed in the literature:

- The American rule – each party pays their own costs, irrespective of the result.
- The English rule – the loser pays all of the winner's costs.

It is important to remember that even when the English rule applies, it is almost *never* the case in practice that the loser pays *all* of the winner's legal costs. Institutions have evolved to limit the kinds of costs that can be claimed. Typically, after a legal trial concludes, the successful party files its bill of costs (which sets out the winner's claim) with the court. An officer of the court then assesses the 'reasonableness' of the costs with reference to legal precedent and a statutory schedule of limits of entitlements of costs. The level of reduction usually means the bill of costs is reduced by between 50 per cent and 70 per cent, depending upon the jurisdiction, and the 'reasonableness' of the bill of costs in the first place. This process is known as the 'taxation' of legal costs. This 'taxation' is not related to the ability of the government to impose commodity or income taxes – the 'taxation' of costs is simply the process of examining – and, where necessary, reducing – the bill of costs of a lawyer. 'Costs' include not only the lawyer's own professional fees, but also the disbursements incurred. Thus, one of the purposes of 'taxation' is to determine the amount of costs a successful party in litigation is entitled to recover from their unsuccessful opponents.

One of the main results in the literature is that aggregate spending is higher under the English rule than it is under the American rule.[2] Intuitively, the American rule reduces the payoff from winning, and increases the payoff from losing, relative to the English rule. The American rule therefore reduces the gap between winning and losing, thereby lowering the overall 'stakes' involved in the case. Thus, less effort is devoted towards trying to win the case (and towards avoiding losing the case) than it otherwise would be. This means that the expected surplus 'in the shadow of the court' is lower under the English system and higher under the American system. Thus, although the American rule may involve lower trial expenditure, it may create incentives for vexatious plaintiffs to file frivolous lawsuits, because the expected surplus from filing a lawsuit is higher. Thus, one prediction is that the English system creates higher costs per trial, but the American system encourages more lawsuits.

The effects of cost-shifting rules on trial expenditures can be easily modelled within our framework. Suppose that the loser of a trial is obligated to pay a fraction $\delta \leq 1$ of the winner's costs. Let P be the per unit price of employing a lawyer. Then the expected payoffs are:

$$B_P = \frac{e_P}{e_P + e_D}[J - (1-\delta)Pe_P] + \frac{e_D}{e_P + e_D}[-Pe_P - \delta Pe_D]$$

$$= \frac{e_P}{e_P + e_D}J - Pe_P + \delta P\left[\frac{e_P^2 - e_D^2}{e_P + e_D}\right]$$

for the plaintiff and

$$B_D = -\frac{e_P}{e_P + e_D}J - Pe_D - \delta P\left[\frac{e_P^2 - e_D^2}{e_P + e_D}\right]$$

for the defendant. The first-order conditions in this game yield:

$$\frac{e_D}{(e_P + e_D)^2}J + \delta P = P$$

for the plaintiff, and

$$\frac{e_P}{(e_P + e_D)^2}J + \delta P = P$$

for the defendant.

The left-hand side of each of these expressions is the marginal benefit of litigation effort. The right-hand side is the marginal cost of litigation effort or hiring a lawyer. Note that when $\delta = 1$ (which is the pure English rule), marginal benefit always exceeds marginal cost, and so there is no well-defined best response for either player. Thus, when $\delta = 1$ – the pure form of the English rule – there is no pure strategy Nash equilibrium.[3]

However, as soon as $\delta < 1$, marginal benefits are diminishing and may reach unity (as long as e_P and e_D are sufficiently high), so best responses are well defined. These two equations imply that $e_P = e_D$. Substituting in to player 1's first-order condition, we get:

$$\frac{1}{4e^{English}} J = (1 - \delta)P$$

so that:

$$e^{English} = \frac{J}{4(1-\delta)P} \tag{11.22}$$

The expected payoffs are:

$$\begin{aligned} B_P &= \frac{1}{2}J - \frac{P}{4(1-\delta)p}J = \frac{1}{2}J - \frac{J}{4(1-\delta)} \\ B_D &= -\frac{1}{2}J - \frac{J}{4(1-\delta)} \end{aligned} \tag{11.23}$$

Note that these payoffs are both decreasing in δ and can be negative, in which case the parties would both be better off if they could agree to set $e_P = e_D = 0$. However, this is not an equilibrium: if the plaintiff agreed to put in no effort, the defendant could choose some small positive effort level of ε and obtain an expected payoff of:

$$\begin{aligned} &-\frac{0}{0+\varepsilon}J - \varepsilon P - \delta P\left[\frac{-\varepsilon^2}{\varepsilon}\right] \\ &= -\varepsilon P + \delta\varepsilon P = (\delta - 1)P\varepsilon < 0 \end{aligned}$$

whereas if he put in zero effort his payoff would be:

$$-\frac{1}{2}J < 0$$

Since ε can be made arbitrarily small, it is never a best response to put in no effort. This means that there is no level of $\delta > 0$ which induces the parties to choose the same level of expenditure as under the American rule.

11.6 The market for lawyers

Somewhat surprisingly, the law and economics literature is mostly silent on many questions relating to the market for legal services. What, if anything, makes the market for legal services similar to – and different from – say, the market for apples? Lawyers provide legal services, which help individuals clarify property and other legal rights. Therefore, over the long run, the legal profession may play an important role in enhancing the efficiency of the allocation of resources. On the other hand, there is also a significant redistributive component to much of the activity in the market for legal services. As a result of such rent-seeking activities, lawyers can also play a significant part in reducing overall economic well-being.

Laband and McClintock (2001), for example, calculate that the vast majority of lawyers (over 600,000 out of a total of 880,000) make absolutely no contribution to productive economic activities in the United States. Epstein (1995) provides preliminary details of the *growth* of 'invisible foot' activities in the United States in the twentieth century, by examining the share of US GDP that is devoted to expenditure on lawyers. Between 1960 and 1987, this share doubled.

Economists are only just beginning to systematically study and understand the process of how and why resources are directed towards establishing, preventing, sustaining, modifying and abolishing wealth redistribution programmes and institutions.[4] These activities have been referred to by various authors as 'rent-seeking' activities (Krueger, 1974); 'directly unproductive profit-seeking' (DUP) activities (Bhagwhati, 1982); 'invisible foot' and 'black hole' activities (Magee et al., 1989); and most recently as 'the dark side of the force' (Hirshleifer, 2001). As a result of these considerations, Magee (1992) has argued that there is an optimal number of lawyers for an economy, hypothesising that long-run economic growth an upside down U-shaped function.

This section develops a framework for analysing the market for legal services, where the demand for such services is driven solely by redistributive considerations, rather than efficiency-enhancing lawsuits. The welfare implications of perfect competition in this market under this extreme assumption are presented and analysed, and the incentive and welfare effects of taxes, price regulation, and government-imposed barriers to entry are considered. The main conclusion is that outcomes in such a market are very different from those we would expect in an ordinary market.

We use the approach outlined earlier in this chapter to examine these issues. Consider a general equilibrium version of the model analysed in section 11.5.1. Assume that there are a large number of plaintiffs and defendants, each of whom has the demand for legal representation given in (11.22). Normalise the size of the population of plaintiffs and defendants to one. Then the aggregate demand for litigation services (assuming an impure version of the English rule is in place) is:

$$Q_D = 2 \times e^{English} = \frac{2J}{4(1-\delta)P} = \frac{J}{2(1-\delta)P} \tag{11.24}$$

Now consider a simple long-run aggregate supply curve for lawyers. Suppose that this long-run supply curve is given by:

$$Q_S = P \tag{11.25}$$

The supply curve reflects the marginal opportunity cost of legal services in their next best alternative. The total opportunity cost is therefore $\frac{1}{2}(Q_S)^2$. In a perfectly competitive market for legal services, the long-run equilibrium price equates supply and demand, so the competitive equilibrium price in this market is:

$$P^* = \sqrt{\frac{J}{2(1-\delta)}} = Q^*$$

The equilibrium is illustrated in Figure 11.6.1 below.

11.6.1 Welfare analysis

One aspect of our market for lawyers that is very different from other markets is the welfare properties of the competitive equilibrium. The consumption of legal services in our model is a little unusual compared to the standard microeconomic model, in the following sense: the consumption of legal services simply redistributes existing resources between plaintiffs and defendants, rather than creating new resources.

Welfare analytics in such a world are very different from the usual microeconomic analysis. On the demand side, each individual's demand curve for lawyers is derived in the usual way, by equating marginal benefit with price – but the marginal benefit for each type of individual depends on the choice of legal services chosen by their opponent. Moreover, in an interior equilibrium, a lower price of lawyers makes no difference to the welfare of both individuals, even though they consume more legal services – this is clear from the payoffs in (11.23). Thus, in contrast to the usual conclusion of microeconomic analysis, the area to the left of the individual or aggregate demand curves is *not* a measure of consumer well-being. Why does this happen? A fall in P induces both types of individuals to consume more legal services in equilibrium. But expenditure on legal services remains the same. The net demand-side effect of a price fall is for both individuals to consume more legal services and to spend the same on those services. More economic activity is devoted to legal services on the supply side, but there is no offsetting benefit anywhere on the demand side. On the other hand, if the price of legal services rises, then both types consume fewer legal services. Spending remains the same, but resources devoted to redistributive activities fall.

In an interior equilibrium, the benefit of each type is given by B_P and B_D as above, and aggregate consumer benefits are simply

$$B_P + B_D = -\frac{J}{2(1-\delta)} = -Q^* P^*$$

The producer surplus is:

$$PS = P^*Q^* - C(Q^*)$$

and so aggregate welfare is simply

$$\begin{aligned} W &= -P^*Q^* + P^*Q^* - C(Q^*) \\ &= -\frac{1}{2}(Q^*)^2 \end{aligned}$$

The change in welfare (dW) as Q^* changes is simply:

$$dW = -C'(Q^*)dQ^* = -Q^* dQ^* \tag{11.26}$$

Therefore, changes in the area under the long-run market *supply* curve can be used to measure aggregate welfare changes in this market. Intuitively, the purchase of legal services simply redistributes resources between plaintiffs and defendants. This redistribution itself has no overall direct welfare consequences for users since both value output equally at the margin. On the other hand, purchases of legal services by plaintiffs and defendants that are used to undertake this redistribution reduce each of their equilibrium benefits. But this loss is offset by an equal revenue gain accruing to the suppliers of legal services. The opportunity cost of producing legal services is therefore a pure social loss, since it is a cost that is not offset by a gain anywhere else in the economy.

These conclusions are illustrated in Figure 11.6.1 below. Consumers of legal services pay $(A + B)$ to suppliers, gaining nothing as a whole, since legal services in this model simply shuffle resources among consumers. This amount of spending is equal to the producer's revenue, and the two payments exactly offset each other. The opportunity cost of supplying the quantity Q^* of legal services, however, is not offset by a gain anywhere else in the economy – it is a pure social loss. We therefore have a result that is the exact opposite of one of the invisible hand result of standard welfare economics that was discussed in Chapter 1: *In the*

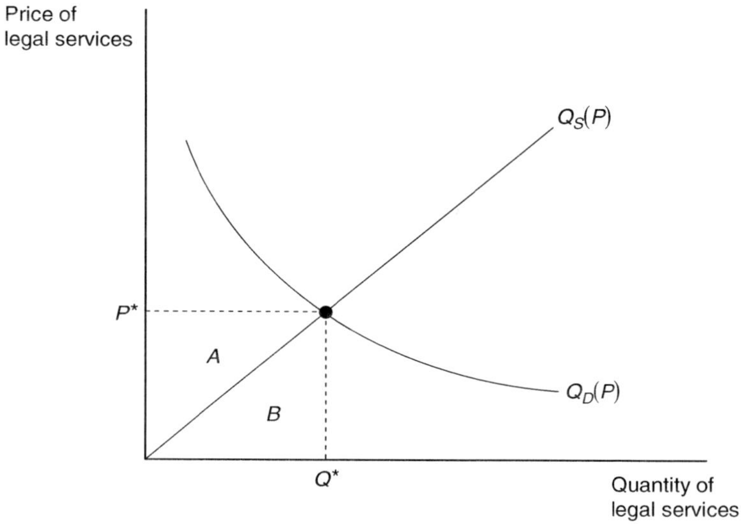

Figure 11.6.1 Competitive equilibrium in the market for legal services

market for purely redistributive legal services, every competitive equilibrium allocation can be potentially Pareto improved upon by another allocation.

11.6.2 Comparative statics

We can also use this simple model to analyse the effects of shocks to each side of the market. Suppose that the demand for legal services shifted out (say, because of a rise in δ, the degree of 'Englishness' of the cost allocation rule). Then more legal services will be consumed and produced in equilibrium, the market price for lawyers will rise, and aggregate welfare is lower by the change in the area underneath the supply curve, which is the area $E + F$ in Figure 11.6.2.

Suppose instead that lawyers become more efficient (so that each unit of legal services can now be produced at a lower opportunity cost than before). The long-run supply curve shifts to the right. Then in equilibrium more legal services are consumed (which all else being equal would be a welfare loss) but each has a lower opportunity cost to produce (which all else being equal would be a welfare gain). With the demand curve in (11.24), and the supply curve in (11.25), these two effects exactly offset each other. To see why, consider Figure 11.6.3. Note that the demand curve in (11.24) as unit elasticity, so revenue accruing to producers does not change as we move up or down along a given demand curve. With

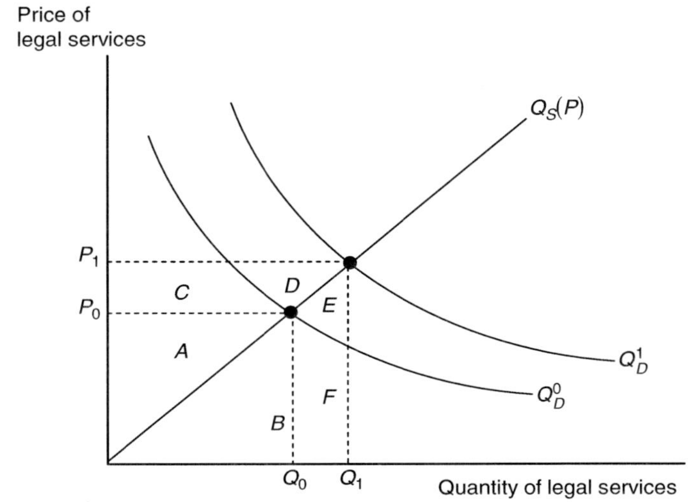

Figure 11.6.2 An increase in demand for legal services

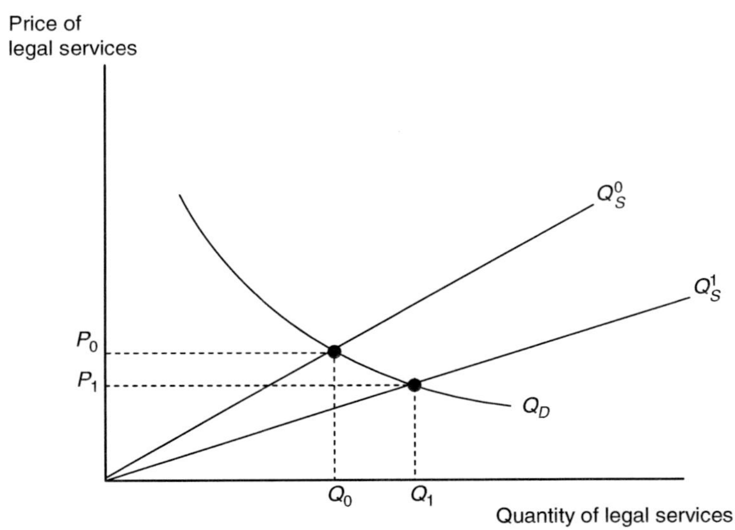

Figure 11.6.3 A reduction in the marginal cost of producing legal services

the supply curve in (11.25), total costs are always equal to the triangle below the supply curve, which is always exactly one half of total revenue. Hence, if total revenue does not change as we move along a demand curve, total cost does not either. This means that welfare must be constant along a given demand curve, and so the positive welfare effects of an efficiency improvement in the delivery of litigation services are exactly matched by negative welfare effects of greater demand for those services.

11.6.3 Welfare effects of policy interventions in the market for legal services

This section considers some possible policy interventions in the market for legal services. Given the previous results, it should not be surprising that interventions in this market can improve - rather than reduce – economic well-being.

11.6.3.1 A tax on purchases of legal services

Suppose that an *ad valorem* tax on the purchases of legal services is implemented, which increases the consumer price to $P_0(1+t)$. This drives a wedge between consumer and producer prices, and fewer legal services are consumed and produced. Total consumer spending on legal services (inclusive of tax) does not change, since the market demand curve in equation has an elasticity of one. The welfare loss is now lower than it was before the tax, because the total opportunity cost of producing the new quantity of legal services is lower. Thus, a tax on legal services can be welfare improving.

11.6.3.2 A price ceiling

Suppose that a price ceiling is introduced in this market. Then consumers of legal services would demand more at this price, but producers would reduce their supply, and the market would be supply constrained. Producer surplus would fall, and expenditure on legal services would also fall. Ordinarily, the ability to consume a good at such a low price would represent a welfare gain to consumers (assuming the good was rationed to high valuation consumers). But this is not the case here: the expenditure on legal services confers no benefit in total and is simply transferred as revenue to producers. There is an overall welfare gain, however, since fewer legal services are supplied and the total cost of resources devoted to providing legal services falls.

11.6.3.3 A price floor

Suppose that a price floor is introduced in this market. Then consumers of legal services would demand less at this higher price, but producers would want to supply more. The market would be demand constrained. Since the demand curve has unit elasticity, expenditure on legal services would not change. Producer surplus would rise, however, since producer revenue would remain the same but total costs would fall. Once again, there would be an overall welfare gain since fewer legal services are supplied and the total cost of the economic resources that are devoted to providing legal services falls.

11.6.3.4 An aggregate quantity constraint

Suppose that a quota is placed on the aggregate supply of legal services – effectively a barrier to entry in this market. The supply curve is effectively perfect inelastic at this new aggregate production level. This drives the equilibrium price up, but again leaves total expenditure on legal services unchanged. Producers are better off, since they receive the same revenue but their total costs are lower. But since total quantity is lower, aggregate welfare must be higher with an aggregate quantity constraint. Thus, an aggregate quantity constraint can be welfare improving.

11.6.4 Summary

This section has constructed a model of the market for lawyers and legal services, in which it was assumed that all activities undertaken by lawyers were purely redistributive. This assumption drives the welfare properties of the model. More generally, it would be possible to examine a similar model in which legal services still impose costs on the economy but also assist parties in negotiating efficient agreements. If this additional assumption is added, then it is no longer true that welfare is uniformly decreasing in the number of lawyers employed in equilibrium. For a sufficiently low level of legal services, the welfare gains that came about from assisting the parties in implementing efficient agreements would outweigh the welfare costs. Eventually, however, as the marginal and total costs of legal services rise, the costs would begin to exceed the benefits. This is exactly the hypothesis put forward by Magee (1992) and which he argues holds empirically.

11.7 Simplicity, complexity and variability of legal rules

In addition to pure rent-seeking considerations, another important source of legal costs comes from their complexity and variability. According to this view, the legal system does not create costs because of redistribution. Instead, it is merely the time and effort spent complying with the sheer volume of laws that creates costs, as well as the effort that must be expended when rules are changed.

Quandt (1983) develops a simple model of the welfare effects of complexity and variability of regulations, which we can modify and extend to legal rules. The basic approach is as follows. Suppose there are two types of firms, 1 and 2. Type 1 firms produce a good, the quantity of which (labelled Q) is consumed. The industry is perfectly competitive. The consumer benefits are $u(Q)$. The price of a unit of output is P. The good is produced with unskilled labour, which receives a wage rate of W. We assume for convenience that the good is produced in fixed proportions, so that Q units of labour produces Q units of output.

Type 2 firms supply legal compliance services, which is also a perfectly competitive market. Now add a crucial further assumption: for Type 1 firms, it takes one unit of labour and $z = z(C, V)$ units of regulatory and legal compliance services to produce one unit of output, where C is a cardinal measure of the complexity of the law, and V is a measure of the variability of legal rules. Let p be the market price of compliance services. Regulatory and legal compliance services are produced with skilled labour, with one unit of skilled labour producing one unit of compliance services. Each unit of skilled labour receives a wage of w.

All else being equal, greater complexity and variability of laws and regulations means that to hire one additional unit of labour and produce an additional unit of output, a Type 1 firm must use more regulatory and legal compliance services. Therefore, we assume that C and V affect z positively, so that:

$$z_C = \frac{\partial z}{\partial C} > 0 \quad \text{and} \quad z_V = \frac{\partial z}{\partial V} > 0.$$

The competitive equilibrium in this model is straightforward to compute. Since both industries are perfectly competitive, price equals marginal cost in each. Marginal cost in the market for compliance services is w, so in the competitive equilibrium we must have:

$$p = w \tag{11.27}$$

Marginal cost in the output market is $W + pz = W + wz(C, V)$, so we must have:

$$P = W + wz(C, V) \tag{11.28}$$

Consumers set marginal benefit equal to price, so the competitive equilibrium quantity obeys:

$$u'(Q) = W + wz(C, V) \tag{11.29}$$

Let $Q^* = Q[W, w, z(C, V)]$ be the quantity that solves (11.29). We have:

$$\frac{\partial Q}{\partial W} < 0, \quad \frac{\partial Q}{\partial w} < 0, \quad \frac{\partial Q}{\partial C} < 0, \quad \frac{\partial Q}{\partial V} < 0$$

From this, we can obtain the equilibrium quantity of legal and regulatory compliance services (and therefore of skilled labour). Recall that each unit of output requires z units of compliance services. Therefore, the quantity of regulatory and compliance services that is purchased in equilibrium is:

$$Q^*z = Q[W, w, z(C,V)]z(C,V)$$

The welfare consequences of increasing C and V are fairly straightforward in this model. An marginal increase in legal complexity, for example, increases z, which increases the marginal cost of the Type 1 good, therefore increasing price and reducing welfare by:

$$dW = -QdP = -Qwz_C dC$$

A similar analysis applies to an increase in the variability of legal rules and regulations.

Predictions regarding the amount of activity and employment in the market for legal and regulatory compliance services are less straightforward, however. If, for example, C rises, then there are two opposing effects on overall activity in the market for legal services, Qz. On the one hand, z rises, which increases activity and employment in that industry. On the other hand, the increase in z reduces Q, as the above analysis showed. The total effect is given by:

$$\begin{aligned} d(Qz) &= \left[\frac{dQ}{dP} pz_C z + Qz_C\right] dC = Qz_C \left[\frac{dQ}{dP}\frac{pz}{Q} + 1\right] dC \\ &= Qz_C \left[\varepsilon + 1 - \frac{dQ}{dP}\frac{W}{Q}\right] dC \end{aligned} \quad (11.30)$$

If demand for good Q is inelastic (so that $\varepsilon > -1$), then $d(Qz) > 0$. An increase in the complexity or variability of legal rules and regulations reduces output of Q, thus increasing the consumer price P and reducing welfare. But activity in the market for compliance services *expands*. Equation (11.30) shows that since $\frac{dQ}{dP}\frac{W}{Q} < 0$, expansion of activity and employment in the market for compliance services can even occur if demand for good Q is elastic – as long as it is not *too* elastic. If activity in both markets is included as part of GDP, and if the demand function in the market for Q is linear (so that elasticity rises as activity falls as we move up the demand curve for Q), we would expect to observe an inverted 'U' relationship between economic activity and legal complexity and variability. This is again consistent with the argument and evidence presented by Magee (1992).

11.8 The common law efficiency hypothesis and the evolution of the common law

The preceding two sections have painted a somewhat pessimistic view of lawyers, legal rules and the legal system. There is an alternative approach, however, which lends itself to a more optimistic view. The *efficiency of the common law hypothesis* begins with the working hypothesis that legal rules that are inefficient tend to be litigated more often compared to rules that are efficient. It then follows that if inefficient legal rules are contested with greater frequency, there is a greater chance that those rules will be overturned. As a result, common law rules will tend to evolve in the direction of efficiency, and lawyers are a source of efficiency rather than inefficiency. This section investigates this hypothesis using some basic principles of evolutionary game theory.

11.8.1 Evolutionarily stable strategies

In an evolutionary game, each player's payoff is a measure of its 'fitness', rather than their subjective well-being. Each player is programmed to follow a certain model of behaviour, which is inherited from its parents or is assigned to the player as a result of 'mutation'. If members of a population follow a strategy s whose fitness exceeds that of an alternative strategy s', then those members who follow s reproduce faster than those who follow s'. A profile of strategies is stable if each member's strategy is a best response to its environment.

The literature on evolutionary game theory has typically focused on situations in which players come from a single population and have symmetric payoffs. Consider, a situation in which pairs of members of a population of organisms are randomly matched with each other. The interaction between the two organisms is modelled as a two-player symmetric game. If a player has a strategy s and his opponent plays s', then the fitness of strategy s is given by $u(s, s')$.

Now consider the notion of evolutionary stability. Suppose that s^* is a candidate for stability. Then this strategy must be able to drive mutations out of the population. So, suppose that a fraction ε of the population mutates and plays the strategy s' instead. The expected fitness to a mutant is:

$$\varepsilon u(s', s') + (1-\varepsilon)u(s', s^*) \tag{11.31}$$

And the expected fitness of a non-mutant is:

$$\varepsilon u(s^*, s') + (1-\varepsilon)u(s^*, s^*) \tag{11.32}$$

For the mutation to be driven out of the population, we require

$$\varepsilon u(s^*, s') + (1-\varepsilon)u(s^*, s^*) > \varepsilon u(s', s') + (1-\varepsilon)u(s', s^*) \tag{11.33}$$

A strategy is said to be evolutionarily stable if there exists a $\bar{\varepsilon} > 0$ such that (11.33) holds for all $\varepsilon < \bar{\varepsilon}$. An alternative but logically equivalent definition is that in a two-player symmetric game, a strategy s^* is said to be evolutionarily stable if and only if:

1. (s^*, s^*) is a Nash equilibrium **and**
2. $u(s^*, s) > u(s, s)$ for every strategy s which is a best response to s^*.

This definition has limited applicability in the context of the evolution of legal rules, however, because the players rarely come from the same population and their payoffs are rarely symmetric. Instead, players usually have different but well-defined roles (such as a plaintiff and a defendant), and each player's payoff bears no resemblance to the payoff of the other – which rules out the possibility of symmetry. In these situations, a different definition of evolutionary stability is required.

Suppose that there are n different populations, with members with each population all identical (for example, in the plaintiff–defendant case, $n = 2$). Let $(s_1, \ldots, s_n)$ be a strategy profile, where s_i is the strategy chosen by a member of population i. The fitness of strategy s_i to a player from population i is $u_i(s_1, \ldots, s_i, \ldots, s_n)$. If there is a mutation in population i so that a small fraction of the population has the strategy $s_i' \neq s_i$, then for s_i to be evolutionarily stable, it must be the case that $u_i(s_1, \ldots, s_i, \ldots, s_n) > u_i(s_1, \ldots, s_i', \ldots, s_n)$. In an evolutionarily stable situation, this must hold for all populations, so that for a profile $(s_1^*, \ldots, s_n^*)$ to be an evolutionarily stable equilibrium, we must have:

$$u_i(s_1^*, \ldots, s_i^*, \ldots, s_n^*) > u_i(s_1^*, \ldots, s_i', \ldots, s_n^*) \tag{11.34}$$

for all $s_i' \neq s_i^*$, and for all populations $i = 1, \ldots, n$. But notice that the condition in (11.34) is just the definition of a Nash equilibrium in the strict sense. Hence finding at evolutionarily stable equilibrium in this situation is straightforward: it is equivalent to finding a strict Nash equilibrium.

In a legal context, evolutionary stability has been studied by Terrebonne (1981). In Terrebonne's model, there are two separate populations: injurers (defendants) and victims (plaintiffs). Pairs of individuals from each population are matched randomly. Injurers have two possible strategies: either to take care (*C*) or not (*N*). Taking care has a cost of $c > 0$. If injurers take care, there is no accident. If they do not take care, then there is an accident which has a cost of $H > 0$.

To maintain the evolutionary spirit of the model, it is assumed that victims acquire their strategies *before* an accident occurs. Hence victims have four possible strategies: they can either always sue (*SS*); never sue (*DD*); sue only when there is an accident (*DS*), or sue only when there is no accident (*SD*). Note that if an accident occurs, victims do not get to decide whether they will sue or not – their behaviour is dictated by the strategy that they have inherited before they know whether an accident has occurred.

The cost to the victim of filing a lawsuit is $L > 0$. The legal rule is characterised by the probability that the victim will be compensated if an accident occurs. Let e_2 be the probability that an injurer who has not taken care is *not* forced to compensate the victim. In other words, this is the probability of a Type II error. The expected payoffs or 'fitness' of each strategy are shown in Table 11.8.1. The first entry in each cell is the expected payoff of the victim, and the second entry is the expected payoff of the injurer.

Let us find the evolutionarily stable strategies of this game. First, note that strategies in which victims sue when an accident has not occurred (the first two rows) will never be evolutionarily stable, since the payoffs to the victim from following the alternative strategies of (*DS*) and (*DD*) are strictly better when the injurer takes care, and are the same when the injurer does not take care. Hence they can never form part of an evolutionarily stable strategy for victims, and we can focus on the last to rows of the game. The transformed game is shown in Table 11.8.2.

Table 11.8.1 Payoffs in the evolutionary litigation/care game

		Injurer	
		C	N
Victim	SS	$-L, -c$	$-H+(1-e_2)H-L,-(1-e_2)H$
	SD	$-L, -c$	$-H, 0$
	DS	$0, -c$	$-H+(1-e_2)H-L,(1-e_2)H$
	DD	$0, -c$	$-H, 0$

Table 11.8.2 The transformed evolutionary game

		Injurer	
		C	N
Victim	DS	$0,-c$	$-H-(1-e_2)H-L,(1-e_2)H$
	DD	$0,-c$	$-H, 0$

To investigate the common law efficiency hypothesis, we need to compare the evolutionarily stable strategies when the common law is efficient, with the evolutionarily stable strategies when the common law is inefficient. If victims only tend to sue when the common law is inefficient, and do not tend to sue when the law is efficient, then this would constitute support for the common law efficiency hypothesis.

Let us consider two broad classes of situations:

- **Case 1:** $c > H$

First, suppose that it is inefficient for the injurer to take care. Then an efficient legal rule will not allow the victim to recover any damages, and so a high value of e_2 is efficient. For any e_2, we also have $c > (1 - e_2)H$, and so the injurer has a dominant strategy of never taking care. On the other hand, if the injurer does not take care, the victim will sue when $(1 - e_2)H > L$, which is only true when e_2 is sufficiently low. But when $c > H$, a low e_2 is inefficient. Hence, victims only tend to sue when the legal rule is inefficient. Hence the efficiency of the common law hypothesis will tend to hold.

- **Case 2:** $c < H$

Now suppose it is efficient for the injurer to take care. In this case, a low value of e_2 is desirable from an efficiency point of view.

If e_2 is sufficiently low, then $c < (1 - e_2)H$, and the injurer's evolutionarily stable strategy is to take care. On the other hand, if the injurer takes care, the victim's evolutionarily stable strategy as shown in the left hand column of Table 11.8.2 is to not sue. Hence, legal rules which are efficient will not tend to be litigated.

The only remaining possibility is when e_2 is sufficiently large, so that the legal rule is inefficient. Then $c > (1 - e_2)H$, and the injurer will have a dominant strategy of not taking care.

In this situation, the victim will sue only if $(1 - e_2)H > L$. In other words, if the legal rule is inefficient and legal costs for the plaintiff are not too large, the evolutionarily stable strategies will lead to an outcome in which plaintiffs litigate. Hence the efficiency of the common law hypothesis will again tend to hold.

On the other hand, if $c > (1 - e_2)H$ but $(1 - e_2)H < L$, the evolutionarily stable strategies will lead to an outcome in which plaintiffs do *not* litigate. In this situation, the efficiency of the common law hypothesis will **not** tend to hold. That is, inefficient legal rules will *not* be litigated, contradicting the efficiency hypothesis.

To summarise, this simple evolutionary model of the common law yields two conclusions:

1. Efficient legal rules will not be contested or litigated.

2. Inefficient legal rules will tend to be contested as long legal costs are not too high.

Taken together, the results support the conclusion that the efficiency hypothesis should hold in a world of sufficiently low legal costs.

11.9 Notes

The link between the Nash bargaining solution and the non-cooperative bargaining approach was first analysed by Binmore et al (1986). Muthoo (1999) is a thorough and highly informative survey of cooperative and non-cooperative bargaining theory. The objection/counterobjection approach to the Nash bargaining solution is due to Rubinstein, Safra and Thomson (1992). The economic analysis of legal conflict began with Gould (1973). Winston et al. (2011) survey the economic research on the market for lawyers and legal services, and argue that the market should be deregulated the approach in this chapter is original, but the general flavour of the basic conclusions have been known by economists for some time. Tullock (1967) is a classic paper on the economics of theft and rent seeking, and the results in this chapter mirror may of those discussed in that paper. Landsburg (1999, pages 272–3) and Friedman (1990, Chapter 20) present simple models of the supply of robbery and the market for theft, the welfare costs of which are similar to those computed in our model of the market for lawyers. The model in section 11.7 is based in part on the approach of Quandt (1983). Schuck (1992) and Epstein (1995) contain excellent discussions of legal simplicity and complexity. Rosen (1992) and Pashigian (1977) analyse the labour market for lawyers.

The approach to legal expenditure as a rent-seeking game outlined in section 11.5 can be found in Katz (1988), Farmer and Pecorino (1999), Hirshleifer and Osborne (2001) and Robson and Skaperdas (2008). Cooter and Ulen (1989) is an early literature survey.

Rubin (1977) is the classic paper on the efficiency hypothesis of the common law. Rubin (2007) collects the most influential papers in this area. Hirshleifer (1980, 1982) is a wide-ranging, book-length discussion. The preliminary discussion in the text of evolutionarily stable strategies in two player symmetric games follows Osborne (2009). The discussion of evolutionarily stable strategies in non-symmetric, multiple population situations follows Harrington (2009). The evolutionary model presented in the text follows Terrebonne (1981) closely.

11.10 Exercises

1. Return to the analysis of Chapter 3, where the factory and the residents have the same quasi-linear utility function. The efficient level of production is $\frac{\bar{Q}}{2}$.
   (a) What are the payoffs to the parties in any bargaining procedure which implements the efficient outcome?
   (b) Write down the expression for the Nash bargaining solution in this situation. Find the solution, and show that the final payoffs to the parties are:

$$\overline{M}_F + u\left(\frac{\bar{Q}}{2}\right) + \frac{u(\lambda\bar{Q}) - u[(1-\lambda)\bar{Q}]}{2}$$

for the factory, and:

$$\overline{M}_R + u\left(\frac{\bar{Q}}{2}\right) + \frac{u[(1-\lambda)\bar{Q}] - u(\lambda\bar{Q})}{2}$$

for the residents.

2. Consider the differing perceptions model of litigation and settlement that was examined in this chapter. Let:

   - ρ_P = plaintiff's perceived probability of winning at trail.
   - ρ_D = defendant's perceived probability that the plaintiff will win at trial.
   - C_P = plaintiff's costs of going to trial.
   - C_D = defendant's costs of going to trial.
   - N_P = plaintiff's costs of settling out of court.
   - N_D = defendant's costs of settling out of court
   - J_P, J_D are the plaintiff's and defendant's common perceived dollar value of judgment if plaintiff wins at trial.

   Suppose that the parties are risk neutral.

   (a) Define the *English Rule* and the *American Rule* for the allocation of legal costs. What is the plaintiff's expected utility under each of these rules if a trial goes ahead? What is the defendant's expected utility under each of these rules if a trial goes ahead?

   (b) Let $S > 0$ be the amount that the parties agree to settle for. Under which conditions which settlement possibilities exist under each cost allocation rule?

   (c) Now consider the following *hybrid* cost allocation rule: if the case goes to trial, the loser must pay a fraction ϑ of the winner's legal costs, where $0 < \theta < 1$. Suppose that if settlement possibilities exist, the parties split any settlement surplus equally. How does the settlement rate depend on ϑ? Are cases more likely to settle if ϑ is higher or lower?

Notes

1 Introduction

1. Hirshleifer (1982) sets out a similar set of propositions.
2. See Demsetz (1969), p. 1.
3. This analytical distinction is due to Buchanan and Stubblebine (1962).

2 Courts, Legal Rules, and Markets

1. See, for example, Benson (1990) for a book-length treatment. Friedman (1994) also discusses some historical examples.
2. The role of private property rights in enhancing the efficiency of resource allocation is further explored in Chapter 7.
3. This term was coined by Joskow and Noll (1981). See also Peltzman (1989).
4. Schelling (1978, page 121) and Brennan and Buchanan (1985, chapter 1) contain discussions of this role of rules within broader contexts.
5. The results of the analysis still go through if instead of depending directly on X, x_i depended on some *function* of X, say $f(X)$, where f is strictly increasing. For example, $f(X)$ could be the average choice of x_i rather than the aggregate of the individual x_i's.
6. These examples are due to Holcombe (1983).
7. The statement of this result is due to Young (1996).

3 The Coase Theorem

1. The role of this simplifying assumption – that individuals 'consume' money – is meant to reflect the fact that money represents purchasing power over all other goods in the economy.
2. This means that we have $\frac{\partial u_F(Q, M_F)}{\partial Q} > 0$ and $\frac{\partial^2 u_F(Q, M_F)}{\partial Q^2} < 0$.
3. This means that we have $\frac{\partial u_F(Q, M_F)}{\partial M_F} > 0$ and $\frac{\partial^2 u_F(Q, M_F)}{\partial M_F^2} < 0$.
4. This means that we have: $\frac{\partial v_R(Q, M_R)}{\partial Q} < 0$ and $\frac{\partial^2 v_R(Q, M_R)}{\partial Q^2} < 0$. The analysis would go through, with appropriate modifications, if the production of Q was assumed to generate a *positive* externality.
5. This means that we have: $\frac{\partial v_R(Q, M_R)}{\partial M_R} > 0$ and $\frac{\partial^2 v_R(Q, M_R)}{\partial M_R^2} < 0$.
6. It is important to note that there may also be cases in which optimality does not require tangency of indifference curves. This can happen, for example, if the indifference curves are straight lines.

7. See Boadway and Bruce (1991), p. 68.
8. Hurwicz (1995) attempted to show that quasi-linearity is not only a sufficient condition, but is also a *necessary* condition. In other words, Hurwicz attempted to show that if preferences are not quasilinear, then the contract curve could not be a horizontal line. However, in an important recent paper, Chipman and Tian (2011) show that a much wider set of preferences yield a horizontal contract curve. In other words, quasi-linear preferences are not necessary for the invariance version of the Coase Theorem.
9. This is the example developed by Aivazian and Callen (1981).

4 Accident Law and Markets, Part I: The Unilateral Care Model

1. The level of care chosen by the monopolist is analogous here to the choice of quality. Since we have assumed that marginal consumption benefits $u'(Q)$ are independent of the level care, this results in the monopolist choosing the efficient level of care. Under a different set of assumptions about the interaction between care and marginal benefits, this result would not, in general, hold. In this more general case, the monopolist may choose an inefficiently high or low level of care.
2. These results are illustrated for the case of CO_2 abatement in McKibbin and Wilcoxen (2002) chapter 5.

8 Contract Law and Markets

1. *Hadley & Anor* v. *Baxendale & Ors* [1854] England and Wales High Court (Exchequer Court), J70.

9 Crime, Punishment and Deterrence – Markets for Illegal Activities and the Economics of Public Law Enforcement

1. The analysis follows Becker, Murphy and Grossman (2006). A series of exercises in Bergstrom and Varian (2009) pp. 299–300, also considers a similar model.

10 Topics in Corporate Law and Competition Law

1. See Grossman and Hart (1980), p. 46.
2. ϕ^{ss} (and indeed all power indices that we compute) have the property that $\sum \phi_i = 1$.
3. Note that this is not quite the same thing as i being critical. Player i can be critical and turn a winning coalition into a losing one, but that does not mean that other players in the coalition are also critical. A minimal winning coalition is one in which *all* members are critical.

11 Litigation, Settlement and the Market for Lawyers

1. This approach is due to Rubinstein, Safra and Thomson (1992). It is also discussed in Osborne and Rubinstein (1994), page 302, and Muthoo (1999), chapter 2.
2. See, for example, Baye et al (2005), Propositions 3 and 5.
3. This result was first stated by Plott (1987).
4. Excellent overviews of recent research are provided in Garfinkel and Skaperdas (1996) and Anderton and Carter (2009).

References

Aivazian, V. and Callen, J. (1981) 'The Coase Theorem and the Empty Core', *Journal of Law and Economics*, 24: 175–81.

Aivazian, V. and Callen, J. (2003) 'The Core, Transaction Costs, and the Coase Theorem', *Constitutional Political Economy*, 14: 287–99.

Alchian, A. (1965) 'Some Economics of Property Rights', *Il Politico*, 30: 816–29.

Alchian, A. and Demsetz, H. (1973) 'The Property Rights Paradigm', *Journal of Economic History*, 33(1): 16–27.

Alchian, A. and Allen, W. (1983) *Exchange and Production: Competition, Coordination and Control*, Belmont, CA: Wadsworth Publishing.

Anderton, C. and Carter, J. (2009) *Principles of Conflict Economics: A Primer for Social Scientists*, Cambridge: Cambridge University Press.

Arlen, J. (1990) 'Re-examining Liability Rules When Injurers as Well as Victims Suffer Losses', *International Review of Law and Economics*, 10: 233–9.

Austen-Smith, D. and Banks, J. (2000) *Positive Political Theory I: Collective Preference*, Ann Arbor, MI: University of Michigan Press.

Austen-Smith, D. and Banks, J. (2005) *Positive Political Theory II: Strategy and Structure*, Ann Arbor, MI: University of Michigan Press.

Bagnoli, M. and Lipman, B. (1988) 'Successful Takeovers Without Exclusion', *Review of Financial Studies*, 1(1): 89–110.

Banzhaf, J. (1965) 'Weighted Voting Doesn't Work: A Mathematical Analysis', *Rutgers Law Review*, 19(2): 317–43.

Barzel, Y. (1997) *Economic Analysis of Property Rights*, Cambridge: Cambridge University Press.

Baye, M. et al. (2005) 'Comparative Analysis of Litigation Systems: An Auction-Theoretic Approach', *Economic Journal*, 115(505): 583–601.

Becker, G. (1962) 'Irrational Behaviour and Economic Theory', *Journal of Political Economy*, 70(1): 1–13.

Becker, G. (1968) 'Crime and Punishment: An Economic Approach', *Journal of Political Economy*, 76: 169–217.

Becker, G. (1974) 'A Theory of Social Interactions', *Journal of Political Economy*, 82(6): 1063–93.

Becker, G. and Murphy, K. (2000) *Social Economics: Market Behaviour in a Social Environment*, Cambridge, MA: Belknap Press of Harvard University Press.

Becker, G., Murphy, K. and Grossman, M. (2006) 'The Market for Illegal Goods: The Case of Drugs', *Journal of Political Economy*, 114(1): 38–60.

Becker, G. (2007) *Economic Theory*, 2nd enlarged edition, New York: Transaction Publishers.

Benoit, J.-P. and Kornhauser, L. (2002) 'Game Theoretic Analysis of Legal Rules and Institutions', Chapter 60 in Aumann, R. and Hart, S. (eds) *Handbook of Game Theory with Economic Applications*, vol. 3, London: North-Holland.

Benson, B. (1990) *The Enterprise of Law: Justice Without the State*, San Francisco: Pacific Research Institute for Public Policy.

Bergstrom, T. (1976) 'Regulation of Externalities', *Journal of Public Economics*, 5: 131–8.

Bergstrom, T. and Varian, H. (1985) 'When Are Nash Equilibria Independent of the Distribution of Agents' Characteristics?', *Review of Economic Studies*, 52(4): 715–18.

Bergstrom, T. and Varian, H. (2009) *Workouts in Intermediate Microeconomics: A Modern Approach*, 8th edition, New York: W.W. Norton.

Bernholz, P. (1997) 'Property Rights, Contracts Cyclical Social Preferences, and the Coase Theorem: A Synthesis', *European Journal of Political Economy*, 13: 419–42.

Bethell, T. (1998) *The Noblest Triumph: Property and Prosperity Through the Ages*, New York: St' Martin's Press.

Bhagwati, J. (1982) 'Directly Unproductive Profit-Seeking (DUP) Activities', *Journal of Political Economy*, 90: 988–1002.

Binmore, K. et al (1986) 'The Nash Bargaining Solution in Economic Modeling', *Rand Journal of Economics*, 17(2): 176–188.

Blume, L. Rubinfeld, D. and Shapiro, P. (1984) 'The Taking of Land: When Should Compensation be Paid?', *Quarterly Journal of Economics*, 99(1): 71–92.

Boadway, R. and Bruce, N. (1991) *Welfare Economics*, New York: Wiley-Blackwell.

Bouckaert, B. and G. De Geest (2000) *The Encyclopedia of Law and Economics*, Edward Elgar. Published on the web at: http://encyclo.findlaw.com/.

Bowmaker, S. (ed.) (2005) *Economics Uncut: A Complete Guide to Life, Death and Misadventure*, Cheltenham: Edward Elgar.

Brennan, G. and Buchanan, J. (1985) *The Reason of Rules: Constitutional Political Economy*, Cambridge: Cambridge University Press.

Brown, J. (1973) 'Toward an Economic Theory of Liability', *Journal of Legal Studies*, 2(2): 323–49.

Buchanan, J. and Stubblebine, C. (1962) 'Externality', *Economica*, 29(116): 371–84.

Buchanan, J. and Yoon, Y. (2000) 'Symmetric Tragedies: Commons and Anti-commons', *Journal of Law and Economics*, 43(1): 1–13.

Calabresi, G. and Melamed, A.D. (1972) 'Property Rules, Liability Rules, and Inalienability: One View of the Cathedral', *Harvard Law Review*, 85(6): 1089–128.

Chipman, J. and Tian, G. (2011) 'Detrimental Externalities, Pollution Rights and the "Coase Theorem"', *Economic Theory*, forthcoming.

Coase, R. (1960) 'The Problem of Social Cost', *Journal of Law and Economics*, 3: 1–44.

Coase, R. (1991) 'The Institutional Structure of Production', Lecture to the memory of Alfred Nobel, 9 December.

Condorcet, M. (1785/1976) 'Essay on the Application of Mathematics to the Theory of Decision-Making', in Baker, K. (ed.), *Selected Writings*, Indianapolis: Bobbs-Merrill.

Cooter, R. and Ulen, T. (2004) *Law and Economics*, 5th edition, Boston, MA: Addison-Wesley.

Cooter, R. and Ulen, T. (1989) 'Economic Analysis of Legal Disputes and Their Resolution', *Journal of Economic Literature*, 27(3): 1067–97.

Cowen, T. (1992) 'Law as a Public Good', *Economics and Philosophy*, 8: 249–67.

Cremer, H. and Gahvari, F. (1993) 'Tax Evasion and Optimal Commodity Taxation', *Journal of Public Economics*, 50: 261–75.
Dahlby, B. (2008) *The Marginal Cost of Public Funds,* Cambridge, MA: MIT Press.
Deegan, J. and Packel, E.W. (1978) 'A New Index of Power for Simple n–person Games', *International Journal of Game Theory*, 7: 113–23.
Demsetz, H. (1969) 'Information and Efficiency: Another Viewpoint', *Journal of Law & Economics* 12: 1–22.
Demsetz, H. (1972) 'When Does the Rule of Liability Matter?', *Journal of Legal Studies*, 1(1), 13–28.
Dixit, A. and Stern, N. (1982) 'Oligopoly and Welfare: A Unified Presentation with Applications to Trade and Development', *European Economic Review*, 19: 123–43.
Easterbrook, F. and Fischel, D. (1991) *The Economic Structure of Corporate Law*, Cambridge, MA: Harvard University Press.
Eide, E. (1994) *Economics of Crime: Deterrence and the Rational Offender*, New York: North-Holland.
Epstein, R. (1985) *Takings: Private Property and the Power of Eminent Domain*, Cambridge, MA: Harvard University Press.
Epstein, R. (1995) *Simple Rules for a Complex World,* Cambridge: Harvard University Press.
Farber, H. (1980) 'Final Offer Arbitration', *Journal of Conflict Resolution*, 24(4): 683–705.
Farmer, A. and Pecorino, P. (1999) 'Legal Expenditure as a Rent-Seeking Game', *Public Choice,* 100(3): 271–88.
Felsenthal, D. and Machover, M. (1998) *The Measurement of Voting Power: Theory and Practice, Problems and Paradoxes*, Cheltenham, UK: Edward Elgar Publishing.
Fiorentini, G. and Peltzman, S. (eds) (1995) *The Economics of Organised Crime*, Cambridge: Cambridge University Press.
Friedman, D. (1990) *Price Theory: An Intermediate Text*, 2nd edition, Cincinnati, OH: South-Western Pub. Co.
Friedman, D. (1994) 'Law as a Private Good: A Response to Tyler Cowen on the Economics of Anarchy', *Economics and Philosophy*, 10(2): 319–27.
Friedman, D. (2000) *Law's Order: What Economics Has to Do with Law and Why it Matters*, Princeton, NJ: Princeton University Press.
Gambetta, D. (1993) *The Sicilian Mafia,* Cambridge, MA: Harvard University Press.
Garfinkel, M. and Skaperdas, S. (eds) (1996) *The Political Economy of Conflict and Appropriation*, Cambridge: Cambridge University Press.
Garoupa, N. (1997) 'The Theory of Optimal Law Enforcement', *Journal of Economic Surveys*, 11: 267–95.
Gibbard, A. (1973) 'Manipulation of Voting Schemes: A General Result', *Econometrica,* 41(4): 587–602.
Gibbons, R. (1992) *A Primer in Game Theory*, New York: Harvester Wheatsheaf.
Gneezy, U. et al (2004) 'The Inefficiency of Splitting the Bill', *Economic Journal,* 114: 265–80.
Gould, J. (1973) 'The Economics of Legal Conflicts', *Journal of Legal Studies*, 2(2): 279–300.

Grossman, G. and Katz, M. (1983) 'Plea Bargaining and Social Welfare', *American Economic Review*, 73(4): 749–57.

Grossman, H. (2001) 'The Creation of Effective Property Rights', *American Economic Review*, 91(2): 347–52.

Grossman, S. and O. Hart (1980) 'Takeover Bids, The Free-Rider Problem, and the Theory of the Corporation', *Bell Journal of Economics*, 11(1): 42–64.

Grossman, S. and O. Hart (1988) 'One Share/One Vote and the Market for Corporate Control', *Journal of Financial Economics*, 20(1/2): 175–202.

Harberger, A. (1971) 'Three Basic Postulates for Applied Welfare Economics: An Interpretive Essay', *Journal of Economic Literature*, 9(3): 785–97.

Harrington, J.E. Jr (2009) *Games Strategies and Decision Making*, New York: Worth Publishers.

Hart, O. (1995) *Firms, Contracts and Financial Structure*, London: Oxford University Press.

Hayek, F.A. (1994) *Law, Legislation and Liberty*, 3 vols, reprint edition, Chicago: University of Chicago Press.

Heller, M. (2008) *The Gridlock Economy: How Too Much Ownership Wrecks Markets, Stops Innovation and Costs Lives*, New York: Basic Books.

Hirshleifer, J. (1980) 'Evolutionary Models in Economics and Law: Cooperation Versus Conflict Approaches', UCLA Department of Economics Working Paper, No. 170. www.econ.ucla.edu/workingpapers/wp170.pdf.

Hirshleifer, J. (1982) *Evolutionary Models in Economics and Law*, Research in Law and Economics, vol. 4, Greenwich, CT: JAI Press.

Hirshleifer, J. (2001) *The Dark Side of the Force: Economic Foundations of Conflict Theory*, Cambridge: Cambridge University Press.

Hirshleifer, J. and Osborne, E. (2001) 'Truth, Effort and the Legal Battle', *Public Choice* 108: 169–95.

Hirshleifer, J. and Riley, J. (1992) *The Analytics of Information and Uncertainty*, Cambridge: Cambridge University Press.

Holcombe, R. (1983) 'Applied Fairness Theory: Comment', *American Economic Review*, 73(5): 1153–6.

Holcombe, R. (1997) 'Absence of Envy Does Not Imply Fairness', *Southern Economic Journal*, 63(3): 797–802.

Hume, D. (1739) *A Treatise of Human Nature: Being an Attempt to Introduce the Experimental Method of Reasoning into Moral Subjects*, reprint, London: J.M. Dent, 1952.

Hurwicz, L. (1995) 'What is the Coase Theorem?', *Japan and the World Economy*, 7: 49–74.

Hylton, K. (2003) *Antitrust Law: Theory and Common Law Evolution*, London: Cambridge University Press.

Johansson, P.-O. (1987) *The Economic Theory and Measurement of Environmental Benefits*, Cambridge: Cambridge University Press.

Johansson, P.-O. (1991) *An Introduction to Modern Welfare Economics*, Cambridge: Cambridge University Press.

Jones, C. (2005) *Applied Welfare Economics*, Oxford: Oxford University Press.

Joskow, P. and Noll, R. (1981) 'Regulation in Theory and Practice: An Overview', in Fromm, G. (ed), *Studies in Public Regulation*, Cambridge, MA: MIT Press.

Katz, A. (1988) 'Judicial Decision making and Litigation Expenditure', *International Review of Law and Economics*, 8: 127–43.

Klein, B. and Leffler, K. (1981) 'The Role of Market Forces in Assuring Contractual Performance', *Journal of Political Economy*, 89(4): 615–41.
Krueger, A. (1974) 'The Political Economy of the Rent-Seeking Society', *American Economic Review*, 64(3): 291–303.
Laband, D. and McClintock, G. (2001) *The Transfer Society*, Washington DC: Cato Institute.
Landes, W. and Posner, R. (1980) 'Joint and Multiple Torts: An Economic Analysis', *Journal of Legal Studies*, 9: 517–56.
Landes, W. and Posner, R. (1987) *The Economic Structure of Tort Law*, Cambridge: Harvard University Press.
Landes, W. and Posner, R. (2003) *The Economic Structure of Intellectual Property Law,* Harvard: Belknap Press.
Landsburg, S. (1999) *Price Theory and Applications,* New York: South-Western College Publishing.
Lave, C. (1985) 'Speeding, Coordination, and the 55 MPH Limit', *American Economic Review*, 75(5): 1159–64.
Lucas, W.F. (1983) 'Measuring Power in Weighted Voting Systems', Chapter 9 in Brams, S. Lucas, W. and Straffin, P. (eds), *Political and Related Models,* New York: Springer Verlag.
Magee, S., Brock, W. and Young, L. (1989) *Black Hole Tariffs and Endogenous Policy Theory*, New York: Cambridge University Press.
Magee, S. (1992) 'The Optimum Number of Lawyers: A Reply to Epp', *Law and Social Inquiry*, 17: 667–93.
Manne, H. (1965) 'Mergers and the Market for Corporate Control', *Journal of Political Economy*, 73(2): 110–20.
Mas-Colell, A. Whinston, M. and Green, J. (1995) *Microeconomic Theory,* New York: Oxford University Press.
McKibbin, W. and Wilcoxen, P. (2002) *Climate Change Policy After Kyoto: Blueprint for a Realistic Approach,* Washington DC: Brookings Institution Press.
Mueller, D. (2003) *Public Choice III*, Cambridge: Cambridge University Press.
Muthoo, A. (1999) *Bargaining Theory with Applications*, Cambridge: Cambridge University Press.
Nash, J. (1951) 'Nonccooperative Games', *Annals of Mathematics*, 54: 289–95.
Newman, P. (1998) *The New Palgrave Dictionary of Economics and the Law*, Volumes I, II & III, London: Macmillan.
Nicholson, W. and Snyder, C. (2009) *Intermediate Microeconomics and its Application*, 11th edition, Mason, OH: South-Western College Publishing.
Nordhaus, W. (1969) *Invention, Growth and Welfare: A Theoretical Treatment of Technological Change*, Cambridge, MA: MIT Press.
Ordeshook, P. (1986) *Game Theory and Political Theory*, Cambridge: Cambridge University Press.
Osborne, M. and Rubinstein, A. (1994) *A Course in Game Theory,* Cambridge, MA: MIT Press.
Osborne, M. (2009) *An Introduction to Game Theory*, New York: Oxford University Press.
Owen, G. (1995) *Game Theory*, 3rd edition, New York: Academic Press.
Palfrey, T. and Rosenthal, H. (1984) 'Participation and the Provision of Discrete Public Goods: A Strategic Analysis', *Journal of Public Economics,* 24: 171–93.

Parisi, F. (2008) 'Coase Theorem' in Durlauf, S. and Blume, L. (eds), *The New Palgrave Dictionary of Economics,* London: Palgrave Macmillan.
Pashigian, P. (1977) 'The Market for Lawyers: The Determinants of the Demand and Supply for Lawyers', *Journal of Law and Economics,* 20: 53–85.
Pashigian, P. (1998) *Price Theory and Applications,* New York: McGraw-Hill.
Peltzman, S. (1975) 'The Effects of Automobile Safety Regulation', *The Journal of Political Economy,* 83(4): 677–726.
Peltzman, S. (1989) 'The Economic Theory of Regulation after a Decade of Deregulation', *Brookings Papers on Economic Activity: Microeconomics,* 1–59.
Pipes, R. (2000) *Property and Freedom,* New York: Vintage Books.
Poisson, S. (1837) *Recherches sur la probabilite des jugements en metiere criminelle et en matiere civile, precedes des regles generales du calcul des probabilities [Investigations into the Probability of Verdicts in Criminal and Civil Matters],* Bachelier, Imprimeur- Librarie, Paris.
Plott, C. (1987) 'Legal Fees: A Comparison of the American and English Rules', *Journal of Law, Economics, and Organization,* 3: 185–92.
Polinsky, M. (1980) 'Strict Liability Versus Negligence in a Market Setting', *American Economic Review,* 70(2): 363–7.
Polinksy, M. and Rogerson, W. (1983) 'Products Liability, Consumer Misperceptions, and Market Power', *Bell Journal of Economics,* 14(2): 581–9.
Polinsky, A.M. and Shavell, S. (2000) 'The Economic Theory of Public Enforcement of Law', *Journal of Economic Literature,* 38: 45–76.
Polinsky, M. (2003) *An Introduction to Law and Economics,* 3rd edition, Boston: Little, Brown & Co.
Polinsky, M. and Shavell, S. (2007) *Handbook of Law and Economics,* vols 1 and 2, New York: North-Holland.
Posner, R. (2007) *The Economic Analysis of Law,* 7th edition, New York: Aspen Law & Business.
Quandt, R. (1983) 'The Welfare Effects of Complexity and Variability in Regulations', *Economics Letters,* 13(2–3): 259–61.
Riker, W. (1962) *The Theory of Political Coalitions,* New Haven: Yale University Press.
Robson, A. and Skaperdas, S. (2008) 'Costly Enforcement of Property Rights and the Coase Theorem', *Economic Theory,* 36: 109–28.
Rogerson, W. (1984) 'Efficient Reliance and Damage Measures for Breach of Contract', *RAND Journal of Economics,* 15(1): 39–53.
Rosen, S. (1974) 'Hedonic Prices and Implicit Markets: Product Differentiation in Pure Competition', *Journal of Political Economy,* 82: 34–55.
Rosen, S. (1992) 'The Market for Lawyers', *Journal of Law and Economics,* 35(2): 215–46.
Ross, S. (2010) A First Course in Probability, 8th edition, New Jersey: Prentice Hall.
Rubin, P. (1977) 'Why is the Common Law Efficient?', *Journal of Legal Studies,* 6(1): 51–63.
Rubin, P. (ed.) (2007) *The Evolution of Efficient Common Law,* Cheltenham: Edward Elgar.
Rubinstein, A., Z. Safra and W. Thomson (1992) 'On the Interpretation of the Nash Bargaining Solution and its Extension to Non-Expected Utility Preferences', *Econometrica,* 60: 1171–86.

Saari, D.G. (1995) *Basic Geometry of Voting*, Heidelberg: Springer Verlag.

Saari, D.G. (2001a) *Chaotic Elections: A Mathematician Looks at Voting*, New York: American Mathematical Society.

Saari, D.G. (2001b) *Decisions and Elections: Explaining the Unexpected*, Cambridge: Cambridge University Press.

Samuelson, P. (1954) 'A Pure Theory of Public Expenditure', *Review of Economics and Statistics*, 36: 387–9.

Samuelson, P. (1955) 'Diagrammatic Exposition of a Theory of Public Expenditure', *Review of Economics and Statistics*, 37: 350–6.

Satterthwaite, M. (1975) 'Strategy-Proofness and Arrow's Conditions: Existence and Correspondence Theorems for Voting Procedures and Social Welfare Functions', *Journal of Economic Theory*, 10: 187–217.

Schelling, T. (1967) 'Economics and the Criminal Enterprise', *Public Interest*, 7: 61–78.

Schelling, T. (1978) *Micromotives and Macrobehavior*, New York: W.W. Norton.

Schuck, P. (1992) 'Legal Complexity: Some Causes, Consequences and Cures', *Duke Law Journal*, 42: 1–52.

Shapley, S. and Shubik, M. (1954) 'A Method for Evaluating the Distribution of Power in a Committee System', *American Political Science Review*, 48: 787–92.

Shapley, S. and Shubik, M. (1969) 'On the Core of an Economic System with Externalities', *American Economic Review*, 59: 678–84.

Shavell, S. (1980) 'Damage Measures for Breach of Contract', *Bell Journal of Economics*, 11(2): 466–90.

Shavell, S. (1982) 'On Liability and Insurance', *Bell Journal of Economics*, 13(1): 120–32.

Shavell, S. (1987) *The Economic Analysis of Accident Law*, Cambridge, MA: Harvard University Press.

Shy, O. (1996) *Industrial Organisation: Theory and Applications*, Cambridge, MA: MIT Press.

Skaperdas, S. (2001) 'The Political Economy of Organized Crime: Providing Protection When the State Does Not', *Economics of Governance*, 2: 173–202.

Skaperdas, S. and Syropoulos, C. (1996) 'On the Effects of Insecure Property', *Canadian Journal of Economics*, 29(2): S622–S626.

Skaperdas, S. and Vaidya, S. (2011) 'Persuasion as a Contest', *Economic Theory*, forthcoming.

Spulber, D. (1989) *Regulation and Markets*, Cambridge, MA: MIT Press.

Spulber, D. (1999) *Market Microstructure: Intermediaries and the Theory of the Firm*, Cambridge: Cambridge University Press.

Stavins, R. (1995) 'Transaction Costs and Tradeable Permits', *Journal of Environmental Economics and Management*, 29(2): 133–48.

Stigler, G. (1988) *Memoirs of an Unregulated Economist*, New York: Basic Books.

Teall, J. (2007) *Governance and the Market for Corporate Control*, London: Routledge.

Terrebonne, R.P. (1981) 'A Strictly Evolutionary Model of Common Law', *Journal of Legal Studies*, 10(2): 397–407.

Tullock, G. (1967) 'The Welfare Costs of Tariffs, Monopolies and Theft', *Western Economic Journal*, 5(3): 224–32.

Ulen, T. (1991) 'Flogging a Dead Pig: Professor Posin on the Coase Theorem', *Wayne Law Review*, 38: 91–105.

Varian, H. (1974) 'Envy, Equity and Efficiency', *Journal of Economic Theory,* 9: 63–91.

Varian, H. (2010) *Intermediate Microeconomics: A Modern Approach*, 8th edition, New York: W.W. Norton.

Viscusi, K. (1992) *Smoking: Making the Risky Decision*, New York: Oxford University Press.

Von Mises, L. (1963) *Human Action: A Treatise in Economics,* new revised edition, New Haven: Yale University Press.

Watt, R. (2000) *Copyright and Economic Theory: Friends or Foes?*, Cheltenham: Edward Elgar.

Weitzman, M. (1974) 'Prices Versus Quantities', *Review of Economic Studies,* 41(4): 477–91.

White, M. and Wittman, D. (1983) 'A Comparison of Taxes, Regulation, and Liability Rules under Imperfect Information', *Journal of Legal Studies,* 12: 413–25.

Winston, C. et al. (2011) *First Thing We Do, Let's Deregulate All the Lawyers*, Washington DC, Brookings Institution Press.

Winter, H. (2008) *The Economics of Crime: An Introduction to Rational Crime Analysis*, London: Routledge.

Wittman, D. (ed.) (2003) *Economic Analysis of the Law: Selected Readings*, New York: Blackwell Publishing.

Young, H.P. (1996) 'Group Choice and Individual Judgements', Chapter 9 of Mueller, D. (ed.), *Perspectives on Public Choice: A Handbook*, Cambridge: Cambridge University Press.

Index